D1548200

ERNST v. HEYDEBRAND und der LASA
(Photograph courtesy of Ullstein
Bilderdienst)

RADICALS AND REACTIONARIES: THE CRISIS OF CONSERVATISM IN WILHELMINE GERMANY

Abraham J. Peck

University Press of America™

Library of Congress Catalog Card Number: 78-62921

FOR MY PARENTS

CONTENTS

Acknowledgements . . . . iv-v

Introduction . . . . vi-xi

List of Abbreviations. . . . . xii-xiii

   I.   The Prusso-German State and the German
       Conservative party (1871-1890)

       Unification: The tip of the iceburg-----The rise
       and fall of the Prussian Conservatives-----The
       alliance of agriculture and industry and the
       founding of a "new" Conservative Party-----German
       Conservatives and the search for political
       stability-----The structure collapses: the
       failure of Bismarck's Germany 1

  II.   German Conservatives Between Conflict and
       Cooperation: *The Bund der Landwirte,*
       Sammlungspolitik, and the Strategy for an
       Agrarian Future (1890-1902)

       The Party adrift: the Conservatives and the
       Caprivi challenge to agriculture-----The Party
       modernized: agrarian politics confronts the era
       of the "carrot and stick"-----*Weltpolitik* and
       the search for conservative preservation
       -----"Fanatical" agrarians and the twisted road
       to economic salvation 17

 III.   From Buelow to Bethmann: *Voelkisch* Stirrings,
       the Dilemma of Taxation, and the Crisis of
       Weltpolitik (1903-1911)

       Back into the fold--and out again (agrarian
       politics in the early Buelow era)-----Economics
       versus the *Volk:* the real face of agrarian
       "nationalism"-----The Conservatives dig in: the
       tax question-----The Pan-Germans succeed where
       Weltpolitik fails 49

  IV.   Pandora's Box: The Election of 1912 and its
       Aftermath (1912/13)

       The Election of 1912-----Anti-Semitism and the
       Volk-----Taxation and isolation 82

   V.   Radicals and Reactionaries in a Period of Crisis
       (1913/1914)

Pan-Germans on the march: success and failure
in the conservative camp-----The *Kartell der
Schaffenden Staende:* fact or fiction?-----The
National Opposition and the coming of war. 107

VI. The German Conservative Party and the "*Machttraueme*
of German Patriots" (1914)

German Conservatives between *voelkisch* movement
and *Volkspartei*-----The hand of friendship is
extended---albeit reluctantly-----The BdL on the
attack...*Burgfrieden* or not-----The ADV: war
aims and the new Germany-----The Pan-German
breakthrough and agrarian strategy-----The gap
widens: growing differences between Pan-Germans
and German Conservatives 135

VII. The Right Gathers: Reality and Illusion in the
German "War-Aims Movement" (1915)

The continuing troubles of the German Conservative
Party-----The BdL moves further to the right
-----Anti-Semitism enters once more-----New moves
against Bethmann 164

VIII. New Parties and Old Politics: The Further
Radicalization of the German Right (1916)

Heydebrand loses control and Westarp responds
-----The BdL faces realities-----The ADV: from
conspiracy to anti-Semitism. 186

IX. Between Fatherland and *Volk*: Increasing
Democratization and the Last Gasp of the Prusso-
German State (1917)

For the German Conservatives the situation worsens
-----The BdL and a return to basics-----Continuity
and action: The German Fatherland Party and Wolfgang Kapp-----Pan-German aims: from the conquest
of land to the conquest of soul. 203

X. The Politics of Preservation and Decline (1918)

The lesson is learned too late-----Adapt and
survive-----The dream is realized 222

Epilogue 236

Notes. 243

Archival Sources 336

Selected Bibliography. 344

Index. 364

Illustrations; Ernst v. Heydebrand und der Lasa. . . . Frontispiece

Cuno Graf Westarp . . . . . Between pages 143-144

Dr. Gustav Roesicke . . . . Between pages 172-173

ACKNOWLEDGEMENTS

Any author whose book has had its beginnings in the form of a dissertation, as has this one, is quite obviously grateful to many individuals and institutions who have aided him along the way.

I should like to thank Professor Volker R. Berghahn who supervised an earlier version of this study at the University of East Anglia, Norwich, England as well as Professor Peter-Christian Witt, who assumed such a responsibility during my stay at the University of Hamburg. I have received advice concerning research problems from Professors Dirk Stegmann, Werner Jochmann, Klaus Wernecke, Hans-Juergen Puhle, Gustav Schmidt and Dietrich Mende as well as Dr. Jens Flemming.

I am also grateful to the archives and libraries that supplied the research materials for this work. I particularly wish to thank the staffs of the Bundesarchiv at Koblenz, the Zentrales Staatsarchiv, sections I and II, the Hamburg Forschungsstelle fuer die Geschichte des Nationalsozialismus in Hamburg, and Dr. Friedrich Freiherr Hiller v. Gaertringen for putting at my disposal a copy of the war-time correspondence between his grandfather, Count Cuno Westarp, and Ernst Heydebrand und der Lasa.

I am grateful to the following publishers for allowing me to quote passages from works published under their imprint: to Yale University Press for allowing me to quote from *The Downfall of the Anti-Semitic Political Parties in Imperial Germany* (1975), by Richard S. Levy; to Rand McNally, Inc., for allowing me to quote from *The Culture of Western Europe* (1961), by George L. Mosse; to Howard Fertig, Inc., for allowing me to quote from *Germans and Jews* (1970), by George L. Mosse. The material from *Army, Industry and Labor* (1966), by Gerald Feldman, is reprinted by permission of Princeton University Press.

The preparation of this study has been made possible by the financial assistance of the Association of Jewish Refugees in Great Britain, the Leo Baeck Lodge-B'nai B'rith, London, the Fulbright-Hays Commission, and the Hebrew Union College-Jewish Institute of Religion, Cincinnati, Ohio.

I would like to thank Gloria Emison for her skillful indexing and Lisa Hebbe for her meticulous typing of the manuscript. I would also like to thank the editors of the University Press of America for their useful technical suggestions.

iv

Radicals and Reactionaries

I could not finish this list of acknowledgements without giving proper credit and thanks to Professor Jacob R. Marcus, director of the American Jewish Archives, Dr. Alfred Gottschalk, president of the Hebrew Union College-Jewish Institute of Religion, and Dr. Uri Herscher, executive vice-president of the Hebrew Union College-Jewish Institute of Religion. It is truly by the grace of their devotion to scientific scholarship and their encouragement that this book has been made possible.

Finally, I would like to thank my parents-in-law for the encouragement they have given me. Above all, I wish to express gratitude to my wife, Jean, and daughter, Abby, for accepting my many research journeys, my special frustrations, and a particularly intense and sometimes remote husband and father.

A.J.P.

Cincinnati, Ohio
April 1978

INTRODUCTION

It has been nearly two decades since Professor Fritz Fischer's *Griff nach der Weltmacht* (Düsseldorf 1961) changed the face of German historiography. Since that time, very few historians have been able to maintain Germany's innocence for the outbreak of the 1914-1918 war. That, indeed, was the essence of Fischer's thesis: that the German *Reich* carried with it the major burden of responsibility for World War I.

The acerbic Fischer Debate,* in which Professor Fischer was attacked with unprofessional bitterness and anger, became a political issue overstepping the bounds of academic exchange. Politicians and journalists alike attacked Fischer with motives seemingly far removed from the search for historical accuracy. No doubt the grounds for their attack lay in the fact that a bit more self-esteem had been chipped from an already damaged German national consciousness.

In many respects, however, the Debate was of positive value. Not only was all of Germany's dirty wash now hung out to dry, but the Wilhelmine Empire, long overshadowed by Hitler and the Third *Reich*, became once more a period of interest and value to students of German history.

Professor Fischer prepared himself well for the barrage of charges and accusations he must have known would follow publication of his controversial thesis. A whole generation of pupils, schooled in the Fischer style, has carried on his work, often writing with an acidity bordering on the polemical style once directed against their mentor. But while they often "gave as good as they got," their contributions to the history of Wilhelmine Germany have been invaluable.

A Fischer pupil's work is easily identifiable: the amount of research done is enormous and the clarity with which it brings into focus a major research problem marks it as being of the highest professional calibre. Two of Fischer's most recent pupils, especially, have set the pattern for the little group of scholars that surround him. Dirk Stegmann, in *Die Erben Bismarcks* (Cologne and Berlin (West) 1970), has focused on the problem of Wilhelmine Germany's ruling elites. Through the research that he has gathered in no less than thirteen archives, Stegmann has striven to prove that the political representatives of German industry and agriculture, despite the twists and turns of Germany's domestic and foreign politics, remained of one mind in

*For an excellent account of the Fischer Debate see John A. Moses, *The Politics of Illusion: The Fischer Controversy in German Historiography*, New York 1975.

their opposition to German social democracy and in
their attempts to maintain the political, social and
economic status quo. Peter Christian Witt, however,
unlike Stegmann, does not attempt to recreate
practically the entire political atmosphere of the
years between 1897-1918. Instead, in *Die Finanzpolitik
des Deutschen Reiches von 1903 bis 1913* (Luebeck and
Hamburg 1970), he has isolated one of the key structural
weaknesses of the Wilhelmine *Reich*, a continual shortage
of funds and a constant inability to find ways of obtaining
them. He has especially demonstrated the manner in which
agriculture and its parliamentary representative, the
German Conservative Party, consistently refused to go
along with attempts to balance the *Reich's* budget through
a federal inheritance tax. He also goes on to show how
such an unyielding position brought about the parliamentary isolation of the German Conservative Party.

Both Stegmann and Witt devote a good deal of attention
to the politics of the German Conservative Party. They
are but two authors among several who have attempted to
deal with particular aspects of this Prussian-centered and
Junker-dominated political organization. In his excellent
study, *Agrarische Interessenpolitik und preussischen
Konservatismus im wilhelminischen Reich (1893-1914)*
(Hannover 1967), Hans-Juergen Puhle has shown how an
agrarian pressure group, the *Bund der Landwirte*,
transformed the German Conservative Party from a Prussian-
oriented, traditional conservative organization into a
largely agrarian-oriented party, devoid of most principles
and traditions. The Bund was anti-Semitic, and exhibited
beliefs oriented towards a mass-integrated *voelkisch* point
of view. It enjoyed great success involving non-*Junker*
elements in its political activities and remained unencum-
bered by parliamentary restraints. Hans Booms, *Die
Deutschkonservative Partei* (Duesseldorf 1954), and Otto
Graf zu Stolberg-Wernigerode, *Die unentschiedene Generation*
(Munich 1968), have demonstrated, on the other hand, that
large parts of the Conservative Party maintained a strong
Prussian orientation, cherished traditional conservative
principles, and were constantly in rebellion against
too much agrarian influence. Marxist interpretations
of the roles played by the *Bund der Landwirte* and the
German Conservative Party have been offered in doctoral
dissertations by Ernst David and Lothar Wallraf. There
are also several older works, most notably by Gerhard
Ritter and Eckart Kehr as well as by Conservative Party
members Cuno Count Westarp, Ernst v. Heydebrand und der
Lasa, and Friedrich Wilhelm Count v. Limburg-Stirum.

Yet there is no single scientific history of the
German Conservative Party. Furthermore, none of the
aforementioned authors has really investigated the
politics of the German Conservative Party beyond 1914
in a satisfactory manner. This book, then, is the first
attempt to deal fully with the Conservative Party both
as a long-time participant in the domestic affairs of
the Wilhelmine Empire and as a conservative political
organization caught between tradition and modernity in
the last three decades before 1918.

The reader will not find in these pages either a
general history of the German Conservative Party or a
statistical and sociological analysis of its membership.
That is to say, I have not attempted to collect statistical
data, analyze voting support or investigate the social
backgrounds of Conservative deputies. This is not to deny
the validity or importance of such an undertaking. But
my purpose in writing this work has been to study the
shifts in Conservative ideology and to investigate the
manner in which the crucial life and death struggle of
the conservative system in Germany during the Wilhelmine
era specifically affected the political organization
known as the German Conservative Party as well as the
activities of the German political Right in general.

Mine is a study in the collapse of an ideological
and political power position under the stresses and strains
of domestic crisis and, finally, "total war." My central
contention is that increasing infiltration of "modern
elements" into old Prussian conservatism brought with it
disastrous results for the survival of the German Conservative
Party. I have written a history of the shifts in the balance
of power and ideology which occurred between the German
Conservative Party, the *Bund der Landwirte* and, especially
during the years 1914-1918, the *voelkisch-* and anti-
Semitic-oriented *Alldeutscher Verband*. I have also
attempted to demonstrate what happened to old-style Prussian
conservatism under the impact of very rapid change in
1914-1918, when a kind of "pre-fascist" politics made itself
a part of the final defense of the Prusso-German state.

Perhaps a word is now necessary to explain some of the
terms and concepts that I employ during the course of my
work. When I speak of "modern elements," I mean the
"genuinely radical Right" as represented by the
Alldeutscher Verband and, to a considerably lesser degree,
the *Bund der Landwirte*. The revolutionary ideology of the
radical Right differs significantly from that of traditional
conservatism. It is quite willing to attack and destroy,

Radicals and Reactionaries

as Professor Andrew G. Whiteside has pointed out,* much that traditional conservatives still deem necessary to society. The main aims of such right-wing radicals are revolutionary change in social, economic and national conditions, and a kind of "national socialism" which may also be termed *voelkisch*. A key aspect of this ideology is the appeal of modernity and the relative meaninglessness of traditionalism. The political style of these elements is geared towards recruitment among the masses and a contempt for aristocratic exclusivity. Most importantly, for this study, is the willingness, even eagerness, of these groups to destroy traditional conservatism when conditions warrant such a step. I will also briefly discuss the problem of *Lernfaehigkeit*, which I understand to be the attempt by traditional conservatism to adjust to changed and unfavorable political and social circumstances.

In my early chapters I attempt to analyze critically the recent studies of Puhle, Stegmann, Witt, H-U Wehler, Dieter Groh, Heinrich August Winkler and Volker Berghahn, among others. I attempt, moreover, to interpret the pre-war history of the German Conservative Party, relying on numerous primary and secondary sources never previously used together in a discussion of Conservative politics. In Chapter I, I propose to trace the collapse of the old, Prussian-centred conservatism and the rise of the "new" German Conservative Party. Why such a different type of Party was necessary in the early *Reich* period will hopefully answer the problem of materialism versus ideology in the Bismarckian Empire. In Chapter II, I hope to show that the "new" German Conservative Party was unable to respond accurately to the governmental attack upon the agrarian sector of the economy and that external elements, in the guise of the *Bund der Landwirte*, took up the flagging agrarian response and also transformed the German Conservative Party. In Chapter II, I also propose to answer the question: how did the conservative system attempt to stabilize political and social conditions in the Reich? Next, I raise the questions: what was *Weltpolitik* and did the Conservatives contribute to it either financially or ideologically? And if not, what elements in Germany did? In Chapter III, I hope to answer these questions and also introduce the *Alldeutscher Verband* and the rise of extreme nationalism. In Chapter IV, I ask: what happened in 1912 as a result of the election of II0 Social Democrats to the German Reichstag? I hope to show that the German Conservative Party suffered both electorally and politically because of this election and that "radical elements" in German politics gained a major ideological foothold among large segments of German society. In Chapter V, I hope to show how the *Bund der Landwirte's*

*Andrew G. Whiteside. *The Socialism of Fools: George Ritter Von Schonerer and Austrian Pan-Germanism*, Berkeley, California, 1975.

concern with the growing atmosphere of democratization drove it into a political alliance with the *Alldeutscher Verband*. The ADV, however, did not enjoy the same degree of success with the German Conservative Party, whose leader, Ernst v. Heydebrand und der Lasa, feared the mass-politics of the *Alldeutscher Verband* as a threat to the aristocratic elitism of the Conservatives. The "all-out attack" against the political Left will be examined in terms of the *Kartell der schaffenden Staende*, a not very practical alliance of agriculture and heavy industry and parts of the *Mittelstand*, as well as the creation of a *voelkisch*-oriented movement, the "National Opposition," controlled by the *Alldeutscher Verband*.

The second half of the book is based largely upon unpublished materials from the files of the Zentrales Staatsarchiv in the German Democratic Republic. This is the center of materials concerning the activities of the German Conservative Party, the *Bund der Landwirte*, and the *Alldeutscher Verband* during World War I. I have also relied quite heavily upon the unpublished war-time correspondence between Count Cuno Westarp and Ernst Heydebrand und der Lasa, the most important Conservative leaders after 1912. In Chapter VI, I hope to demonstrate how the ADV, equipped with plans for a "new" Germany, introduced a programme of foreign territorial acquisitions at the outbreak of war, with much success in gathering support from many quarters, but with little success in convincing the Conservatives. Agriculture's role in the war-economy is likewise discussed. How, in fact, did the German Conservative Party, or rather its individual members, react to the new direction of German politics as represented by the Pan-Germans? In Chapter VII, I hope to demonstrate the growing split in the Conservative Party between those fearful of the new direction and a more "modern" or radical grouping pushing for an orientation toward the Pan-Germans. I also hope to demonstrate that the BdL was deeply involved in ADV politics and that anti-Semitism was once more an issue in radical politics. In Chapter VIII, I hope to show how Heydebrand fully discredited himself in the eyes of the German Right, and that Westarp assumed actual control of the Party. What, then, was to be done about the German Conservatives? The ADV was bombarded by members wishing to create a "Great Party of the Right," in effect threatening the continued existence of the Conservative Party. In this chapter, the BdL is shown to have realized that it no longer enjoyed parity with the ADV, but had instead become one more organization manipulated and controlled by the ADV.

Radicals and Reactionaries

The ADV is also shown to have increased its emphasis
upon anti-Semitic activities. In Chapter IX, I hope to
show that the Conservatives became obsessed with the
growing question of reform in the three-class Prussian
voting Law. But what of the agrarians and the ADV? The
Bund der Landwirte, I hope to demonstrate, was instrumental
(along with heavy industry) in forming the German Fatherland
Party in an attempt to maintain the Prusso-German state
and its lucrative material benefits. The ADV, however,
abandoned its war-aims programme in favor of convincing
the German nation of Jewish responsibility for the
increasingly disastrous war. In Chapter X, I propose
to demonstrate that the resentment against Conservative
policy and leadership exploded among the members and the
Party was fully split between "traditionalists" and
"modernizers." As the Was seemed lost, the Party vainly
attempted to alter its programme and adopt a more flexible
attitude to political change. But the effort was not
enough and came much too late. The Party was lost. The
BdL, however, used its political cunning to preserve its
position of power. So did the ADV, which declared "war"
upon Jewry and made a racial "struggle to the death" its
primary post-war concern. If the Conservative Party
collapsed in 1918, was traditional conservatism dead?
In the Epilogue, I attempt to answer this question by
analyzing the tactics of the radical Right and the creation
of the DNVP (German People's Party), which emerged as the
successor to the German Conservative Party. The old
Conservative leader, Count Westarp, resurfaced in the
mid-twenties to become chairman of the DNVP. But his
attempts to restore Conservative policies were beaten
down by ADV intrigue. A changed political climate during
the Weimar Republic and the triumph of the "modernizers"
made traditional conservatism forever obsolete.

ABBREVIATIONS

ADB	Alldeutsche Blaetter
ADV	Alldeutscher Verband
BA	Bundesarchiv Koblenz
BdI	Bund der Industriellen
BdL	Bund der Landwirte
CdI	Centralverband der Industriellen
DHT	Deutscher Handelstag
DLR	Deutscher Landwirtschafts Rat
DNVP	Deutschnationale Volkspartei
DRP	Deutsche Reformpartei
DSP	Deutschsoziale Partei
DTZ	Deutsche Tageszeitung
DZ	Deutsche Zeitung
DZA I	German Central Archives, Potsdam
DZA II	German Central Archives, Merseburg
HC	Hamburgerische Correspondent
HE	Hamburger Echo
HFr	Hamburger Fremdenblatt
HFs	Hamburg Forschungsstelle fuer die Geschichte des Nationalsozialismus in Hamburg
HN	Hamburger Nachrichten
H-W	Heydebrand-Westarp Correspondence
HZ	Historische Zeitschrift
KE	Kleine Erwerbung

KdBdL	Korrespondenz des Bundes der Landwirte
KZ	Kreuzzeitung
MGM	Militaergeschichtliche Mitteilungen
NL	Nachlass
NLZ	National Liberale Zeitung
RDMV	Reichsdeutscher Mittelstandsverband
St.A.Hbg.	Staatsarchiv Hamburg
VZG	Vierteljahrshefte fuer Zeitgeschichte

CHAPTER I

The Prusso-German State and
the German Conservative Party (1871-1890)

i. Unification: the tip of the iceburg

One of the most remarkable facts of Germany's
unification in 1871 was its lack of social unity. From
the very beginning of the German Empire, class differences
were a constant source of domestic tension. The external
appearance of a great solidarity belied the inner schisms.

One did not have to search widely for the sources
of this difficulty. A Prussian conservative named Otto
von Bismarck stood at the political tip of the newly-
created *Reich*. Instead of counting his main support
from the members of his own social class, the conservative
Prussian nobility *(Junkers)*, Bismarck had found it more
useful to work towards unification with middle-class
liberals. Adding to their difficulties, the *Junkers*
were unable to reconcile the inclusion of Prussia into
a federal *Reich* with the presumed loss of their own
political strength.

Also contributing to the dissension within Germany
was an increasingly militant working-class party whose
presence would one day constitute the growing danger of
a "revolution from below." The rise of the Social
Democratic Party struck a further note of domestic
unrest in a nation just liberated from its historical
disunity. It is little wonder that one historian has
concluded that "Bismarck unified the German states, not
the Germans."[1]

In the initial period of German unification the
economic situation was also far from stable. Although
Germany had come to the stage of an accelerated industrial
growth at a relatively late period, the Industrial
Revolution was in full swing at the time of the *Reich's*
inception. With big business speculations predominating,
millions were being made and lost by a relatively small
group of financial entrepreneurs. Although it remained
politically and socially anachronistic, Germany was
undergoing a "transformation" of essential values in
its economic and moral traditions. Led by stock
speculators and the rise and fall of big city finance,
the antiquated, agrarian-based structure of the German
economy changed to such an extent that "industrial
economy now became predominant and...Berlin became the
centre of German economic life."[2]

Radicals and Reactionaries

Capitalistic attitudes spread rapidly throughout the middle classes and even to the aristocracy. The prospect of receiving large dividends from relatively small investments allowed a traditional aristocratic aversion to finance to lose much of its meaning. Fritz Stern, in an essay on the relationship of the social aristocracy to these schemes, has highlighted the extent to which many *Junkers* (including Bismarck) were swept along by the investment fever.[3] The outward appearance of a nineteenth-century *Wirtschaftswunder* brought with it the uneasy feeling that this capitalism was not a part of German tradition. Yet, at the same time, values, which for centuries had led the *Junkers* to look upon money-making as a less than respectable profession, were rapidly falling by the wayside. In addition, the financiers were often unethical; and for the very pillars of German society to have become involved in such goings-on must have worried many traditionalists in the newly "unified" German nation.

A number of serious economic fluctuations began to affect Germany in 1873. Part of a world-wide trend, economic stability was not disrupted by a sudden and "spectacular breakdown."[4] It was, rather, a varied depression, leading initially to violent crashes and panics in Germany, Austria, and America and to "recession" periods in France and England. The effects of this eventful turn in economic affairs managed to perpetuate themselves in Germany until the year 1896. So much of the social and political thought of the Bismarckean *Reich* was shaped by economic fluctuations that no study of the years after 1871 can omit the economic and psychological effects of the "Great Depression."[5]

The great crashes ended the speculative mania of the brief but hectic *Gruenderjahre* (1870-1873). Dreams became financial nightmares and the *Junkers* did not remain unaffected. A kind of national guilt feeling developed and it did not have long to wait in order to erupt into a full-blown moral revulsion. Scapegoats were quick to be found.

The focus of national distaste came to rest upon those elements in German society whose actions were most associated with the "un-German" events of the preceding half decade. The Jew and the liberal, by virtue of their seemingly deep involvement, bore the main burden of blame. Their vilification allowed the German aristocracy to disassociate itself quietly from the financial fiasco. The *Junkers* were able, once more, to assume their traditional role as guardians of the "true and eternal" German values.

2

The political issue, never far from the surface of the *Junkers'* complaint, was central to the mood of aristocratic resentment. The loss of power and the minor role which this conservative elite seemed destined to play in the new nation only intensified its anger at the "influential" Jewish and liberal circles. Such resentment was shown by the *Kreuzzeitung*, the printed voice of the ultraconservative *Junkers*, which not only attacked the policies of the new *Reich*, but labeled them as "Jew politics" *(Judenpolitik)*.[6] The "un-German" elements were natural targets. According to them, both groups had influenced Bismarck to the detriment of the aristocratic class. They cited the fact that Bismarck's closest financial adviser, Gershon Bleichroeder, was a Jew; and they pointed out that the National Liberal Party had become Bismarck's closest political ally.

The two decades following the end of the *Gruenderjahre* were years of extreme unhappiness and embitterment. While the nations that surrounded her looked on as Germany established a formidable position in European affairs, the social dilemma within grew steadily worse. A feeling of unqualified *Angst* at such a state of domestic friction was voiced as early as 1876 in a letter from Felix Freiherr von Stein to Eduard Lasker:[7]

> The voices of the villages and small country
> towns are being raised against the large cities,
> that of the landowners against the might of
> capital, and the voices of the agrarians and
> tradesmen against the representatives of big
> industry and trade... In the repressed sectors
> (i.e.: the working class-AJP) of the population
> a great displeasure about the situation of things
> is developing.

ii. The rise and fall of the Prussian Conservatives

As Germany struggled to resolve her social and financial dilemmas, Bismarck saw in the turmoil of the post-*Gruenderjahre* a perfect opportunity to rid himself of the now "unhealthy" liberal support. By continuing to maintain such support, he stood to gain little beyond the further wrath of an aroused, anti-liberal feeling that permeated large parts of Germany.[8] A conservative at heart, Bismarck's political philosophy remained unchanged despite the period of close cooperation with the National Liberal Party. He had used liberalism as

a means to unification rather than as a political goal.
With the liberals' usefulness in helping to forge the
Reich at an end, Bismarck could now hope to return
Germany to its proper conservative state. The destruction
of liberalism as a political force and the end of a
short-lived liberal age in Germany were at hand.[9]

Historical judgement has come to regard the
Bismarckian state as a testament to the creative genius
of the Iron Chancellor. Bismarck is acknowledged to
have played the key role in creating a political,
economic, constitutional, and social structure which
lasted until the end of the Second *Reich*. This is an
important link in the chain of "continuity" which,
according to some historians, stretches from Bismarck
to Adolf Hitler.[10] It is possible to advance such a
thesis precisely because the politics of Bismarck's
Germany so clearly bear the indelible stamp of continuity
in several areas: the conflict of classes, the
maintenance of a feudal-aristocratic rule amidst the
dynamics of a modern industrial state, and, especially,
the absence of a meaningful liberal-democratic political
force. All were common to its history.[11]

The development and maintenance of a conservative
German Empire became the chief concern of Bismarck's
political life. In order to achieve this aim it was
essential that he enjoy the confidence of those who
would stand to benefit most from his vision and who
would strive to aid him in ensuring its success. No
group was as important to Bismarck or more difficult
to accomodate than the Prussian conservatives.

A conservative philosophy existed in Germany well
before the outbreak of the French Revolution.[12] It
was not until the Revolution of 1848, however, that
the philosophy was organized into a political movement.
Prussia, Germany's most populous state both before and
after unification, became the center of German
conservatism.[13]

The Revolution of 1848 had been a warning to
conservative interests in Prussia. Their compact little
world, which had remained intact for several decades,
was severely shaken by the liberal-democratic demands
of the "48er" revolutionaries. Not since the "frightful
time of the French," as the Napoleonic invasion of
Prussia was called, had such an alien spirit threatened
the predominance of conservatism as a way of life.
Forced to organize politically, the various components

4

of Prussian conservatism-aristocratic landowners, the
Lutheran clergy, and top-level bureaucrats-may have
been vague in the specifics of a party programme, but
they maintained a united opposition to all liberal
demands. Specific liberal calls for the introduction of
parliamentary government, a broadening of the vote, and
the unification of the numerous German states only
intensified conservative opposition. It was the last of
these demands which most threatened conservative interests.
Closely related to the industrial-capitalistic development
of Germany, a unified *and* industrial nation could only
damage the economic and social standing of the primarily
agrarian conservatives and the influence of the Prussian
state.

What was this last-minute conservative creation?
At first, the Prussian Conservative Party was little
more than a *Glaubenspartei* embracing "...diffuse
principles rather than specific programmes."[14] The
Party believed that only a conservative movement could
save the declining prestige of King Friederich Wilhelm IV.
Convinced of their historical importance to Prussia,
aristocratic Conservatives viewed the state as a naturally
evolving organism in which the monarch served as the "head
of society" and they as the brains.[15]

Such a relationship between monarch and noble acted
as the essential determinant in the Conservatives'
appraisal of society. The Christian-monarchical-
aristocratic order was viewed as having no national
borders; rather, it was considered to be the essence
of society in eastern and central Europe. This did not,
however, preclude an almost fanatical belief in the
legitimacy of the individual state.[16]

Another equally important factor in the early
Weltanschauung of the Prussian Conservative Party was
its firm dedication to the concept of the "corporate
state" *(Staendestaat)*. The earliest form of the
Staendestaat, the "Estates of the realm," was originally
conceived as a fourteenth-century method of power-sharing
between princes and noble diets. Its nineteenth-century
form reflected the special privileges granted to the
landed aristocracy when Friederich Wilhelm the Great
Elector destroyed the power of the diets in the middle of
the seventeenth century. The *Staendestaat* remained the
conservative ideal of German society and, as a result,
"sharpened the division between lord and peasant, noble
and burgher. Henceforth, the *Staendestaat* came to mean
the separation of society into Estates with special
privileges and duties associated with each..."[17]

5

During the 1850's, the conservative politician and
ideologue, Friedrich Julius Stahl, modernized the
Staende by defining them in terms of land, industry,
and the professions. Yet the concept of the
Staendestaat retained its feudal image of a socially
dominant nobility. A three-class voting law was soon
introduced to make certain that social divisions did
not become blurred and that agrarian predominance in
Prussia remained intact.

The "modernization" of conservative thought, as
reflected by Stahl, could not arrest the destruction
of the traditional corporate world. This was so
despite the fact that a small group of Prussian
Conservatives (the so-called court *Kamarilla*) was able
to direct the policies of the Prussian state during
the decade that followed the 1848 Revolution.[18] A
gradual urbanized industrialization began to wear away
the foundations of this feudal concept. Especially
after 1866, when Bismarck and the North German
Confederation began to destroy most of its aims, the
Prussian Conservative Party began to disintegrate into
"old" (anti-Bismarck) and "new" (pro-Bismarck) Conservatives. Such a division was a serious obstacle to the
maintenance of a unified Party. Between 1867 and 1870,
three Conservative parties emerged: one each in the
North German *Reichstag*, the Prussian Chamber of Deputies,
and the Prussian House of Lords. Between 1866, and the
abandonment of the principle of legitimacy, and 1871,
when they grudgingly accepted national unification, the
"old" Conservatives in Prussia fought an unsuccessful
battle to preserve the *Staendestaat* concept.[19]

The reorganization of county government *(Kreisordnung)*
in 1872[20] was the last act in the tragedy of the Prussian
Conservative Party. With the passage of the *Kreisordnung*
laws, the idea of the *Staendestaat* as the primary source
of conservative power ceased forever.[21] The *Kreisordnung*
dilemma also brought severe defeat to the Conservative
members in the Prussian House of Deputies during the
elections of 1873 and 1874.[22]

Clearly a new type of Conservative Party had to
emerge. The old conservative shibboleths were outmoded
and too many issues, once opposed by Prussian Conservatives,
had already been achieved. Fortunately for Prussia's
conservatives, the collapse of their political movement
coincided with the onset of Germany's economic instabilities.
Prussian agriculture, especially in the sparsely populated
areas east of the Elbe River, could not escape the harsh

realities of an economic crisis nor the more long-term
effects of a structural one.

iii.   The alliance of agriculture and industry
and the founding of a "new" Conservative Party

Apart from the great schism over Bismarck's
politics, an equally significant difference of opinion
could be noted in Conservative circles during the early
years of the Second *Reich*. Dissident voices had already
expressed dissatisfaction with Conservative aims when
the corporate-patriarchal idea had received its most
powerful impetus in 1848. The "Association for the
Preservation of the Material Interests of all Classes
of the Prussian People,"[23] a group influential in
founding the Prussian Conservative Party, had stressed
that material protection of *Junkers* was more important
than ideological rigidity.[24] It was therefore not
surprising to note that by 1873, as the Prussian Conservative
Party floundered in self-administered impotence, a hard
core of Conservative materialists had long since abandoned
the dead world of conservative principles.

All of this meant that Prussia's conservative
groups, especially the *Junkers*, could no longer look to
an organized movement to buttress their exalted position
in Prussian society. Indeed their position was made less
tenable by the economic miseries that befell east Prussian
agriculture during the late 1870's. The varying strains
of conservative thought were forced to recognize the
importance of a healthy agricultural sector as the key
to a stable conservative Prussia. The growing influx of
cheap American wheat left the *Junkers* unable to compete
for domestic markets. The profitable free-trade policies
which they had steadfastly maintained (as long as prohibitive
transportation costs had kept U.S. and Russian grain
imports at a minimum) were no longer acceptable.[25]

Industrial Germany also fell victim to the impact of
cheap foreign imports. Equally dissatisfied with free
trade, which remained a legacy of the discredited liberal
period, major industrial firms banded together to press
for a systerm of protective tariffs. The *Verein Deutscher
Eisen und Stahl Industrieller* (Association of German Iron
and Steel Industrialists) was formed in 1874 in order to
influence government policy. Foremost among their demands
was the dismissal of Rudolf von Delbrueck, President of
the Imperial Chancellors' Office and the chief architect
of the liberal free trade policy.[26]

The agrarians, however, wanted no part in an anti-free trade movement. *Junker* concern, despite the continued pressures upon their livelihood, lay in another direction. They were awaiting the result of Bismarck's new policy, which used "the fear of the menacing social question as a new power capable of integrating Germany." The renewed turn to conservatism, a direct aim of this policy, could only benefit Prussian reactionary interests and ensure Prussia's predominance in the new *Reich*.[27] To the agrarians, foreign imports[28] did not seem as menacing or as politically useful as the danger of international Catholicism or the working-class movement.[29]

At the turn of the year 1875/76, two events occurred which would prove of enduring consequence for the remainder of the Second Empire. The first of these resulted from Bismarck's failure to secure much needed *Reichstag* support for two of his major aims, a financially independent *Reich* and a successful outcome to his *Kulturkampf* against Catholicism. The primary reason for this lack of success was Bismarck's inability to establish a firm basis of support among the conservative parties. He was still considered either a liberal by the conservatives or the opposite by liberals. In such a situation, he gladly accepted an offer of assistance by industrial interests in the *Reichstag*. They offered Bismarck support in his major policies, if he would assure them, on a *quid pro quo* basis, of Delbrueck's removal and the introduction of protective tariffs upon industrial goods. The Chancellor immediately acquiesced to the first demand, but left the second unresolved. He also urged industry to come to an unqualified understanding with agriculture.[30]

The second event of the new year was the dramatic fall of domestic wheat prices.[31] No longer able to remain inactive, the *Junkers*, led by east Prussian landowners, organized and founded the *Vereinigung der Steuer und Wirtschaftsreformer* (Association of Tax and Economic Reformers).[32] In February 1876, the Association stressed that "we live in an age of material interests," clearly reflecting the shifting emphasis of conservative thought.[33] Of the original 481 members of the group, nearly nine-tenths were *Rittergutsbesitzer*[34] whose concerns no longer centered upon ideology.[35] The Tax Reformers' statutes, drawn up in February, stated that the members of the Association were "opponents of protective tariffs." Yet they treated the issues of import duties and consumption taxes as "open questions."[36]

8

Bismarck's courting of the protectionist groups went beyond the need for industrial or agrarian tariffs: "Bismarck's aims were, first, to interweave the interests of the various producing classes of Prussia and to satisfy them in the economic field, and second, to bind these classes to the monarchial state led by him."[37] The new pressure groups of industry and agriculture would serve those aims. So would a "national" Conservative Party which would reflect the merger of Prussian conservatism with the federal *Reich*. Only then could Bismarck lead a truly Prusso-German state.[38]

Within six months of its founding, the Association of Tax and Economic Reformers had drawn the various Conservative factions into a "new" German Conservative Party. It created an organization which would not only realize its demands (which included, finally, the call for protective agrarian tariffs) but which would be a reliable supporter of Bismarck's policies. The narrowly defined demands of the Tax Reformers were an important aspect of the Party's programme.[39] Yet the German Conservative Party had to pay continued lip-service to arch-conservative insistence on the necessity for organic and corporate institutions.[40]

The creation of the German Conservative Party stands as one of the most important events of the Bismarck era. From this source one can trace the succession of events which helped to create and solidify the conservative mood of "illiberalism" which defined and dominated the Second *Reich*. Not only did it represent a first step towards "...the attempt to make the conservative Prussian element a parliamentary political factor," but it allowed, in the words of Max Weber, "an economically sinking class" to retain, both as an interest group and in parliament, a source of power and authority.[41]

The protective tariff alliance between agriculture and industry which occurred in 1879 was a major development in Conservative Party strategy during the era of Bismarck. Yet nearly as important as the alliance between rye and iron was the Conservatives' conversion to a "national" party. As a group of approximately twenty-five thousand individuals (half of them *Rittergutsbesitzer* from east Prussia), the agrarians did not constitute a formidable group in sheer numbers.[42] The real strength of this class lay in the ability to perpetuate itself at a time when rapid industrialization acutely threatened its place in society. After 1878, the Conservative Party came to the conclusion that it could no longer alone wage a struggle against the dynamics of industrial-capitalistic modernity.

9

Although it was still influenced by the arch-conservative
Kreuzzeitung group within the Party, the protectionist
element was able to "modernize" most Conservatives into
accepting the arrival of an "epoch of permanent revolution."[43]
To counteract this threat to their conservative world,
feudal-thinking *Junkers* were able to form alliances with
farmers and craftsmen, a technique Friedrich Naumann had
already described at the beginning of an increasingly
democratic age.[44] *Junkers* were able to think of themselves
as "national" without necessarily thinking of the "nation."[45]
The "coming role of the Conservatives" *(Messerschmidt)*
meant the new-found ability to include elements of a
middle-class ideology[46] within their feudal-aristocratic
Weltanschauung. This did not mean that control of the
Party changed hands. Its real strength and leadership
remained in the grip of "authoritarian and hierarchic"
east Elbian landowners.[47]

Such concessions to modernity, by which "...the old
order prolonged its life,"[48] were illusory. The promise
of a new Conservative Party did not mean a changed role
for the *Junkers*. They were content to allow the effects
of economic instabilities and the subsequent wide-spread
revulsion against liberalism, Judaism, and the fear of
socialism to do their work for them. With the aid of
such conservative institutions as the student fraternities,
universities, reserve officer corps,[49] and the Prussian
bureaucracy,[50] the Conservative Party was able to strengthen
the level of conservative influence among the traditional
and new elites in German society.[51] Caught up in the
midst of economic insecurity and an industrial revolution,
Conservatives, who functioned as *"Herrenmenschen mit
demokratischen Handschuhen"* (F. Naumann), found that
modernity could be used to perpetuate the past. Liberalism,
as a competing political philosophy, could never hope to
triumph in a system where modernity meant that "instead
of the *Junkers* being liberalized, the bourgeoisie became
feudalized."[52]

While incorporating the diffuse and opposing varieties
of conservative belief, the new German Conservative Party
also managed to exploit the economic plight of east
Prussian agriculture and gain the aid of Bismarck's
domineering hand. By 1879/80, the Party, Prussian-
centered and controlled by *Junkers*, stood like a Phoenix,
whose rise from the ashes of political sterility had
transformed it once more into a major voice in German
political life.

10

iv.   German Conservatives and the search
      for political stability

The German Conservative Party did not exercise its
greatest degree of power in the national *Reichstag*.
Instead, the Prussian legislature *(Landtag)* became,
after 1879, the center of consistent Conservative
majorities.

The nature of the federal constitution, which had
been constructed by Bismarck to give the Prussian state
an enormous degree of power, made certain that whoever
maintained a majority in the Prussian *Landtag* was assured
of a great deal of influence upon *Reich* matters.   In this
manner, the Conservative Party managed to remain "small
but powerful."   Its greatest political achievement, however,
was the maintenance of the Prussian state as a stronghold
of reactionary thought.   Predominant in a political system
which resembled the *Kamarilla* period, the Conservatives
were able to maintain that position of power with the aid
of a three-class voting law, unchanged constituency
boundaries in east Prussia, and the numberous political
and social institutions of the Prussian state.   During
the latter part of Bismarck's chancellorship, Conservative
influence grew so strong that it became impossible to
rule Germany without them.[53]   In the era of Bismarck,
the German Conservative Party became more than just a
political party or parliamentary representation; it was
the political vehicle for a set of beliefs and a system
of rule determined to survive against all odds.

However effective the Conservatives may have been
in controlling the political situation in Prussia, their
Reichstag position was never as secure.   The Conservatives
were not viewed with much enthusiasm outside of Prussia.
Throughout its existence, the Party was unable to win
more than a quarter of all *Reichstag* seats in an election
decided by (unlike in Prussia) universal, direct and open
suffrage.   An alliance of some sort became a common
practice for the Party's *Reichstag* representation.

During the 1870's and 1880's this was normally
managed with either the Catholic Center Party or, more
preferably, the National Liberals.   The Free Conservative
Party or *Reichspartei* (its *Reichstag* representation) was
conservative in principle, but maintained a strong
industrial orientation after leaving the Prussian
Conservative Party in 1866/67.   It did not possess a
large enough representation (never more than 41 seats)
to be effective in an individual alliance.

11

The Center Party was the choice of the extreme right-wing Conservatives who represented the *Kreuzzeitung* faction. They were primarily concerned with the place of ideology among Conservatives and the place of the Lutheran Church in Prussia. They shared with the Center certain similar views on religious and social questions. Fearful of the future direction of Bismarck's attack upon the Catholic Church, the *Kreuzzeitung* Conservatives joined with the Center to persuade Bismarck to abandon the *Kulturkampf*.[54] The ultraconservative Party members were able to play an influential role in Conservative politics, especially after 1881.

In that year, the editorship of the *Kreuzzeitung* newspaper and the leadership of the ultraconservatives was assumed by W. v. Hammerstein-Schwartow. Also in 1881, the *Kreuzzeitung* faction came under the influence of Adolf Stoecker, a court preacher and head of the *Berliner Bewegung*, a movement oriented towards the working class.[55] In Stoecker's opinion the masses could be led to a "social conservative" point of view. This ideology would replace social democracy as the philosophical power base of working-class politics and lead the workers to a true conservative position. Stoecker's anti-Semitic opinions blended in well with those of v. Hammerstein. Together, the two groups were a constant source of irritation to Bismarck's plans for the development of a German Conservative Party which would be free of ideology and function solely as a pressure group.

Bismarck and the majority of agrarians were in favor of an alliance with the National Liberal Party.[56] Although generally approving Bismarck's policies, ultraconservatives could not bring themselves to support such an alliance. They feared the anti-religious and strongly capitalistic attitudes of the National Liberals. The materialists in the Conservative Party, too, remained hesitant, since the National Liberal Party contained an extremely liberal left-wing. The situation was eased somewhat for the protection-oriented Conservatives by the emergence, in 1884, of Johannes v. Miquel as leader of the National Liberal Party. In that same year, the left-wing National Liberals joined the more progressive left Liberal coalition in the *Reichstag*.[57]

From 1884 until 1887, the German Conservatives and National Liberals struggled to make Bismarck's policies secure. During this period, Bismarck was in need of parliamentary assistance with several of his most important

bills. Above all, he needed help to insure state
support for the continuation of the Anti-Socialist
Law, first passed in 1878. But the coalition of
Conservatives and National Liberals was unable to
offer much aid. It was not until Bismarck dissolved
the *Reichstag* in 1887 (on the pretext of its failure
to pass an army bill), that the coalition was able
to triumph in the so-called *Septennatswahlen* of 1887.
Even then, the *Kartell* of 1887 (now expanded to include
the *Reichspartei*) was at best a loose but continuous
Reichstag coalition. Not only did the *Kreuzzeitung*
Conservatives make a full alliance impossible, but the
victory of 1887 was made possible only by Bismarck's
manufacture of a "war scare" with France. There were
no assurances that in the next election, to be held
in 1890, Bismarck would again find a winning issue.

In the third decade of Bismarck's rule, Germany's
social question was far from being settled. Bismarck,
unable to find an answer in purely domestic solutions,
gave reluctant approval to a policy of "industrial and
colonial" expansion.[58] He visualized a new area of
expansion for German industry and a future source of
economic growth. Moreover, he felt that such a policy
would allow the continued support, with state
intervention, of the alliance between industry and
agriculture.[59]

Through the use of a "manipulated social
imperialism" (P. Kennedy), Bismarck sought to export
the social and political tensions of the *Reich* and to
further his own aims whereby "the raising of national
enthusiasm...became a factor in national integration."[60]
Colonies and their material benefits meant very little
to Bismarck's over-all political strategy. If they
were able to become, however, a viable release for the
tensions of the German "age of neuroses" (Hans Rosenberg),
then he would give them a significant measure of his
support. In addition to "social imperialism", Bismarck
manufactured an anti-English resentment in an effort to
strengthen the ideological meaning of the "nation."
He was able to blame Germany's internal difficulties
upon "outside" sources. Finally, Bismarck sought to
achieve a political basis for the *Kartell* through his
colonial policy. No clearer example of Eckart Kehr's
argument for the "primacy of domestic politics" can be
demonstrated.[61]

Yet by 1890, Bismarck had abandoned most of these
schemes to concentrate upon a new danger, one which
threatened his personal position of power. He had become

convinced that Germany's new Kaiser, Wilhelm II, was
bent on exercising the power to dismiss the Chancellor
which the Constitution of 1871 had granted him. Desperate
for defensive schemes to prevent such an occurrence,
Bismarck hit upon the idea of wrecking the *Kartell*.
With such a measure, he hoped to create a situation of
anarchy in Germany's domestic and international affairs.
This, he believed, would demonstrate his "indispensibility",
thus retaining for him not only his position as Chancellor,
but, in effect, limiting the Kaiser's aims regarding
one-man rule.[62] The *Kartell* was futher weakened by a
dispute over colonial policy between Bismarck and the
National Liberals. By 1890 there was every possibility
that the Party would leave the coalition.[63]

v. The structure collapses: the failure
   of Bismarck's Germany

The "permanent threat of a *coup d'etat*" (M. Stuermer)
became, after 1878, the secret weapon of conservative
Germany against the forces of liberalism and socialism.
Throughout the remainder of Bismarck's rule, it served as
a constant veto on any attempt to translate the results of
rapid industrialization into political forms unwelcome
to the conservative system. The *coup* never, of course,
took place. It was, rather, a psychological weapon
designed to produce a progress-arresting fear in liberal
and socialist circles. Yet it is more important as a
factor in the evaluation of the Bismarckian state. It
served as the one continuous feature which more than any
other, pointed to Bismarck's inability to resolve the
social tensions within the Empire and instill a measure
of self-confidence in Germany's conservative system.[64]

The alliance between agriculture and industry was
essential to the development of a conservative and
politically-stable *Reich*. One historian has labeled
this alliance as the "second founding of the *Reich*."
According to this interpretation, the year 1878/79, when
the alliance was formed, can be understood as having
more significance than 1871 since "...1879 saw a radical
redistribution of power, and 1871 did not." The alliance
promised to secure for Bismarck the necessary balance
between his need for political domination and economic
expansion. Whereas the differences between agrarians
and industrialists and conservatives and liberals had been
real and serious issues in the second decade of Bismarck's
office, this situation seemed on the way to a permanent

14

solution by 1878/79. It was in that year that Bismarck began his attacks upon the Social Democratic Party. With the subsequent division of German society into *staatserhaltende* and *staatsverneinende* elements,[65] into "friends" and "enemies" of the State, the aim of maintaining a political and economic union of interests took on an even greater meaning.

Yet the alliance between industry and agriculture was never as firm as Bismarck would have liked. Anti-industrial prejudice on the side of the agrarians and the desire for profit weakened the relationship. After higher protective tariffs were introduced in 1887, agricultural prices increased sharply. Higher agricultural prices meant the need for higher industrial wages to offset the increases. Even earlier, in 1885, an agrarian group, the Pomeranian Economic Society, had introduced proposals calling for the doubling of rye and wheat tariffs as well as a number of anti-capitalist, anti-industrialist demands.[66]

On both the economic and political level, Bismarck's hopes for a stable conservative system proved to be more illusion than reality. By 1890, the agrarian-industrial dispute had developed into a serious dilemma. In the *Reichstag*, the *Kartell* was at an end.

In an age which Michael Stuermer has described as "...men living with an abysmal fear of social and political revolution from below and under the threat of a *coup d'etat* from above,"[67] the achievement in Germany of something resembling internal stability had become an enormous and virtually impossible task. During a time of great domestic dilemma, Bismarck's attempt to assume the position of the "strong man" in German politics was doomed to failure. What on the surface appeared as a victory for the *status quo* only achieved, in the words of Hans Rosenberg, the "appearance of stability."[68] Behind this facade one found, at best, conflicting economic interests only superficially merged; and, at worst, one found the intensification of class antagonisms, as "in" groups struggled to maintain political control of the Empire. Despite the genius of Bismarck's political manipulations, and despite the fact that a *Bildung* and *Besitz* union of liberals and conservatives had been achieved, the "dead end" of the Bismarckian system was at hand. Not even the conversion of various *Reichstag* parties into "neo-corporate interest groups...without responsibilities or political control..."[69] was enough to save the grand design.

Radicals and Reactionaries

Instead of total consolidation, 1890 saw a still
incomplete nation-state deeply divided by class strife
and a growing agrarian-industrial conflict over the
direction of Germany's economic future.[70] The German
Conservative Party and the conservative system seemed
everywhere preponderant, yet nowhere secure. Such a
situation reflected the bankruptcy of a manufactured
political environment whose superstructure of merged
interests could not conceal the glaring weaknesses at
the very foundation of its existence.

CHAPTER II

German Conservatives Between Conflict and
Cooperation: The *Bund der Landwirte*, *Sammlungspolitik*,
and the Strategy for an Agrarian Future (1890-1902)

i. The Party adrift: the Conservatives
    and the Caprivi challenge to agriculture

1

The *Kartell* collapsed in the elections of 1890. Not
much later, in March of that year, Bismarck was dismissed
from office by Wilhelm II. The fragile union of interests,
which had allowed competing economic sectors to maintain
an uneasy peace, was broken--a victim of agrarian fear
and hostility.[1] As a result, both the German Conservative
Party and agriculture soon found themselves in similarly
hazardous positions.[2]

Conservative fears were intensified as Wilhelm
followed Bismarck's dismissal with the appointment of
General Leo v. Caprivi as the new German Chancellor.
Caprivi's self-styled description as a man "without an
acre of land or a blade of straw" *(ohne Ar und Halm)* was
viewed as decidedly hostile to the future of German
agriculture. His departure from the rigidity of Bismarck's
conservative politics was a further blow to agrarian hopes
of a secure position in the configuration of Germany's
political and social elites. But his ultimate decision
to sacrifice agriculture and thereby insure an expanding
industrial sector was viewed by the *Junkers* as nothing
less than an agrarian disaster.

The German Conservative Party was far from ready to
accept the challenge offered by Caprivi's actions. As
the self-appointed defenders of Prusso-German agriculture,
the Party was a logical choice to lead that economic
sector's response. Instead, the long-standing differences
between the *Kreuzzeitung* faction and pro-Bismarck
Conservatives led by v. Helldorff-Breda continued to
surface and ensured political disunity within Party ranks.
Yet v. Helldorff's own leadership qualities had been
questioned by Bismarck on more than one occasion.[3] It
was this Conservative's well-documented blunder in
"misunderstanding" Bismarck's intentions that had caused
the Party to vote against the renewal of the Anti-Socialist
Law in 1890.[4] The weakness of Conservative leadership,
however, had long been evident. Conservative politicians
had always been among the most numerous representatives
of the *Honoratioren*, a curious breed of "amateurs who
could afford to hold political office without financial
reward..."[5] Part-time politicians with only a part-time

17

ability to lead were no longer in line with the needs of
a (supposedly) "modern" party such as the German
Conservatives. Instead, the existence of the Conservative
Party as a political power demanded a high degree of
organizational and individual skill. Faced with Caprivi's
threat to agriculture, the Conservative leadership responded
with only a minimal amount of effective political opposition.

This deplorable state of Conservative affairs could
not have been otherwise. Despite the fact that the
Party recognized the need for economic self-interest, it
had done little to modernize its internal structure. It
remained "a loosely knit organization held together by
an unwritten code rather than by an active party
machinery under centralized leadership."[6] Thus when
Caprivi dismissed the importance of agricultural participation in the German economy, the Conservative-agrarian
outcry was great but its initial response was muted.

Surprisingly, the early period of Caprivi's government
was, in marked contrast to that of his predecessor,
conflict-free. A noticeable lack of conservative-agrarian
influence in political matters was not the only feature
of the time. For his "New Course" in German politics,
Caprivi was able to find support in various sections of
the non-Conservative *Kartell* parties, the left Liberal
coalition, and even in the ranks of the Social Democratic
Party. His policy of "compromise and moderation" received
little criticism from conservative circles.[7] Caprivi
seemed in control of matters to a degree thought unlikely
for one so much in the shadows of the Bismarckian era.
Economic conditions, too, were favorable for the years
1890 and 1891;[8] grain prices had been higher than for
some time. It was now only left for the new Chancellor
to continue his moderate policies in order to assure
himself of political success.

Caprivi, however, had assumed the office of
Chancellor with a vague but active desire to "shake up"
the rigid bureaucratic system in Prussia. He instructed
his fellow Prussian ministers (the German Chancellor
was also head of the Prussian Ministry of State) to
assert deliberately their independence in the face of
strict bureaucratic procedure; in the process, however,
Caprivi alienated reactionary forces in the upper
echelons of the Prussian bureaucracy.[9] The *Junkers*,
too, gradually turned against Caprivi when, backed by
a Center-left Liberal coalition, he reorganized the
Prussian system of local administration. This legislation,
the *Landesgemeindeordnung* of 1891, "...cut further into

the old *Junker* privileges and granted the rural
communities a modicum of self-government."[10] Caprivi's
main threat to the *Junkers'* interests, however, came in
the form of fifteen international trade treaties that,
in late 1891 and early 1892, stood ready for renewal.[11]

Bismarck, it will be remembered, had successfully
bridged the political gap between conservative and liberal
interests.[12] His ability to weld together seemingly
divergent interests had not, however, extended to the
area of economics. This was especially true of economic
protection. It was evident, for example, that high
tariff rates were essential if the *Junkers* were to break
even, let alone make profits. Protection was important
to German industry in terms of its domestic markets. But
industrialists were also beginning to see the need for
overseas markets for their goods. In that case, a policy
of moderate protection was necessary so that a risk of
tariff war could be kept to a minimum. As one historian
has described the situation, "industrialists wanted to
conquer the world market; agrarians wanted protection
from it."[13]

Caprivi was faced with several choices regarding the
series of protectionist treaties that he had inherited
from Bismarck. He could have continued, firstly, to
support a policy of high tariffs against foreign grain
and industrial goods. But with the union of German
agriculture and industry finished, there seemed to be
no useful purpose in continuing such strong protectionist
measures. The risk of economic retaliation seemed too
high a price to pay for the benefits of economic protection.
Secondly, Caprivi could have continued a policy of strong
agricultural protection and reduced the amount of support
given to industry. Yet this would not have eliminated the
threat of tariff wars and would have deprived Germany of
the most expansive and least vulnerable part of her
economy.[14] Caprivi's third choice seemed most logical.
He had to eliminate agricultural protection, which was
proving the most vulnerable and least useful in the
economics of international competition. By lowering
agricultural tariffs, the new Chancellor was prepared
to open Germany's internal grain markets to a deluge of
foreign supplies. By supporting industry with the
establishment of long-term tariff rates, Caprivi hoped
to "stimulate exports by providing German manufacturers
with guarantees against sudden changes in foreign import
duties."[15]

Radicals and Reactionaries

A further aspect of Caprivi's policy, equally important but rarely considered, was his plan to establish a Central European tariff group against the industrial competitiveness of Great Britain, Russia, and, above all, the United States.[16] This important objective--which would dominate Germany's foreign economic and political objectives for decades--could only become operative once Germany proved herself prepared to make concessions to her neighbors--once more necessitating the lowering of protective tariffs.

The combination of these factors thus threatened to deprive agrarian interests of a dominant place in Germany's social hierarchy. They also threatened the very fragile position of agrarian economics, already existing only with state concessions.

If this were not enough, Caprivi's political activities indicated a strong desire to remove himself from the administration of Conservative needs and interests, something which had been an essential part of Bismarck's policy. In a dispute that arose over the School Bill of 1892,[17] Caprivi not only retired from the top ministerial position in Prussia, but also withdrew from an active involvement with the internal politics of the Prussian state.[18] For the *Junkers*, this was a direct signal that Caprivi was, in effect, withdrawing from Conservative affairs.[19] They could no longer deny the fact that agriculture would receive neither political nor economic aid from a Chancellor who refused to administer Prussia--the stronghold of Conservative and agrarian Germany.

The growing feeling against Caprivi combined with an earlier antipathy towards industry and big business to form the essence of agrarian discontent. No longer satisfied merely to voice their opposition to the present state of affairs, Prussia's agrarian conservatives began to contend that action in any form was their sole method of salvation. One possible solution lay in the ability of their political representative, the German Conservative Party, to alter a course that seemed headed for certain disaster.

2

On December 14, 1891, Count Limburg-Stirum, Chairman of the Conservative group in the Prussian *Abgeordnetehaus* (Chamber of Deputies), published an article in the *Kreuzzeitung* filled with bitterness at the plight of the "most loyal supporters of the *Reich*, the Prussian agrarians."[20] His frustration and anger reflected the

20

mood of radicalism among sections of the Conservative
Party. These members viewed opposition to the Government
as essential. They were fearful of a future dominated
by Caprivi's anti-agrarian policies and were suffering
from the effects of a sudden grain-price slump. It
was these agrarians who would play the key role in the
rise of a movement dedicated to organizing such unhappiness
into an effective political force.

A large part of that unhappiness centered around the
lack of an assertive Conservative leadership.[21] A
significant portion of the Party remained committed to
a vision of the *Kartell* and the need for governmental
allegiance. As such, members of the Helldorff-Breda
Conservatives blindly supported most of Caprivi's policies.
In their adherence to the concept of governmental
cooperation, they were unable to grasp fully the severe
crisis facing Prussian agriculture.[22]

The pro-Caprivi position of these Conservatives
was countered by Stoecker and v. Hammerstein. But since
the latter two were committed to particular forms of
Christian piety, mass-movement politics, and anti-Semitism,
their appeal was limited to a small number of Conservatives.
This had already been demonstrated by the ease with which
Bismarck succeeded in blocking their attempts to gain
control of the Party. But with Bismarck gone, and
Caprivi declining to meddle in Conservative affairs, their
position improved. Changing agrarian interests now
demanded a strong and enlarged Conservative influence.
Not Helldorff-Breda's uncritical views, but a "mass-
movement for the Right and led by the Right" was the new
agrarian demand.[23] Only in this manner might pressure
be brought to bear upon Caprivi.

The question of Conservative leadership finally
reached a crisis point in the controversy following the
governmental withdrawal of the Prussian School Bill.
Helldorff-Breda's governmental views led him to oppose
the Bill, which was extremely pro-clerical in its intent.
A full confrontation between pro-Government moderates
and religious pietists was now inevitable. Helldorff-Breda
attempted to force Conservative members to purge Stoecker
and v. Hammerstein as a step towards reasserting his
moderate leadership. Most Conservatives, however, were
aware of the general agrarian dissatisfaction with their
politics.[24] They completely rejected Helldorff-Breda's
contention that "anti-Semitism and narrow economic
interests" were alien to the traditions of the Conservative
Party.[25] Instead of solidifying his powers, Helldorff-Breda

lost his position in both Conservative factions, the
Reichstag and House of Deputies. He resigned as Party
Chairman in May 1892.[26] The *Kreuzzeitung* Conservatives
along with Stoecker now dominated Conservative politics.

A changed leadership did not resolve Conservative
difficulties. Otto v. Manteuffel-Krossen, Helldorff-Breda's
replacement as Party Chairman, was actively involved in
several unsuccessful attempts to defeat Caprivi's policies,
but his reluctant desire to oppose the Government reflected
a persistent Conservative dilemma.[27]

If the Conservative Party was to satisfy the needs
of its supporters, it had to establish itself in several
directions. There was the need to save agriculture's
position as an integral part of the conservative state.
This position was being threatened by Caprivi's aim of
severely lowering agricultural tariffs; an organized
resistance was of the utmost importance. Also necessary,
because agrarians were restricted in numbers, was a link
with other social groups who found themselves (or could
be convinced they were) in a similarly threatened state.

Such groups, furthermore, had to be organized in a
manner that would serve agrarian needs. The ability of
aristocratic agrarians to meet changing social conditions
with remarkable forms of compromise and innovation in the
organizational sphere was soon made evident. Foremost
among the illustrations of such flexibility was the
agrarian relationship with Stoecker's Christian Social
Party and the *Radau* anti-Semites.

The Christian Social Party[28] had already been a part
of Conservative politics for over a decade since first
associating with the *Kreuzzeitung* group in 1881.[29] Its
peculiar position within the Party--that of maintaining
its own Chairman, newspaper, and Party Day--had never
convinced the great majority of *Junkers* that the Christian
Socials were an integral part of Conservative thought and
action. The friction between aristocratic *Junkers* and
"popular" politicians like Stoecker remained unresolved.
Yet Stoecker's presence was tolerated because it gave the
agrarians an opportunity to improve upon their own
organizational and demagogic skills through observation
of this magnetic personality.[30] After the creation of an
agrarian pressure group, the *Bund der Landwirte*,[31] the
need for Stoecker and his supporters diminished. Consequently,
Stoecker was dismissed from the Party in February 1896.
Christian Social influence remained a negligible factor in
Party affairs for the next two decades.[32]

In the midst of their struggle against Caprivi,
agrarian Conservatives were faced with a serious challenge
from an unexpected source. A vigorous anti-Semitic
and anti-Conservative movement, led by lower middle-class
agitators Hermann Ahlwardt and Otto Boeckel, had by 1890
greatly increased its representation in the *Reichstag*.[33]
These *Radau* (rowdy) anti-Semites challenged and defeated
the despised "Cohn-servatives" in subsequent by-elections.[34]
The existence of such a political and social movement
threatened to diminish Conservative influence, even within
"safe" constituencies.[35] At a time when agrarians
desperately needed to maintain and increase strong links
with the peasantry and middle-classes *(Mittelstand)*, the
presence of a force that threatened to reduce and perhaps
destroy this connection could not be disregarded. Repellant
as the vulgar, racial anti-Semitism of the *Radau* elements
may have been, agrarian despair necessitated the inclusion
of such a group.[36]

Conservative agrarians, though temporarily dominated
by Stoecker and v. Hammerstein, were gaining the knowledge
and confidence to leave behind these hesitant and
unpopular elements. Radical agrarians were aware that
the great majority of *Junkers* were unwilling to follow
a political party whose position and whose actions did
not allow it to directly confront the enemies of agriculture:
Caprivi, industry, capitalism, Jewry, and Social Democracy.

The lessons that the agrarians had learned from their
close connection with non-Conservative groups became
evident during the Conservative Party Day held in Berlin's
Tivoli Brewery on December 4, 1892. The new Party
programme reflected agrarian demands for high agricultural
tariffs, closer ties with the *Mittelstand* and the need
for economic parity with industry. It also attacked the
elements considered most dangerous to agrarian interests:
high finance, Social Democracy and Jewry.[37]

Tivoli thus marked a significant change in the
politics of the German Conservative Party. It gave
vent to the question of agriculture's continued participation in the German economy. It permitted the
Conservatives to make known the fact that they would
stop at nothing in order to ensure a stable agrarian
future. The ideas of the radical anti-Semites and
Christian Socials contributed to the success of the Tivoli
meeting. These groups were present because their strengths
were needed to eliminate Conservative and agrarian
weaknesses. Those pockets of popular and racial anti-
Semitism that had been scattered and unorganized were
now made a part of the legitimate world of Conservative

23

politics. Their radicalism was maintained but not
allowed to dominate. It was channeled into an effective
agrarian link with various economic and social classes.[38]
The pseudo-democratic and mass-based techniques of the
Stoecker movement, too, were to be used for agrarian
needs and their aims revised.

The Tivoli meeting was, above all, a "dress rehearsal"
for the creation of an agrarian-dominated and Conservative-
supported pressure group, the *Bund der Landwirte* or
BdL (Agrarian League).[39] Tivoli provided the ideological
platform from which the BdL (founded barely two months
later) would launch a "counter-revolution" against Caprivi
and his attempts "to strengthen (industrial) influence
in the power system at the expense of the *Junkers*..."[40]
Armed with newer, more refined weapons of reaction, agrarian
Conservatives completed the break with tradition and with
industry. Yet they did not necessarily abandon the aims,
set forth by Bismarck, which both agriculture and industry
recognized as vital to the existence of the Prusso-German
state.[41]

ii. The Party modernized: agrarian politics
     confronts the era of the "carrot and stick"

1

In 1908 Oscar Stillich saw the salient feature of
German political life as being "...the hunger for power."
Political parties were no longer filled with ideals,
he wrote; rather, their defined roles as political
groupings were based on "...economic and social questions..."[42]
The observation was noteworthy in at least two respects:
it was a general conclusion reached amidst the specific
investigation of the role played by the German Conservative
Party and it seemed such a commonplace, necessary, and
entirely visible feature of German political life--a fact
based, however, on an entirely different set of historical
origins.

Previously, those political parties which had endorsed
(and therefore accepted) the fundamental principles of
the nineteenth-century Prusso-German state had justified
their course by formulating appropriate political theories.
They had scarcely been able to conceive of the possibility
that anything could have driven them to oppose the State.
This position had altered, however, with the onset of
wide-ranging changes in the economic and social structures
of the *Reich* during the decades after unification.
Economic self-interest was the first weakened link in

24

the relationship between government and party. Yet it
was hardly all-embracing. Governmental acquiescences
to the harsh realities of unnatural shifts in the
power structure of the state (protective tariffs to
counter increasing economic instability for agriculture
and heavy industry) clearly showed Bismarck's
manipulative genius. Furthermore, the emergence of the
"nation" as an idealized possession of the Right insured
that the relationship between the State and the conservative parties remained strong.

It was rather in those groups of political
"survivors" who had suffered as a result of Bismarck's
"integrative" excesses that an atmosphere was created
where total or partial opposition came to be the normal
state of affairs and, as in the case of the Center
until its *volte*-face in 1897/98, politically profitable.[43]
This gradual decline in loyalty to the government finally
produced changes in the *staatserhaltende* groups as well.
Under the Caprivi administration, the Conservative
Party was brought to the brink of open revolt against
the man and the policies considered a danger to agrarian
well-being. Through various tactical measures, the
agrarian section of the Party was able to integrate
elements of "popular" anti-Semitism and lower and
middle-class demagoguery into an organization which
would otherwise have become increasingly directionless
and impotent.

By the end of the Tivoli meeting in December 1892,
the core of agrarian opposition no longer felt itself
able to remain within the German Conservative Party.
Barely three weeks after Tivoli had demonstrated the
extent of agrarian willingness to cooperate with entirely
non-Conservative elements, an obscure landowner writing
in a little-known agrarian newspaper (the *Bunzlauer
Provinzblatt fuer Bauern*), demanded the creation of a
large agrarian party in order to "...try and win more
influence upon Parliament and legislation." The *Aufruf*
suggested the highly provocative notion that agrarians
could no longer depend upon Conservative parliamentary
representation to solve their long-standing political
and economic difficulties. Agrarians, according to the
author, had to "...stop voting and being liberal,
ultramontane or Conservative."[44] The agrarian spokesman,
Conrad Freiherr v. Wangenheim, re-emphasized this mood
at the end of 1893 when he wrote to his brother that
"our goal remains the same: the gathering together of
all elements who wish to maintain the Christian Monarchy.
We are of the view that this goal can only be achieved on

the basis of the present economic movement since the
nation is *'tired of political parties'* (italics mine-AJP)
and all political parties have shown their incompetence."[45]

Such was the mood which nurtured the agrarian
movement known as the *Bund der Landwirte*.[46] It was
founded on February 18, 1893, one of several extra-
parliamentary organizations established in a year noted
for its "transitional" character. The basis for this
transition was a reduction in the significance of
parliamentary parties as the basic vehicle for political
dissatisfaction and, relatedly, the appearance of
organized sections of German society disenchanted with
the "dead-end" function of parliament and embittered
over Caprivi's foreign and domestic policies.[47]

The *Bund der Landwirte* was an agrarian "pressure
group" formed by malcontents within the Conservative
Party and, beyond, in the ranks of east Prussian
landowners. The ostensible basis for its creation was
the immediate necessity for agrarians to combat Caprivi's
economic policies. In addition, however, there were
more deeply-rooted problems in German agriculture which
were equally in need of remedy. Chief among these was
the steady increase in the structural and economic
crises of the agrarian sector.[48] The *Junkers* were
moreover, unwilling to acquiesce to the gradual
abandonment of the Bismarckian system and the loss of
their own social and economic significance. Consequently,
they were no longer prepared to accept the authority of
the State as all-embracing. While they understood the
immense importance of the relationship between their
social position and the authority of the State (especially
as a guard against the working class) that relationship
could only continue at the cost of political and
economic concessions.[49] The conscious decision on the
part of the agrarians to alter the long-standing symbiotic
relationship between State and Conservatives was symptomatic
of a long-range situation in which the *Bund* "...constituted
a radical opposition against the government, and was
certainly ready to learn organization from Social
Democracy, but passed itself off as *staatserhaltend* and
truly conservative."[50] Beyond this the *Bund* was not only
seeking a greater degree of social and economic aid from
the state but an increased share in its source of power.[51]
The State, for its part, was aware not only of the change
in Conservative-agrarian politics, but of the imminent
crisis that such a change, combined with an agrarian-
industrial antagonism, might produce. This recognition
was a primary factor in the attempts of later governments
and the monarchy to remedy the situation and to reinstate
a form of understanding between the two sectors based
upon mutual political and social interests.

26

The search for survival at any cost and the need
for profitability at the cost of someone else were the
motivating forces behind the *Bund*.[52] It played a role
independent of the German Conservative Party yet was
able to complete the transformation of the Party into
"...a great agrarian class party with a *mittelstaendischen*
wrapping."[53] The economic[54] and the ideological[55] bases
of the agrarian movement were practical applications of
Tivoli principles combined with radical agrarian innovation.
In particular, the *bund* character, which was enough of
a development in the "political style" (Puhle) of the
time to warrant sociological classification,[56] was a
complex mixture of both restoration and radicalism,[57]
anti-Semitism[58] and *Mittelstand* politics,[59] and of
Social Darwinism[60] and anti-capitalism.[61] Essential to
the understanding and evaluation of the interest group
in general and, more specifically, of the "pressure
group" as exemplified by the *Bund* is the premise that all
of these organizations, despite self-interest and surface
disagreements, were "...a relatively united defensive
front against the emancipatory demands of the workers'
movement."[62] In fact they are also of the utmost importance
in a general evaluation of the ruling system of the
Second Empire. The emergence of interest groups like
the *Bund der Landwirte* was hardly a boon to the spread of
democracy. Despite the supposed proliferation of
legitimate group interest the "...constellation of
parliament, party, and interest groups was such that
the broadening of political participation in Germany did
less to strengthen democracy than to make more inevitable
the ultimate appearance of the 'plebiscitarian dictatorship'."[63]

2

The changes within the Conservative Party, both in
terms of structure and ideology, were the significant
factors in the role it would come to occupy in the
spectrum of parties and politics of the Wilhelmine *Reich*.
The founding of the *Bund der Landwirte* not only determined
that role but was the key factor in the process of change.
The agrarians in the Party had been forced to attempt an
act of salvation in a rapidly declining situation--one
that foresaw the economic destruction of the *Junkers*
east of the river Elbe. The most radical of these had
opted for a solution based upon the need for extra-
parliamentary agitation and a broadly-based re-evaluation
of Conservative aims and principles. Included in this
rupture with a tradition-dominated ideology was the
appearance of non-Conservative ideas and social attitudes.

Radicals and Reactionaries

The working relationship which emerged between the
Bund and the Conservative Party and between *Junker*
and middle-class agitator allowed the BdL to exert
an enormous influence and to chart the course for
future agrarian survival. It also forced the Conservatives
to lose their identity as a self-standing political unit.
To be sure, this was a situation made possible only by
the closest cooperation between *Bund* demagogues and
Conservative members; in other words, there was more
acceptance of *Bund* domination than opposition to its
presence.

The individual conceptions of Conservative
politicians began to emerge into clear-cut divisions.
What was once an essentially Prussian royalist, moderate
and Estate-bound view was now forced to acknowledge,
if not accept, a vast new army of BdL functionaries,
drawn from differing social backgrounds, who served
to create and put into practice the nationalist, Social-
Darwinist, and corporate state ideology of the
Bund der Landwirte. Among them Hahn, Oertel, Malkewitz,
Endell, Kaufhold, and Kiesenwetter were the most
important.[64]

Conservative ideology and Conservative leadership
no longer bore any resemblance to the simplistic view
of society based on the existence of harmonious Estates;
nor was it blindly rooted in adherence to the Prussian
state and strict cooperation with monarchy and government.
The *Bund der Landwirte* had "transformed" them both into
a "new look" centered upon radical anti-Semitism, opposition
to governmental policy and above all, the development of
an agricultural romanticism. In so doing it was not
only breaking new ground for the defense of the agrarian
sector, but reinforcing older positions against the
renewed demands of the German working class[65] and the
danger of industrialization.

3

During the period after unification, agriculture
and industry, the traditional and new elites of the
German *Reich*, had experienced vastly different economic
fortunes. As a consequence, the Caprivi regime, where
this divergence was at its zenith, clearly reflected
the importance of economic distress as a factor in the
instability of political systems. With the Bismarckian-
inspired destruction of the *Kartell* and the "sacrificial
lamb" position of agriculture, the Wilhelmine ruling
system and its interests momentarily lost sight of the
"friend-foe" alignments within the Empire. In one of

its frequent attempts at the political seduction of the German working class, the *Reich* abandoned an outright persecution of Social Democracy. When combined with the conflict between agriculture and industry this resulted not in seduction but in a further strain upon the system and, relatedly, an increase in both actual and perceived instability.

This may be more readily explained if one considers the Marxist contention that two basic political methods were employed by both Bismarck and the elites of the Wilhelmine period to defend and maintain the conservative system: 1. a method of repressive violence and 2. a method of reform liberalism.[66] This is essentially the "carrot and stick" theory which some historians have labelled "negative integration."[67] The Caprivi era represented an attempt to concentrate upon the latter method while essentially scrapping the classical Bismarckian forms (Anti-Socialist Law *and* social welfare schemes). In so doing, the Caprivi government and the brief period of the "peoples" Kaiser represented one of the few attempts to "integrate" the German working-man without actively persecuting his political representatives.[68]

The attempt at a liberal-reform control of the working class seemed at first to have achieved a measure of success. The number of strikes and strikers declined significantly after 1890/91 and did not rise again to any level which approached that of 1890. The dismissal of Caprivi, however, and the appointment of Prince Hohenlohe-Schillingsfurst as Chancellor reversed this trend.[69] This cannot be attributed to an increased demand for wages[70] nor can it be shown to be strictly the result of an increased revolutionary consciousness on the part of the working class.[71] It can only be understood as an awareness by the German worker that his links with Social Democracy were not to function unimpeded.

This was clear from the increased totals secured by the Social Democrats in the election of 1893. Moreover, influential government circles were calling for renewed cooperation between agriculture and industry. There was, too, a growing awareness by these groups that the essential threat to the *Reich* consisted not only in the danger of Social Democracy but equally in the vacuum of power created by the friction between agriculture and industry. The problem remained one of uniting the conservative forces and halting the increasing recruitment of the working class by the Social Democrats with their chiliastic message. The renewed efforts of a *Sammlung* of *staatserhaltende* forces, as well as the *Umsturzgesetzes* of 1894/95 and the *Zuchthausvorlage* (Workhouse Bill) of 1899 were clear indications that the *Reich* perceived the danger to its stability and intended to correct the situation. They were also useful indicators of the manner in which "psychological moments" played a key part in the process of "negative integration": the working class was offered the "carrot" when the system felt itself strong enough to mount such an attempt (correctly or otherwise); but the moment that the attempt produced negative results, the stick was hurriedly pulled out again. After 1894 the stick was not removed until the outbreak of "total war" in 1914 when the "psychological moment" once more dictated its withdrawal. Expressed in another manner, the Caprivi period may be seen as an indication of the ability of the Conservative system and its interests to make certain that all "internal differences always found their limits, if the struggle of the workers' movement touched a nerve in the system of exploitation and class rule."[72]

An immediate solution to the crisis of an unstable ruling system was not, however, at hand. The Conservatives and especially the *Bund der Landwirte* were in no mood to consider such a solution. The anger and hostility with which the *Bund* attacked the tariff negotiations and agitated for Caprivi's dismissal caused the normally conservative publicist Hans Delbrueck to condemn the "national fanaticism" which believed that it could tread upon the laws of humanity.[73]

Another group of conservatives was also concerned with the increased radicalism of the parliamentary Conservatives. Their uneasiness was directed at the growing opposition which the *Junkers* were displaying towards the monarchy. Thus, for instance, Waldersee, the Conservatives' choice to replace Caprivi, noted in March of 1894 that within the Prussian provinces "...a great change of ownership is being carried out in the country...The real conservative elements of Prussia are being destroyed, and with that a good portion of the monarchial loyalty is being lost..."[74] A further, more certain sign that there was indeed serious worry over the mood of the *Junkers* came in the form of a speech delivered by Wilhelm in September of 1894. In his talk, the Kaiser emphasized the importance he attributed to Conservative strength in Prussia. He, as King of Prussia, could not remain without the Conservatives, he said. But he also warned the Party that it would be unable to achieve any of its demands unless the Kaiser had full Conservative cooperation.[75]

It was, in fact, only after Caprivi had been purged from office by the "feudal-agrarian and social reaction" (Gustav Schmoller) that the chances for a reconciliation between the feuding economic sectors became possible.[76] The impetus for such a scheme had already existed since 1891. In March of that year the Free Conservative leader v. Kardoff, reflecting the more far-sighted politics of his party, had written of the need for a "preservation of economic policy through a connection between agrarian and industrial interests."[77] Several further moves in the direction of such a plan, namely the founding of a "National Party" with protective tariffs and the *Mittelstand* as its bases or the creation of a "German Economic Party" as successor to the "Economic Association" of 1878, found the agitation and non-cooperation of the radical agrarians too great a barrier; each floundered after initial starts.[78]

The new direction of *Reich* politics away from the anomaly of the Caprivi years was instituted by the Kaiser. At the beginning of 1895 he ordered the newly-appointed Chancellor Hohenlohe to emphasize more strongly the "Prussian line." He also instructed him to prepare an economic program that would be acceptable to the agrarians. This would include government subsidies to agriculture in the form of credits and a partial acceptance of the *Grosse Mittel* demands of the BdL by the introduction of reforms for the German stock exchange. Industry, too, was to be appeased as much as possible. Paramount in this was the end of any social policy of extended friendship to the working class. The *Mittelstand* was to receive the protective hand of the government and the trade unions were to receive its wrath. It was the Kaiser's opinion that the "social question"--as reflected in the increasing unionization of the working class and the election gains of the Social Democrats--could best be neutralized by exporting it in the shape of an increased nationalism based upon a slogan of "world politics." In this he was reaching back into the era of Bismarckian social imperialism without relying on merely the issue of colonies. Integration, it was felt, would have to be achieved on the basis of another issue.[79]

The aims of such a complete turnabout in the politics of the Crown and the Government were varied and, factually, quite diverse. The anti-social policies were initiated

31

not only as precise points on the road to a nearly-
complete appeasement of the social elites but had, of
course, the end aim of renewed and full cooperation
between monarchy, government and *staatserhaltende*
interests. They also helped to complete the Kaiser's
cleansing from the system of those ministers
sympathetic to the "New Course" and Caprivi. This
was achieved in 1896/97 with the dismissal of
Boetticher, Marschall, and Berlepsch. Together with
Lohmann they had constituted not only a dangerous threat
to the renewed emphasis upon an agrarian-industrial
understanding, but had also stood in the path of the
Kaiser's aim of achieving for himself the role of the
"decisive integrating factor" in German politics;
furthermore, Wilhelm would now be able to achieve his
"personal rule" of the German state. The emergence
of men such as Buelow, Tirpitz, Miquel and Posadowsky
meant a Ministry which could put into practice the
decisive factors in the Kaiser's strategy: Buelow as
the minister to propagate the theme of "world politics";
Tirpitz to find the key integrative theme through
the building of a large naval fleet; and Miquel as the
chief strategist behind the renewed cooperation of the
economic elites.[80]

To a very great degree the opinion and mood of the
Conservatives and the BdL played a key factor in the
success or downfall of the new slant in German politics.
Each and every aspect of the overall approach to the
crisis of the conservative system--and the renewed emphasis
upon a *coup* by both the Kaiser and Waldersee[81] underscored
the perceived threat--was dependent upon the cooperation
of all the conservative interests. Heavy industrial
interests had been prepared to support the agrarian
sector since the impressive gains of the Social Democrats
in the election of 1893. Cooperation was seen as the
best defense against the "democratic tendencies" now
threatening the *Reich*.[82] Influential advisors to the
Kaiser also felt that the key to the success of much
of his planning depended upon Conservative support.
This was made evident by Philipp Eulenburg in a letter
to Buelow[83] in which Eulenburg was of the opinion that
the Kaiser "must have his natural support among the
Conservatives--the Conservatives in the good sense of
the word--and this is in line with a glance at Prussian
history. For the King of Prussia cannot long remain
without the Conservatives...A King of Prussia...and a
Conservative Party which adopts democratic-demagogic
allures are not only mutually incompatible--but must
also be brought together again..."

Among moderate Conservatives there were strong
indications that this process of reconciliation was
achieving some success. At the Conservative Party
conference, the first since Tivoli, in November of
1896, moderate Conservatives such as Manteuffel-Krossen
and Limburg-Stirum played a key role in policy decisions.
This was not to deny the continuing influence of the
BdL. The less extreme agrarians had, however, abandoned
the radical Kanitz proposal for a nationalized grain
market. The cooperative policy of the government in
state subsidies to agriculture and the renewed hope of
higher tariffs upon agricultural products had been
positive signs that the extreme demands of Kanitz
would now be merely agitational in purpose.[84] Furthermore, Conservative influence had suffered after Caprivi's
dismissal. They had not been strong enough to achieve
either Waldersee's nomination for Chancellor or Georg v.
Heydebrand's as Agriculture Minister.[85] The realists
within the Party were perceptive enough to understand
that the success of their struggle could no longer be
secured merely on the basis of total opposition. The
political winds were now blowing not merely to restore
the agrarians to influence but to insure their ultimate
economic and political survival.

iii. *Weltpolitik* and the search for
conservative preservation

The reactionary politics of the conservative elites
in Germany assumed, after 1897/98, a clarity of purpose
unknown since the fall of Bismarck. This was greatly
enhanced by a crisis situation which made itself felt
as a permanent part of the political background. The
Kaiser and his newly-empowered team of ministers
perceived a situation fraught with the dangers of
system instability and political revolution. A lack
of response would have been tantamount to the admission
of a "dead-end" role for the conservative system.

The awareness of such a grave challenge to the *Reich*,
however, did not dictate a simple solution. Apart from
the ordinary difficulties involved in the consolidation
of groups with differing social and political outlooks,
there was the special problem of the agrarians. This
was the greatest difficulty of all for it entailed the
coordination of a basic and seemingly unbridgeable split
between the industrial sector and the agrarian extremists
of the *Bund der Landwirte*. The BdL had taken the agrarian
struggle for economic and political survival over the

brink of fanaticism and, apparently, no longer contained
the essential moderation and interest necessary for a
more general defense of the Prusso-German state.
Nevertheless, political solutions for the resumption
of the Bismarckian union of *Schlotbarone* and *Krautjunker*
were devised. The resulting institutions in the form
of Miquel's *Sammlungspolitik*[86] and the Tirpitz-inspired
naval fleet[87] contributed (at least in appearance) to
a reunion of the old *Kartell* partners and further concentrated efforts to defend and secure the threatened
position of the "German authoritarian state" (Eckart Kehr).

The carefully considered plan which the Kaiser now
saw as the guarantee against *Umsturz* and *Revolution*, and
upon which he had labored for nearly two years, was
gradually introduced to the German nation. It was thus
only fitting that Wilhelm should have been the person
to give the first public indication of the political
policies which he hoped to pursue. In September of
1895 he labelled the Social Democrats a "horde of people
who were not worthy enough to carry the name of Germans."
In less than six months' time he had introduced the
slogan of "world politics" into a political vocabulary
that was desperately in need of a unifying term. Both
utterances were clearly intended to show that he, Wilhelm,
was prepared to follow the lead of the ruling classes in
pursuing the Socialist "spectre." Wilhelm also indicated
that he was willing to enlist the aid of those social
and political groups who were not involved in the direct
running of the State, but who had been historically
corrupted, time and again, by the "revolution from
above."[88]

The particular responsibility for the implementation
of these aims was transferred to three of Wilhelm's
ministers, Johannes v. Miquel, Alfred v. Tirpitz and
Bernhard v. Buelow. Each seems to have been best suited
to his particular task: Miquel had been the leading voice
in the call for the resumption of a working cooperation
between agriculture and industry; Tirpitz was an individual
of great political foresight and was in full agreement
with the Kaiser's wishes. His dedication to the building
of a great fleet was matched only by his rejection of
Social Democracy: "In my opinion, Germany will quickly
sink from its Great Power status if the general sea
interests are not systematically, and without loss of
time, driven forward...because in the new great national
task and the economic benefits which go with it there lies
a good antidote to educated and uneducated Social Democrats."
And Buelow, destined to become Chancellor, echoed these
sentiments when he stated that "only a successful foreign
policy can help to reconcile, calm, rally, unite."[89]

It is not without surprise--but entirely within
the tradition of the German ruling elites--that what
began as a plan for the concentration of powers and a
stabilisation of the system should have ended in only
partial success and a greater division between the
forces entrusted to bring about that unity. But in a
very real sense this was the outcome of a policy which
saw two powerful forces in the person of Miquel and
Tirpitz, each emphasizing very different and
uncomplementary solutions toward a single goal.

The Miquel conception was above all an attempt to
unite heavy industry and agriculture. It was to provide
the "erection of an agrarian-industrial Condominium
against Social Democracy."[90] Furthermore, in achieving
this aim, Miquel was prepared to use a combination of
"manipulative social imperialism, restoration of the
protective tariff cartel, anti-socialism, and *Mittelstand*
politics."[91] He first presented this programme in a
speech at Solingen on the 15th of July 1897 and repeated
these proposals in the Prussian *Landtag* on the 23rd of
July. It was here that he first used the word
Sammlungspolitik (rallying or gathering policies).
Miquel's aims were not only a direct attempt to renew
the Bismarckian *Kartell* but were actively aided by a
newspaper article written by the former Chancellor,
now an isolated legend living in bitterness and intrigue,
in which Bismarck called for a "cartel of productive
Estates."[92] The joint efforts of Miquel and Bismarck
resulted in an understanding between the heavy industrial
Central Association of German Industrialists (CDI) and
the moderate agrarian group known as the German Agricultural
Council (DLR). These negotiations, held in the summer
and autumn of 1897, were followed by the creation of a
working committee, the *Wirtschaftlicher Ausschuss*. Both
interest groups, joined by the commercial interests of the
Deutscher Handelstag (DHT) and government-sponsored
representatives, found the appropriate institutional
setting where the *Sammlung* relationship could be developed
along the lines of economic and ideological solidarity.[93]

At about the same time these events were shaping the
earliest stages of the revived *Sammlung* between industry
and agriculture, the renewed concern over the Social
Democratic threat, and protection of the home markets,
a bolder, more wide-reaching scheme was being established
by Tirpitz. Through the building of a great fleet, Tirpitz
saw the "ingredients for a *Sammlung* at home and an
awakening in far continents."[94] Briefly sketched, the
concept was divided into two major parts: On the one
hand, it sought to create a firm and expanded power base

for the Kaiser. This would be achieved by establishing
Wilhelm as the "plebiscitarian-acclaimed Caesar" at
home and as the powerful leader of a nation which had
attained "Great Power" status abroad. Furthermore, the
domestic position at home could be made much more secure
by the building of a fleet than by the potentially
explosive act of the oft-discussed *coup d'etat*. For if
Wilhelm wished to strengthen the authoritarian parts of
the German constitution and render the *Reichstag* politically
impotent, then the limiting of its budgetary powers
(through a strong armaments policy) would be most effective.
Hence the first part of the Tirpitz plan was dedicated to
the strengthening of the Kaiser as the essential figure in
the power structure of the Prusso-German state.

On the other hand, Tirpitz had obviously taken to
heart the formula of the British imperialist Cecil Rhodes
that "if one wishes to avoid a civil war, one must
become an imperialist."[95] "Jingoism" would be used to
integrate those parts of the bourgeoisie not directly
involved in ruling the state or gaining economic benefits
from the building of a fleet. Politically, a broad
Reichstag majority would almost be certain if the
bourgeois parties (most notably in the Center) would
find the fleet issue a useful common denominator.
Most importantly, a world power status achieved through
this policy would eventually come to mean increased
wealth for all, and the working class would no doubt
receive its share. Political neutralization of the
"Fourth Estate" would then be possible, perhaps even
its integration. The net result of this kind of naval
policy would be stability and a cementation of the
status quo. Primary among the envisioned successes
would be to have the power of the Kaiser secured.[96]

A careful comparison of the Tirpitz and Miquel
versions of *Sammlungspolitik* reveals a number of basic
differences: 1. The Miquel version was centered on
the renewal of the Bismarckian coalition of heavy
industry and agriculture, whereas Tirpitz (at least
until 1900) was an "enemy" of protection and considered
the Hanseatic interests and the liberal wing of industry
more important as a basis for his naval building program.[97]
2. Miquel attempted to base his *Sammlung* on a short-term,
narrowly-based(Prussian)involvement with the "ruling
classes" of the state. Although Miquel and the Free
Conservatives attempted to influence the heavy-industrial
wing of the Center,[98] it was never a central part of his
programme nor did it hold much promise of success.
Tirpitz was aiming at the political manipulation of the

whole *Reich* and, relatedly, large sections of the
bourgeoisie. This was much more likely to prove the
basis for a workable majority in the *Reichstag* and to
make possible the pursuit of a "positive" conservative
policy.[99] 3. Miquel's scheme was hardly new. It meant
only the "stabilization and rebalancing of the alliance
constellation that was secured through Bismarck in 1879.
Far from being original, it was only a modified edition
of the *Kartell* of 1887 which Bismarck had created on
tactical grounds."[100] Tirpitz, on the other hand, was
more innovative. The fleet was seen as a last stand
involving as its essential component a "world historical
game of chance" (Holstein). 4. The Tirpitz plan was
leading away from and going beyond the idea of a *Sammlung*
as developed by Miquel. This was evident in at least
two respects:[101] First, the important role which
industry would play in the Tirpitz plan would give that
sector an additional advantage over agriculture; it
would reinforce industry's role in the future of the
Reich. Miquel feared this as it would only further
exacerbate the agrarian sector (especially the BdL) and
complicate the task of reconciliation between agriculture
and industry. Second, after 1897/98 the Tirpitz strategy
began to run the risk of being closely intertwined with
a separate variant of imperialism as conceived by groups
close to Friedrich Naumann of the *National-Sozialer Verein*
and Barth of the left Liberal *Freisinnige Vereinigung*.
This so-called "liberal *Sammlung*" (Stegmann) also aimed
at a strong imperialist role abroad but combined it with
full-scale reform of the Prusso-German political system
at home.[102] While in the short-term such a movement
seemed to possess little chance of success, its long-term
competitive role weakened the Tirpitz strategy and forced
it to depend upon elements totally opposed to its major
aims, especially the continued domination of the *Junkers*.[103]

Differences such as these were never totally resolved
during the *Sammlung* period, 1897-1902. In fact, what
emerges, perhaps more clearly defined than the factual
implementation of a *Sammlungspolitik*, is a disturbing
sense of a disunity and of power-struggle among the
conservative forces. A pattern emerges which seems to
suggest that 1897-1902 must not only be seen in terms of
the search for conservative stability but as a period
where the boundaries of political decision-making destined
to emerge from that search remained largely undefined
and unresolved. Several factors may be put forward
for this hypothesis and there are several related
questions which need clarification:

Radicals and Reactionaries

1. The means to secure the new balance developed into institutionalized ends. The differences in the conceptions of Miquel and Tirpitz destroyed the integration of the monarchial guidelines as put forth by Wilhelm. Instead of being a struggle of conservatives against socialists, conflicts arose between Miquel and Tirpitz, between the conception of a fleet and one of the old Bismarckian *Kartell*, and between the idea of an all-powerful Kaiser and the renewed political strength of industry and agriculture.

2. This last point prompts the question as to the specific political responsibilities and roles which the Kaiser as "plebiscitarian Caesar" and industry and agriculture as the reunified and strengthened "ruling classes" were intended to play in the future conservative state.

3. In what sense did the powers of political decision-making rest in the hands of the Kaiser, in the hands of Miquel, Posadowsky, Buelow and the economic interests they represented?

4. Was it possible that the role of "plebiscitarian Caesar" was no longer possible given the new economic circumstances of the period after 1897? Could the Kaiser have come to dominate, manipulate and control agriculture and industry (in the manner of Bismarck) given the fact that his strongest weapon--the economic crisis of 1873-1896--was no longer a relevant factor?[104]

5. While Buelow and Eulenburg may have supported the Kaiser in his "pose of caesaristic autocracy",[105] did the *Fronde* around Miquel mean more than a description of an opposition to the social imperialist content of naval policy?[106] Did it, in fact, imply a deeper opposition to the motive behind the Tirpitz plan--the political role of the Kaiser?

6. And finally, did the question so often asked in the period before 1897-1902, "Who rules in Berlin?" actually disappear in 1897? Was it equally applicable during the period immediately succeeding it in a conflict between a monarch striving toward omnipotence and ruling elites determined to rule?

iv. "Fanatical" agrarians and the
     twisted road to economic salvation

1

If the various advocates of *Sammlungspolitik* could
find little basis for agreement in method and purpose,
they were unanimous about the importance of the *Junkers*.
For Tirpitz an essential aim (with a priority next to
that of strengthening the Kaiser's position) was the
retention of the *Junkers* in the political and economic
system of the *Reich*.[107] Miquel viewed the agrarians as
the vital factor in the success of the *Sammlung* and the
ruling elite which would be most difficult to convince
of the *Sammlung* merits.[108] The "liberal" Sammlung, on
the other hand, while also concerned with the East
Elbians, was most intent on destroying their power position
in order to be able to initiate domestic reforms.[109]

The continuing struggle of the agrarians to reclaim
their declining economic and political standing did not
cease with the era of *Sammlungspolitik*. While moderate
elements, most notably "traditional" agrarians like
Limburg-Stirum, Manteuffel-Krossen and Schwerin-Loewitz,
were gradually adopting a less-hardened and more realistic
attitude towards industry, more extreme groups were
prepared to see the dissolution of the *Reich* as a step
leading to the establishment of a "Greater Prussia" and
a renewal of their powers. As Hohenlohe noted in his
diary on December 15, 1898, "...the *Junkers*...don't
care a straw *(pfeifen)* for the *Reich* and would rather
abandon it sooner than later."[110]

Apparent in the relations between the German
Conservatives and the *Bund der Landwirte* was a sharp
difference of opinion over the degree of cooperation
with Miquel. For many of the leading Conservatives
the idea of the old Bismarckian *Kartell* was still a
vivid memory. If Miquel could never approach the stature
of the old "Iron Chancellor", he was at least prepared
to imitate his political strategy. A number of factors
give support to the contention that a considerable
group of Conservatives was steadily won over to the
side of Miquel and the *Sammlung*. The key factors were
the issues of the fleet and the *Wirtschaftlicher Ausschuss*.

As has been stated, Miquel's political strategy
viewed the fleet as only one "instrument" of *Sammlungspolitik*.
Before 1897/98, and the emergence of the rival Tirpitz plan,
Miquel had shown an open willingness to support the policy
of an expanded navy. Through his influence upon Waldersee,

he was able to maneuver various sections of the
Conservative Party into adopting a similar view. The
Kreuzzeitung, for example, suggested an increase in
naval strength as early as 1896.[111] And under the
persuasive argument of Miquel, Limburg-Stirum, the chairman
of the powerful Conservative Party faction in the Prussian
House of Delegates, was convinced of the political need
to support the fleet.[112] The necessity of an outlet
for national enthusiasm as a means of "national integration"
did not escape Miquel's calculations. As the heir to the
system developed by Bismarck, Miquel, too, was a cautious
but realistic exponent of a modified social imperialism.[113]
The Tirpitz plan, however, which by the end of 1897 had
emerged with a full arsenal of propaganda in support of
industry and especially commerce, so threatened to
aggravate the agrarian fears of unilateral industrial
growth as to jeopardize the whole *Sammlung* scheme.
Miquel's response was a piece of brilliant tactical
maneuvering. Instead of a violent reaction to Tirpitz,
he swung over to a full acceptance of the Admiral's
demands for the legislative approval of naval expansion.
But as an ultimate reward for his efforts and as a means
of securing agrarian support for the *Sammlung*, he devised
a compromise between the two economic sectors: "No grain
tariffs, no fleet!" The industrialists found this a
suitable compromise. It was not only the agrarians who
desperately needed the tariffs; industry too would
find them useful. To finalize the success of his tactic,
Miquel assented to the creation by the industrialist
Krupp of the agitational *Flottenverein* (Naval League).[114]
The Conservatives, for their part, gave the compromise
ultimate legitimacy in April 1898, when Manteuffel-Krossen
and Schwerin-Loewitz joined the Naval League as members
of its governing board.[115]

Success, too, seemed to be the key word in the
second of Miquel's political and economic fronts--the
Wirtschaftlicher Ausschuss. The organization, while
economic in principle, was seen by Miquel as a crucial
"political factor"[116] which would highlight the extent of
the *Sammlung's* ability to deter the growth of Social
Democracy--especially in the forthcoming *Reichstag*
elections scheduled for early summer 1898. This short-
range aim (the long-term one being the eventual change
in the existing tariff rates) led, after a period of
delicate and often heated debate, to the publication in
early March 1898 of an "Economic Election Manifesto"
signed jointly by delegates from heavy industry, moderate
Conservatives, *Bund der Landwirte* members, Free Conservatives,
and National Liberals.[117] The key points of the manifesto

emphasized the rejection of the existing tariff treaties and the shelving of all party political differences which might have damaged the economic interests of the groups concerned. To a very great degree, Miquel's commitment to Bismarck remained unimpeded, as the basic objective of the latter point was the attempt to re-establish the *Wirtschaftliche Vereinigung* of 1878.[118] The election of 1898, which was to be the first test of the political strength of the *Sammlung*, ended in disaster: the German Conservative representation in the *Reichstag* dropped from 72 to 56 seats, the *Reichspartei*-Free Conservatives from 28 to 23 and the National Liberals from 53 to 46. The only concrete gains went to the Social Democrats who rose from 44 to 56 and the Center which achieved a modest rise from 96 to 102 seats. The reason for the decisive failure of the *Sammlung* can be attributed to a number of factors: the inability of the *Sammlung* parties to create a working relationship with the Center, the strong party loyalties which refused to disappear in the face of the call for cooperation without regard to party[119] and the especially damaging effects of a fourth *Sammlung* in the guise of the agrarian extremists of the *Bund der Landwirte*.

It was evident that as a call for a *Sammlungspolitik* developed into a narrowly-based coalition between heavy industry and moderate Conservatives, it was bound to exclude large and potentially disruptive elements from its midst. This was true of industrial concerns with a vital need for export. The chemical industry, especially, saw the potential increase in tariffs, which comprised one of the bases of the *Sammlung*, as a genuine threat to its own economic interests. It did not hesitate to take the initiative in forming interest groups whose essential aim was to counter protection.[120]

The *Bund der Landwirte*, too, saw Miquel as a threat. Though they were hardly excluded from the *Sammlung*, they made a deliberate effort to subvert it. They viewed the *Sammlung* as a threat to their self-proclaimed role as the real "national *Sammlung* of the producing powers."[121] The *Bund* programme, in which the radical agrarians retained complete faith, was seen as the key to the renewed political and economic strength of agriculture and the *Mittelstand*.[122] The *Bund* paid a relentless court to parliamentary representatives who might be induced to sell their votes to the *Bund's* objectives in return for the promise of electoral aid. Their agitation cut across party loyalties and sectional differences. With 118 members of the *Reichstag* committed to their programme, the *Bund* emerged as the greatest

41

victor of the 1898 elections. Their extremism and
unyielding position had alienated National Liberals
and heavy industry to a point where the Miquel *Sammlung*
was lost among a sea of recriminations between the
Sammlung partners.

Moderate Conservatives were especially at the
mercy of the *Bund*. During the Conservatives' convention
at the start of February 1898, Manteuffel pointed out
the duty of the *Bund* not to forget Conservative interests
in the impending elections. Such a warning was necessary
since the *Bund* had been cultivating a growing anti-Semitic
movement with interests directly opposed to those of
the Conservative Party. The BdL reaction was sharp
and clear: "Why should that be our duty? Are we
vassals of the Conservative Party?" was the question
posed by the *Korrespondenz der BdL*.[123] The extent of
the antagonism between *Bund* and Conservatives was
further demonstrated in 1900 as the *Bund* launched a
vicious campaign of attacks against two of the leading
moderates, Manteuffel and Mirbach. In December 1900
the *Kreuzzeitung* answered by questioning what the
responsibilities of the Conservative Party were towards
the BdL and whether there was any need for the Party
to associate itself with the speeches of BdL agitators
such as Hahn, Roesicke, and Luecke: "What do these
gentlemen have to do with the Conservative Party?"[124]

The reaction of the *Bund* to the fleet issue was
hardly a consistent one. From the viewpoint of the
Bund, the fleet could only serve the benefits of
industry. This was clearly a situation in which the
anti-industrial orientation of *Bund* ideology would have
given the fleet a high priority upon its hate list. But
the tactical use of the fleet did not escape the notice
of BdL tacticians such as Hahn. The fleet was seen
as the logical area where a compromise could result in
the acceptance of the grandest of *Bund* issues--the Kanitz
proposal. The agrarians had earlier made an unsuccessful
bid to push through the Kanitz motion during the
parliamentary discussions of March 1-2, 1895. The theme
of the *Reichstag* debates had been concerned with naval
increases. The BdL radicals had thrown forth the
challenge: "No Kanitz, no boats" *(Kein Kanitz, keine
Kaehne)* but met with little response to their blatantly
selfish scheme.[125] It was not until 1897/98 and the
highpoint of Miquel's *Sammlung* that the fleet once again
promised to be of political advantage. This time the
Korrespondenz der BdL and Hahn both came out in favor
of the fleet.[126] The tactic was obvious: It was to

confuse the still undecided moderate Conservatives to
such a degree that the *Sammlung* would have been in
serious danger. Miquel's strategical response to
Tirpitz[127] was also directed against the disruptive
tactics of the *Bund*. His call for "No tariffs, no
fleet", was not only aimed at maintaining Conservative
participation, but was also used as a weapon against
the fathers of the "No Kanitz, no boats" slogan--with
the new variation of the tariff. That the *Bund* understood this tactic completely was demonstrated in
October of 1899 as the other BdL-oriented publication,
the *Deutsche Tageszeitung*, now published a bitter attack
on the Second Naval Bill and Hahn and Roesicke began
to agitate against the fleet rather than give it support.[128]

In 1899 the road to a successful *Sammlungspolitik*
as envisaged by Miquel received further setbacks. The
most damaging came in the form of the Mittelland Canal
Proposal and its defeat in the *Reichstag*. The Canal
Bill had originally been sponsored in 1894 as part of
a plan calling for the creation of a canal stretching
from Dortmund to Ems. It had been rejected then, mostly
on Conservative votes. They feared correctly that it
would serve as a means of "cheap transport" of foreign
grain into Central Germany and as an attempt by industry
to penetrate agrarian strongholds.[129] Five years later
Wilhelm decided to send the Proposal back to the
Reichstag for another reading. This time he asked
Miquel, of all people, to reintroduce it. Miquel was
aware of the strain such an issue would put on the
Sammlung. He reluctantly introduced the proposal,
only to see it bitterly attacked and defeated by all
the conservative parties and the Center. The Kaiser
was outraged, the more so since several of the sharpest
attacks had come from civil servants who doubled as
Conservative members of the parliament. Only by the
sheer cunning of a hardened and desperate politician
was Miquel able to hold on to a rapidly diminishing
conception.[130] The defeat of the Canal Bill and of the
"Workhouse Bill" (*Zuchthausvorlage*) some months earlier
(a bill with a decidedly anti-Socialist intent drawn up
by the Kaiser) were clear indications that Wilhelm was
becoming dissatisfied with the course of Miquel's
politics. It was also clear that the Kaiser's own
efforts at decision-making and political action were
meeting with a resistance hardly anticipated by a
monarch who was assuming the position of "autocrat"
among his own government ministers.[131]

It was only a matter of months and the beginning
of a new century before the struggle between Miquel and
Tirpitz reached its final stage. The matter was decided
in a curious way. At the end of February 1900, and
worried by the danger to the Second Naval Bill that was
posed by the BdL extremists, Tirpitz was forced to
reconsider his whole position concerning the agrarian-
industrial *Sammlung*. In early February, Schwerin-Lowitz
had presented moderate Conservative feeling toward the
fleet. His was a speech marked by a hesitant, low-key
approval of the fleet in terms which made it almost
difficult to distinguish between acceptance and rejection.
Schwerin was clear on one issue--the Conservatives would
accept the increased fleet only as a source of military
defense and *not* as a source of grain import or foreign
trade.[132] Tirpitz then opted for a policy of agrarian
protection thereby undermining Miquel's "No fleet, no
tariffs" position. In so doing, Tirpitz also abandoned
Hansa interests.[133] Yet it was hardly Miquel's hour
of glory. He had become too involved in the Kaiser's
own attempts at political intervention. The remainder[134]
of his political life was spent in relative impotence.
Instead it was Tirpitz that now dominated *Reich* politics.
He conspired with Posadowsky and Thielmann of the *Reich*
Treasury Office to secure the approval of the other
German states in the matter of agrarian protection in
the forthcoming trade negotiations. On May 1, 1900,
Thielmann gave official status to the question of
agrarian protection.[135]

That moment should have belonged to Miquel. It
did not. In a struggle which contained the key to the
future of the Prusso-German state, there was hardly
enough space for two victors. This applied equally to
the struggle between the forces of reaction and those
of democratization--and that struggle had not yet reached
its climax. The agrarians had been given the new lease
of life that they had required. It was now only left
to see to what extent that lease (in the size of the
tariffs) would satisfy their most radical exponents.

2

After 1900 the attention of the Government was
focused much more directly on the agrarians. The
appointment of Buelow to the office of Chancellor
in October 1900, brought to that position a politician
who considered himself "a friend of the agrarians" and
seemed committed (as he was to every interest) to their
political primacy.[136] Yet Buelow, too, was faced not

only with the task of having to find a reasonable set
of tariffs which would satisfy industrialists and moderate
Conservatives, but discount the extreme demands of the
BdL. An attempt to please the radicals with the
appointment of v. Podbielski, himself a BdL functionary,
to the position of Prussian Minister of Agriculture did
not suffice. Nor did a firm commitment by the Chancellor
promising the agrarians in the Prussian House of
Deputies that they could be certain of increased
protective tariffs.[137] If anything, the early months of
1901 saw the start of a propaganda campaign of vast
proportions, aimed at obtaining the exaggerated tariffs
of the BdL.

The situation was complicated further by the
determined mood of the Kaiser. He had not given up his
plans for the Mittelland Canal Project. This had been
the essence of the government's *quid* in exchange for the
quo of higher agrarian tariffs. It was a clever move on
the part of the Kaiser. With the popular Buelow making
the request in the Prussian house and the promise of
increased tariffs as the incentive, the Kaiser hoped to
reverse the humiliation of the previous reading. The
Conservatives, counseled by the BdL, however, indicated
that a favorable response would not be forthcoming.
The Kaiser threatened to cancel the rise in tariffs if
the Conservatives did not tow the line. Kanitz and
Wangenheim kept the Conservative forces in line and
vowed that the Proposal would never pass until the
agrarians received *Reichstag* approval of a satisfactory
grain tariff.[138] Again the bill was withdrawn in May
of 1901.

The remainder of 1901 and nearly the whole of 1902
were spent attempting to work out an acceptable set of
tariffs. The BdL made its aims clear in an article of
June 24, 1901, published in the *Deutsche Tageszeitung*.
In it they instructed Buelow to remember that his "aim
should not be to make agriculture's situation bearable,
but to restore it to primacy in the economy."[139] By
the autumn of 1902 at least four different sets of
proposed tariff rates were before the *Reichstag*.[140]
An impasse seemed the only possible outcome. Furthermore,
the BdL had hit on a way to destroy the remnants of
Miquel's *Sammlung*. They demanded that the tariff on
iron, the sacred cow of industry, be reduced. This was
done in response to the announcement of the CDI on
October of 1901 that a double tariff (a maximum and
minimum rate) as demanded by the agrarians was not in
the interests of industry.[141] Apparent in the war of
demands between the industrial and agrarian interests

45

were the widely divergent aims of the two economic
sectors: the agrarians, to insure a "closed" economy,
wanted a complete curtailment of foreign trade relations,
while the industrialists of heavy industry were, at best,
searching for "compensating" tariffs in view of the
numerous moves toward protection by competing industrial
nations.[142] This was a fact which had been pushed to
one side as the enthusiasm of Miquel and the more
important factor of a common defense against the Left
had guided the early *Sammlung*.

The breakthrough came in the form of a compromise
suggested by the Free Conservative-Reichsparty politician,
v. Kardorff.[143] In spite of furious attacks by the BdL
and the stalling tactics of the Social Democrats, the
compromise was accepted by a majority of the *Reichstag*.[144]
Industry as represented by the iron and steel magnates
found the compromise to their satisfaction. The raw iron
tariffs had been maintained and the ability of the
industrialists to meet the inevitable wage demands
resulting from high agricultural protection seemed best
served by the terms of the new compromise.[145]

Moderate Conservatives, too, were satisfied. They
had voted 30 to 13 in favor of what they had seen as the
basis of their economic salvation. The tariffs held a
number of highly lucrative rewards for them. Above all,
the profitability of their land would rise as a result
of the reduced competition.[146] If the relations between
the *Bund* and the Conservatives had suffered because
of the tension of the tariff debates, this would prove
to be of only temporary duration. The angry feelings of
some Conservatives against the actions of the *Bund* and
v. Wangenheim[147] were based more on the heat of the
moment than the fire of a long-term discontent. Equally,
if the *Bund* had lost the membership of v. Kardorff[148]
this was due to the call by v. Wangenheim for the elimination
of all "middle parties", an obvious reference to the fact
that the Kardorff compromise, whose "spiritual father,
through the policy of *Sammlungspolitik*, had been Miquel",[149]
and the Free Conservatives were seen as the successors to
the Miquel *Sammlung*.[150]

Yet the agitation of nearly a decade and the
ideological fervor with which the *Bund* had maintained
so successful a political role were not viewed as
complete. The *Reichstag* which was to be elected in
1903 (and which would have the responsibility for
negotiating the new treaties) might prove to be of a
complexion which would favor even higher agrarian tariffs.

It was for this reason that the *Bund* conducted a campaign
of agitation and reprisal against those Conservatives
who had voted for the Compromise and who might be persuaded
to change their minds in a *Reichstag* vote. There was,
however, a further reason: the unshakeable belief of
the *Bund der Landwirte* in the strength of its own
programme and political future. This had led it to
oppose the Compromise and all those not committed to
the radical agrarian course of action. In a letter to
Hermann v. Arnim, explaining the reason behind his
resignation from the *Bund*, v. Kardorff hinted at the true
motives of the *Bund der Landwirte*, its relation to the
Conservative Party, and the ultimate aim of its decade
(1893-1902) of "agrarian demagogy":[151]

> The *Bund der Landwirte* was founded as
> an association of agrarian interests without
> regard to party. Instead, Wangenheim immediately
> made the attempt to become master of the
> Conservative Party. He proclaimed, quite
> openly, that he would make propaganda only
> for this party, since it was the only party
> that could give the Socialists a helping
> hand, and that a year of lasting distress
> in agriculture and industry (which would have
> come about through the rejection of the
> protective tariff) would have been a desirable
> situation, because only then would the Crown
> fall back upon the men (namely the agrarians
> of the BdL-AJP) who could save the nation as
> well as lead it.

The new tariffs became law in 1906. On that occasion
the Conservative and BdL member, v. Oldenburg-Januschau,
proclaimed with satisfaction that "...from today onward,
the German state will no longer be known as merely
industrial, but will be recognized as both an industrial
and agricultural nation."[152] Agriculture had achieved
the sort of concessions necessary to insure its permanence
in the socio-political structure of the Prusso-German
state. And what of the German Conservative Party? It,
too, had emerged as a more permanent part of the
conservative system. Its political course was intertwined
with that of the BdL's. Whereas the Party had failed,
limited as it was by the nature of its parliamentary
participation and unsatisfactory leadership, in its
initial defense of Prussian agriculture, the *Bund* had not.
The BdL had assured that economic sector's survival with
its relentless pursual of influence, power and the
integration of non-agrarian elements. Though this was,

47

to be sure, an achievement of immense value to the
Conservatives, it was so strictly in an economic sense.
Politically, the Conservative Party was "modern" but
filled with elements bitter at the ideological price
they felt the Party had paid. Organizationally, and
in terms of its new propaganda techniques, the Party
had acquired a "new look." Yet to the Conservatives
sitting in the Prussian *Herrenhaus*, it was a look that
threatened to push Prussian conservatism in a direction
far different from its aristocratic past. Yet these
were troubles destined to crystallize in another period.
For the time being, all conservatism rejoiced in the
knowledge that Imperial Germany could now remain tied to
the semi-feudal system that constituted its most
notorious characteristic.

CHAPTER III

From Buelow to Bethmann: *Voelkisch* Stirrings,
the Dilemma of Taxation, and the Crisis
of *Weltpolitik* (1903-1911)

i. Back into the fold--and out again
    (agrarian politics in the early Buelow era)

1

     Eckart Kehr, perhaps Germany's most perceptive and
able historian of the twentieth century, was convinced
that the tariff debates of 1902 had resulted in a
"...three-fold tendency: for industry the fleet,
Weltpolitik, and expansion; for the agrarians the
tariffs and the upholding of the social supremacy of
the Conservatives; and as a consequence of this social
and economic compromise, political hegemony for the
Center."[1] The effects of this renewed cooperation
between the social and economic elites, which in many
respects resembled a kind of "third founding of the
Reich" (Stegmann), was also significant in another
sense. It strengthened those aspects of reaction,
both political and social as well as foreign and
domestic, which would be used to suppress the working
class and ensure the expansion of German imperialism.
It also increased the chances for the extra-parliamentary
influence of economic "pressure groups"; the continuing
calls for a corporate representation of Parliament
reflected further the political degeneration of that
institution.[2]

     The wording of Kehr's thesis reflects an interesting
appraisal of the political realities of the time; it is
correctly interpreted yet insufficiently analyzed. While
it allocates the "political hegemony" of the *Reichstag*
to the Center, it fails to understand that, as we have
seen, *Reichstag* "hegemony" was a peculiar kind, and was
by no means equal to the actual influence possessed by
the economic-interest groups. It concludes, furthermore,
that the concessions given to both agriculture and heavy
industry resulted in an equally-divided balance of power:
the domestic supremacy of the agrarians would be matched
by heavy industry's use of the fleet and the chance for
overseas profits with unlimited potential. Yet, this,
too, is deceptive, for although he correctly concluded
that it was the feudal economic system that "...gave the
politics of the *Reich* their goal and direction",[3] Kehr
spent little time analyzing the relative political
strengths of the *Sammlung* partners and the Center's
position. As has already been demonstrated in this
work, these political strengths were used to procure
widely-differing economic ends.[4]

Radicals and Reactionaries

Political aims, too, were barely complementary.
The continuing attempts of the BdL to promote their
own form of *Sammlung* did not coincide with heavy industry's
readiness to work within the Tirpitz and Miquel variants.
It was apparent that the iron and steel magnates and
the *Junkers* were united in a "negative" sense only and
that the "...rejection of Social Democracy...enabled
a joint action."[5]   The idea of mutual concessions, similar
in degree, is erroneous. The *Sammlung* "...entailed not
the full sharing of political power but shadowy concessions
by the *Junkers* to maintain the essence of power."[6]   Such
"shadowy concessions" (removal of the *Antrag Kanitz*, the
willingness to compromise upon tariff rates) were trivial
compared to industrial readiness to succumb to the
prestige of ennoblement. The "feudalization of bourgeois
capital" (Max Weber) in which the "...tariffs were a
tour de force, whereby the *Junkers* demonstrated their
ability to use political influence to fortify their
source of wealth", resulted in the "...complete
feudalization of the industrialists, who found it more
congenial to oppose the impotent mass of Social Democrats
than the determined grip of the *Junker* oligarchy."[7]

In order to assess the relative influence of the
Sammlung partners upon the decision making process,
Hans-Juergen Puhle has suggested several areas in which
such power could be demonstrated: economic potential
in view of total development; protection of own interests;
traditional position in the politics and economics of
the whole system; real influence on the concrete decisions
of governmental administration and Parliament; influence
upon parliamentary acts; and, finally, influence upon
political "style." Puhle's findings demonstrate the
degree to which agriculture appears to be the far more
influential sector. Among other things, Puhle lists
the positive influence of the following factors upon
agriculture's position: unlike the late-comer, heavy
industry, it had always belonged to the ruling system;
it had the tradition of the Prussian *Obrigkeitsstaat*
on its side; agriculture employed state aid and governmental intervention; it maintained a lively and effective
opposition to the Government until 1902. Only in the
lack of economic development does agriculture receive
negative marks.[8] Furthermore, industry did not maintain
an effective representation in either the Prussian
Herrenhaus or *Abgeordnetenhaus*--not to mention in the
Reichstag. The lack of a direct access to the bureaucracy
was also a hindrance, whereas the agrarians not only
had ready access to this important political link, but
made up an especially large part of it, primarily in
the army and among the *Landraete*.[9] Agriculture constituted

the strongest element of organized resistance to democracy
and the strongest buttress against the collapse of the
Prusso-German state. In this capacity, too, it held a
far more influential position than industry. It was
industry's role in furthering the idea of *Weltpolitik*
as a social-imperialist venture which "...covered up
the increasing political disintegration of Prusso-Germany."[10]
Agriculture, however, was the front-line defense against
the disintegration of the state and against the parliamentary
onslaught of the political Left; in that role, the agrarians
were protecting the vital interests of the industrial
bourgeoisie as well.

The strength of organized agriculture remained
undiminished as did its ability to adapt its organization
and propaganda techniques to the changes arising from
an increasingly industrialized society. The aggressive
techniques of the BdL and its growing influence upon
the German Conservative Party emerged unchanged from the
tariff battles. In one sense the agrarian crisis had
been very real, necessitating cooperation with heavy
industry. In another sense, however, the BdL had entered
into an alliance without ever desiring to relinquish its
hold over agrarian positions of power. This was hardly
Sammlung in the sense that Dirk Stegmann has seen it, i.e.,
"...a policy of compromises for the procurement of definite
economic, social, and political aims..."[11] The agrarians,
in fact, were unwilling to compromise over any social or
political goals. This was the logical area in which they
had to maintain their predominance if the Prusso-German
state were to function, indeed, survive. Economically,
agriculture was satisfied with maintaining special
subsidies in the form of brandy rebates and grain transport allowances, while giving heavy industry the main
slice of the economic pie. This was hardly a concession.
Instead it was the perpetuation of a favorite agrarian
slogan learned early in the battle for predominance
and survival: "Learn to complain without actually
suffering!" This the agrarians seemed prepared to do,
all the while carrying the German Conservative Party
further down the path to political "modernity."

2

For the Conservatives the period directly after the
acceptance of the Kardorff Compromise proved to be one
of bitterness and anger at the agitation created by the
Bund der Landwirte. The more moderate elements within
the Party reacted by threatening direct action against
v. Wangenheim. A number of them, led by Conservatives

51

such as Hohenlohe, Count Roon, Praetorius and, above all,
Kroecher, drew up a motion that was aimed at excluding
v. Wangenheim from the Conservative Party. The desire of
the overwhelming majority of Conservatives, however, was
to avoid an internal civil war, with the net result that
moderate anger subsided without causing irreparable
damage. This did not deter v. Wangenheim from seriously
considering the formation of a new party. A number of
radical agrarians were prepared to back his plan.[12]

That it never materialized was due to the disastrous
results of the 1903 elections in which only 4 of 55
BdL-supported candidates were elected. A further reason
was the diplomacy of the Party's Chairman, v. Normann,
and Ernst v. Heydebrand und der Lasa, who not only
managed to strengthen the political bond between the
Bund and the Conservatives, but finally capitulated to
the *Bund's* argument that the majority of Conservatives
had been "stupid" in accepting the tariff rates.[13]

After 1902, the predominance of the *Bund* over the
direction of Conservative politics became a gradual and
discernible fact. If one had previously been able to
distinguish between a Conservative and an "agrarian"
policy this was now less true. Part of the reason
for this change was the desperate need by the Conservatives
to obtain the *Bund's* extraordinary integrative talents.
There was a strong indication for this need in the
comments of v. Wangenheim at the 1904 "meeting of
reconciliation" with Conservative leaders. The *Bund*
Chairman predicted the "end of the Conservative Party"
if the direction of Conservative policy did not change
course from one of "chumming about with the top"[14] to
one where the Conservative base among the masses was
greatly strengthened. Opinion polls, if they had been
in existence, would have undoubtedly shown that "since
the turn of the century, the large and middle-sized
farmers viewed the *Bund der Landwirte*--much more than
the German Conservative Party--as the representatives of
their political and economic interests."[15] In fact the
central issue at the 1906 Conservative Party Day was
the need to become a "popular" *(volkstuemlich)* Party.
The arguments for such a move were provided by two
non-aristocratic BdL members, Meyer and Kaufhold. Both
men criticized the abundance of *Junkers* within the Party
and Kaufhold summed up his speech by calling for the
inclusion of "...elements from all ranks of the population.
The liberals, whenever they agitate, always portray the
Conservative as a Party that contains only *Junkers*, other
nobility, landowners and three renowned craftsmen."[16]

A process of reconciliation was also taking place between the BdL and the Chancellor. Relations between the Government and the agrarians had reached a low point during the tariff debates. The exact feelings of the Government were made clear by the State Secretary of the Foreign Office, v. Richthofen, in a conversation with the Austrian ambassador. V. Richthofen stated that the Government had been surprised at the losses suffered by the *Bund* in the 1903 election, but it had not been "an unpleasant surprise."[17] The end of the tariff debates and the gradual reduction of the BdL's campaign of agitation meant the "...disappearance of the decisive points of difference between the BdL and the Government."[18] By 1905, conditions had become favorable enough for a series of meetings between Buelow and v. Wangenheim. Held on February 7 and April 11, the discussions were marked by the high degree of conciliation demonstrated by both sides. The idea to hold these discussions had been put forward by the Prussian *Generallandschaftsdirektor*, Wolfgang Kapp (involved at the time with the Eastern Marches question) and arranged by Undersecretary of State Friedrich Wilhelm v. Loebell, Chief of the Reich Chancellery, who acted as the middleman between various nationalist groups and the Chancellor.

The discussions that took place on these days were classic examples in the use of political tactics. Each side had come into the negotiations quite prepared to refrain from any hostile words. They were also ready to offer new ideas towards a mutual understanding and cooperation. V. Wangenheim told Buelow that the *Bund* was not an end in itself and was quite willing, if the domestic problems of the *Reich* could be settled, to dissolve as a political entity. Not to be outdone, Buelow rejected the offer with the reply, "No, the *Bund* must remain, and not only that, it must not become *gouvernmental*" (governmental).[19] Neither side was prepared to contribute much in the way of actual concessions. Buelow's attitude was influenced as much by his growing dissatisfaction with the Center Party as by his need to have the agrarians rejoin the governmental *Sammlung*—especially in light of continued criticism by the nationalist organizations. The *Bund*, on the other hand, was convinced that it represented the final fortress against the growing threat of revolution. As the most successful pressure group in the *Reich*, the BdL was not really prepared to destroy itself at short notice. Its offer of dissolution was in reality a challenge to Buelow—it knew that the Chancellor was far from solving the difficulties of the Prusso-German monarchy.

53

Also working in the *Bund's* favor was the climate
of political feeling in the *Reich*. Ever since its
formulation in 1893, the BdL's platform had gradually
become integrated into the more general framework of
conservative ideology. If the strength and purpose
of the *Bund* had originally received its motivation
from the struggle for agrarian survival, it was now
able to draw further inspiration from a nationalist-
oriented public:[20]

> ...bourgeois public opinion came more
> and more under the influence of the interest
> groups and the nationalist-imperialist
> propaganda organizations. The public opinion
> of the *Reich*, of which the government had to
> take notice, was not only nationalistic and
> imperialistic, but with few exceptions, also
> anti-democratic; above all, however, anti-
> socialist, wide parts anti-liberal and anti-
> Semitic as well. The majority of public
> opinion...strengthened the Prusso-German leader-
> ship section in its authoritarian and feudal
> convictions and behavior patterns...

3

The concern for the future of Germany's domestic
situation was matched by an equally uncertain future
abroad. Kehr has shown the effect of agrarian policies
upon Germany's relations with Britain and Russia.
Agrarian hatred of England's industrial-oriented values
played a role in the naval competition that developed
between the two Powers; the agrarians pushed for a defense-
oriented fleet in the North Sea rather than one devoted
to the protection of overseas trade.[21] On the other
hand, the need to protect German grain markets proved
a firm barrier to any Russo-German alliance based upon
a "dynastic" friendship.[22] In fact, the years between
1904 and 1906 saw Germany become more and more isolated
from both of these nations. Especially in the period
between 1905-1906, a "turning point" seemed to develop
in the whole complex of German foreign policy. An
increased awareness of *Weltpolitik's* ultimate consequences
(which included the possibility of war with England
over the fleet) contributed to an ultimate question of
choice--continued competition or understanding with
England?[23] Also, Buelow's carefully constructed *Weltpolitik*
conception had, by 1906, all but fallen apart. Barbara
Vogel has demonstrated how Germany's failure to ratify
the treaty of Bjoerkoe[24] and the unsuccessful results of
the Algeciras conference[25] helped to destroy that conception.

But perhaps most damaging of all, again according to
Vogel, was the growing anger of Russian rye exporters.
After 1906, these exporters were shut out of the German
Reich as a result of the 1902 tariffs. Yet German
grain exporters still played a predominant role in
Russia's domestic markets. Russia could no longer
serve as the cornerstone of Germany's and Buelow's
Weltpolitik.[26]

At the beginning of 1906, Buelow's ability to
govern as Chancellor was being seriously questioned.
At the end of January, Conservatives in the *Herrenhaus*
publicly reproached Buelow for his ineffectiveness in
dealing with the "Socialist danger."[27] And Heinrich
Class, steadily assuming the role of the ultra-nationalist
voice in the Pan-German League, felt that he would have
to fight against the Chancellor, whose government had
become little more than a "purely bureaucratic authority
for the administrative work of the day, but no longer
the leader of the people."[28] There was undoubtedly a
crisis at hand, and the main question seemed to be
whether Buelow would be able to survive as Chancellor.

Uppermost in Buelow's considerations were the
questions of the fleet and the serious effect of the
powerful *Reichstag* Left upon the political stability of
the Empire. The fleet was becoming the most obvious
tool in his fight against German Social Democracy.
Buelow was more and more inclined to see the demands
for the fleet as a means whereby, with an unacceptable
budgetary demand, he would be able to dissolve Parliament
and conduct a nationalistic campaign to weaken the Left.

The fact that such plans were being discussed months
before the actual dissolution is an indication of the
intensive preparations that were being drawn up and
of the acute awareness by Buelow of the potential danger
facing not only himself but the entire Prusso-German
constitutional system. A further indication of this
is a reflection that Buelow had written several years
after the events of 1905/06:[29]

> Our present monarchical and conservative
> system (including world position of the *Reich*
> and Prussia) will only fall if socialism and
> liberalism, worker and *Kleinbuerger* unite. In
> this manner only were the revolutions of 1789,
> 1830, and 1848 successful. The English
> aristocracy had the sense to see that that
> never happened. Therefore, I always applied

> the English formula in the years between
> 1903 and 1906 in order to discredit Social
> Democracy in the eyes of the educated
> bourgeoisie... After I prepared the battle
> in this manner (without careful and lengthy
> preparation, no victory!) I went ahead in
> December 1906.

The *Reichstag* was dissolved on December 13, 1906 after rejecting government demands for financing a Southwest African "defense" force. In many instances, the election campaign represented a more important and truer reflection of the future course of *Reich* politics than the actual election results. Foremost among the campaign techniques employed by Buelow was his heavy reliance upon the so-called "nationalist" groups. As the theme of the campaign was ostensibly one dealing with national and foreign political issues (nicknamed the "Hottentott" Election), the logical step for the Chancellor was to have employed groups whose agitational skills were employed primarily in those directions--and against the Social Democratic Party. In a now-famous letter of December 31, 1906 (Sylvester's Eve),[30] Buelow informed General v. Liebert, head of the *Reichsverband gegen die Sozialdemokratie* (Imperial League against Social Democracy) and member of the *Hauptleitung* of the Pan-German League that the "...fight is against Social Democrats, Poles, Guelphs, and Centerists." In addition to v. Liebert, Buelow also sought the services of General Keim,[31] a vociferous exponent of the Navy League and later head of the *Wehrverein* (Army League). The election struggle was marked by an organized press campaign against the Social Democrats and the Center. In addition, "emergency" government decrees prohibited Social Democratic speakers from using certain facilities.[32]

Oddly, the most powerful "pressure group" in the *Reich* was all but silent amidst the tumult of the other nationalist groups. The *Bund der Landwirte* remained only an interested onlooker, aiding Buelow with his campaign against the Social Democrats, but insisting that they could not agree with the part of Buelow's letter of December 31 in which he had called for a sacrifice of party interests on behalf of the common fight. The *Bund* continued to insist that it was the only *Sammlung* able to lead the fight against the Left.[33]

The election results reflected the hard work of the "nationalist" groups. The Government parties, known as

the *Block*, won an overwhelming mandate and the Social
Democrats lost nearly one-half of their *Reichstag* seats.
The Center, however, gained in the *Reichstag*, due to
the reluctance of the Conservatives and Free Conservatives
to join the Government's battle against them.[34] But it
was the National Liberals who had gained the least.
They had decided to avoid any pact with the Center and
had no choice but to enter into Buelow's *Block* and to
abandon further whatever had been left of their "liberal
substance."[35]

The election of 1907 was notable in that it assured
Buelow of a *Reichstag* majority capable of maintaining
the *Sammlung* impetus, and continuing the pro-fleet
policy of previous *Reichstage*. But the results included
more ominous aspects as well. Buelow had won the undying
hatred of the Center and in a conference later that year,
the Party leaders decided that it would be their goal to
"...break the *Block* apart and make the Chancellor's
policies impossible...Here lies the next task of Center
policy."[36] This the Party implemented almost at once
as right-wing members began to make contact with the
Conservatives aiming at close cooperation in the forthcoming tax reform.[37] An unknown quantity were the
"nationalist" groups. They had found success in their
campaign against the Social Democrats. They had,
furthermore, been unleashed upon the political scene
and seemed to offer a viable addition to the Government
Sammlung. The majority of these organizations, however,
had no desire to participate in anything remotely
parliamentary, no matter how similar the end goals may
have been. Finally, there was the matter of the *Block*
itself. From the beginning, it met with the hostility
of the more radical Conservatives. Wolfgang Kapp wrote
to Buelow in September of 1907 that,[38] "...this policy,
as cannot otherwise be expected, is in no way supported
by the Left or by the Right on the grounds of political
unity. It is simply being used out of tactical
considerations. This unity can only be described as
a very loose one." The view of the Conservatives, as
expressed by v. Oldenburg-Januschau, was equally
pessimistic:[39] "The Buelow *Block* was in the long run
a very unhappy experience. In it there were plenty
of forces opposed to us."

ii.   Economics versus the *Volk*:
      the real face of agrarian "nationalism"

The reluctance shown by the BdL and the Conservatives
to give their full support to the "nationalist" election
of 1907 underscored the increasing difficulty which the
agrarians had in justifying their "national" viewpoint.
This was due, in part, to the growing dissatisfaction
among German nationalists with agrarian refusal to
support wholeheartedly, in financial terms, the political
aims of *Weltpolitik*. It was also due to the rise of
organizations whose basic philosophy and general political
orientation made the deification of the German people
(Volk) into a central tenet instead of merely using it,
like the agrarians, as a kind of window dressing for
social and political survival and economic self-enrichment.
The issue of inner colonization was a clear indication
of the latter point.

When Buelow declared war upon the "enemies of the
Reich", prominent members on his black list were the
Prussian Poles. In various parts of East and West
Prussia, Silesia and Posen, they formed a large, if not
major, portion of the urban and rural populations.
Since the end of the eighteenth century, when the
various partitions of the Polish state changed their
citizenship, they had been displayed by the Prussian
state as a shining example of the civil toleration
with which this feudal region had attempted to disguise
the true nature of its minority policies. Toleration
and pride gave way to persecution and hatred, however,
when a democratic movement within the Polish community
challenged the pro-Prussian Polish aristocrats and estate
owners who represented the Prussian Poles in the *Reichstag*.
In the election of 1881 eighteen Poles won parliamentary
seats and the Prussian government began to fear, above
all, a Polish-democratic domination of the far-eastern
regions of the state known as the *Ostmarken* (Eastern
Marches).[40] This fear was supported with repressive
policies against the Polish culture and language,
designed to "Germanize" the Poles and the *Ostmarken*.
Its true purpose was to crush the democratic forces.[41]

At first the idea of inner colonization by German
settlers seemed to hold the promise of great benefits
for the *Junkers*. Put at its simplest, the *Junkers*
wished to encourage settlement of the area not only
as a means of protection against Polish domination, but
as a scheme whereby German farm workers would be less

inclined to leave the land.[42] The plan, however, was destined to have only a brief existence. During the early 1890's a radical-nationalist presence began to make itself felt in the *Reich*. It led, on the one hand, to the formation of the *Bund der Landwirto*, which used both radicalism and nationalism in the struggle for agrarian survival. A second variant, on the other hand, led to the founding of the Pan-German League and, in the case of the *Ostmarken*, the creation, in 1894, of the "Association for the Advancement of Germandom in the Eastern Marches." In 1899 the organization shortened its name to the "German Eastern Marches Association" (DOV) but was more popularly known as the "H-K-T Society" or the *Hakatisten*.[43]

The Pan-German League and the DOV were much more emphatic than the agrarians in their opposition to the Poles. Even though all conservative groups agreed upon the necessity to institute measures which would ensure the predomination of German culture and language, only the *voelkisch*-oriented Pan-Germans and *Hakatisten* insisted upon the exclusion of Russian-Polish seasonal workers from the *Reich* and especially the Prussian provinces.[44] This struck directly at the interests of the agrarians, in whose eyes the continuing exodus of farm workers to industrial centers was beginning to make the mass importation of Slav workers a distinct possibility. As a source of cheap labor, these workers obviously lost their ominous national and cultural threat. It also highlighted the question of economic interest versus ideology, a question which would be a point of permanent tension in Conservative-agrarian politics for the duration of the Second Empire.

From its very founding the DOV was regarded by the BdL as a rival organization. Despite repeated attempts by BdL functionaries to gain a predominant position in the group and to bring it under *Bund* control, this was not achieved. Instead, the recruiting tactics of the DOV established it as a body led and dominated by bureaucrats from the larger cities. By 1895, the DOV had turned its attentions to a nation-wide drive to gather support for its anti-Polish activities; agrarian influence was minimal and the rivalry of the two organizations had become hostile.[45]

Concentrated efforts to make inner colonization a success made little progress in the period between 1894/95 and 1902. The attempts to buy up Polish-owned estates for break-up into small plots of land for German settlers resulted in near-total failure. As quickly as

they were purchased, their former Polish owners were
able to use the purchase money to acquire new estates
from bankrupt German landlords.[46] In addition, the
enterprise was weakened by the constant rivalry between
Hakatisten and agrarians. Their only form of close
cooperation was in the bitter exchange of criticisms,
the most damaging of which labelled the agrarians as
egotistic and unpatriotic.

It was not until after the turn of the century
that inner colonization began to resemble the type of
undertaking which brought it into line with other
reactionary schemes in the Empire. Among these, the
struggle against Social Democracy was predominant. The
most direct influence upon the new course was Alfred
Hugenberg. As a member of the Pan-German League and as
an individual with close connections to industry (he
was later to join the Supervisory Board of Krupp) and the
CDI, he had already advocated in 1899 the idea of
creating "small landowners" and "independent producers",
tasks which he saw as part of a "landworker and farmer
policy" designed to act as a counterweight to Social
Democracy.[47] The fundamental purposes of inner colonization remained intact: to stop the flow of farm labor
to the cities and to halt the Polish influence in the
Prussian state. To this combination was added a third
fundamentally more serious and far-reaching plan, which
was at the same time nationalist-*voelkisch* and industrial-
led (and assumed complete agrarian cooperation):[48]

> Undoubtedly the most effective method in
> the struggle against Social Democracy...lies in
> the fact that the State is striving to make the
> workers sedentary *(sesshaft)* to fasten them to
> the earth and to achieve (a state-AJP) where
> grandfather, father, and son build a home and
> grow fond of it; for out of this develops the
> love of the fatherland, and the faithfulness
> to the homeland and the state...

The opposition to Social Democracy was an area
in which the BdL and the Conservatives not only played
an active part but often a leading one. The presumption
that the BdL was prepared to join the industrial-agrarian
Sammlung or one with the ADV or DOV for the purposes
of inner colonization was, however, without solid
foundation. The inability of the *Bund* to accept anyone
but itself as the head of such a movement made the
cooperation with "radicals" like Hugenberg and Leo Wagener
an uneasy one. This was not to deny the fact that a

radical-national feeling was part and parcel of *Bund*
ideology or that the aims of the nationalist groups
coincided with those of the Conservative Party. This
was especially evident in extremists like Diederich Hahn
who in 1906 demanded that stricter controls be established
against the immigration of "foreign races" into the
Reich, demands which were, in the main, anti-Semitic
but were no doubt equally directed against Slav laborers.[49]

The Social Democratic threat to the conservative
state meant a stepped-up pace in settling German workers.
The Government, backed by the nationalist groups, was
forced to suspend the idea of buying up Polish properties
and resettling Germans on them. Instead the Government
opted for the outright expropriation of these settlements.
Legislation passed in 1904 did not go far enough in this
direction. Hence, a new set of laws was prepared which
would give the Government even more far-reaching powers.
The action was fully supported by the BdL and the Conservative
Party with the exception of the *Herrenhaus* and Posen
Conservatives.[50] These dissident groups formed the
heart of the landowning elements whose continuing
suspicions about the radical social aims of the *voelkisch*
groups were confirmed in 1908 when the new Expropriation
Act did not specify whether the expropriated properties
would be Polish or German. A government promise to
restrict the amount of expropriated property, however,
led Ernst v. Heydebrand und der Lasa to support the
measure and assured its ratification.[51]

After 1908 the agrarian BdL and the Conservative
Party became outspoken advocates of Polish expropriation
and inner colonization. Led by Wolfgang Kapp and the
functionaries of the BdL, every effort was made to
spread the idea of inner colonization into the previously
immune province of East Prussia. The importance of
keeping landowners on the land was obvious, but Kapp
directly challenged the *Junkers'* notion of the importation
of Slav workers[52] and attempted to arouse an enthusiastic
response to colonization among the generally suspicious
landowners.

Unlike the nationalist-*voelkisch* demands, however,
which refused to differentiate between the expropriation
of Polish and German estates, the *Bund* and Kapp made
this distinction the essential point in their support
of inner colonization in East Prussia. Protection of
agrarian interests was spelled out by Kapp in a pamphlet
written in 1909. In it he was able to promise the
Junkers that the goal of keeping the landworkers
"sedentary" would not be achieved by the "...breaking-up

of whole estates", since the *Grossgrundbesitz* was a
"...national cultural factor" whose destruction was
against the "state interest."[53] Edgar Jaffe, in a review
of the Kapp pamphlet, summarized the reasons behind
the ostensibly "nationalist" aims of the East Prussian
programme. Kapp, wrote Jaffe, was the "...driving factor
of a movement which is working for a complete transformation
of the previous policy of inner colonization. Instead
of the break-up of large estates and their conversion
into smaller areas, and hence the replacement of
Grossgrundbesitzer by farmers, there will instead be
a...strengthening of the large estates..."[54]

This should have surprised no one familiar with
agrarian ideology and aims. The apparent attempt to
retain and protect their economic interests went against
the over-all policy of inner colonization and threatened
to destroy its *voelkisch* and *Sammlung* contents. The
latter threat was made clear by the industrialist Krupp
von Bohlen und Halbach[55] who voiced obvious distress at
reports that the *Grossgrundbesitzer* were "...enemies of
inner colonization, and that without their aid...a large-
scale systematic inner colonization and especially the
settling of workers..." was impossible. These fears
were, for the most part, correct. The lack of good
faith on the part of the Government in refusing to stop
expropriation of German estates as well as the unabated
activity of the *Bund* in furthering its own aims[56] led
to an open break between the agrarians and the DOV. By
1911, the real intentions of the agrarians had been
made public. Instead of expropriation they now advocated
a number of measures to increase the German estates
and also to maintain existing ones.[57] That such a
position was discernable had already been demonstrated
a year earlier in a speech by one of the staunchest
agrarian supporters of inner colonization, Graf Schwerin-
Loewitz:[58] "...the whole success of inner colonization
depends, in the last analysis, on the fact that we get
profitable prices for our agricultural produce..." It
was obvious that it would take more than a *voelkisch*
movement or the plans of industry to change the course
of agrarian politics.

iii.   The Conservatives dig in: the tax question

The creation of the *Block* signalled the rejuvenation
of the policies begun in 1902 with the Kardorff-majority
and the question of protective tariffs.[59] The elimination

of the Center from its seven year position as the "key"
party in the *Reichstag* meant that Buelow had to work
with the two Conservative parties, the National Liberals
and the recently-added left Liberal faction. Of these
the German Conservatives held the dominant position in
the *Reichstag*. This was made painfully clear by Lujo
Brentano in a letter to Friedrich Naumann.[60] In it,
Brentano spoke of the debacle of his own left Liberals,
whose parliamentary strengths had been sacrificed in a
desperate effort to avoid the possibility of a Center-
Conservative majority. "In fact," concluded Brentano,
"it is the German Conservative Party that rules."

The defeat of the Social Democrats at the polls and
the creation of a parliamentary majority favorable to
the Government did not, however, ensure that Buelow
would be able to return to a stable conservative system.
A far more urgent and potentially damaging issue remained
unresolved, namely the problem of the *Reich* budget which,
since the turn of the century, had developed into a losing
struggle of increased expenditure versus insufficient
revenue. The factors behind the financial "crisis" of
the *Reich* were extraordinarily complex.[61] They can,
however, be broadly listed:

1. In the highly "dualistic" system of the
German *Reich*, the federal autonomy of the various German
states was legally guaranteed. The practical applications
of this duality were no more than the sanctioned predominance of the Prussian state. This dualism was
reflected in the collection of *Reich* revenues. The
federal government was responsible for raising indirect
taxes (without "regard" to person or class such as
those upon tobacco, beer, brandy and tariffs), and the
individual states direct taxes (on income, accumulated
wealth, inheritance and death duties), some of which
were then, and in certain circumstances, transferred
to the federal government in the form of so-called
Matrikularbeitraege.[62]

2. Directly related to the manner in which
Reich expenditures were collected was the way in which
they were spent. As much as 90% of expenditures went
for defense. Such an outlay upon armaments was the
direct result of a political and social system which
saw its survival in terms of "friend-foe" alignments,
social integration and the defeat of Social Democracy.
The decision to strive for a Great Power status, the
inevitable result of Germany's conceived choice between
a "hammer or anvil" position in European and world

politics, was made at the turn of the century[63] and was
related to the search for stabilizing the monarchical
system. It was not the army, however, which would provide
this impetus. Instead, the weight of the financial
burdens that such a grand scheme would entail (as well
as their general unavailability) led the leadership of
the *Reich* to put all of its hopes into the building of
a great naval fleet. Hence, since 1899 that leadership
had consigned the military to second place. The army
was seen as the *ultima ratio* in *Reich* policy in case
of civil war. What was needed was an army composed of
troops firmly dedicated to the monarchy, not conscripted
soldiers whose proletariat background might be cause
for them to join the Left in the event of a final
struggle for control of the nation. b. The "dead certain"
calculations worked out by Tirpitz called for the
construction of the fleet *without* the need for direct
taxes, additional *Matrikularbeitraege* or a rise in indirect
taxes; in short, it would not involve the changes of a
tax system designed for the profit of the few and exploitation
of the masses. c. The fleet was viewed as the most effective
means of integrating German society.[64]

The finance and tax policy of the Wilhelmine *Reich*
did not support the national economy as such, rather it
tended to finance and support the alliance between the
Junkers and the industrial bourgeoisie. *Sammlungspolitik*
was in effect paid for by the broad masses of the
population.[65] One had only to be aware of the effects
of the various agrarian tariffs and subsidies--which ran
the gamut from tariffs on grains (which raised the price
of bread and beer) to those various premiums or *Liebesgaben*
given to the *Junkers*--to realize that it was the worker
who was expected to bear the financial burdens of
Weltpolitik.[66] Furthermore, several million marks
worth of foreign grain was kept out of the *Reich* by the
highly protective tariffs. This fact not only severely
weakened the economic potential of the *Reich* but made
a mockery of the agrarian-industrial position which
stated that they were protecting "national work"--a
fanatical and totally misrepresented objective in view
of the cartells and monopolies which often delivered
materials to foreign ports at costs considerably less
than those in the home markets.[67] The arms race
financial crisis became a permanent part of the *Reich's*
difficulties from 1900 to 1908 and had a profound effect
on the future course of Conservative-agrarian politics.

    As a result of the ever-increasing need for
finances, an obviously worried *Reich* Government was
forced to seek funds in areas which had previously
been considered untouchable. One plan was to introduce
a direct *Reich* tax upon inheritance. Successive heads
of the *Reich* Treasury Department, beginning with
v. Stengel, made frequent and totally unsuccessful
suggestions in this direction. The attempted reforms
of the *Reich* financial system in 1903/04 and 1905/06
resulted in half-hearted measures to introduce such a
tax. Their subsequent failure was due in part to the
objections of the federal states who saw in the tax
an incursion into their special areas of independence and
power and to the objections of the agrarians who used
their strength in the Prussian House of Representatives
to block any attempts to obtain the necessary legislation.[68]
This was especially evident during the 1905 reform when
the Prussian Minister of Finance, v. Rheinbaben (who was
also active in the drive for inner colonization), followed
up the successful threat to withdraw Conservative support
for the Government by extorting the watering-down of a
governmental proposal for a comprehensive inheritance tax.[69]

    Conservative reaction to a *Reich* inheritance tax
took on the form of a double-layered opposition. The
"official" position comprised a set of ideologically-
tainted arguments designed to support a distinct
Conservative point of view. Oldenburg-Januschau, for
instance, felt that such legislation would be contrary
to the method created by Bismarck whereby all direct
taxes were collected by the state. To change such a
system would, according to Oldenburg, lead to the eventual
destruction of all principles. To show, furthermore, the
"human and compassionate" side of the Conservative
opposition, he complained that such a tax would strike
relatives of the deceased when they were most vulnerable
financially.[70] Heydebrand, too, felt obliged to show
dissatisfaction with the tax. His avowed objection was
that it would serve as a vehicle in the hands of a
parliamentary body elected by equal suffrage.[71] The
Conservatives officially viewed the tax as a "communist"
threat to federalism and as a danger to patriotism[72]--a clear
indication of how valuable the concept of the "nation"
remained in their thought and action.[73] Both politicians
could not, however, refrain from dealing with a fear much
closer to Conservative concerns. Both felt that an
inheritance tax would "...endanger agrarian possessions
in the extreme..." and would furthermore lead to an
eventual expropriation.[74]

Radicals and Reactionaries

It was at this level of oppostion, which involved the self-interest of the agrarian class, that Conservative resistance found its real incentive. This was also the level at which the tax threatened two fundamentals of Conservative existence:

1. The tax violated the *de facto* base of Conservative strength--their ability to exist on the basis of a "free ride" in economic matters, provided by a system which operated on the principle of giving to the Conservatives their assured subsidies while receiving their political support. It also threatened to upset the favorable balance of power which the Conservatives had achieved against (and with) heavy industry on the basis of the tariffs of 1902.

2. More importantly, perhaps, it threatened to reveal the dishonesty and tax manipulation regularly practiced by the *Junkers* with the help of the Prussian *Landraete*, who, in their capacity as tax officials, served to support their fellow aristocrats in evading income tax. [75]

Buelow's ineptitude in fiscal matters and the extraordinary range of freedom that he allowed Rheinbaben in subverting any proposals for a suitable tax compromise kept the inheritance issue from driving a wedge between the Government and the Conservatives. [76] The maintenance of the *Block* seemed to outweigh all other considerations although Buelow was not averse to pressing for a coordination of *Reich* and Prussian policy and a reasonable approach towards the Political Left. [77]

By 1908, however, the huge gaps in the financial budget made the acquisition of new taxes (to the tune of 500 million marks) a vital necessity. Furthermore, banks, which held a large part of the Government's debt, demanded a stop to the growing budgetary imbalance. Buelow saw the implementation of a lasting finance reform as a "...question of survival" for the German nation. [78] There seemed to be no alternative to introducing a *Reich* inheritance tax despite the fact that it would mean the pursuit of an anti-Conservative policy. But Buelow's fears of the destabilizing effects of the financial crisis and his growing impatience with the obstructive tactics of the Conservatives made such a tax inevitable. For the specific purpose of assuring that his decision would be successful, Buelow acquired the services of Professor Ernst von Halle, chief of the "Scientific Propaganda Section of the *Reich* Navy Office" to organize a large public campaign in support of the reform. The "nationalist" organizations including the ADV, the Navy League and the Colonial Society offered their combined services to ensure that the movement towards reform would be a "popular" and anti-Conservative one.[79]

The reaction of the Conservative Party and the *Bund der Landwirte* was swift and to the point. As early as February 1908 the BdL made it known that it would not tolerate any attempt by Buelow to introduce the promised reforms. From the outset of the struggle between agrarians and Government--which, prolonged as it was for nearly eighteen months, brought the "...agrarians to the barricades"[80]--the *Bund* acted as chief tactician on the side of the agrarians. As a first step the BdL made clear that it was ready to lead the Conservatives out of the *Block*. In so doing, it resorted to its most resourceful tactic--the insistence that the *Bund* was the recognized leader of any *Sammlung* movement of *staaterhaltende* organizations. Thus a speaker at the 1908 general meeting of the *Bund* made the point that "the right kind of *Block* still has to be founded and the *Bund der Landwirte* is that *Block*."[81] It was, furthermore, apparent that Buelow was no longer acceptable to the agrarians. His dismissal from office became, along with the break-up of the *Block*, the predominant aim of agrarian policy. The subsequent events of the Daily Telegraph Affair in which Buelow lost a considerable amount of his power and gained the Kaiser's wrath, proved to be the needed catalyst in bringing about the fall of the Government. Taking full advantage of the strained relationship between Kaiser and Chancellor, Roesicke passed the BdL sentence upon Buelow. His remarks on the 11th of November, 1908 tactfully but incorrectly indicated that the *Bund* regarded its position as a natural outgrowth of the Kaiser's own view: "No one-- not even the Kaiser--can rely on Buelow. Are we expected to act any differently?"[82]

The ideological and political influence of the *Bund der Landwirte* was visible throughout the entire controversy over finance reform. Especially evident was the ideological stamp that was imprinted upon the so-called "Kolberg" programme. Formalized in the town of Kolberg in the early part of September 1908, the programme was a creation of BdL (Wangenheim, Roesicke) and Conservative leaders (parliamentary chairman v. Normann, Freiherr v. Oppenfeld). Stating that the BdL and the Conservative Party were agreed upon the "need to prevent

a material burden upon the large landowners and the
prevention of a voting reform in Prussia", the programme
went on to state eleven further agrarian demands and
conditions:[83]

1. The agrarians were against a federal
    income and property tax.
2. They were against the extension of
    an inheritance tax upon descendents.
3. They agreed to a raising of the state
    Matrikularbeitraege demanded by the
    Government as part of the reform but
    were against interference with the
    freedom of the states to decide how
    their contributions were to be raised.
4. They called for a rise in the beer tax.
5. They called for a rise in the tobacco tax.
6. They were against a one-sided raising of
    the taxes upon brandy but agreed to the
    monopolization of manufacturing concerns.
7. They called for a tax increase on stock
    exchanges.
8. They called for a tax upon dividends.
9. They called for the introduction of a
    federal trade monopoly upon petroleum.
10. They called for a tax upon bearer
    securities.
11. Lastly, the agrarians concluded by
    stating that they were prepared to
    continue within the *Block* only if
    points 1, 2, 3 and 6 were carried out.

To ensure that the *Block* would not survive and that
their ability to defeat the reform was based upon
realistic strengths, the Conservatives furthermore
entered into a "marriage of convenience" with the
Center Party. This alliance allowed the Center to
achieve not only the objectives formulated at the
end of the election of 1907[84] but the chance to regain
its key position in the *Reichstag*.

The combined aims of the agrarians were achieved
in rapid succession. On June 24, 1909 the rejection
of the vital inheritance tax paragraph marked the end
of Buelow's near-decade of rule. A last minute telegram
from the Kaiser to Buelow instructing him simply to
force *(oktroyieren)* the tax law upon the parliament
went unheeded. Not surprisingly, he resigned as
Chancellor on July 14.

68

Viewed from the standpoint of the agrarians'
ability to preserve their most vital interest--namely
their economic one--the "victory" on the issue of an
inheritance tax must stand as their most spectacular
parliamentary achievement. Combined with their
"*Block*-busting" techniques and their contribution to
Buelow's resignation, the events of 1908/09 might be
viewed as an indication, more appropriately as an
affirmation, of agrarian strength not only in their
own Prussian-based areas but throughout the *Reich*.
Subsequent events, however, added a new dimension to
the course of agrarian fortunes and especially to
those of the Conservative Party:

1. An immediate result of the failure of
the reform legislation and the inability to ease the
burden of indirect taxation was a Social Democratic
"backlash." The tax legislation reflected the
Conservative and Center preferences for the tax burden
to remain on the shoulders of the working man. The
increases upon basic necessities such as tea, coffee,
and matches were answered with strong disapproval
at the polls. In the *Landtag* election in Baden
(October 1909) all the bourgeois parties suffered a
decline in the number of seats, while the Social
Democrats gained. This prompted the Prussian
representative in Baden, Eisendecher, to place the
responsibility "...for the highly regrettable electoral
decline..." squarely upon the shoulders of the
Conservative Party.[85]

2. The destruction of the *Block* left the
National and left Liberals in a state of confusion.
The disgust at the selfish tactics of the Conservatives
drove the left Liberals (now united in an anti-agrarian
stance) in the opposite direction--towards a closer
cooperation with the Social Democrats.

3. A feeling of betrayal was equally
concentrated in the National Liberal Party.[86] The
economic interests within the Party, especially those of
light industry, commerce and banking, joined together
in a direct attempt to break the agrarian strengths
in the *Reichstag* and among middle and small landowners.[87]
From these efforts emerged the *Hansabund* and the
Deutsche Bauernbund. The position of heavy industry
and the CDI was much more cautious. The common interests
of *Grossgrundbesitzer* and heavy industrialist made such
a caution necessary and the underlying role of both as
the direct representatives of the ruling elites could

69

not bear a long-term antagonism which might damage the
entire conservative system. Nevertheless, the
agrarians had suffered considerable damage to their
image among those groups whose support they had so
eagerly cultivated. This was, in the first instance,
among certain sections of the *Mittelstand* who now
declared that "the Liberals promote the practical
needs of the *Mittelstand* while the Conservatives only
observe sentiments friendly to the *Mittelstand*."[88] And
in a related fashion the Conservatives had shown their
unwillingness to enter fully into the radical-national
drive to exploit the consequences of *Weltpolitik* by
larger and more direct contributions to armaments and
the spread of the "nationalist" message. This they
had achieved by their less-than-wholehearted support
for "inner colonization"[89] and by opposing the obvious
desires of the nationalist organizations for the passage
of the Buelow reforms. The myth of the "national" image
so fervently expounded by the agrarians since the era
of Bismarck lost its force precisely at a time when
the national-*voelkisch* movement was beginning to have
its first serious effects upon Wilhelmine politics and
society.

    4. Just as the aftermath of the 1902 tariffs
had led to a bitter confrontation between the BdL and
elements within the Conservative Party, so too did
the rejection of the inheritance tax in 1909. Less
than a week later, dissatisfaction with Conservative
policy could be noted from within Party ranks.[90] The
unhappiness centered, as in 1902, upon the role and
influence of the *Bund* within the Conservative Party.
The result of this feeling was the creation of a
"Young Conservative Association", also known as the
"Pankower Movement" after the section of Berlin where
it was founded. Led by the Berlin attorney Bredereck,
Dr. Beutler (Dresden), and, most notably, by Major
General v. Loebell, brother of the former *Reich*
Undersecretary of State, the movement reflected growing
concern with the overwhelming agrarian influence of the
BdL. This "governmental" group, which pictured itself
as a "young Conservative" opposition within the
Conservative Party, aimed at the following goals:
a. the reduction of agrarian influence within the
Conservative Party and the renewal of the strained if
not broken relationship between the Conservatives and
parts of industry and commerce; b. the creation of a
Conservative *Volkspartei* (People's Party); c. and finally,
the attempt to establish a Conservative Party base in the

larger German cities and towns. The movement met with
severe hostility from the assembled delegates at the
Conservative Party meeting in December of 1909 and
eventually fell back into line without being able to
maintain the impetus of its protest. Its main
achievement lay in the fact that it served to demonstrate
to the BdL more than to the Conservative leadership,
the necessity of keeping firm its old alliance with
the CDI and heavy industry as well as the need to take
a more careful look at the *voelkisch*-imperialist movement which in several important matters resembled the
ideology and aims of the *Bund der Landwirte*.[91]

5. The combination of the above-mentioned
factors helped to make the Conservative position at
the end of 1909 less than favorable. Certainly their
situation in Prussia remained unchanged. Yet the
mere fact that they had been unable to turn the
financial crisis to their advantage and had, instead,
merely postponed the question of direct taxes for a
while, indicated a general weakening of that position.
This was in addition to the great outcry that followed
Buelow's resignation--the contention being that the
Conservatives had contributed to the creation of an
atmosphere which had resembled a parliamentary veto of
the Government. Much more important, however, than
the hypothesis that the *Kaiserreich* stood at the
"crossroads", between a government appointed by the
Crown and one appointed by Parliament[92] was the question
of Conservative resistance to change. If the Conservatives
had been willing to accept the bulk of the finance reform,
the pseudo-constitutional system would have taken an
important step toward a strengthened party system.[93]
At best the Buelow *Block* was a parliamentary majority
cooperating on issues of secondary importance. It was
rather the Conservative Party in whose hands the relevant
choices lay--and whose parliamentary future would be
most affected by their consequences:[94]

> The Conservatives opted for a stand against
> Buelow, against the National Liberals and against
> every material sacrifice and for the Kaiser, for
> the Center and for their purse. That they paved
> the way for all that they hated, Social Democracy,
> trade unions, democracy and parliamentarism
> was only a logical consequence of this decision.

iv. The Pan-Germans succeed where *Weltpolitik* fails

1

The fifth Chancellor of the German Empire was
Theobald von Bethmann Hollweg. He assumed the position
on July 14, 1909 amidst a flurry of politicking which
saw various candidates hoping to succeed Buelow.[95]
As Secretary of State in the *Reich* Office of the
Interior and Vice-President of the Prussian Ministry
of State, Bethmann had gained the former Chancellor's
confidence as an extremely capable administrator. When
the time came to appoint Buelow's successor, Wilhelm
agreed to Bethmann's nomination despite earlier reservations. Bethmann seemed the best man to handle the
serious domestic crisis.

Historians have always pondered over Bethmann,
attributing to him and his politics a host of varying
characteristics. The lack of a clear consensus has been
due, in part, to Bethmann's own complex nature which
mixed practical politics with moments of genuine
philosophical anguish. This was especially evident
in the latter part of his Chancellorship. It is not
surprising, then, that the political parties which
would have to work with or against him in the *Reichstag*
also greeted the appointment with differing views.
The Conservatives, worried because of the negative
results of their tax struggle, felt that Bethmann
"...appears ideally qualified to unite the divided
parties with impartial government and sober legislation."
The Center, on the other hand, maintained a cautious
silence while the National Liberals feared him. The
left Liberals saw in him a representative of liberalism
based upon morality; but it was the Social Democrats,
as the outsiders in German politics, who were able to
view him realistically and with detachment. Bethmann
was, they claimed, no less than his predecessor, a
staunch exponent of *Sammlungspolitik*.[96]

The Social Democratic view was correct. Bethmann's
political aims all too clearly resembled those of Buelow.
The only major difference lay in Bethmann's more
moderate approach towards the Left. Otherwise his goals
were characteristically oriented towards *Sammlung*. He
sought to close the split among bourgeois and conservative
parties, while politically dissociating himself from the
left Liberals and Social Democrats. He advocated little
in the way of more basic reforms and yet he was aware
that some reform was necessary if the system was to
survive.[97] The duality of this approach to governmental

72

rule is a reflection of the difficulty of a clear-cut
interpretation of Bethmann's rule: one historian has
termed Bethmann's approach as a policy of "strategic
defence";[98] another has called it "evolutionary
conservatism";[99] while a third has referred to it as
a pre-war "policy of the diagonal."[100]

Bethmann's soft-handed approach to Social Democracy
did not mean that he was willing to allow it either
governmental recognition or parliamentary power. As
he once wrote: "A chancellor who tried to argue for
the Social Democrats would have been signing his own
political death-warrant."[101] A fear for the vulnerability
of his office guided Bethmann's relations with Germany's
ruling powers. In practical terms his politics were
middle of the road placations of industry and agriculture:
"The slogans 'Defence of national work' and 'Support
of autarchic agriculture', which justified the 1879
and 1897 compromises between agrarians and industrialists,
were the foundations of Bethmann's economic credo."
This was especially evident in his political appointments.
For the industrialists his appointment of Kiderlen-
Waechter to the post of Foreign Secretary was an
indication of Bethmann's acknowledgement of the important
link between a vigorous foreign policy and a strong
export industry.[102] Similarly, his other appointments
in the summer of 1910 reflected a concern to please
the agrarians: as Interior Minister he appointed the
highly conservative v. Dallwitz and for the sensitive
post of Agriculture Minister he selected Baron v.
Schorlemer-Lieser, a member of the Prussian *Herrenhaus*
and the "Committee of Fifty" of the Conservative Party.

The expressions of satisfaction with which the
Conservative Party had greeted Bethmann's appointment
soon faded. It was evident from the outset of their
relationship that Bethmann recognized the importance of
the *Junkers* to the conservative state. Bethmann made
this clear in a letter to Gustav Schmoller. In this
letter, however, he also indicated hope for the agrarian
cooperation that contained the seed of almost unavoidable
conflict:[103]

> Our landed aristocracy is certainly not
> free from error, but they do provide us with
> sources of manpower for our army and
> administration. And these we need as much
> for our future as we did for our past. We
> can never do without this class, only hope
> for its modernization.

Not only did Bethmann hope for a change in the policy
of the Conservative Party; his first major piece of
parliamentary legislation also indicated an active
desire to provide the impetus. The government proposal
was a reform of the Prussian Voting Law. It did not
alter the three-class vote but offered only watered-
down plans designed to receive Conservative approval.[104]
The Conservatives' reaction was far from favorable.
Despite protestations to the contrary, it was their
attitude which forced Bethmann to abandon the legislation.[105]
When Bethmann next dared propose that the *Reichsland*
Alsace-Lorraine should receive three votes in the
Bundesrat, the Conservatives were shocked. To Bethmann
such a move meant a step towards winning Alsatian
allegiance to the *Reich*. The Conservatives, through
Oldenburg-Januschau, considered it "a blow against
Prussian honour and prestige." At the bottom of this
reaction was a proposal that the three Alsatian votes
would count only if they were to be no threat to a
Prussian majority in the *Bundesrat*. Bethmann saw
something "...unclear and dangerous" in this agrarian
position. The Conservatives, he felt, had demonstrated
their "...personal, social, religious and political
hubris and intolerance..." He began to have serious
doubts about being able to work with them. Perhaps,
he thought, they would have to "...pass through the
hard school of *Reichstag* elections" before they would
understand their responsibility to the Kaiser and the
Prusso-German state.[106]

Inside the Conservative Party there was a mood of
bitter pessimism and grim determination. Nowhere was
this mood better reflected than in the person of
Ernst v. Heydebrand und der Lasa.[107] Nicknamed the
"uncrowned King of Prussia" by the Left and the
"Little One" by the Right, Heydebrand made up for a
small physical frame with an enormous grasp of
conservative principles and aims.[108] A traditional
Conservative, his leadership qualities had made him the
power behind the fight against the inheritance tax.
While v. Normann, characterized as "...dutiful...but
no great speaker and less politically creative [than]
Heydebrand",[109] remained Party chairman in the *Reichstag,*
it was the "Little One" who dealt with the crisis
situation facing the Conservative Party.

Such a description of Conservative politics in
1909/10 was not an exaggeration and could be noted
at several levels: 1. The departure of the National
Liberals from the *Block* meant the loss of an important

ally in the *Reichstag*. The National Liberals subsequently found an issue for cooperation with the left Liberals in the demand that the inheritance tax be passed into law. To the Conservatives this action was one step from a formal alliance with the Social Democrats. The left Liberals had themselves been dismayed at Conservative tactics and merged in March 1910 into the *Fortschrittliche Volkspartei* (Progressive Peoples' Party) with a pro-SPD position. 2. Perhaps the most disturbing event in the aftermath of the finance reform was the creation of the *Hansabund*, founded in the summer of 1909. Represented in the organization were the most influential members of German trade, commerce, industry, banking and the "old" and "new" *Mittelstand*. The avowed purpose of the *Hansabund* was to smash those agrarian politics which had led to the failure of the finance reform. It was, in part, a revenge on the agrarians for their recent refusal to aid bourgeois business interests in the pursuit of *Weltpolitik*. It was also a recognition by the more liberal interest in the *Hansabund* of the "doomed" nature of feudal politics. Through the *Hansabund* the foundations had been laid for a bourgeois challenge to the agrarian grip on German society.[110]

2

A political crisis like the one facing the Conservative Party demanded the tightening of agrarian ranks. This meant an even closer relationship between the Conservatives and the BdL. By 1910 whatever tension may have existed between *Bund* and Party, in the form of an anti-BdL minority, had all but vanished. Instead, as the conservative Polish aristocrat, Hutten-Czapski, told Bethmann, the Conservatives were "everywhere bowing and submitting" to the *Bund* and supporting its campaign against the National Liberal Party.[111] To Heydebrand, who was aware of the increasing pressures upon his Party from within and outside of the *Reichstag*, such a relationship was neither new nor unwelcome. His cooperation with the *Bund* extended back to the time of the 1902 tariff debates.[112] He was an open supporter of the BdL's agitation and was the first Conservative leader to be clearly thankful for the various services provided by the radical agrarian pressure group. Apparently these outweighed the fact that many Conservative difficulties could be directly attributed to BdL tactics.

The weakened standing of the Conservatives and the loss of a certain amount of political self-confidence within the Party made it a natural target for the

recruiting campaigns of the nationalist organizations.
No group was more eager to add Conservative members to
its lists than the Pan-German League. Ever since
Heinrich Class had taken over command of the ADV, it
had pursued a vigorous search for individuals who would
embrace its *voelkisch* ideology. The Pan-Germans had
always maintained a certain number of Conservative
members, even counting Mirbach-Sorquitten as one of its
original founders. But Conservative membership had
never exceeded fifteen percent.[113] Class now attempted
to recruit Conservative members at the local level,
hoping that the Party's obvious dilemma would give the
ADV's ideological message more appeal. But his lack
of success led Class to suspect that orders of non-
cooperation had come from the Conservative leadership.

Thus, sometime in 1910, Class paid a visit to
Heydebrand. The meeting was a disaster. Despite
Class's insistence that the ADV, in its search for
Conservative members, would in no way constitute a threat
to the Party leadership, Heydebrand was unconvinced.
He told Class to stay out of the "still uncontaminated
east", an obvious reference to the fact that he wished
to keep East Prussia free from the unsavory ideology
of the ADV, an ideology whose mass-political appeal
sharply differed from the aristocratic/agrarian views
of the Conservatives. Furthermore, the Conservatives were
in no position to challenge an invasion of the supreme
bastion of Prussian conservatism by a force which
threatened to deprive the Party of its most crucial
political and social base.

Instead Heydebrand suggested that Class join the
Conservative Party and establish a Party base in
southern Germany. Class needed little perception to
realize that Heydebrand's warning to him was made from
a position of fear and contempt: fear that one more
anti-Conservative straw would break the Party's back
and contempt for an ideology that threatened the basis
of conservative existence in Prussia. For Class this
meeting was the beginning of a struggle to gain the
ideological management of both the Conservative Party
and the BdL as well as the destruction of Heydebrand's
grip on East Prussian politics.[114]

While Heydebrand and the Conservatives were seeking
ways to boost their sagging political fortunes, their
newest political opponent, the *Hansabund*, was faced
with an equally difficult problem. The *Hansabund*,
whose members liked to think of themselves as the

"neglected children of German legislation",[115] was comprised of those business interests most adversely affected by the tariffs of 1902 and the anti-capitalist campaigns of the BdL. As such they were uncomfortable with the CDI, whose position as one of the two main interests to benefit from the 1902 government legislation hardly qualified it as a "neglected child." This strange bedfellow, perhaps out of some deep-seated loyalty to its economic sector, had signed the original manifesto calling for the creation of an organization to support the rights of industry, trade, commerce, and banking. But the CDI's spirit was never really in the *Hansabund*. From the beginning, the obvious political and economic differences between Bueck and Roetger of the CDI and the leading *Hansabund* figure, Jacob Riesser, made the CDI participation at best half-hearted. Most importantly, the CDI had never abandoned the desire to continue its long history of cooperation with agriculture.[116] It could not support an action which called for the conquest of the agrarian sectors of power.

Nevertheless, until the beginning of 1910, the Conservative and BdL reaction to the CDI was in line with their general criticism of the *Hansabund*.[117] This was due in part to the CDI's connection with the National Liberals, a party much despised by the agrarians. It was also due to CDI criticism of agrarian action in the question of finance reform. The latter point was over-shadowed still more by CDI criticism of the agrarian position on foodstuff tariffs, which the agrarians saw as necessary to their particular economic and political situation but which the CDI saw as the essential reason for a steep rise in workers' wages.[118] From 1910 onward, however, until its final break with the *Hansabund* in the summer of 1911, the CDI followed through a process of gradual reconcilliation with the agrarians.[119] Both sides contributed important concessions. The CDI carried out a progressive separation from the National Liberal Party and accepted, despite higher industrial wages, the agrarian tariffs. From the agrarian side came the abandonment of their negative view of industrial trusts and cartels: this as a result of similar agrarian cartels in sugar and spirits and of the BdL venture into the potash industry. By 1911, the Conservative leader in the Prussian *Landtag*, v. Pappenheim, was enthusiastically supporting the construction of a Rhineland-Westphalian coal cartel.[120] Together the agrarian and industrial interest groups pursued the call for "exceptional" laws against the Social Democrats as well as jointly opposing any changes in the Prussian voting system.[121] The bond between heavy industry and agriculture was once more secure. On the interest group level, at least, the agrarians had managed to secure valuable aid against the growing onslaught of the liberal Left and the SPD. The ruling elites, in the guise of the "sister" organizations of the BdL and CDI, renewed an old but familiar set of demands: "maintain the economic policies of the *Reich*" and "struggle against the destructive tactics of the Social Democratic Party."[122]

With the departure of the CDI out of the *Hansabund*, the agrarians no longer felt directly threatened. The desire of the *Hansabund* to form a sort of "BdL of industry and trade"[123] proved to be incapable of realization. Despite shipping magnate Albert Ballin's call for a Diederich Hahn or a General Keim of the Left,[124] no such skilled demagogue directed *Hansabund* affairs. The *Hansabund* was more of an indirect threat, however, in that it offered a place of refuge to unhappy sections of the *Mittelstand*—a development which threatened to limit severely the mass base of BdL politics.[125]

3

Bethmann Hollweg's domestic objective had been to continue the *status quo* by rallying together the *staatserhaltende* forces. In this he had not been particularly successful, since the *Sammlung* attempt of 1910 was a notable failure. Yet in foreign policy, Bethmann's objective was quite the opposite. Instead of rallying together, Bethmann was chiefly interested in breaking-up the three-power *Entente* which was gradually forcing the *Reich* to be totally isolated in its Great Power relations. Hampered by a hostile public opinion, made more hostile by the propaganda of the ADV, Bethmann's efforts in trying to woo Russia away from the Entente amounted to little. Bethmann then turned his attention to Great Britain. A German-British understanding, it was felt, based upon a reduction in naval tensions between the two nations, contained the key to the future dissolution of the *Entente*. Once again, little was achieved in terms of practical results.[126]

Since the beginning of 1910, Bethmann had come under increasing criticism from the ADV. At one point he had foreseen no possibility of working with the Pan-Germans, whom he angrily denounced as "idiots."[127] But the growing importance of the ADV as a source of German public opinion seems to have changed that view. Bethmann's Foreign Secretary, Kiderlen-Waechter, was

especially eager to employ the Pan-Germans on the side
of the Government. In an April 1911 meeting with
Class, he informed the ADV leader that the Government
wanted to "share" with the Pan-Germans the task of
arousing German public opinion on the question of
Germany's acquisition of a large portion of Morocco.
It is quite probable that the meeting took place with
Bethmann's consent. The Chancellor may have hoped to
lessen, perhaps eliminate his most vociferous and
potentially dangerous critics.[128] Class, realizing
his good fortune, published a pamphlet, *West-Marroko
Deutsch*, within days of the meeting.[129] It was this
pamphlet which gave the ADV the national exposure it
had been seeking.

Bethmann's distinct failure in the Moroccan question,
in which Germany acquired 263,000 square kilometers of
the French Congo (and the accompanying swamps and
disease-bearing insects) instead of resource-rich
Morocco, was announced to the *Reichstag* on November 9, 1911.
It was at this precise moment that Heydebrand, scheduled
to speak after the Chancellor, chose to demonstrate that
the Conservatives were indeed a *nationalgessinte* Party.
Referring to the "worthless" agreement that Bethmann had
attempted to place in a positive light, Heydebrand
proclaimed that "these yieldings, these agreements, these
understandings will not secure us peace...only our good
German sword can do that."[130] It was as sharp a critique
as would be heard among the many that were levelled at
Bethmann that day. Bethmann was aghast at Heydebrand's
behavior. He felt that Heydebrand was leading the
Conservatives "down demagogic paths."[131] It had not
been the first clash between Bethmann and Heydebrand,
neither was it to be the last. Although Bethmann was
still uncertain as to the exact direction of Heydebrand's
hostility or to its ultimate purpose, Kurt Riezler felt
certain that he understood the Conservative leader's
intentions. On a separate occasion, when Conservative
and Chancellor had clashed over policy, Bethmann's
secretary and intimate advisor had written in his diary
that "Heydebrand wants to bring the Chancellor down."[132]

The year 1911 and the Moroccan crisis marked a
turning point in the domestic and foreign policy of the
Wilhelmine Empire. The combined sense of diplomatic
shame and growing international isolation felt by the
German public made the Pan-German League a force that
could no longer be ignored by either Bethmann nor
Heydebrand.[133] The Conservative leader had been among
the first to recognize this and it may have accounted

for the exaggerated vehemence and nationalism of his
Reichstag speech. In order to reestablish the importance
of the army ("the good German sword") in German military
plans (in Conservative eyes, the real defender of the
conservative State) and the image of the Conservatives
as more than just profit-motivated agrarians, Heydebrand
was prepared to attack the German Chancellor. Yet both
men faced an important *Reichstag* election in a few
weeks' time as well as the very real problem of the
Pan-German League. In this sense the many differences
which separated them seemed to decrease in magnitude
when compared to the threat posed by a small group of
fanatics who challenged the very basis of their
political existence. Bethmann could very well have been
echoing Heydebrand's sentiments near the end of 1911
when he wrote that "like the craters growing on Mount
Aetna, the crises in our politics continue to grow
without interruption."[134]

In fact, the period from 1903 to 1911 had not been
a very successful one for the German Conservative Party.
While its relationship with the BdL remained steady,
anti-BdL forces within the Party had expressed their
views more openly than ever. In the early part of this
period, traditional conservative feeling against the
Bund was extremely pronounced, forcing v. Wangenheim
to consider founding a new Conservative Party--something
other radical agrarians would also contemplate at a
later date. Indeed, the *Bund*, through its non-aristocratic
membership, attempted to force the Party to adopt a more
mass-based appearance. While this effort was not
successful, the Conservatives were forced to rely even
more on BdL support in their struggle against a *Reich*
inheritance tax.

Although the Conservatives, with the aid of the
agrarian pressure group, were able temporarily to
thwart such a tax, new voices in the Party were raised
against the BdL. But these voices, because of their
extreme views, threatened to shake the Party to its
political roots. The Conservative leadership, fearful
of the Party's weakened *Reichstag* position, could not
allow such an occurance. It was this weakened state,
not only in parliament but among bourgeois elements
angry at the Conservatives' selfish refusal to support
Weltpolitik, that was the cause for much concern among
Party leaders. Especially frightening was the attempted
invasion of east Prussia by the Pan-German League, an
extra-parliamentary organization whose techniques and

ideology bore a close resemblance to the manner and beliefs of the *Bund der Landwirte*. In coming years, this similarity would threaten to create the most disastrous consequences for the German Conservative Party.

CHAPTER IV

Pandora's Box: The Election of
1912 and its Aftermath (1912/13)

i. The Election of 1912

The German nation had barely recovered from the
New Year's festivities of 1912 when it faced the serious
issue of a national election. On January 12 the country
went to the polls.

What were the aims of the Conservatives as they
prepared for this less-than-welcome test of their
political appeal? For the most part, the Party was
content to remain in a "defensive" position, a
situation it had been unable to alter since 1909. It
hoped especially to retain its cooperation with the
Center in the "Black-Blue" *Block*. This was an important
prerequisite for success in the *Stichwahl* (final ballot),
held several days after the main vote. A second aim
was the defense of Conservative strongholds in areas
east of the Elbe River, where in 1910 the National
Liberals had captured a by-election seat in Oletzko-Lyck
and the Progressives had triumphed in Labiau-Wehlau.
These Liberal and Progressive forays into traditional
Conservative regions, along with a notable lack of new
Conservative voters and an increased pressure from
both the *Hansa*-and *Bauernbund*, forced the Conservatives
to intensify their search for voters west of the Elbe
and in the larger cities and towns. Finally, the Party
increased its attacks against the Social Democratic
Party, hoping, in this manner, to form a "union" with
heavy industry during the elections.[1]

As in previous elections, the Conservatives were
able to look forward to the organized assistance of
the BdL. But, as in earlier campaigns, they had to
tolerate the relentless drive of the *Bund* for non-
Conservative supporters of the agrarian programme. As
a result, the politics of the BdL in Westphalia and
the Rhineland threatened to upset the delicate relations
between the Center and the Conservatives. This situation
was further intensified by some rather indelicate anti-
Center comments made by Schwerin-Loewitz in the summer
of 1911. Moreover, any chance for a Conservative-
National Liberal reconciliation during the election was
ruled out by the *Bund*.[2]

The position of the Government towards the Conservatives
was one of extreme caution.[3] Bethmann most wished for
a *Reichstag* that would deliver up the necessary legislation
for a popular and successful governmental policy.[4]
While the Government, in its election manifesto, listed

aims similar to the Conservatives, namely the "defense
of national work" and the struggle against the Social
Democrats, its support was far from enthusiastic.[5]
Although Bethmann certainly hoped for a successful outcome
for the Party, he was, at the same time, highly sceptical
of its chances. He felt that the Conservatives had lost
a considerable amount of "unconscious" sympathy in areas
outside their own *Junker* circles.[6] It would have been
highly damaging to the image of the Government to have
been so closely associated with a Conservative loss.

On election day 84.9% of those eligible registered
their vote. This was the highest turnout in the history
of the *Reichstag* elections.[7] That such a large voter
response was recorded lay, in the first instance, with
the fact that a significant part of the bourgeois
population—not to mention the working-class—was extremely
unhappy with the course of events in the period since
1907. It was not the anti-SPD slogans of the Right which
determined their vote but the actual problems facing
the nation: the failure of the finance and Prussian
voting reforms, the debacle of the Morocco policy and
especially, since the summer of 1911, the steep rise in
food prices. The stubborn agrarian adherence to a policy
of high protective tariffs at a time when animal fodder
and foodstuffs were short proved to be the greatest weapon
possessed by the anti-agrarian forces.[8]

The election campaign was especially noteworthy
for the massive role played by the extraparliamentary
pressure groups. What in 1907 had been an election
concerned with a "nationalist" issue, was, in 1912,
significant for its emphasis upon economic and social
questions.[9] The social element was especially strong
in the electoral politics of Count Westarp[10] who, in
the course of five short years, had assumed, along with
Heydebrand, the "official" leadership of the Conservative
Party. His constituency was the partly Polish district
of Meseritz-Bomst (Posen) and Westarp's entire campaign
was fought on an anti-Polish and anti-SPD basis. His
Polish opponent, Professor v. Karwowski, conducted a
similar campaign against the Conservatives. He appealed
to the Catholic Poles of the district not to be fooled
by an apparent Conservative-Center coalition. As one
of his election pamphlets put it: "Five years ago they
(the Conservatives-AJP) joined the greatest enemies of
our Church in the battlecry—'Out with the Center'."[11]

When the results of the main vote were recorded, it became apparent that the *Block* parties and their allies would suffer losses; these, on the whole, were acceptable. The Conservatives, for instance, sent more candidates in to the *Stichwahlen* (held on January 20, 22 and 25) than in 1907. But indicative of the problems to come was once again Westarp's own constituency where, in the *Hauptwahl* (main vote), he received less votes than his Polish opponent.[12]

Despite massive assistance from the Center, Conservative results in the *Stichwahlen* were disastrous. Its *Reichstag* representation dropped from 60 to 43 seats. Even more serious was the extent of National Liberal gains in Conservative strongholds, especially East Prussia.[13] The BdL had fared even worse; Hahn, Roesicke, Lucke, aus dem Winckel and Oldenburg-Januschau—practically the entire leadership—had not been reelected and returned to the BdL to work in an extra-parliamentary role. The *Bund*, in fact, had only been able to return 78 politicians pledged to its programme compared with 138 in the 1907 election. The position of the other *Block*-associated groups was not much better. The Free Conservatives (26 to 16 seats), the anti-Semites (22 to 13 seats) and the Conservative-allied Economic Union (*Wirtschaftliche Vereinigung*—18 to 10 seats) also suffered significant losses. Only the Center (102 to 91 seats) was able to avert such losses.

The left-wing of the National Liberals and the Progressives had, on the other hand, cooperated during the *Stichwahlen* and both parties suffered only a minimal setback. They had achieved their aim of damaging the base of agrarian power. Not only did they make significant inroads into east Elbian areas, but the *Hansabund* had managed to return 56 of its own members (among them 17 National Liberals and all but 3 of the Progressive representatives) and 32 others committed to their programme. This was achieved at the expense of heavy industry which, despite massive funding, was only able to elect 41 of 120 financially-supported candidates. For the CDI and heavy industry the results of the election only further confirmed the limited desirability of the *Reichstag* as the basis of their economic and political representation. Furthermore, the German voter had totally rejected any idea of an agrarian-industrial *Sammlung*. In its place sat 110 newly-elected members of the *Reichstag*. They all belonged to the German Social Democratic Party.[14]

84

Radicals and Reactionaries

The *Reichstag* election was a clear warning to the
Right. The enormous Social Democratic and Liberal
presence in the national parliament was an ominous
indicator of a none-too-bright conservative future.
To the forces of the *status quo* there seemed no more
appropriate or necessary moment to regroup their
numbers and prepare the struggle against the
deterioration of a system for which time was running
out. In this respect 1912 was very much the year of
conservative decision. It served as a starting point
for a last ditch effort to save the Prusso-German state.
In some of its more successful forms, conservative
resistance extended to the year 1918 and beyond,
remaining intact even though the political and social
system it defended had ceased to exist.

What forms did the conservative opposition assume?
From 1912 onward it maintained both an offensive and
defensive character. In imperialism and militarism,
its offensive variants, it sought to sustain and broaden
the search for national integration. At the same time,
the ruling classes sought to expand the search for their
own material profit. Finally, it was a reaction (but
in an offensive sense) to an increasingly hostile and
dangerous external threat.

In its more defensive form, conservative opposition
attacked the growing danger of Social Democracy, not
only directly but through the uses of anti-Semitism and
anti-parliamentarism. None of this was new, having made
at one time or another, since Bismarck, considerable
impact upon the course of anti-democratic thought in
the German *Reich*. What separated the period after 1912
from any since 1871 was the extensive loss of self-
confidence experienced by those forces that represented
the conservative state. As v. Wangenheim wrote in the
summer of 1912, the struggle against the Left "had to
be total."[15] This was one more way of saying, that,
in essence, the long-dreaded "dead-end" of the Bismarckian
system was now becoming a reality.

ii.   Anti-Semitism and the *Volk*

In an effort to find the "key" to a successful
political role, both the Conservative Party and the
BdL had traditionally made effective use of anti-Semitism.
Prior to German unification there had already existed
in conservative circles a view that the Jewish religion
posed a grave danger to the continuation of a pious and

Christian nation. Extending back to the financial
collapse of the *Gruenderjahre*,[16] anti-Semitism was
used to divert the impact of Conservative failures in
the economic sphere and to forge the bonds which
connected the *Junkers* with large elements of the lower
middle class as well as with non-aristocratic farmers.
This task was lightened by the fact that the SPD
avoided making contact with these groups and the dismissal of their value by a state interested primarily
in big agriculture and heavy industry.[17] Eventually,
the manner in which anti-Semitism came to serve
Conservative-agrarian purposes accurately reflected
the shifting emphasis from ideology to economics,
which emerged as the chief Party concern. By the
early 1890's, Conservative opposition to Jewry no
longer focused exclusively upon the Jewish religion
but upon the Jew as the embodiment of the liberal spirit
in economics and culture.

Parallel to the growth of Conservative anti-Semitism
was the development of several small anti-Semitic
parties which maintained a numerically insignificant
yet highly visible representation in the *Reichstag*.[18]
Although they were of one mind in their opposition to
Jewry, these groups were divided in their relationship
to the Conservative Party. One "democratic" wing
viewed aristocratic *Junkers* and supposedly usurious
Jews as equally responsible for the economic oppression
of the poor farmers and *Mittelstand* elements who formed
the bulk of the anti-Semitic support. A more
"conservative" part, however, sought good relations
with the Conservatives and especially with the *Bund
der Landwirte*.

By 1894, the two largest anti-Semitic parties,
the German Social Party (DSP) and the German Reform
Party (DRP) had united into a single political
organization. Yet the German Social Reform Party (DSRP),
as it was called, maintained, at best, a precarious
unity. Not only did the two wings fail to reconcile
differences in political direction (the DSP social
demagogic and agrarian oriented; the DRP social reformist
and *Mittelstand* oriented) they also accentuated, as the
Leipziger Neueste Nachrichten reported, the most crucial
political dilemma of the decade after 1890, "...the
contrast between city and country."[19]

The basic differences between the two halves of the
DSRP were further complicated by the development of a
strong political relationship between the "conservative"
DSP and the BdL. By the middle of 1897, the

Norddeutsche Allgemeine Zeitung could report with some
accuracy that the German Social Party wanted to convince
the BdL of its anti-Semitic merits and that since the
BdL was "anti Semitic to the bone" they would have
little difficulty in achieving that aim.[20] If at
first, however, the desire for political cooperation
had been more on the side of the DSP, by 1898, it had
swung over to the BdL. Strengthened by the close
friendship between the DSP spokesman, Max Liebermann v.
Sonnenberg and BdL Director Diederich Hahn, it was
clear, from remarks made by v. Wangenheim in August
1898, that the BdL was intent upon achieving control
of the organization and, in turn, of the entire
anti-Semitic movement. It planned to do so, in the
words of v. Wangenheim, by aiding the Liebermann
faction "...in gaining ascendency in the anti-Semitic
movement."[21] To achieve this the BdL had to make
certain that the parent DSRP would no longer function
as a political party. In so doing, the agrarians were
intent upon accomplishing another objective--the
capture of the emerging *Mittelstand* movement which,
under the influence of the DRP, threatened to develop
an anti-agrarian bias. The importance of the
Mittelstand to the agrarians was highlighted by v.
Wangenheim in the same speech, as he criticized the
Bund's closest ally, the Conservative Party, for failing
to maintain a "convinced following in the *Mittelstand*."
A year later, v. Wangenheim, in a speech in Gotha,
gave the signal for the dissolution of the DSRP when
he made it known that he regretted the existence of such
a political entity.[22] The signal was taken by Liebermann
and the DSP, which withdrew from the DSRP during its
Magdeburg convention in October of 1900.[23]

In time the BdL was successful in dominating both
the anti-Semitic and *Mittelstand* movements.[24] At the
head of each group stood an individual dedicated to the
interests of the agrarian sector and the importance of
the struggle against Jewry: Max Liebermann v. Sonnenberg,
head of the German Social Party and founder of the
Economic Union *(Wirtschaftliche Vereinigung)* and Theodor
Fritsch, head of the Saxon *Mittelstand* Union and founder
of the Imperial *Mittelstand* Association. Both movements
served as vehicles for the spread of the agrarian and
anti-Semitic doctrine. At the time of Liebermann's
death in 1911, the Economic Union and its loose
confederation of small *Reichstag* parties and interest
groups gave the BdL an "agrarian" party in every German
state parliament.[25] Fritsch, on the other hand, stood
at the head of a large organization and was able to

give the BdL enormous influence over non-agrarian
sections of German society. It is important to note
that the success of BdL politics after 1900 was, in
large part, due to the flexibility of its approach
to politics. Unlike the Conservatives, the BdL was
not hemmed in by the confines of parliamentary affairs.
When, after 1912, its *Reichstag* representation was
dramatically reduced, it was at once able (as will be
seen) to join forces with a growing extraparliamentary
force. Such was not the case with the Conservative Party.

Although it remained part and parcel of agrarian
politics, anti-Semitism was largely restricted to the
demagogic speeches of the BdL's annual gathering in
Berlin's Circus Busch auditorium. Apart from this,
the "party-political anti-Semitism" (U. Lohalm) of the
Economic Union maintained a steady, economically-
motivated attack against the "liberal" Jewish spirit
in German life.[26] Important changes, however, were
taking place in the development of an anti-Semitic
ideology. Existing alongside economic and cultural
anti-Semitism was a far more vicious strain, intent
upon proving the racial threat of the Jewish people.

2

We have already noted that in Conservative
circles, religious anti-Semitism, the earliest form,
had all but lost its primacy to the more economic
and cultural types. This "second stage" in the
development of German anti-Semitism replaced the
religious motive with an emphasis upon and opposition
to the Jew as banker and newspaper editor. And
whereas earlier anti-Semitism had prescribed religious
conversion as the logical solution to the "Jewish
Question", here the call was for the Jew to become
German.

The importance of this shift in anti-Semitic
thought cannot be overemphasized. It meant, in effect,
that the newer stage of anti-Semitism developed a much
more metaphysically constructed difference between
Germans and Jews. Central to this difference was the
existence of a German *Volk*, "a metaphysical entity,
an eternal and unchanging ideal which encompassed all
the German people."[27] Although German preoccupation
with *voelkisch* ideology was in existence as early as
the eighteenth century, its relation to anti-Semitism
was a phenomenon closely associated with the industrial
revolution and the era of mass politics. *Voelkisch*

thinkers tended to reject the accompanying uprootedness
and cultural sterility of the industrial society.[28]
Instead, they longed for a return to the Middle Ages
and the predominance of an agrarian society.   In
Wilhelmine Germany they found the antithesis to all
their ideals.   They saw the "soul" of Germany being
gradually destroyed by the cultural bareness of
Zivilisation, which meant little more than the spread
of industry and the growth of big cities.   Coupled
with these symbols of a decadent age, the "image of
the Jew" came to dominate all that was rotten in
industrial Germany.   The urban and supposedly rootless
Jew became the epitomy of *Zivilisation:*   a sterile,
anti-German construct who demeaned and destroyed the
vitality of the *Volk* and repressed true German *Kultur*.
Yet, in spite of almost total opposition to the Jewish
"stereotype", many *voelkisch* ideologists continued
to hold out hope for individual Jews.   They felt certain
that some Jews might be able to shed their destructive
"spirit" in exchange for entry and assimilation into
the German *Volk*.[29]

But anti-Semitism was unable to confine itself within
the limits of religion, culture and economics.   A
sizeable number of anti-Semitic works reflected a
fascination with the racial differences between Germans
and Jews.   Writers, such as the French diplomat
Arthur de Gobineau in his major work, *Essai sur
l'inegalite des races humaines* (1853), stressed the
racial purity of the Aryan race (of which the Germans
were a part) and its aristocratic external and internal
qualities.   Gobineau, however, was a prophet of racial
doom.   He foresaw the racial extinction of the Aryan
race through its bastardization by lesser races.[30]

His warning was echoed by *voelkisch* thinkers in
Germany.   Although Gobineau's actual theories did not
make their appearance in Germany until 1894, several
theorists had already applied similar findings to their
own racial situation by as early as 1880.   Among the
most prominent were the journalist Wilhelm Marr and
Eugen Duehring.   Marr founded the first political
organization which carried an anti-Semitic title--The
Anti-Semitic League--in 1879.   A year later, Duehring
published the *Jewish Question* which examined, for the
first time in Germany, the "Jewish question" in racial
terms.   In his book, Duehring came to four extremely
important and influential decisions: 1. the Jewish
threat to German culture and morality was an inherent
racial trait contained within each and every Jew;

89

2. Unlike the religious and economic-cultural anti-Semites, Duehring ruled out Jewish conversion in Christianity as a means to assimilation or the ability of certain Jews to become German; 3. He found the Jews an obstacle to the progress of the German *Volk* and concluded that such progress could only be attained in a future death struggle between the German and Jewish races; 4. He saw his particular form of anti-Semitism tied to the "will" of the German *Volk*--in short, he advocated a kind of *voelkisch* democracy.[31]

Despite their vehement opposition to "modernity", most *voelkisch* critics of Wilhelmine Germany were either unwilling or unable, as George Mosse has pointed out, to deal with its economic or social consequences.[32] Instead, their retreat into a world of embittered cultural despair kept them far from the realities of the Industrial Revolution as it was experienced by millions of threatened Germans. The first practical application of Duehring's theories were the rural, anti-Semitic and democratic movements of Boeckel and Ahlwardt. As noted, they contained a strong element of anti-agrarian feeling.[33] But, as we have seen, the agrarians within the Conservative Party and the BdL adopted much of the *voelkisch*, racial anti-Semitism of the "Radau anti-Semites" in order to maintain their control over large groups of peasants and small farmers. They combined this with a pseudo-democratic appeal whose success was demonstrated in the membership figures of the BdL: by 1911, nearly ninety percent of the BdL was comprised of peasants and small farmers.[34]

After the collapse of these "democratic" movements, racial anti-Semitism lost much of its virulance.[35] Many ultra-Conservatives found the combination of democracy and racial anti-Semitism not only distasteful but dangerous to their class interests. As a result, much of the anti-Semitic movement went "underground." It developed a theoretical emphasis on racial anthropology and couched a continuing stress on building racial hatreds with scholarly references and academic jargon. Even Theodor Fritsch became a "cultured anti-Semite." He now advocated the spread of the *voelkisch* and anti-Semitic doctrine through the process of education.[36] For Fritsch and the BdL, however, this was a superficial change in tactics. The agrarian element was concentrating on another victim of industrial Germany--the *Mittelstand*. The general trend towards *voelkisch* and anti-Semitic education by the written word was an ideal method for capturing the educated bourgeois. As a result, many of these social groups--small merchants, entrepreneurs and

artisans from the cities--found themselves in alliance
with agrarian demagogues from East Prussia. They
and the BdL were strange bedfellows indeed; but necessary
ones if both were to survive the threat that the effects
of industrialization posed to their economic and social
well-being. The BdL was able to translate the cultural
anguish of *voelkisch* thought and the academic racialism
of the anthropological journal into a straightforward
political terminology. Agrarian ideology transformed
the tension between *Zivilisation* and *Kultur*, and between
German and Jew into a political struggle between the
envisioned triumph of the proletariat and the return
to an agrarian *Staendestaat*. It was primarily for this
reason that much of the *Mittelstand* movement became so
willing a recipient of the agrarian ideology. In
allowing the BdL to exert a great deal of influence
upon it, this large segment of German society was
responding to the promise of a return to economic and
social stability. It viewed the "new" Germany not
with an eye towards the future but with the vision of
a revitalized past.[37]

3

　　By the first decade of the twentieth century
racial anti-Semitism in Germany was a broadly-based,
firmly entrenched institution. No segment of the
German *Volk* was beyond its praise and no aspect of
Jewish life was safe from its demeaning "scientific"
analysis. Furthermore, several racial assumptions had
become integral parts of the *voelkisch* ideology.
Duehring's theory of the inevitable death struggle
between the Aryan and Jewish races, for instance, was
greatly strengthened by the general popularity of
Social Darwinism and its theory of the survival of the
fittest. In addition, the historical pessimism of
Gobineau had been replaced by a much more favorable view
of historical direction. *Voelkisch* theory now rejected
the idea of an eventual end to the Aryan race through
racial admixture. It developed, instead, a kind of
messianic complex in which it saw a pure and noble
Aryan race as the savior of Western culture.[38]

　　Perhaps the most outstanding contributor to the
development of these ideas was Houston Stuart Chamberlain.
An Englishman by birth, Chamberlain spent most of his
life in Germany where he eventually became a German
citizen. Like many an enthusiastic immigrant, he strove
to become more "native" than those born in the country.
One expression of this enthusiasm was his marriage to

91

the daughter of the *voelkisch* composer, Richard Wagner.
Another was Chamberlain's deification of the German
Volk. In his most important work, *Die Grundlagen des
19 Jahrhunderts* (The Foundations of the Nineteenth Century)
(1899), Chamberlain sought to combine science and
mysticism into a coherent tool for the analysis of
civilization. But his fanatical worship of the Aryan
race and of all things German deprived Chamberlain of
his claims to a scientific method in all but the most
elementary areas. Instead, his "analysis" produced
the conclusion that most of the great figures in human
history, including Jesus Christ, had been of the Aryan
race. And since he claimed that the ancient and present
Teutonic peoples were the carriers of Western culture,
Chamberlain had no difficulty in viewing the two
greatest forces of the modern age, science and religion,
as distinctly German. When he attempted to deal in
scientific terms with the question of race, Chamberlain
concluded that it was in the measurement of the human
skull and the outward appearance of the brain that the
internal character or soul of a person could best be
identified. Later racist thinkers would use this
approach to distinguish between an Aryan and a Jewish
appearance.

However unscientific his claims may have actually
been, they added a certain legitimacy to racialist theory
of the kind that metaphysics alone had been unable to
provide. In elevating science to an equal position,
Chamberlain was the first *voelkisch* thinker to accept
modernity and see its redeeming value. It was, of
course, a qualified modernity: one which was in German
rather than in Jewish hands. Yet no less important
was the friendship between Chamberlain and the Pan-German
leader, Heinrich Class, and the influence of racialist
thinking upon Pan-German members, especially those in
academic life. But perhaps Chamberlain's most important
contribution came in one of his more mystical pronouncements. He advocated a revolution of the German *Volk*
in order to recognize its true spirit and to free it
from the domination of Jewish influence. It was to
be an internal--not social--revolution that stressed
an upheaval of the spirit. But in so doing, Chamberlain
was touching the heart of political reality. He was
providing one of the weapons which a conservative system
intent on preventing just such a social upheaval would
use to defend itself and the social classes that ruled
it.[39]

4

By the time the *Reichstag* election of 1912 was
imminent, the vast majority of conservative Germany
was overtly anti-Semitic. After more than a decade of
"respectability", the "Jewish question" now regained
the virulence that had characterized its *fin de siecle*
period. A meeting of the Prussian Ministry of State
on the day before the Election reflected the new mood.
A discussion on whether to appoint a Jew to the Prussian
Herrenhaus was quickly abandoned. All the assembled
Ministers felt that at "this particular time" such
a recommendation to Kaiser Wilhelm "would be without
purpose."[40] Why was there such a renewal of outright
anti-Semitic hostility? To describe it simply in terms
of an intensification of racial hatred would be
incomplete. To be sure, twenty *voelkisch* organizations
were founded between 1910 and 1913 for just such a
purpose.[41] But that was only one motive among several
that lay beneath the surface of the renewed attacks
upon Jewry.

In the decade since racial theory had become the
chief concern of the *voelkisch* forces, its stature as
a unifying factor between social groups had attained
international recognition. Racial theories were to be
found in most European nations and in the United States,
much like the theories of the nation-state that gave
rise to the Age of Nationalism. Like the nation, race
became symbolic of a common striving; both were also
subject to the influence of Social Darwinism: one variant
"characterized by the doctrine of progress through the
elimination of unfit nations, the second...marked by
the elimination of unfit individuals."[42] Both
symbolized the "antidotes to potential social revolution"
employed by political systems desperate to survive.[43]

As the election of 1912 drew nearer, the German
Conservative Party found itself without a strong campaign
issue. The struggle against Social Democracy, of course,
remained a constant. Its effectiveness had been highlighted by the electoral losses of the SPD five years
earlier. That campaign, however, had cost both the
Conservatives and the BdL dearly. Although they had
temporarily reversed the political growth of the
extreme Left, their steadfast refusal to subordinate
class interests to a united effort led by "nationalist"
organizations destroyed their most potent political
weapon: they were no longer able to hide their narrow

political and economic aims under a "nationalist"
claim.[44] The battle over tax reform brought the true
interests of the Conservatives and agrarians into full
public view.[45]

With the emergence of "race" as a full-blown social
and political ideal, the BdL was able to recapture some
of its national respectability. The strong undercurrents
of racism inherent in BdL ideology placed it in direct
cooperation with the nation-wide *voelkisch* movement.
Moreover, by using anti-Semitism as the main link, the
agrarians were able to cultivate their control over the
Mittelstand and non-aristocratic farmers under fully
legitimate pretensions. Such tactics did not apply to
the Conservative Party. Despite a strong attempt by the
BdL to reroute Conservative principles in a more racially
anti-Semitic direction, racial moderates and ultra-
Conservatives blocked all such measures.[46] As late as
1910[47] and 1911,[48] Conservatives directed nearly as much
criticism against the excesses of *voelkisch* racialism
as against German Jewry.

The seriousness of the Social Democratic threat,
however, combined with a deteriorating position in the
Reichstag and a generally declining political influence,
forced the Conservatives to reassess the advisability
of such a stand. As a result, anti-Semitic agitation
was increased: not as an end in itself, but as an
additional base from which to attack Social Democracy.
Thus the *Kreuzzeitung's* final pre-election attack against
the SPD defined it as a "Jewish disciplined" organization.[49]
And within days of its staggering losses in the Election,
the Party, already looking toward the next election in
1917, announced its long-range campaign strategy which
would include "agitation and the catchwords: Down with
international Jews and Social Democrats."[50]

This particular theme was picked up by all Right-
wing organizations. The "golden" and "red" international
became the twin spectres that haunted the German nation.
Especially during the winter and spring of 1912, the
tirade against the Jews reached fantastic proportions.
Letters poured into newspapers and journals from ordinary
Germans attacking the "destructiveness of the Jewish
spirit and Jewish capital."[51] To many, the danger of
Jewry presented an even greater threat to Germany than
did Social Democracy. All this did not go unnoticed
by the elements most opposed to the social upheaval
that threatened the conservative system. And most
were quick to seize upon anti-Semitism as the key to its

94

defense. V. Wangenheim practically said as much when
he predicted that "we will see the rebirth of an anti-
Semitism more ideal, but equally as strong as is
preached by Theodor Fritsch."[52] To v. Wangenheim the
"totality" of the struggle against the extreme Left
was dependent on the ability to mobilize all
staatserhaltende forces. Toward this end, Fritsch was
empowered to found the *Reichshammerbund* to coordinate
the spread of the anti-Semitic message to as much of
German society as possible. In addition, the BdL
directed the creation of a major *voelkisch* organization,
Der Verband gegen die Ueberhebung des Judentums (The
Association against the Presumption of the Jews), which
included leading Pan-Germans and racial anti-Semites.[53]
This was a major step in attempting to gather all
voelkisch elements under one banner. The *Verband* was
financed not only by the BdL but by heavy industry as
well. Its other purpose was to ensure that the liberal
interests of the *Hansabund* did not influence large
sections of the *Mittelstand* to reject the BdL. This
possibility greatly worried v. Wangenheim, as he
admitted to Major Endell: "If we want to reach our
goal, we must bring the Middle with us and make sure
that it does not go with the wind *(Hansabund)*."[54] A
strengthening of the anti-Semitic link would achieve
this aim. As if to ease v. Wangenheim's fears, the
Hamburg *Mittelstand* leader, Henningsen, wrote in the
Deutschsoziale Blaetter, only a few weeks after v.
Wangenheim's letter to Endell, that "the *Mittelstand*
movement must come quite naturally to the battle against
the Jewish spirit. In this sense it must be anti-Semitic
or it will cease to be."[55]

Another prominent figure of the German Right was
also distressed by the *Reichstag* election of 1912. He
was Heinrich Class, head of the influential Pan-German
League, confidant of heavy industry and friend and
disciple of Houston Stewart Chamberlain. More than
any other figure of the political Right, Class was heir
apparent to the title of *voelkisch* leader. A believer
in the truth of Social Darwinism as it applied to nation
and *Volk* and an advocate of the death struggle between
the Germanic and Jewish races, Class personified the
combination of *voelkisch* theory and practical politics.
Before 1912, the Pan-German League had limited itself
mainly to the drive for a "Greater Germany", in the
form of increased continental and colonial holdings
and for a strengthening of the "Germanic spirit" among
Germans residing outside the *Reich's* borders. Now,
however, Class was convinced that the German nation

stood at the edge of disaster. In May of 1912 he published a book entitled *Wenn ich der Kaiser waer (If I Were the Kaiser)*, which enjoyed five printings up to 1914. Fritz Fischer has called this work "the first model for an authoritarian state."[56] To this must be added a further description; it was a model for the first practical application of Chamberlain's call for an internal revolution of the German *Volk*. Despite the wide-ranging reforms, both internal and external, that were advocated in Class' book, it was evident that one major reform was predominant: the extermination of the Jewish "spirit" in German life. By advocating the application of an alien status upon German Jewry as well as practical measures designed to restrict its right to a normal existence (the loss of all public offices; no voting rights or military service; no Jews as lawyers, teachers, bank directors, estate owners) Class took the first steps toward the total elimination of any Jewish influence in German life. By separating him from the German *Volk*, Heinrich Class made identification of the Jew that much simpler--just in case "elimination" would not involve his "spirit" alone.[57]

In 1912 anti-Semitism became a major force in right-wing German politics. Because of the Social Democratic threat, it had been taken beyond the confines of the Circus Busch and out of the pages of the political-anthropological journals to serve as a rallying point of the German Right. To the BdL the Jew represented new-found credibility among the "national" movements and a link with the forces necessary for the "total" struggle against the Left. The Pan-Germans viewed him as the source of all dangers to the *Reich* and the one factor whose "spiritual" elimination was deemed necessary to allow the German *Volk* to pursue its predestined greatness. For most of the German Right the Jew was an alien force who would never fit within the context of a true German *Volk*. Only the Conservative Party was unwilling to proceed to this extreme view as an article in the *Konservative Monatsschrift* of December 1913 clearly showed. In the article, entitled "The Jewish Question and anti-Semitism", the author severely criticized the existence of an "instinctive and naive racial hatred." It was true that Jewry possessed a different spirit and character, he concluded, but "what anyone who works on the Jewish question really wants is that the Jews become different than they are, that they become Germans."[58] This divergence in opinion on an issue

which was crucial to the continued existence of the
conservative state could not and would not be taken
lightly. To many on the far right of German politics,
such hesitancy on the part of the Conservatives
indicated not only faulty Party leadership, but a
contribution to the defense of the system that was
too little and, in terms of Conservative credibility,
too late.

iii. Taxation and isolation

     With their *Reichstag* position weakened, the
Conservatives took precautions to guard against further
encroachments into areas considered important to their
predominance. Especially sensitive was the continuing
question of taxes. It will be remembered that this
matter had been postponed from the reform struggles of
1909 without a satisfactory conclusion.[59] At the
heart of the matter was the question: should the *Reich*
have the right to levy a direct inheritance tax
against the *Junkers*? For a time, the Conservative
Party and the BdL had successfully thwarted a positive
response to this query but had been unable, at the
same time, to contribute a lasting solution to the
growing financial difficulties of the *Reich*.

     The issue of direct *Reich* taxes, in fact, had
never resolved itself. Moreover, it had saddled the
Conservatives with an "unpatriotic" label which
Heydebrand attempted to refute during his "Morocco
speech" in November 1911. The Conservatives were
willing to give for the purpose of armaments, he said,
but it would have to be from the wealth of the living
and not from the dead.[60] *Reichstag* chairman v. Normann
reaffirmed the Conservatives' position and added a
further reason: the Party's negative position was a
"matter of honor."[61] Such wafer-thin excuses had
little effect upon anyone--least of all upon the
bourgeois electorate. The Conservatives were repaid
for their resistance to a just taxation with a
resounding political defeat. Of those who stood in
direct conflict with the Conservatives, the one to
gain least satisfaction from their debacle was
Bethmann. His hopes for a renewed government *Sammlung*
were apparently shattered. While in theory there existed
the possibility of a slight majority based upon a
Bassermann-Bebel grouping, the basic conservatism of
Bethmann's "politics of the diagonal" could not allow
for such a situation.

Forced to think of acquiring *Reichstag* majorities based more upon issues than governmental loyalties, Bethmann, nonetheless, did not completely abandon his original hopes. Several days after the Election, he resumed his attempt of *Sammlung*. The first of the *staatserhaltende* groups to react was the BdL. Through v. Wangenheim they rejected his "serious and meaningful" call and declared themselves "in opposition to Herr v. Bethmann" on the matter.[62] In actual fact, the agrarians regarded Bethmann's action as superfluous and perhaps even harmful. The *Bund* was equally determined to rally the conservative forces of the Empire under its leadership. They were part of a general trend which was beginning to emphasize the fact that the struggle against the Left had moved more and more outside the confines of the *Reichstag*. If the Social Democrats could not be defeated at the polls, ran the thinking of the extraparliamentary opposition, perhaps their ticket of entrance--secret, direct, equal and universal suffrage--could be eliminated. Any why not eliminate the *Reichstag* altogether? It certainly did not represent the true interests of the nations' productive Estates. In doing away with the *Reichstag*, such groups sought to eliminate not only the vehicle but the source of the threatened democratization and parliamentarization of the Wilhelmine Empire.

Military considerations during the early part of 1912 quickly revived the question of taxation and brought the *Reichstag* effectiveness of the Conservative Party into serious question. An urgent need to find funding for large increases in army manpower forced Bethmann to once again consider a *Reich* inheritance tax. It could not have come at a more inopportune moment. Calling for such a tax was certain to arouse the opposition of both Conservatives and the Center. But Bethmann was also aware of the growing estrangement between the "Black-Blue" *Block*. Both the Center and the National Liberals had come under the influence of moderate forces unwilling to see the agrarians maintain such overwhelming control of Germany's fate. Bethmann and *Reich* Secretary of the Treasury Wermuth saw Conservative compliance with an inheritance tax as a "golden bridge" to the other bourgeois parties and a positive step toward the renewed government *Sammlung*.[63] Such hopes were, however, futile. The Center and, especially, the Conservatives renewed their opposition to the tax. In view of such opposition, Bethmann sought to ease his demands. Wermuth, on the other hand, stubbornly insisted on the inheritance tax. It

was then that Bethmann, out of desperation, struck
upon the idea of eliminating the tax exemption or
Liebesgaben for brandy. It was, no doubt, a dangerous
step, sure to inuriate the agrarians. But the
exemption had always been an irritant to the bourgeois
parties and the Chancellor was still hopeful of some
sort of *Sammlung*.[64] In fact, Bethmann had no other
choice. The conservative *Bundesrat* had rejected a
subsidiary inheritance tax to be paid through
Matrikularbeitraege and Wermuth continued to press
demands unacceptable to either Conservatives or
Centrists. Wermuth was promptly forced to resign and
his deputy Kuehn appointed to the post. The brandy
tax bill that resulted from the elimination of the
Liebesgaben was accepted by the Conservatives, only
because it seemed, when compared with the inheritance
tax, the lesser of two evils. Just before the bill's
passage, however, Erzberger of the Center and Basserman
of the National Liberals attached a rider calling for
a "general taxation on property" within a year. But
the exact nature of the tax had not been properly defined,
leading to disagreements among all the *Reichstag* parties.
Only Bethmann was pleased by the cooperation of the
bourgeois parties and the army increases they had passed.
The tax question, however, had not been settled only,
once again, postponed.[65] And in May, a month after
the bill's introduction, when the Conservatives tested
the strength of their *Reichstag* alliances by introducing
a bill severely limiting the activities of the social
democratic trade unions and the coalition rights of
workers, they found only the right-wing of the National
Liberals and the Free Conservatives in support. The
Center, increasingly sensitive to the feelings of its
own Catholic trade-unions, voted against the bill and
assured its defeat.[66] Contrary to Bethmann's hopes,
the parties were far from a *Sammlung* situation; and
the Conservatives, the rug pulled out from underneath
them by the Center defection, found themselves with
few allies. Both Heydebrand and Westarp, in later
reflections, pinpointed these events as the beginning
of the *Reichstag* isolation of the Conservative Party.[67]

During the summer of 1912 the question of taxation
and finances remained in the background of *Reichstag*
affairs. By late autumn, however, it once again
occupied center stage. In part, this was due to
pressing military considerations, the result of a
military and political crisis in the Balkans. Both
Wilhelm and Bethmann recognized that the new situation
warranted immediate military increases. Of primary

importance to this consideration were two questions:
by how much should the army increase and where could
additional funds be found to cover the cost?[68] If
this was not enough to create a new financial crisis,
then *Reich* Treasury Secretary Kuehn provided the
additional impetus. He informed Bethmann that the
deadline set for the implementation of the *Lex* Erzberger-
Bassermann (April 30, 1913) was growing short. No
decision had been taken upon the specific form of
taxation although several proposals had been suggested.
The constant opposition of the Conservatives to any
form of death duty had left the situation in hopeless
deadlock.

As in previous questions of taxation, Bethmann
had to somehow balance the need to create a broadly-
based *Sammlung* of *Reichstag* parties with his desire to
protect the interests of the stubborn and seemingly
unappreciative Conservatives. Equally problematic
was the best method to avoid a collision with the
Bundesrat on the question of direct *Reichstag* taxation.[69]
Mindful of these problems, Bethmann considered Kuehn's
suggestions. According to the Treasury Secretary only
a direct *Reichstag* tax upon property or inheritance
capital gains was appropriate to fulfill the *Lex*
Erzberger-Bassermann. Furthermore, only the property
capital gains tax stood a chance of receiving Conservative
or Center support. On January 4, 1913 Bethmann approached
the *Bundesrat* with his proposal.

Normally, Bethmann would never have taken such a
plan before the federal states, knowing beforehand that
he would find almost total opposition to his suggestion.
In the changed circumstances of the new *Reichstag*, however,
any insistance upon a direct inheritance tax would have
almost certainly made him dependent on a majority of the
Left. Moreover, the Chancellor was under the impression
that Heydebrand had spoken positively about a capital
gains tax on property.[70] With this in mind, Bethmann
went to the *Bundesrat* only to find the opposition about
as total as he could have expected. The federal states,
always sensitive to their constitutional rights to tax
income and property, refused to consider any proposal
which would have diminished that right. They did,
however, suggest to Bethmann that they would support a
Reich inheritance tax. This they were willing to do
since the *Reich*, in 1906, had already managed to obtain
a death duty on distant relatives and the states were
prepared to concede the remainder of the inheritance tax
rather than allow a new area of encroachment upon their
independence. Only Prussia objected to this suggestion.[71]

Radicals and Reactionaries

Frustrated by the opposition of the *Bundesrat*,
Bethmann began to consider, however remotely, the
possibility of introducing a direct inheritance tax
On January 7, during a meeting of the Prussian
Ministry of State, he suggested, somewhat naively,
that perhaps the Conservative position had changed, since
"the inheritance tax no longer simply serves the purpose
of fulfilling the law of June 14, 1912 (i.e. Erzberger-
Bassermann-AJP)." Bethmann was now prepared to include
the Army Bill as part of the finances to be covered
by the tax. Obviously hoping that this would appeal
to the Conservatives' sense of patriotism, he argued
that if only they would accept the inheritance tax as
a means of paying for the Bill, "it could contribute
to the raising of their image", and "really deflate the
Liberals."[72] But Bethmann's hopes, based as they were
upon a misunderstood conception of Conservative
patriotism, were quickly dashed. On February 21, the
Chancellor met with Heydebrand and the aged and nearly
senile Count Kanitz. They informed him that the
Conservative position was clear: they could not
accept either *Reich* tax nor could they help in finding
an alternative. Resorting to standard agrarian
ideology, they told Bethmann to get the money from the
"stock market" interests. Three days later the Center
also rejected the inheritance tax.[73]

Faced with an intolerable situation, Bethmann hit
upon the idea of testing the "patriotism" of the
remaining *Reichstag* parties and the federal states.
Developing a plan that Kuehn had first mentioned at
the end of 1912, Bethmann now suggested that perhaps
the Army Bill might even serve to solve a large part
of the *Reich's* financial plight. With a cost of over
a billion marks, there was no possible way that the
Reich could have paid for the Bill without a major tax
reform. But, argued the Chancellor, what if the non-
repetitive costs could be covered by a single donation
in the form of a "defense contribution" *(Wehrbeitrag)*?
As it would be levied only once it could not be
construed as a direct tax. It would be, rather, the
type of "patriotic" contribution that he had so
desperately desired from the Conservatives. Moreover,
the Army Bill would also cover the *Lex* Erzberger-Bassermann
and hopefully, persuade the Center and the Conservatives
to enter into a government *Sammlung.*[74]

The correctness of this approach was shown by the
enthusiasm that the "defense contribution" received
from the press and civilian authorities. After the

manpower increases had been set, final estimates put
the non-repetitive costs at close to a billion marks
and the "running" costs (those to be paid more than
once) at nearly 200 million. Although there was
general enthusiasm from the states and all bourgeois
parties except the Conservatives towards the "defense
contribution", no solution seemed forthcoming on how
the running costs would be financed. Bethmann, still
seeking to protect Conservative interests, continued to
hold out for a capital gains tax on property. Although
the Conservatives and Center had softened their opposition
to such a tax,[75] the majority of the south German states
and the Hansa cities continued to oppose it. The
traditional rivalry between north and south Germany
and the recurrent economic differences between the
shipping interests of the Hanseatic cities and the
protectionism of the east Prussian agrarians contributed
to this position. The Chancellor could conceivably
have got the *Bundesrat* to pass the property tax.
Prussia and the other north German states held the
majority of votes in the *Bundesrat* and the Prussian
Finance Minister, Lentze, had come out for such a tax.
But Bethmann considered it politically impossible to
encourage such a move.[76]

The result was further compromise. The running
costs would be met by the states as increased
Matrikularbeitraege to be raised through higher direct
taxes on either property, income or inheritance. If
an individual state parliament could not ratify this
agreement by the end of 1914, then the *Reich* property
tax on capital gains would come into effect. It was
an agreement that pleased no one, but it was eventually
passed by the *Bundesrat*.[77]

Trouble arose when the Army Bill and the *Bundesrat*
compromise came before the *Reichstag*. Although the
"defense contribution" was passed with a minimum of
difficulty, the parliamentary commission established
to deal with the Army Bill and *Bundesrat* compromise
proved more difficult. As a result of at least two
questions (the number of princely adjutants to be
allowed the states and a cut of cavalry regiments from
six to three) the *Reichstag* was nearly dissolved,
essentially at the Kaiser's request.[78] The Right was
able to combine, however, to overcome the obstruction
tactics of the Social Democrats and pass the Army Bill
nearly intact. Bethmann helped secure its favorable
outcome with constant appeals for patriotic duty and by
painting a gloomy picture of the *Reich's* increasing
"encirclement" by hostile powers.[79]

Radicals and Reactionaries

The question of running costs was next on the
Commission agenda. Only the Conservatives voiced a
positive opinion for the *Bundesrat* compromise and then
only hesitantly because of the *Reich* subsidiary tax.
The remainder of the bourgeois parties were more
inclined to favor the *Reich* capital gains tax on
property. The SPD and the left Liberals, on the
other hand, demanded the introduction of a *Reich*
inheritance tax. Bethmann was able to overcome both
these plans, the first by direct vote and the second
through the lack of a majority. But the Center
refused to remain passive. It next introduced a
proposal to change the subsidiary tax to a primary one.
Despite frantic efforts by the Conservatives to
maintain the subsidiary tax, the Center measure was
passed by an alliance of National Liberals, Left
Liberals and Social Democrats.[80] At the end of June
the *Reichstag* was prepared to vote upon the whole bill.
During the second reading of the property tax, the
Social Democrats, with National Liberal approval,
proposed also to tax the princes of the *Reich* in the
"defense contribution." Bethmann at once asked for
and received full authority from the Kaiser to dissolve
the *Reichstag*. The National Liberals backed down,
fearing both the blame for bringing down Parliament and
the uncertainty of new elections.[81] The proposal was
defeated but on the same day the primary *Reichstag*
capital gains tax on property was approved. The Center
and the National Liberals had combined with the left
Liberals and the SPD for 280 "yes" votes against only
63 "no" votes that could be mustered by the Conservative
parties and the Economic Union.

The *Reichstag* decision sent waves of shock through
the Conservative Party. For the first time a major
piece of tax legislation had been approved despite its
opposition. As a feeling of complete and utter isolation
set in, the Conservatives looked to Bethmann as to the
source of all their difficulties. Although the Chancellor
had been responsible in obtaining the largest military
increase in the *Reich's* history, it was not this success
but rather his failure in protecting their interests
that motivated their critique of Bethmann. He had,
according to their view, been unable to protect them
in the question of running costs. This, in actual fact,
stemmed from several misconceptions that Bethmann had
maintained about the Conservatives. Firstly, his original
idea (that the property tax would protect the agrarians
from the threat of an inheritance tax) was false. The
agrarians had never viewed the taxation issue as an

"either-or" situation. They were instinctively opposed
to both *Reich* taxes and held Bethmann to blame for not
aiding them in maintaining the subsidiary tax. Secondly,
in trying to gain new finances for military needs,
Bethmann had been unable to perceive the nature of
agrarian "patriotism." This concept viewed the interests
of the nation and the material class interests of the
Conservatives as one. Whatever, including direct taxes
for defense, damaged their own position also damaged
the nation. It was this myopic view of national affairs
that continued to keep the question of finances an
unresolved issue, and turned Bethmann into a political
enemy.[82]

Following the events of June 30, 1913, the Conservatives
stood alone. Not only was their *Reichstag* power base
in a shambles, but they had once again, in early 1913,
failed to secure legislation directed against the Social
Democrats. The agrarians took this to mean that the
Reichstag was in serious danger of becoming completely
democratized and that the next target would be Prussia--the
heart of agrarianism. While Bethmann was able to tell the
Kaiser that "the tax compromise reached by the Majority
bourgeois parties may foreshadow some lessening of our
political antagonisms",[83] the Conservatives were
preparing to dig in for an extended struggle. Only
days after the June defeat, Heydebrand wrote a congratulatory
letter to Count Westarp who had just become chairman of
the *Reichstag* Conservatives upon the death of Kanitz.
In this letter, Heydebrand acknowledged that Bethmann was
taking the "unfortunate position of our group in the
Reichstag" rather lightly. But Heydebrand sought to
reassure the worried Westarp that Bethmann's politics
would not extend into sacred Prussia. He confidently
predicted that the centers of conservative power in that
state--the *Herrenhaus*, the Ministry of State, the
predominance of the Conservatives in the *Abgeordnetenhaus*,
the bureaucracy and Wilhelm--the "pentagon", as he termed
it, would overcome both Bethmann and his politics.[84]

The political isolation of the Conservative Party
was, in fact, only of several significant changes in the
politics of the post-1912 *Reichstag*. Writing in his
political journal, *Die Preussische Jahrbuecher (The
Prussian Yearbooks)*, at the end of 1913, Professor Hans
Delbrueck commented upon one aspect of this change: "We
now have numerous parties and groups", he stated, "who
come together and form new combinations with each political
question." This, he felt, had finally put an end to
the myth of a *Reichstag* divided into two opposing groups,

"a Black-Blue *Block* on the one side and the combined liberals on the other."[85] What Delbrueck described was part of the process of "block-building and blockage" which has been analyzed by Gustav Schmidt[86] and indicates the state of German domestic politics in the final years before World War I. In essence, this was a situation in which the individual *Reichstag* camps--the conservative parties on the right, sections of the Center and National Liberals in the middle and left Liberals and revisionist Social Democrats on the left--"were able successfully to block each other and thus make impossible any real political progress."[87]

Crucial to this development was the political demise of the Conservative Party and the emergence of the political center. The latter grouping had been a part of the domestic scene since the creation of Tirpitz's fleet.[88] At that time, however, the ruling classes had maintained complete predominance. Social reformers such as Naumann and Barth had been unable to pursue successfully the twin aims of the so-called Liberal *Sammlung*: greater social reform at home and a strong German international presence. Since 1909, however, with the creation of the *Hansabund*, the size of its political base had increased while that of the conservative powers declined steadily. By 1912, large sections of the Center Party and National Liberals (Young Liberals) were entering into majorities without and, often, against the Conservatives. The middle rejected the inconclusive efforts of the conservative Right in its struggle against Social Democracy. They saw only the German bourgeoisie as holding the key to the integration of the working-class movement.[89] Furthermore, they viewed the problem as a power-struggle between themselves and the ruling elites for the future leadership of the *Reich*: for whoever controlled the masses would control the nation. They planned to achieve this by capturing the revisionist wing of the SPD (which was in basic agreement with the reform movement) and by offering alternatives to the SPD (such as the Center Party with its strong emphasis upon trade unionism).[90]

The problem was that there were just too many obstacles in the way of a center *Sammlung*. Chief among them, as Schmidt has shown, was the retention of partisan political loyalties which refused to yield to a general reform movement.[91] Also, despite their revolutionary rhetoric, the SPD "needed the existing monarchical order as the tree to bark at in order to prevent a split in their own ranks into a revolutionary and revisionist party." This was exactly the situation of the ruling

classes who needed a revolutionary SPD in order to
maintain their credibility and, indeed, the existence
of the Prusso-German state.[92] The resulting situation,
as Volker Berghahn has noted, was one of "an almost
total impasse."[93] Within the *Reichstag* the various
blocs were able to cancel each other with the consequence
that "the political initiative went more and more to
the agitation organizations" outside of the national
parliament.[94] This had an especially disastrous effect
upon the Conservatives. By the middle of 1913, the
Party had not only been humbled by a Center-Left
coalition in the *Reichstag* but had lost the confidence
of both agriculture and heavy industry.

CHAPTER V

Radicals and Reactionaries in a Period of Crisis (1913/14)

i. Pan-Germans on the march: success
    and failure in the conservative camp

     In mid-April 1913, Heinrich Class received a letter
from a Baltic German named Erich v. Oettingen.[1] It
had been v. Oettingen's task to approach the Agrarian
League chairman, Conrad v. Wangenheim, on behalf of
Class, with the suggestion of political cooperation
between the ADV and the agrarian organization.[2] Class
had already extended the hand of friendship a year
earlier by praising the *Bund* in his book *If I Were Kaiser*.[3]
Now the fruits of his and v. Oettingen's labor were
reflected in the contents of the letter. In his discussions
with Class's emissary, v. Wangenheim had revealed himself
to be eager for cooperation. The BdL was "looking for
aid in furthering the *Mittelstand* psychology"[4] and
needed the support of the nationalist organizations
in achieving this aim. V. Wangenheim, convinced by
v. Oettingen that Class was "conservative through and
through", hinted that the BdL might be of great aid to
the Pan-Germans in achieving ADV aims. The agrarian
leader felt that it was "purely a matter of bad direction
that the ADV seemed somewhat utopic." Finally, v. Wangenheim
listed one more request: if Minister of Agriculture
Schorlemer-Lieser were to replace Bethmann-Hollweg as
Chancellor, then he, v. Wangenheim, wanted the post of
Agriculture Minister.

     After a June meeting with Class, in which v. Wangenheim
found him impressive and "totally disinclined to adopt an
ultra-nationalist stance",[5] both leaders returned to
their respective organizations for approval of a meeting,
the details of which were to be kept secret. On July 6
the two groups met at BdL headquarters in Berlin. Class
was accompanied by Admiral Breusing and Senator Neumann
of Luebeck; joining v. Wangenheim were BdL officials,
Aus dem Winkel and Wadehn. The two sides quickly agreed
that it was "necessary to have a *Sammlung* of all
staatserhaltende forces in the area of domestic politics
against the increasing democratization and atomization
of the German *Reich*."[6] In a report of the meeting,[7]
Neumann outlined the basic agreements: both organizations
entered into a formal alliance; the ADV would advise
the domestic and interest-oriented agrarians on matters
of foreign and "national" policy while the agrarians
would expect the Pan-Germans to spread the *Bund*
ideology (especially on inner colonization) through
the ADV ranks; finally, there would be a coordinated
press policy and an exchange of speakers. "There was
much satisfaction on both sides," concluded Neumann.

The formal alliance between the ADV and BdL
"cannot", in the words of Fritz Fischer, "be emphasized
enough in its meaning for the development of the internal
and external politics of the *Kaiserreich* before the
outbreak of the (First) World War."[8] The close association
between two groups with similar views on racial supremacy
and on the importance of agriculture provided both with
opportunities to add new dimensions to their ideological
frameworks and increase the sphere of their influence.
This was especially true for the BdL. Wangenheim's
proposal for a joint cooperation with the ADV was
unanimously approved by the *Bund* on July 30.[9] Class,
however, did not inform the ADV of the proposed alliance
until August 20 and then not without a certain degree
of opposition from some quarters. Admittedly a political
union of the organizations was impossible. The ADV was
unable to support the agrarian-interest politics of the
BdL if it wished to maintain the support of its anti-
Junker members in southern and western Germany. This
was exactly the point raised by newspaper publisher and
ADV Executive Committee member Heinrich Rippler who
felt that the agrarians were merely seeking support
"for the achievement of victory in the coming tariff
struggles."[10] Similarly, the Pan-Germans were unable
to sanction fully BdL cooperation with right-wing
Centrists and un-German "ultramontanism."[11] Class was
able to argue successfully against such objections by
painting a picture of 400,000 agrarians becoming
nationalists under the "influence" of the ADV. This
opinion was shared by Lieutenant-General v. Liebert
who saw an increasing decomposition of the political
parties and a forced politicization of the economic-
interest groups. Class summed up his reasons for an
alliance in the following manner: "I see in the fact
that nearly 400,000 members of the BdL wish to work
with the far smaller ADV, a recognition of the meaningful
position that we have struggled for in public life."[12]

The specific aims of the agrarians are not as
clearly defined.[13] There is no doubt, however, that
Rippler was correct in his reference to agrarian
concern over the forthcoming tariffs.[14] Too, Admiral
Breusing formulated a very perceptive opinion after his
meeting with the agrarians:[15]

> The struggle of democracy against agriculture
> endangers the German nation at its very root. The
> democratic attack has become so strong that
> agriculture has been unable to oppose it merely

through a defense of economic interests. The
danger to the nation by this attack must be
emphasized more than ever. Related to this is
the fact that the *Bund der Landwirte* concerns
itself more than ever with national questions
and has set national aims for itself. Since
the *Bund* is really not at home in this field,
working together with us is especially welcome.

Yet however much the *Bund* stood to achieve through its
relationship with the Pan-Germans, a certain amount of
danger was also present. In *If I Were the Kaiser*,
Class had made clear the Pan-German view that agriculture
was the most important basis for the national well-being,
survival and independence of the Empire. At the same
time, he had also stressed that large landowners would
have to part with significant portions of their property
wherever "inner colonization" made such a sacrifice
necessary.[16] Here, agrarian and Pan-German ideology
clearly disagreed. It appears, then, that an extremely
important part of cooperation with the ADV was based
upon the *Bund's* (and v. Wangenheim's) desire to pursue
the aim of eliminating or modifying this grave threat
to the economic survival of the *Junkers*. Thus, while
Fritz Fischer sees v. Wangenheim's appearance as a
speaker at the ADV's Stuttgart convention in early
1914 as "the most noteworthy event in this development
of cooperation between BdL and ADV-AJP)", the content
of his speech equally suggests the former aspect of
the relationship. In his speech, v. Wangenheim spoke
of the need to avoid "a purposeless destruction of
existing property." Furthermore, "the firmly-established
large land-owner must remain sacrosanct" and be the
"leader, teacher and carry the burden of honorary
officers" of any "inner colonization."[17]

2

The Pan-Germans found relations with the German
Conservatives much more difficult. This was especially
true with regard to Heydebrand. The Conservative
chairman had maintained a wary distance between himself
and the ADV since his disastrous meeting with Class in
1910.[18] Thus the Conservatives were not represented at
the *Plauener Verbandstag* of the ADV in 1912, a meeting
where many of the "national" aims of the Pan-Germans
and their allied organizations were formulated.[19]
Class did not hesitate to criticize the Conservatives
in *If I Were the Kaiser* for the "purely opportunistic
and governmental tendencies that have remained in the

Party for too long and have not yet been overcome."[20]
His evaluation of Heydebrand was restrained yet
sufficiently critical: "Herr Heydebrand is quite a
character but not the ideal leader of a great German
Party. He is too much an advocate of his party in the
sense of being one-sided...too much only Prussia...and
too much of a *Junker* and unideological type to
evaluate correctly the moving spirit of our times."
Part of that "spirit" was *voelkisch* racialism and Class
further criticized the Party for the "restraint with
which the Conservatives approach the question of
racial teaching."[21] He, nevertheless, held out the
hope "that we will be able to move closer to the
Conservative Party."[22]

According to Alfred Kruck,[23] Class and the ADV
attempted once again to persuade Heydebrand to join
him in a formal alliance along the same lines as the
one with the BdL. But, as in 1910, Heydebrand refused,
guided by the same fear of political rivalry from the
Pan-Germans in the heart of Conservative East Prussia.
"The Conservatives think," Class wrote to his second-
in-command, retired Bavarian General Constantin v. Gebsattel,
"that we have the ambition of serving as the center of
a great national party of the future."[24] This was in
June 1913. A month later the *Kreuzzeitung* defined
exactly its position towards such an alliance:[25] "We
have absolutely nothing to do with the Pan-German League.
There is certainly no kind of organizational tie nor
is there a personal one." And in an obvious rebuff to
the growing Pan-German call for the territorial growth
of the nation, the *Kreuzzeitung* stated that "the
Conservative Party has no need to endorse the annexations
of European territories by the German Empire in order
to appear patriotic." Rejected in his attempts to deal
directly with Heydebrand, Class turned to subtler means.
This was evident from a letter which Class wrote to
v. Klitzing, the Director of the Prussian Land Credit
Association and a leading Conservative.[26] Class reported
that he had succeeded in persuading v. Wangenheim to
take over the role of "middleman" between the ADV and
the Conservative Party. With the aid of the BdL he
hoped "that the present mistrust will be overcome," and
that the Conservatives "will be able to have the same
trust in us as exists today in the BdL." Class was
also intent upon mobilizing support from within the
ranks of the Conservative Party. Pan-German sympathizers
such as v. Klitzing could be used effectively "in the
direction of our *Sammlung* attempts if the Conservative
leaders receive a statement from within the Party which

expresses the same goals" as the ADV. Class was
counting on the "anger and bitterness" of the Conservatives
against Bethmann and their "indignation" over the course
of German foreign policy as a step toward overcoming
Heydebrand's opposition. "One other thing," Class
wrote, "one of our members, Franz Sontag, who formerly
worked for the *Post*, has been called to the *Kreuzzeitung*
as a chief editor. At the beginning, of course, he
must handle himself very cautiously, but he hopes
gradually to influence that newspaper to adopt a Pan-
German point of view."

ii. The *Kartell der Schaffenden Staende:*   fact or fiction?

1

Since 1912 both agriculture and heavy industry had
witnessed the gradual erosion of their respective *Reichstag*
positions. For the agrarians, this had meant not only the
loss of parliamentary seats held by BdL Members (Hahn,
Roesicke, v. Oldenburg-Januschau, Lucke and Aus dem
Winckel) but a significant reduction in the number of
Reichstag deputies committed to the agrarian programme.
Worse still, the chief responsibility for the support
of that programme had fallen to the increasingly isolated
and ineffectual Conservative Party.

The situation of the CDI and heavy industry was
even more frustrating. Never in possession of a sizeable
group of deputies who were able to represent its interests,
the CDI soon found itself dependent upon a handful of
Conservative and National Liberal politicians. To add
further to this dilemma, heavy industry had to contend
with the anti-industrial hostility of the Conservative
leadership, as Heydebrand, for example, openly displayed
in a 1910 speech:[27]

> It is a mistake to believe that it would be
> of any value to our Conservative aims if the
> representatives of industry were brought into
> the Conservative Party. The Conservatives, let
> us not labor under any illusions, are partial to
> the rural areas, smaller and middle-sized towns.
> The economic conceptions...of industry differ
> from our own.

It was with a knowledge of the growing CDI dissolusion-
ment with *Reichstag* policies that the BdL held its annual
conference on February 17, 1913. The session was highlighted

111

by speeches from Hahn and v. Wangenheim. Both speakers
attempted to play upon the unhappiness of heavy industry,
both in its relations to the *Reichstag* and the *Hansabund*.
Hahn welcomed the CDI "back to the old comradeship-in-
arms...that Prince Bismarck had created at the end of
the 70's. We can now give our expression of relief
that heavy industry has left the *Hansabund* and now
represents a view similar to ours." V. Wangenheim,
on the other hand, outlined the direction that a renewed
and strengthened relationship between the two economic
sectors would take:

> As long as our government does not recognize
> the SPD for what it is...there will be no change
> on our part. We will come to a situation, which
> the SPD wants, that will not go away without a
> revolution. Our patience is exhausted. We will
> join together in an anti-Socialist organization
> and struggle against the SPD in every area.

He concluded his speech by emphasizing that the
cooperation of the two groups would not only be based
on an anti-SPD alliance: "It is also necessary to
show the *Mittelstand* and industry that our interests
go hand in hand. For the first time, it is necessary
to wipe away all that separates us and to show unity
between city and country in the area of tariff policy."[28]

Not surprisingly, the BdL's call for a full-scale
attack against the SPD and support of the existing
tariff system was enthusiastically greeted by heavy
industry. The *Deutsche Arbeitgeberzeitung*, a leading
CDI exponent, openly called for a union of industry
and agriculture "in battle against Social Democracy."[29]
Similarly, the BdL was further supported by the agrarian-
led Association of Tax and Economic Reformers under Count
Mirbach-Sorquitten and, of course, by the RDMV where the
basis for the renewed partnership had first been constructed
during 1911 and 1912.[30] In May, v. Wangenheim informed
Roesicke that the *Bund* was prepared to work with the
militantly anti-Socialist Hamburg Association for the
Combatting of Social Democracy and also with the
Ex-Servicemen's Association.[31] These were but two of
the many extra-parliamentary groups whose growing concern
over the political and economic state of the Prusso-German
Empire began to find a focal point in the unifying
efforts of the *Bund der Landwirte*.

If, in fact, there had been any lingering doubts
as to the gravity of the situation facing Germany's
ruling interests, these were quickly dispelled by the

112

beginning of July. Two events, occurring in rapid
succession, were seen as convincing evidence of the
disintegrating conservative position. The first of
these was the Prussian *Landtag* election held at the
beginning of June. The election results were not
distinguished by dramatic gains or losses. The most
notable consequence was a clear loss of strength by
the left-wing of the National Liberal Party. But the
combined loss of 14 seats by the two Conservative parties
(hardly significant in terms of their already overwhelming majority in the *Landtag*) and a gain of 4 seats
by the SPD and 2 by the left Liberals seemed to
constitute, to an already frightened group of Conservatives,
a definite "shift to the Left."[32] Even more important,
however, was the calamitous result of the financial
question which, at the end of June, left both agrarians
and industrialists with a feeling that the new direct
taxation, voted in by a combination of the Center,
National Liberals, left Liberals and SPD, was "the
first step toward the confiscation" of a large section
of private and individual wealth.[33]

The gravity of the situation forced agriculture
and heavy industry to accelerate their plans for
cooperation. At the beginning of July, the BdL and
CDI met to draw up final confirmation of a political
bond which they hoped to disguise as "non-political"
and thus avoid an attack by the Left. Also present
were the RDMV and the Christian Farmers Associations
(CBV), a group which represented views similar to the
BdL's in southern and western Germany.[34] At the same
time, the more concrete guidelines and aims of the
economic groups, which the RDMV had already proposed
in May, were formally presented to the nation by the
Conservative (Prussian *Abgeordnetenhaus)* deputy and
Mittelstand leader, Walter Graef. In his article, in
the newspaper *Tag* (red), Graef disclosed that "within
the past few weeks," a new organization had been
founded, known as the "Circle of Producers." Comprised
of the BdL, CDI, RDMV and the CBV, the newly-founded
group had built a *Reich* committee "for the economic
cooperation of industry, agriculture and the *Mittelstand*."
Graef saw the necessity of a strict tariff and social
policy as the twin pillars of defense against the
"destructive politics of pure speculation and mobile
finance," an old BdL demand, and the creation of a
force to counter "the democratic wave which is once
more spreading over Germany." As the major aims of
the "Circle of Producers", he proposed the following
points:

113

1. The struggle against all abuses of our economic organism.
2. The preservation of authority in all economic sectors.
3. The maintenance of suitable prices and the protection of willing workers.
4. The defense against Social Democracy and the false teachings of Socialism.

As with the "non-political" meeting between agrarian and industrial interests in early July, Graef now claimed a similar "purely economic" motivation for the "Circle of Producers."[35] This attempt at political delusion fooled no one, least of all the leader of the left-wing of the National Liberal Party, Ernst Bassermann. Amidst an outpouring of denunciations and a complete rejection of their plans by the Left, he, most clearly, recognized the true aims of the right-wing movement:[36]

> The conservative wirepullers will not rest; they want to create ties between the Central Association, BdL and the anti-Semitic RVDM. That means: high protective tariffs; *'lueckenlose'* tariffs; anti-Socialist law; no reform of the Prussian suffrage system; a quiet struggle against the *Reichstag* voting right; the battle against everything liberal; the struggle against Bethmann-Delbrueck and the hope for the strong leader...

The accuracy of this opinion was demonstrated a week later in a letter from v. Wangenheim to Roesicke in which the agrarian leader discussed his hopes for the forthcoming *Mittelstand* Day to be held in Leipzig. V. Wangenheim was optimistic not only that there would be complete success in the coordination of the various economic interests but that "the negotiations concerning our efforts toward the fight against Social Democracy, through the drawing in of the working population, will fully overlap."[37] From August 22 until August 25, the "Circle of Producers" met in Leipzig at the third annual meeting of the RDMV. From that meeting emerged the *Kartell der Schaffenden Staende* (Cartel of the Creative Estates) who, once they had agreed upon their course of action, no longer needed to masquerade under an assumed title. Their new name testified to the fact that their alliance was based upon the spirit of Bismarck and that the bond which now connected them could be traced back to the year 1879.

114

What were the real aims of the *Kartell*? The four-point programme adopted at the *Mittelstand* Day convention was merely a reaffirmation of the Graef proposals published nearly two months before the Leipzig meeting. They were points long maintained by the BdL and only point 2, "The preservation of authority..." could be interpreted as the specific contribution of the CDI and its authoritarian *Herr-im-Haus* point of view. Instead, one must look beyond the stated aims, evaluate the prevailing mood within agrarian and heavy industrial circles and assess the changes in German society, both politically and economically, since the Election of 1912. Only then can the *Kartell* be understood as a kind of *Schutz und Trutz Bund* (Defensive Alliance) of *staatserhaltende* forces engaged in an all-out effort to retain their status in a society undergoing enormous social and political change.

2

"The political parties are dead. Long live the new formation of professional Estates in our politics. This is what one often hears in industry today." So wrote the *Hansabund* leader and industrialist Otto Brandt in September 1913.[38] The *Frankfurter Zeitung* echoed Brandt's sentiments in a September leader: "The big entrepreneur is unhappy and demonstrates this unhappiness because in the last few years things have been going contrary to his wishes. He doesn't like the *Reichstag* and he doesn't like the government."[39] That such an expression of anti-parliamentary and anti-governmental feeling was possible in the late summer of 1913 is not surprising. A latent hatred of the *Reichstag* and universal, direct suffrage had been an established part of conservative ideology since 1881. In that year Bismarck had proposed the creation of a *Volkswirtschaftrat* (National Economic Council) as a means of representing the interests of the "productive Estates." The agrarians and the *Mittelstand* had been the first to jump aboard the corporative bandwagon. At the 1909 convention of the Conservative Party, Diederich Hahn, on behalf of the BdL, had pleaded for the recognition of a body of professional Estates. Furthermore, there had been an increase of such feeling each time the SPD had scored significant gains in its *Reichstag* representation.[40] Thus, by the middle of 1913, with 110 SPD seats in the *Reichstag* an accomplished fact, and the direct *Reichstag* tax a clear indication of the leftish slant of that body's political direction, heavy industrial interests of the Right were more than prepared to join the agrarians in the establishment of an "independent, secondary system

115

of societal powers," which not only existed along side
the political parties "but stood in direct competition
to them."[41]

Although the *Kartell* sought to demonstrate a sense
of unity in its political objectives, the divergent
needs of agriculture, heavy industry and the *Mittelstand*
soon became evident. To be sure, all groups within the
Kartell paid lip-service to the anti-democratic and
anti-parliamentary proposals that were suggested during
the autumn of 1913 as antidotes to the growing "democratic
flood." Among these, the most widely quoted were plans
for the establishment of an upper house of the *Reichstag*
to deal with the interests of the professions and the
creation of an economic chamber that would function
apart from the federal *Reichstag*.[42] These proposals
were, by far, the almost exclusive aims of heavy industry
and the *Mittelstand* which saw in them the answer to
their declining *Reichstag* representation and a source
of direct access to the all-important bureaucracy.[43]
This view was not as strongly shared by the agrarians,
who already possessed such a bureaucratic link. The
only real non-industrial support for these demands came
from Professor Johannes Unold of Munich University,
the war-time constitutional consultant to the Conservative
Party. Yet even Unold's proposal differed somewhat from
industrial suggestions in that he pleaded for the continued
existence and primacy of the traditional party political
framework. His *Volksvertretung* (National Representation)
called for the "priority of economic interests" as the
most suitable area of inter-party relations. Only then
could such a "National Representation" serve "as a basis
for the professional groups."[44]

In the agrarian camp the *Kartell* was seen as a
political extension of that group's long-time effort
to dominate and lead a *Sammlung* of parties and interest
groups against Social Democracy. Even before the *Kartell*
had become an established fact, v. Wangenheim's short-
range priorities had centered on this issue. In an
optimistic letter to Class he revealed his intentions:
"I have a view towards calling together all those
corporatives this autumn who wish to take up the battle
against democracy of all shades. I hope that the current
mood [of the nation-AJP] will allow us to create a
great organization against democracy."[45]

By the end of September, the battle against the
Social Democratic threat had become the BdL's overriding
concern. This was due, in part, to the collapse of any

116

real political unity that the *Kartell* may have at one
time possessed. Not only had each of the *Kartell*
partners expressed primary aims which were considered
secondary by the other members, but the exaggerated
economic demands of the BdL (the so-called *lueckenlose*
tariffs) had become intolerable to a large part of
heavy industry.[46] Furthermore, the *Kartell* had been
attacked from the very beginning by both the *Hansabund*
and the left wing of the National Liberal Party, who
now rebuffed the CDI's efforts to draw them into a
heavy industrial *Sammlung*. This was followed in
November by the failure of the CDI to establish a
working relationship with the BdI.[47] In another letter
to Class, this time at the end of September, v. Wangenheim
noted the "uproar against the understanding between
agriculture, industry and the crafts [which] is noteworthy for the political and economic circles that are
behind it." Here was meant, of course, the *Hansabund*
groups, the left wing of the National Liberals as well
as the SPD, which had succeeded in popularizing the
Kartell as the *"Kartell der raffenden Haende"* (the
Cartel of greedy hands). Despite this, the agrarian
leader remained hopeful that "something useful can
be made out of this understanding." V. Wangenheim
had already proposed, he told Class, that the *Kartell*
partners meet "on the neutral ground of the battle
against Social Democracy."[48] What seemed like a
last-ditch effort to salvage the disintegrating unity
of the *Kartell* was, in actual fact, designed to
strengthen the political hand of the *Bund der Landwirte*.

If the search for a *status quo* position in
politics was an overwhelming *Kartell* concern, so too
was the desire for some sort of economic stability.
Economics, after all, was the mask with which the
Kartell partners had attempted to disguise their
reactionary, if diversified, political aims. It was
also, perhaps, a more suitable area for compromise,
possessing the memory of the Kardorff Majority of
1902 as a clear-cut historical precedent. Yet it
must be remembered that the BdL had opposed this
tariff solution as all too moderate and had waged
a vicious, if unsuccessful, campaign to reverse its
results.[49] Could the *Bund* now restrain its natural
inclincation to oppose any area of compromise which
did not place the interests of the BdL in the forefront
of its economic considerations? Apparently not,
thought the National Liberal *Hamburgerische Correspondent*,
commenting on the results of the Leipzig meeting:[50]

> The demands of the agrarians--*lueckenlose*
> tariffs and the further complication of necessary
> trade treaties--all this points to a rejection
> of any unity between the majority of German
> industry and the BdL. This is especially true
> of the BdI, whose manufacturing and export
> industries will stay away from such an association.

Such a reaction by the BdI was not surprising--it had,
along with the *Hansabund*, remained opposed to any
notion of agrarian preponderance in politics and
economics.

But the *lueckenlose* tariff demands were more than
merely the demand for a simple retention of the Kardorff
tariffs that were due to expire in 1917. They sought,
as the name implied, to close any "holes" in the
existing tariff structure: and by that was meant the
introduction of protective tariffs on a host of further
agricultural products such as milk, potatoes, vegetables
and herring. Adhering strictly to their ideological
notion of a closed, autarchic economy, the BdL came to
Leipzig prepared to compromise only upon its own terms.
Even before the Leipzig meeting had ended, dissident south
German members of the CDI refused to work with the
agrarians. They had been led to believe - on the basis
of liberal newspaper reports - that the CDI fully
supported the *lueckenlose* tariffs and was yielding to
BdL pressure. Fortunately for the CDI directorship,
it was able to calm south German apprehensions without
ever fully eliminating that regions' antipathy towards
the BdL. The much sought-after compromise between the
economic sectors was partially achieved. But it was
done so more from a fear of liberal demands in the
Reichstag--that a "check" be made with an eye toward
lowering the existing agricultural and industrial
tariffs--than from a willing partnership between the
economic associations in the *Kartell*.[51] The retention
of the 1902 tariffs became the focal point of both
industry and agriculture, as the *Kreuzzeitung* was able
to report with a degree of accuracy in October 1913.[52]
Yet the economic and political situation in Germany
during 1913/14 was such that a lasting union of the
Kartell partners on the basis of the Kardorff Majority
had become a near impossibility--especially for the
agrarians.

About the middle of 1913 the German public, through
various press reports, began to sense that something
was desperately wrong with the Imperial economy. Despite
optimistic reports to the contrary (circulated by a
frightened banking community) and impressive business
statistics for the years 1909-1912, it was not long
before the German economy was being characterized as
"fast asleep" with little hope for an immediate
recovery.[53] Translated into economic terms, this meant
simply that, during the year 1913, Germany had slipped
into a period of deep economic stagnation or "recession."
The crucial indicators of recession were all present:
on the banking side, a shortage of capital and high
interest rates that kept new commercial and industrial
involvements at a minimum; over-production and a sharp
drop in prices in both agriculture and industry; and
among the working class, a sharp rise in unemployment.[54]
This last factor was especially problematic, particularly
when viewed with an eye toward the continuation of a
conservative social and political system. The recession
hurt an already weakened working class whose economic
fortunes had been on the decline since the end of the
nineteenth-century. In fact, for the worker, the "boom"
period for industry and commerce, 1909-1912, had meant
only the continued halt to wage increases and a
further decline in purchasing power as basic necessities
continued to rise in cost. A further reflection of
working-class unhappiness was the steady growth of the
SPD, which in one year, 1910-11, added 16.2% to its
overall membership. What the recession would contribute
to that already frightening sum was the nightmarish
speculation that faced the Prusso-German state.[55]

What about the ruling groups in the Empire? Did
they, too, suffer under the impact of a weakened economy?
An immediate reply must be no. During the period of Germany's
economic recession of 1912-14, there was little or no
slump in the agricultural or heavy industrial sectors.
This is not to say, however, that these essential components
of the conservative system found in continued economic
prosperity the social stability they so desperately
desired.

In fact, for both groups there had been numerous
warnings that, domestically, the trend was moving away
from the predominance of their types of output toward
other areas. In industry, it was a trend toward finished
and consumer goods; in agriculture, it was in the direction

of horticultural cultivation and away from East
Prussian grain. This transition was apparent throughout
the period from 1896-1913--and not only for economists.
Junkers and iron and steel magnates, too, became aware
of these shifts long before they were able to damage
production in either area. Guided by the "producer"
ideology of the ruling elites, whose maxim stated that
"economic policy must be made with the producer in
mind--and not the 'pure' consumer", the answer for rye
and iron had been to export. This was the key to the
"boom" period, 1909-1912. Along with export, the
heavy industrial powers had been able to gain governmental cooperation in the sale of "forced" armaments,
beginning in 1912. As a result of these significant
accomplishments, agriculture and heavy industry, allied
in their traditional policy of economic *quid pro quo,*
blossomed during the recession. While the policy of
high protectionism secured their internal markets, they
were able to penetrate a number of foreign markets, most
notably Russia.[56]

Such was not the case, however, with other sectors
of the German economy. Finished industry, for instance,
felt the full effects of the recession in the domestic
sphere. Textiles were able to corner only about
one-third of the foreign export market, compared to
over one-half for the semi-finished products. In 1914,
these dramatic differences between heavy and light
industry became part of the deep divisions that were
already separating the German *Reich* into several
opposing camps. As Arthur Feiler, the economic editor
of the *Frankfurter Zeitung,* noted:[57]

> Thus, social tensions are growing and so
> is the gaping gulf between heavy industry and
> the finished goods industry, between the
> beneficiaries of our economic policy and those
> who are disadvantaged by it, between the
> propertied and the property-less classes,
> between capital and labor. And the trend
> is that this gulf will become even bigger in
> the course of the recession.

As mentioned above, economic security in a time
of financial uncertainty was no guarantor of social
stability. Feiler put this problem very clearly.
What seemed more of a dilemma, however, was the fact
that certain aspects of the Bismarckian system, which
had been the source of the intended political and
economic stabilization of the German *Reich,* were now
adding to the systematic unravelling of the thread

120

that bound together the Prusso-German state. This was
most notable in the area of agrarian protectionism.
Historically, heavy industry and agriculture had benefitted
mutually from their cooperation in a protectionist economy.
This had remained the case until 1913/14, when heavy industry
found that an unwilling *Reichstag* and a chronically
underfinanced *Reich* treasury threatened to put a stop
to the profitable armaments policy that industry had
helped to initiate. Dealing with the *Reichstag* was merely
a question of a *coup* from the Right or a "revolution
from above."[58] The former solution, especially, as
has been noted, found a sizeable following in the period
after 1912. The lack of governmental finances, however,
was a much more difficult problem. The *Reich* seemed
unable to purchase armaments for one outstanding reason:
massive governmental subventions to agriculture, to the
tune of 25 billion marks during one three-year period,
were rapidly emptying the *Reich's* coffers. Thus, one
of the *Sammlung* partners, agriculture, was seemingly
responsible for the other's financial problems. It
was hardly a positive sign for the future when, by 1914,
one of the pillars of the classical *Sammlungspolitik*
had become a hindrance rather than a boon to the continued
economic stability of the conservative system.[59]

This was but one aspect of a many-layered dilemma
which, at the beginning of 1914, remained as much
unresolved as in the past; how was the German Empire
to reconcile a world-oriented economic policy with an
obligation to protect its own economic elites through
the use of highly protective economic tariff barriers?[60]
Especially problematic was a situation in which this
global orientation was not the exclusive domain of
agriculture and heavy industry. The *Hansabund*, BDI and,
to some extent, the SPD were also in favor of such a
policy with the notable exception that they did not
share the state's devotion to economic protection. They
were in favor of either lower tariffs or their total
elimination and the reintroduction of free commerce.[61]

The left-wing, of course, was a political "outsider"
on most matters and its calls for the abolition of the
tariff walls fell upon deaf governmental ears. Until
1914, the ideological glue which held together government,
heavy industry and agriculture proved too strong an
obstacle. The agrarians, especially, felt extremely
secure in the knowledge that they held the full support
of the German government in economic matters. This even
led to excesses on the part of the agrarians such as in
March of 1912, when, during the Conservative Party
convention, they boldly proclaimed that "if our previous

slogan was 'No Kanitz, no boats', today it is no
guaranteed maintenance and perhaps increases of the
high protective policy--no defenses or army corps."[62]
Although unsuccessful in this particular appeal, the
agrarians, nevertheless, profited handsomely from their
government's export-oriented policy. Through the system
of *Einfuhrscheine* (import certificates), by which
exporters of grain could avoid paying duties on grains,
coffee or petroleum from other lands, a market developed
where *Junker* exporters sold their certificates to
importers at handsome profits. Because of this system
of "veiled" export premiums, Germany, although not
self-sufficient in grains, became, by 1908, a grain-
exporting nation. Much of this grain was shipped to
Russia, which, by the commercial treaty of 1905, had
conceded extremely low tariffs on German agricultural
produce. Russia, however, was deterred from exporting
more than a fraction of its grain to Germany because
of that nation's high protective tariffs.[63]

This particular situation remained in effect until
1913. By that time the landowning aristocracy in Russia
could no longer tolerate such an unequal state of affairs.
It finally became aware of the extent to which the 1905
agreement with Germany was damaging its own economic
viability. Grumblings could also be heard from the
Austro-Hungarian Empire, where Hungarian farmers were
almost as cruelly exploited as the Russians as a result
of a similar commercial agreement. As early as March
1913, the unhappy condition of Russian farmers came to
the attention of the BdL. Roesicke, in a worried state,
addressed himself to the question:[64]

> The Russian trade treaty (coming up for
> renewal in 1916/17- AJP) is tied to the tariff
> freedom of our grain to Russia. For the future,
> we must concern ourselves only about the Russian
> government's views on these tariffs.

That the BdL expressed concern about a treaty that
would not be acted upon for nearly four years was not
merely a matter of excessive worry about the terms of
the agreement. It was also based upon the fact that
the trade advantages granted by the 1905/06 agreements
were one of the few remaining sources of strength left
to the agrarians at a time when they had lost most
others. Time had caught up with the *Junkers*, and their
position in society was fast becoming untenable since
"from the social...point of view, the upper middle-class
was about to become the dominant group in German
society."[65] Along with the growth and threat of the

122

working-class movement, the commercial agreement of
1905/06 had allowed the agrarians to maintain a
substantial part of their old political and economic
influence. Surrounded by a hostile *Reichstag* and an
unenthusiastic Chancellor, agrarian apprehensions were
now grounded in the firm belief of an impending
economic and social disaster of a magnitude unprecedented
since the time of Caprivi. Roesicke expressed a fatalism
toward such a situation quite out of character with the
usual confidence of the agrarians. But, at the end of
1913, such a fatalistic outlook was in keeping with
the growing dilemma facing the Prusso-German state:[66]

> For the second time since Bismarck was
> ousted from the Chancellorship, there threatens
> the collapse of our national economic policy.
> As with the ratification of the Caprivi trade
> agreements, our agrarian tariffs will be reduced...
> Every tariff reduction, on our agricultural
> products in the 1917 agreements, will directly
> aid our competitors, just like the Caprivi
> treaties were followed by the terrible
> Argentinian competition of 1894-95.

To relieve agrarian worry, Delbrueck, on behalf of
the Government, assured the agrarians, on January 20,
1914, that "the protective tariff system must be
maintained, but it will not be raised."[67] This was
cold comfort to the agrarians, who viewed the speech
negatively and felt that it put Germany in a passive
position vis-a-vis Russia.

Another point which served to heighten the tensions
between Russians and Germans was the question of the
Polish seasonal workers. The use of these laborers
on East Elbian estates during harvest periods was one
manner in which the *Junkers* kept their production
costs at a minimum. No social security or welfare
benefits were paid to the Poles, and they had to be
fed only during the harvest period. To the Russian
landowner, this was outright poaching of badly needed
workers and an unnecessary burden that was placed on
the Russian government, which had to maintain the Poles
during non-harvest periods. Thus the Russian landowning
aristocracy was faced with a number of severe problems:
high tariff barriers that kept their exports from German
markets; massive quantities of German grain which
competed against their own on the domestic market;
and the problem of the Polish seasonal workers, who
benefitted the German *Junkers* much more than their
fellow Slavs in the Russian aristocracy.[68]

In March 1914, south Russian exporters took steps
to correct this situation. They stated flatly that
Russia "should liberate itself from its economic dependence
upon Germany, which is humiliating for a great power."
They also called for close ties to nations with no
agricultural barriers and expressed a desire to keep
German industry from their border. Forced to act upon
these demands as a result of the intensity of
aristocratic unhappiness and determination, the Russian
parliament approved immediate tariff increases on
grains coming into the country. It was becoming quite
clear that the advantages enjoyed by the East Elbian
agrarians for nearly a decade would be at an end once
a new commercial treaty with Russia was to be signed.[69]

Faced with the loss of an economic advantage it
could not do without, German agriculture reacted
accordingly. In March, the Conservative *Reichstag*
deputy, Hoesch, announced that his Party was not afraid
of a tariff war.[70] And Heydebrand went even further:
he called for a showdown between the two nations, and
only thinly veiled a threat which seemed to imply
military action: the Russian authorities in St. Petersburg,
concluded the Conservative leader, understood "very well
the language of force."[71] Despite cooler heads, such as
Professor Otto Hoetzsch, who tried to preserve the
ideological and historical connections between the
Russian and German aristocracies, it was obvious that
the economic factor had all but eradicated any such ties.[72]
Agrarian concern was focused on the possibility of even
higher tariffs on German grains, the possibility of a
Russian border closing to the Polish laborers and the
economic decimation of the ports of Danzig and Koenigsberg.
In light of the possibility of such disastrous consequences,
the agrarians began to consider various solutions to
avoid the possibility of social and economic extinction.
As such, they were but one of the various components
of a conservative system which felt that its list of
realistic options, in terms of finding a solution to
its foreign and domestic problems, were rapidly dwindling
and that the most feasible option left was military
conflict.

The potential plight of heavy industry and, above all,
agriculture (with regard to the loss of the lucrative
Russian markets) only served to intensify further their
domestic struggle against the Left. For, as has been
noted, there existed a sizeable internal voice against
high tariffs and excessive profits. During the first
part of 1914, this struggle resulted in a stop to most

social legislation in the *Reich*. Enough pressure was
exerted by the powerful economic organizations
represented in the *Kartell der schaffenden Staende* to
influence the Government in that direction. Thus, for
example, at a meeting of the Prussian Ministry of State
on November 31, 1913, Bethmann Hollweg announced that
there would be no action on a reform of the Prussian
Voting Right during 1914, and that no mention of it
would be made in the Kaiser's message to the nation.
On January 10, 1914, Delbrueck formally announced a
stop to further social legislation. He rejected,
however, the *Kartell* idea of an auxiliary *Reichstag*.[73]
As this was followed, within days, by Delbrueck's
assurances to the agrarians that the protective tariff
walls would be maintained, there can be little doubt
of the Government's basic sympathy with and, most
probably, fear of the *Kartell* forces. Yet it must
also be mentioned that there was little similarity between
Bethmann's hopes for a *Sammlung* of all national groupings,
and the essentially non-governmental, indeed even anti-
governmental, posture of the *Kartell der schaffenden
Staende*.[74]

The total effect of the *Kartell* upon the direction
of German politics in 1914 remains a problematical issue.
One of the leading German historians to have dealt with
the *Kartell* has termed the stop to social legislation
as a "semi-victory" for the *Kartell*.[75] Assessing its
major failures, however, makes one hesitant to support
this view. As Thomas Nipperdey has stated:[76]

> All in all, the *Kartell* was an undoubtedly
> noteworthy collection of powers who wished to
> modify and stabilize the system against the gains
> of the Left. But as a block of the Right that
> went beyond Party boundaries, that served as a
> basis for the destruction of the political parties
> in favor of economic and social interests, that
> made forays into the National Liberal Party or
> in the Center, or indeed, changed the system--in
> all that it failed.

Not only did it fail in these efforts, but the *Kartell*
was never able to establish itself as an institution
beyond the local level. The CDI's directorate made its
position quite clear in a memorandum of September 14, 1913:
"The feeling between both sides should continue and should
be renewed from situation to situation. Thus, the idea
of a future, concrete organization of these relations
can remain in the background."[77]

125

Furthermore, the historic antagonisms between agriculture and industry were not fully resolved by the spectre of a common foe. The chronic insecurity of their economic and social position was a constant part of any political action undertaken by the agrarian sector. The real possibility of lower tariff rates, as demanded by the German left, was the focus of agrarian concern throughout 1913/14. When added to the possible reduction or loss of their governmental subsidies as demanded by the Left and made necessary by the possibility of an armaments crisis facing industry, it is not surprising that more was not accomplished by the *Kartell* partners.

Agrarian fears for their economic stability gradually forced them to single out Bethmann as their bitterest foe. While in June 1913, v. Wangenheim could tell Roesicke that "Bethmann's whole policy convinces me that we will have to oppose him in a subtle and quiet manner, but not in the same intensity as that against Caprivi", his position at the end of 1913 had changed completely: "As Count Caprivi, without wanting it, became the founder of the BdL, so will Bethmann, if he continues with his present policy, become, against his will, the founder of the merging of all the productive Estates."[78]

There seemed little that the agrarians could successfully do to ward off an almost unavoidable economic disaster. Luckily, for them, however, the clouds of war were slowly moving over the European continent. By May of 1914, there was a general concern in the *Reich* about Germany's preparation for war. Among the most important issues was that of grain supplies for the production of basic foodstuffs. On May 25/26, Secretary of State Delbrueck convened the *Wirtschaftlicher Ausschuss*, composed of industry, commerce and agriculture, to discuss, ostensibly, the question: "how are we to organize ourselves economically in order to provide food for our nation in case of war and what will we do with our unemployed industrial workers?"[79] The meeting was dominated by v. Wangenheim and the BdL and it served as the vehicle for an agrarian tactic designed to save that economic sector for the second time in less than twenty-five years.

The background developments to this meeting are worth reviewing. For years, the *Reich* had been unable to meet its grain needs strictly on the basis of domestic production. This necessitated the import of foreign grains and other foodstuffs at prices which, because of the German tariff barriers, were exceedingly high. Despite this fact, the agrarians of the BdL

126

continued to insist that they were able to provide
more than enough produce for the entire German nation.
This claim was part of their ideological and economic
program, developed in the 1890's, which called for a
self-sufficient German economy.[80]

But, by the beginning of 1913, the agrarians were
no longer certain that the demand for an autarchic
economy would disguise their huge and profitable grain
exports. As noted, they faced an increasingly hostile
Left and a politically uncertain Chancellor. For this
reason, they shifted the emphasis of their grain sales
back to the domestic market. During a meeting of the
German Agricultural Council on February 12, 1913,
Roesicke informed the Kaiser that "there is no doubt
German agriculture is technically capable of providing
the most important foodstuffs in sufficient quantities
for not only our present population but a much larger,
future, one." Among Roesicke's suggestions for insuring
such a boast were the following: 1. Each export of
grain for the making of bread and other foodstuffs was
to be sharply curtailed; 2. To secure sufficient grain
supplies, these were to be stored in nationally-constructed
central warehouses; 3. The preliminary step for all of
this, however, was to be an official price ceiling.
Roesicke claimed that the Ministry of Commerce felt
that a large boost of grain prices would be the best
regulator against the mismanagement of Germany's grain
supplies.[81] It is quite evident from the notes of the
meeting that its main purpose had been to discuss the
problem of foodstuffs in case of war. Prominently
listed as another of Roesicke's suggestions was that
"foodstuffs in *occupied* [italics mine-AJP] nations
are to be used for feeding the army and local population."[82]

In 1913, war was a speculation; in May 1914, it
was a strong possibility. When State Secretary Delbrueck
called the *Wirtschaftlicher Ausschuss* together, his
questions were factual and demanded realistic answers.
The agrarians, for their part, were gripped, as has
been noted, by a pessimistic view of future export
possibilities. They had continued to stress the idea
of an autarchic economy during 1914, and attempted to
claim self-sufficiency for non-grain items such as beef.[83]
Now, in response to Delbrueck's queries, they presented
a programme quite similar to Roesicke's of February 1913.
V. Wangenheim declared that the present situation made
it necessary to immediately implement the basic points
of the old Kanitz proposal. Essentially, this would
include an "immediate closing of our borders to any
grain export and the collection of large supplies of

human and animal foodstuffs." Again, v. Wangenheim
asked for the erection of grain storage centers and the
availability of interest-free government capital to
store the grains.[84]

The meeting broke up on the 26th with unanimous
agreement that the agrarian proposals had been correct.
Delbrueck assured the Committee members that he would
implement the BdL suggestions at once. The following
day, v. Wangenheim informed Roesicke of the meeting's
results: "At the meeting I stressed that the moment
had come for our old demands of the Kanitz Proposal
to be introduced. Also our idea of transferring
industrial workers to the land in case of war succeeded.
This is a secret--but I believe we have got through the
demands of the agrarians and the BdL."[85]

Those "demands" were intended to secure for
agriculture a continued role in the German economy.
Certain that their grain exports to Russia would greatly
diminish or disappear, war or no war, the agrarians
had decided to receive their profits from domestic
markets. These would be obtained either at the expense
of the Government--for the Kanitz plan also called for
a nationalization of the grain trade--in the form of
Liebesgaben,[86] or the mass of the population, in terms
of highly inflated price ceilings. Furthermore, the
problem of the Polish seasonal laborers would be solved
by the transfer of unemployed industrial workers to the
land. For the first time in decades, the agricultural
sector would enjoy a kind of *Stadtflucht*--or *Landflucht*
in reverse.

iii. The National Opposition and the coming of war

A group parallel to the *Kartell*, but by no means
identical in its aims, was the so-called National
Opposition. If the *Kartell* was no more than a "point
of contact, a demonstration and a programme of right-wing
economic associations", whose essential interest lay
in a "retention of the economic and social status quo...",[87]
then the National Opposition and its guiding spirit, the
Pan-German League, represented far more radical change.

The National Opposition was founded in 1912, in the
post-Morocco Crisis, post-Election era of widespread
criticism against Bethmann Hollweg. During a meeting
of the Pan-German League at Plauen, a highly critical
Heinrich Class delivered a devastating assessment of

Bethmann Hollweg's policies, both foreign and domestic. The speech, printed as *A Balance of the New Course*, became a kind of manifesto for the organizations which were to carry forth the struggle against a weak government and a *Reich* which leaned toward democracy.[88]

By 1913, the Pan-German League had gathered under one organizational umbrella the *Kolonialverein, Flottenverein, Deutsche Handlungsgehilfen Verband, Wehrverein, Kyffhauserbund, Jungdeutschlandbund*, and the *Reichsverband gegen die Sozialdemokratie*. As a kind of "holding company" of the Right, the Pan-German League was able to coordinate the ideological content of the National Opposition to the point where the latter's social darwinistic, *voelkisch*, and imperialistic outlook differed little from the parent group.

It did not take the Pan-German League long to make its opposition to Bethmann, the *Reichstag* and direct suffrage a matter of public record. With the publication of *If I Were the Kaiser*,[89] Heinrich Class/Daniel Frymann revealed to the German nation his blueprint for a new Germany. Mainly, this consisted of a proposed *coup* against the *Reichstag*, its dissolution, the forced imposition *(Oktroyierung)* of a new *Reich* constitution and the replacement of the *Reich's* universal suffrage through the introduction of a plural vote.[90] Interesting to note in these demands was that, for the first time in *Reich* history, a proposed *Staatsstreich* had not emanated from monarchical or active military sources.

In early August 1913, Class met with his second-in-command, retired General Constantin Freiherr v. Gebsattel, to discuss the contents of a memorandum written by the latter. Together, they reviewed the main areas that Gebsattel felt were most dangerous to the Prusso-German state. They decided not to finalize the draft until it had been sent to several Pan-German sympathizers in the Government as well as the Crown Prince, a known ADV admirer.[91]

Days later, the economic associations met at Leipzig to formalize the founding of the *Kartell*. Included among the *Kartell* associations was the BdL, which in July had formed a working relationship with the Pan-Germans.[92] Initial Pan-German reaction to the *Kartell* was enthusiastic, as the *Alldeutsche Blaetter* made clear:[93]

> Our seed is beginning to sprout, the fruit of our labor is beginning to ripen. We are moving forward, we are beginning to triumph...The recognition

of the goals which we have set for the German
people, the path on which we wish to lead the
Germans to these goals, is growing before our
very eyes.

During a meeting of the Central Committee of the
ADV on September 5, the question of the Leipzig *Kartell*
was discussed. Especially important was point 6 on the
agenda: "The ADV and *Sammlungspolitik*." Although
there was general agreement on the usefulness of the
Kartell, there was little enthusiasm about a formal
relationship between it and the ADV. Reismann-Grone,
for instance, felt that "among the industrialists, at
least nine-tenths of them are not national, and are
ready to sacrifice *voelkisch* interests for economic
advantages. The estate owners are, in this sense,
only a little, but only a little, better."[94] In spite
of a resolution, at the conference of the *Reichsverband
gegen die Sozialdemokratie* in Breslau on October 25/26,
which fully endorsed the *Kartell* and was signed by the
other members of the National Opposition,[95] there
remained a distinctive difference between the two
organizations. Both recognized the dangers that
threatened the Prusso-German state: the growing swing
to the Left in the *Reichstag*, the threat to Prussia of
a direct and universal vote, and the possible consequences
of democracy. Yet the *Kartell* viewed these dangers
through spectacles tinted with the color of economic
interest while the National Opposition searched for
ways in which to cleanse the *Reich* of their presence.
The agrarians, especially, were repeating their well-
developed practice of pseudo-nationalism, which industry
soon found useful.

Thus, it is not surprising that, although it became
the focal point of right-wing activity after 1913,
Sammlungspolitik never achieved its designated aims--
neither on the party political, economic group or
voelkisch level--before the outbreak of World War I.
It is also important to recognize the non-monolithic
form of *Sammlungspolitik* (and to this may be added a
governmental *Sammlungspolitik)* which allowed several
forms to co-exist simultaneously.

When Class and Gebsattel received the Crown Prince's
reaction to the memorandum, they were overjoyed. It
was positive to the point of enthusiasm. The ADV had
found an extremely useful ally. In fact, it was the
old Conservative and BdL politician, v. Oldenburg-
Januschau who had secretly been influencing the Crown
Prince at v. Wangenheim's request.[96]

The Gebsattel memorandum was no less than a list of the repressive measures necessary to bring about the realization of Heinrich Class's new Germany. Entitled *Gedanken ueber einen notwendigen Fortschritt in der inneren Entwicklung Deutschlands (Thoughts about a Necessary Progress in Germany's Internal Development)*, Gebsattel occupied himself with a discussion of the "three buring issues in Germany today:" 1. The abolition of universal suffrage; 2. a "solution of the Jewish question;" 3. and finally, a strict press law which would eliminate all Jewish and Social Democratic influence.[97]

Both Bethmann and the Kaiser received a copy of the Gebsattel memorandum in mid-November. The timing was perhaps not accidental, since the difficulties in the Alsatian town of Zabern had just gotten underway.[98] It seems quite possible that the Pan-Germans chose this time to test the Chancellor's political mood: if his reaction to Zabern could be shaped by Gebsattel's ideas in a positive manner, then all the previous talk about a Chancellor purge could be abandoned; if not, then it could move ahead at full blast.

Whatever the reason, both Chancellor and Kaiser reacted, for the most part, negatively: The Kaiser perhaps out of a fear of being upstaged in his own *Staatsstreich* plans, of which he often spoke, and Bethmann, because he felt that, both internally and externally, the conservative forces in the *Reich* were no longer in an advantageous enough position to successfully bring about a coup. Both men feared the consequences of a revolution as a result of Gebsattel's recommendations.[99]

Although unsuccessful in influeucing either Chancellor or Kaiser, Class and Gebsattel continued to pursue their objectives, although along somewhat different lines. Essentially, this consisted of three major aims: 1. the attempt to spread the nationalist message by means of an ADV *Sammlung;* 2. the continued "invisible" struggle against German Jewry; 3. the formulation and dissemination of ADV "war" aims.

The first of these was spelled out by Gebsattel in June. In a letter to v. Liebert, he stated that:[100]

> The ADV will rally (italics mine- AJP) all Germandom to maintain the care and spread of the German *Volkstum*. This is only possible where the

131

> domestic situation has been straightened out.
> We can depend on all the political parties that
> support the monarchy. We can also fight the SPD
> but still support South German Liberalism which
> is less averse to our movement than North German
> Conservatism.

As part of their *Sammlungspolitik*, the ADV concentrated
a large portion of its effort upon the *Reichstag*.
Whereas the *Kartell* groups had all but abandoned
parliamentary politics as worthless, the Pan-Germans
sought to bring about a reconciliation between the
National Liberals and the Conservative Party while
courting the Center.

The Conservative Party continued to be a thorn in
the side of the ADV. Despite excellent relations with
several Conservatives, the ADV was unable to surmount
Heydebrand's influence or his intransigence. The
Conservative leader's total rejection of the Pan-German
presence in East Prussia frustrated all attempts at
an ADV-Conservative understanding. The Pan-Germans
were even tempted by the idea of a "new" Conservative
Party, with Heydebrand and others like him conspicuously
absent. But the fear of losing even the little support
they already possessed was enough of a deterrent. At
one point, Gebsattel appeared without much hope of
an eventual ADV success:[101]

> Is our work with the Conservatives so hopeless?
> With Kleist, Wangenheim, Wadehn and the Kreuzzeitung,
> I have the feeling that it is not. A new Party
> is now impossible. We must work parallel (with
> the Conservatives) but a common path would be better.

Conservative members had participated in the ADV
since its founding. After 1912 there were more, but two
stood out: Prince Salm-Horstmar and retired Admiral
v. Grumme-Douglas. Along with Albrecht v. Graefe, they
represented what might be termed a "modernizing" trend
within the Conservative Party, dealing with concepts
and ideologies almost completely lost upon old
traditionalists like Heydebrand.[102] Their importance
increased during the War. But between the two extremes,
however, stood younger, more pragmatic Conservatives.
Outstanding among them was Westarp, who had risen to
a leadership level in the Party, but whose careful
politics left him unlinked either to full or non-commitment
to the Pan-German movement. It also left him as the target
of ADV persuasion by such Pan-German Conservatives as
v. Liebert:[103]

132

> I will talk to Westarp and ask him if it
> is not tactically wise to join with the ADV. He
> is a party leader who believes politics is an art.
> As a private individual, he surely has the same
> opinions as you. Westarp will think of the ADV
> as an *avant garde* movement which precedes a storm
> and will look at the results before he commits
> the main body of the German Conservative Party.
> But he will not accept our aspirations as the
> Party's if there is a misadventure on our part.
> It would make impossible a *Sammlung* of the
> *staatserhaltende* forces (Liberals, Center) that
> can still be achieved if Bethmann's influence
> is overturned.

Part of the ADV's difficulties with the Conservatives
was the Pan-German preoccupation with the "solution of
the Jewish question." Too many traditional Conservatives
found these racist, anti-Semitic views to be distasteful.
Others, such as v. Oldenburg-Januschau, although
sympathetic to the ADV and its political aims, found
the "Jewish question" overemphasized. Despite Gebsattel's
emotional confession that "I live and die on the conviction
that in recent times the Jewish question has been the
most serious issue to face the German nation",[104] the
"Jewish question" was quietly relegated, out of necessity,
to the privacy of ADV meetings. Its controversial nature,
which even divided the general membership of the ADV,
was not allowed to damage other aims, although measures
against Jewry continued to be a topic for discussion
among the ADV members.[105]

The threat of war, so much a reality in early 1914,
presented the theoretician of the Pan-German League,
Heinrich Class, with a formidable task: to formulate
a set of territorial aims that would encompass Class's
concept of the social-darwinistic struggle between
nations, the ADV's quest for a "greater" Germany and
Gebsattel's fanatical belief in the necessity of
agriculture as the basis for Prusso-Germany's survival.
In July, these plans had already been drawn up, although
only Class and a few intimates knew about them. In a
letter to Gebsattel, Class gave some indication of the
kind of program he had produced:[106]

> In word and print, we must hold up our
> war aims to our people : free land, free of people.
> And we must so construct public opinion that
> nothing else matters than the achievement of
> these war aims.

133

Radicals and Reactionaries

To the National Opposition, then, war took on a metaphysical character, assuming messianic-like qualities. Franz Sontag, for instance, saw war "not as the great...destroyer but as the renewer and maintainer, the great physician...who accompanies humanity on its way to a higher form."[107] That "higher form" was the *voelkisch* state, in which, as Reismann-Grone described it, "the old terms have to be changed: instead of religion, language and artistic intuition; instead of humanity, the race."[108] What made the idea of war so attractive to the radicals was that, according to theorists like Class, a new Germany would arise whether the war was won or lost:[109]

> A war would only hasten reform. If it ends successfully, then we can count on a nationalist majority in the *Reichstag*. If it ends in Germany's defeat, however, then only the powerful will of a dictator, supported by the allegiance of all patriots, can carry out the necessary constitutional reforms.

The new Germany was only threatened by anyone and everyone who stood in Germany's path to internal and external greatness. This would come to include even such traditional conservatives as Heydebrand who refused to accept or could not understand the terms set forth by the radical Right.

CHAPTER VI

The German Conservative Party
and the "*Machttraeume* of German Patriots" (1914)

i.   German Conservatives between
     voelkisch movement and *Volkspartei*

     For the Conservatives 1914 began much as 1913 had
ended: isolation in the *Reichstag*; a definite loss of
credibility among the economic-interest associations;
the increasing fear of future threats to the Prussian
three-class electoral system; the fear of further
property taxation and a growing Russian opposition to
agrarian grain exports. Yet, relatively speaking,
the Conservatives were in a far better position than
many *Reichstag* parties. Most of the other *Reichstag*
groups were beset by severe left-right splits: this
was true of the Center, the SPD (between orthodox and
revisionist views), the National Liberals, and the
left Liberals (between domestic reform and imperialism).
Only the *Reichspartei*-Free Conservatives, the leading
Reichstag exponents of *Sammlungspolitik*, had escaped
such internal rifts; but their lack of mandates precluded
an important role in parliamentary tactics.

     The Conservatives, however much an anti-BdL,
traditional Conservative attitude prevailed in the
Prussian *Herrenhaus*, found their party essentially
intact. Yet the *Reichstag* Conservatives were unable to
benefit from this distinct advantage. The constellation
of parties in the post-1912 parliament was such that
the Conservatives were continually on the defensive and
isolated in terms of political maneuverability. They
were unable to adequately represent the interests of
the BdL nor were they, in 1913, so industrially-oriented
that they were able to follow the lead of the Free
Conservatives--a position the latter party had maintained
since the 1890's.

     As a result, the movement towards a defense of the
conservative status quo and an attack upon the forces
of the Left shifted away from Conservative anti-Socialist
motions in the *Reichstag* to the various extra-parliamentary
organizations. By 1913, the *Kartell der schaffenden
Staende* and the National Opposition were clearly the
centers of such a movement: the former concerned about
the future of their economic interests and the latter
defending the German *Volk* from both its internal and
external enemies. Despite the basic differences between
them, both organizations were united by a bond of radical
imperialism and anti-democratic agitation. The BdL
played a special role in this relationship: by virtue

135

of their membership in the *Kartell* and special position
with the Pan-Germans, the agrarians were able to maintain
a vital communications link between the two groups.

1

The German Conservative Party was not as fortunate.
Since the election of 1912, its political strength had
declined to a dangerous low, reflecting, among other
things, a serious financial shortage and a stagnant,
if not declining, share of the national vote. Part
of the problem was the Party's lack of an adequate
organizational machinery. There was little in the way
of active provincial voter recruitment or fund raising.
And while the creation of a *Fuenfziger Ausschuss*
(Committee of Fifty) helped to reflect a fairer representation
of provincial Conservatives, most decision-making powers
remained with the aristocratic and Berlin-centered *Elfer
Ausschuss* (Committee of Eleven).[1]

But problems of voter recruitment and finances were
not, strictly speaking, merely difficulties of a post-
1912 nature. As early as 1910, Heydebrand, in a speech
to Hannover Conservatives, had hinted at their existence
and spoken of the need for Conservatives "to get closer
to the cities", since, he concluded, "a Conservative
Party that cannot understand this has no right to play
a leading role in the life of our nation."[2] At the
same time, conservative groups in Hamburg were considering
the possibility of gaining a foothold for Hanseatic
business interests within the Conservative Party. Headed
by Dr. A. Koch, the *Hamburg Konservative Vereinigung*
(Hamburg Conservative Union) was founded in March 1912.
In its first public statement,[3] it declared that:

> We want to pursue a healthy conservative
> policy in association with both of the great
> conservative parties of the *Reich*. Yet we
> also wish to maintain an independent support
> of Hamburg's trade, ship-building and commerce.

While the existence of a conservative group in a
large north German city brought neither voters nor
finances to the Conservatives, it accounted for a
considerable furor within the ranks of the Party
members. The BdL attacked the Party's decision to
cooperate with the Hamburg organization on the grounds
that "...one will surely sacrifice our deep rural roots
in order to win an extremely uncertain basis in the big
city." The *Konservative Monatschrift*, on the other hand,
believed that "if conservatism is not to be destroyed by
the big city, it must build in the big city."[4]

Until the beginning of 1914, however, connections
between big city and rural Conservatives were limited.
But by early 1914 the situation for the Conservatives
had become desperate. The Party found itself with
even less finances and new recruits than in 1912. That,
and the _Reichstag_ isolation of the Party, forced the
leadership to intensify its concentration upon large
urban areas. Furthermore, the new relationship between
agriculture and heavy industry, as reflected in the
Kartell, also meant the possibility of financial aid
to the Party from the immensely wealthy industrial
concerns. Primarily for these reasons, Heydebrand
spoke to the Hamburg Conservative Union (January 1914)
in the most conciliatory tones imaginable for the
usually sharp-tongued Conservative head. In essence,
he appealed to industry to forgive the German Conservative
Party:[5]

> Yes, we belong to those people who can learn,
> and especially since we Conservatives have gone a
> bit too far in this or that direction. Certainly,
> we are far from being an enemy to industry.

Despite a vehement attack against Hamburg by Diederich
Hahn of the BdL in February,[6] the Conservatives went
ahead with their renewed efforts to establish a base
in large urban areas. In the middle of March, the
Kreuzzeitung ran a series of articles by the Christian-
Social minister, Rev. Julius Werner on "The Possibility
and Necessity of Conservatism in the Big Cities." The
Konservative Monatschrift ran an article in May on
"Conservative Movements in the West." Finally, on
June 12, Werner addressed the Inner Directorate of the
Conservative Party on "How Conservative Thoughts in
the Cities, and Especially the Big Cities, can be
Implemented with More Success." Immediately thereafter,
a commission was formed, with Westarp as chairman, to
consider Werner's suggestions.[7]

Ideologically speaking, the Conservative turn to
the big city was a startling development. To the
Conservatives, places like Berlin and Hamburg had long
been considered the enemy: they corrupted national
values, they were the heart of Jewish finance and the
seat of the hated Social Democrats. For the _Junkers_
to now have to enter them meant a dilemma far greater
than either the lack of money or votes.

In August 1912, the _National Liberale Zeitung_ had
published an article strongly critical of Conservative
demands for a "strong man" to replace the much-despised

137

Bethmann. The *NLZ* questioned the motive behind the
call and concluded that its purpose was "only to retain
Conservative influence in our nation, an influence that
is rapidly disappearing."[8] Three years earlier, the
Berliner Tageblatt had spoken in similar terms:[9]

> It is the inadequate leadership of the
> Conservative Party that is to blame for its
> difficulties (*Reich* finance reform-AJP)--not
> its programme. Our leaders have lost touch
> with the *Volk*. Most of them belong exclusively
> to the ranks of the agrarian estate owners.

At that time, the Conservative leadership had paid little
attention to these warnings. In subsequent years,
however, the problem of agrarian influence in the Party
remained an active, if not always visible, issue. As
in previous Conservative outbursts against agrarian
predominance (1902, 1909), the issue in 1912 seemed
to ignite, fizzle and disappear, always tempered by
the reality of the agrarian contribution to Conservative
politics: without the BdL, the German Conservative Party
would have sunk into political oblivion long before 1912.
With its ties to the *Mittelstand*, the BdL provided a
cover for the reality of the blatant aristocratic
exclusivity prevalent within the Party.

2

The growth of the *voelkisch* movement in the period
after 1911--and the creation of the National Opposition--
introduced a new element into German politics and society:
a much more popular type of political movement, oriented
toward the social masses and opposed to anything not
directly related to the "good" of the *Volk*.

The Conservative leadership, led by Heydebrand,
resisted all efforts of the Pan-German movement in its
drive to incorporate the Conservative Party. As long
as the *voelkisch* movement gathered strength in an
extra-parliamentary environment, the Conservatives were
able to escape direct pressure. But in 1912/13 the Party
lost much of its parliamentary influence and entered a
period of almost total isolation. Its confidence was
especially shaken by two events that occurred in 1913.
The first of these was a pamphlet published by the Free
Conservative Ernst Deetjen entitled *Freikonservativ!
Die Nationale Mittelpartei*. Essentially, Deetjen was
capitalizing upon renewed attempts at a *Sammlung* of all
bourgeois parties. According to the author, the Free
Conservatives were the ideal party to lead such a *Sammlung*.

As a "Party of the Middle", the Free Conservatives hoped
to draw into their ranks "the former right-wing of the
National Liberal Party and the left-wing of the German
Conservatives." There was no doubt that Deetjen was
dealing in illusions--the Free Conservatives were a
badly-beaten and totally uninfluential *Reichstag* presence.
Nevertheless, his comments upon the position of the
German Conservatives probably reflected a widespread
feeling within the political Right:[10]

> The Conservative Party...has shown that it
> cannot stop the general evolution of a swing to
> the left in parliament. It is no longer a popular
> party since it has shown a too strongly-pronounced
> representation of one interest and has failed to
> understand the dramatic changes in the development
> of our *Volk*.

The second event was the establishment of close ties
between the BdL and the ADV. Unwilling (or unable) to
follow the lead of the *Bund*, Heydebrand attempted to
counter both the lack of a broad political base and the
growing strength of the National Opposition. His decision
was to resurrect one of the earliest phrases that the
Conservative Party had used to cover up its one-sided
pursuit of agrarian interests. From 1913 onwards, the
Party attempted to pass itself off as a *Volkspartei*. It
was a recognition by the Party that narrow sectional
appeal was no longer enough to guarantee its political
survival. With their main link to the middle classes
and small farmers, the BdL, now deeply involved with
voelkisch elements, the Conservatives had the choice
of following suit or establishing an identity, albeit
a false one, which would allow access to non-*Junker*
groups. This was one of the main points brought out
by Otto Pfister in his pamphlet entitled *Deutsch-
Konservativ* (introduced by Heydebrand):[11] "We were and
are a true *Volkspartei* that has set out to be the choice
of the whole *Volk*, and are independent from top to bottom."
In May 1914, Heydebrand re-emphasized this point in a
speech to the *Patriotische Vereinigung* (Patriotic Association)
of Altona:[12] "The Conservative Party is a *Volkspartei* and
must remain one if it is to exist."

Grudgingly, but with its knack for political survival
still intact, the German Conservative Party recognized the
era of mass politics, something which the BdL had done
several decades before. Yet recognition hardly implied
acceptance to the degree in which the *voelkisch* movement
was moving towards the creation of a new Germany. This
was especially true with regard to "inner colonization"

which the Conservatives feared as a threat to the
continued economic existence of the *Junker*. Ever
since Class had stressed (in *If I Were the Kaiser*)
the possibility that large landowners might have to
give up portions of their property to further inner
colonization, agrarian interests (v. Wangenheim) had
attempted to modify the Pan-German approach.[13]

Yet inner colonization was not a monolithic
concept. There were several views as to its ultimate
purpose: industry favored the resettlement of urban
workers to the land as one method of fighting social
democracy; for the BdL, inner colonization was "the
greatest national task of our time," whose ultimate
purpose would be to guarantee Germany a greater chance
at autarchy as well as lessening Germany's reliance
upon Polish seasonal workers, whose future use was
seen as questionable; the *voelkisch* movement saw it as
a battleground between Germandom and Pan-Slavism and
as additional *Lebensraum* for Germany; finally, the Left
was in favor of a speeded-up inner colonization so that,
in the words of v. Wangenheim, "they can quickly destroy
the hated *Junkers* in the hope that the Socialists could
then dominate the smaller landowners."[14]

Because of their self-proclaimed *Volkspartei* image,
the Conservatives were unable to take an active part in
combatting the potentially destructive aspects of
voelkisch inner colonization. This was made evident
by Mirbach-Sorquitten on April 6, 1914 in a letter to
Westarp. Apparently several *Junkers*, not directly
associated with the Conservative Party (among them Count
Spree and v.d. Borght), had formed a *Schutzverband fuer
Deutschen Grundbesitz* (Protective Association for Landed
Property). Mirbach cautioned Westarp that the Conservatives
were not to identify openly with the *Schutzverband* but
that the *"Schutzverband's* aim of retaining landed property
deserves our support...above all it deserves our support
against the subversive strivings of all landreformers."[15]

However tactical the Conservatives may have been in
covering their true interests concerning inner colonization,
they simply had no choice in the matter of Prussia: for
Prussia was the heart of a reactionary conservatism (and
a supreme reactionary stronghold). Writing in the
Kreuzzeitung in January, Limburg-Stirum outlined the
three greatest dangers facing Germany:[16]

1. An extension of the constitutional rights of
   the *Reichstag* until the establishment of a
   full parliamentary system.

2. A reduction in the Kaiser's "absolute powers of command."
3. The democratization of Prussia's Electoral Law, or if that cannot be reached, the neutralization of Prussia and the other Federated States through the destruction of their financial independence.

Because of the consequences of the election in 1912, the first and second points already had some basis in fact and the *Reich* finance reform in 1912/13 had caused many to share Limburg's opinion about Prussia's financial situation. In fact, only the three-class Electoral Law remained firmly in the hands of over- whelmingly Conservative Prussian Houses of Deputies and Lords.

The defense of Prussia, therefore, ultimately rested upon the defense of the Voting Law. To ensure Prussia's survival as the leading German state and guiding light of the nation, the Conservative Party helped create the *Preussenbund*. Between January and April 1914, the *Preussenbund* mounted a large propoganda campaign with the aim of gaining as much support for Prussia as was possible. Yet the narrow-minded base of *Preussenbund* politics was reflected in attacks against Bavaria at its first "Prussia Day" in January. Well-known Conservatives were not among the leading figures in the *Preussenbund*, but, interestingly, several industrialists were members. After April, the *Preussenbund* was not heard from again until 1917.[17]

If the Pan-German-inspired *voelkisch* movement stood for anything it was for the purity of the German race and the elimination of the Jewish "spirit" from German life. During the year 1912, as already noted, this preoccupation with the Jewish "danger" reached significant proportions. Only Conservative publications had maintained a restrained attitude toward this national fanaticism. The Pan-German drive against the Jews remained active (but underground) throughout 1913 and into 1914. On the agrarian side, the BdL continued to present its annual anti-Semitic sideshow (with Diederich Hahn as the keynoter) in the Circus Busch--and 1914 was no exception.[18] But on the same day that Hahn was repeating his tired platitudes against German Jewry, a more important event was occurring at a meeting of the *Vereinigung der Steuer-und Wirtschaftsreformer* (Association of Tax and Economic Reformers), the group directly responsible for the creation of the German Conservative

141

Party in 1876. Chaired by Mirbach-Sorquitten and attended by v. Arnim, v. Schwerin, v. Wilamowitz-Moellendorf, Count Yorck and several other leading Conservatives, the session was devoted to a full discussion of the *Judenfrage*. This in itself was not unusual, since the Association had always been anti-Semitic and, as Mirbach stated, "has never underestimated the danger which Jewish predominance in finance and domination of the press has presented." Ways in which this predominance could be overcome were presented at the meeting. One method suggested was the proper financial maintenance of the estates--so that Jews would be unable to purchase them from debt-ridden *Junkers*. A further suggestion was the creation of a rival press, without Jewish influence. At this point, the BdL anti-Semite, v. Bodelschwingh, addressed the Association. The effect of his speech, outlining the ways in which Jews had to be excluded from all aspects of German life, was electric. Mirbach immediately proposed the following motion:[19]

> The Association of Tax and Economic Reformers has, until now, not felt it to be correct that Jews, simply because they were Jews, were to be excluded. But as a result of Herr v. Bodelschwingh's speech, that Jews are to be excluded from everything, as far as possible and at once, I now propose the following : every Jew, even if he supports the Conservative Party and recognizes its programme, is to be denied membership in the German Conservative Party.

A short time later, the *Kreuzzeitung* opened its columns to regular attacks against Jewry. The co-founder of the *Preussenbund*, Wolfgang Eisenhart, in a May article,[20] attacked Jewish "high finance" as the key behind the threatened "liberalization of Prussia." In July, the Pan-German, General v. Kleist, summarized six reasons why there were no Jews in the officer corps and why "we must never allow Jewry to hold the sword in its hand to protect the Throne--I would rather see the Crown in ruins."[21]

Conservative tactic or *voelkisch* influence? Most probably it was a combination of both forces. The Conservative Party, in attempting to refashion its national image in a *Volkspartei* direction, could not stand too near the *voelkisch* fire without being burned. Also, despite the relative homogeneity of Conservative aims and principles, there was no denying the fact that some Party members may have actually felt a genuine

attraction to the new political and social movement.
Hence, in searching for ways in which to maintain its
basis in German life, without being swallowed up by a
Pan-German whirlwind, the German Conservative Party
was unknowingly creating the seeds of internal conflict
and opposing a force less definable and more powerful
than anything before it.

3

On December 18, 1913, Westarp sent Heydebrand his
assessment of the Conservatives' *Reichstag* position and
suggestions for the future political tactics of the
Party.[22] Westarp felt that "the struggle over the
growth of Parliament's power will form the basis of our
future action," a struggle in which the Conservatives
would "fight for the rights of the Kaiser." More
importantly, Westarp was ready to throw overboard
any cooperation with Bethmann in favor of a "relentless
criticism of the Government." As a consequence of the
Conservative struggle against the further democratization
of Parliament and the attacks against Bethmann, Westarp
was hoping for "a dissolution of the *Reichstag*."

Two days later, Heydebrand replied. Unlike the
vigorous call to action put forth by Westarp, the
Conservative leader maintained a calm and almost
reserved tone:[23]

> Undoubtedly there is a closed front here, that
> includes the National Liberals and Center, against
> us...It is also true, as you say, that we would
> be unwise to remain this isolated, because it
> hurts our coalition strength. In short, I agree
> with you on all your points, but I warn you, above
> all else, to be cautious,

This would not be the last time that Heydebrand's
caution and Westarp's aggressive manner would be at
odds over a political issue. In July, in the midst
of a grave diplomatic crisis, the Conservative leadership
was involved in a difference of opinion over the creation
of a political group called the *Jungkonservativen
Reichsverband* (Young Conservatives Imperial Association).
It is not clear how large the group was or how many
local and district branches it possessed. Apparently
it was centered in Bonn and contained essentially young,
politically-unknown Conservatives.[24] The formation
of the Young Conservatives brought favorable comments
from the parent Conservative Party and the *Kreuzzeitung*.[25]
The Young Conservatives advocated a type of Conservative

CUNO GRAF WESTARP
(Photograph courtesy of
Ullstein Bilderdienst)

idealism, the kind that had been associated with early
conservative thinkers such as Stahl and v. Gerlach.
This was quickly seized upon by National Liberal
newspapers, who painted the organization as representing
"a strong reaction against the official agrarian-feudal
interest politics" of the German Conservative Party.[26]

Heydebrand's attitude toward the organization was
one of anger and suspicion:[27]

> Either these people (Young Conservatives-AJP)
> belong to our party--then they are superfluous--or
> they pursue some special aim--and then they are
> questionable and dangerous, despite being sympathetic
> to our basic ideas. I would have thought we
> learned from the Young Liberals. I don't agree
> with the *Kreuzzeitung's* favorable treatment of
> them and have ordered the paper to make no more
> mention of this group.

Westarp did not share Heydebrand's view:[28]

> Actually the people in Bonn seem to have
> every intention of towing the Party line. I
> believe we will have to tolerate them. Later
> on we can make the following changes : reduce
> the group to a very local character and
> therefore set aside the name *Reichsverband*;
> restrict membership to those under 25 years
> of age.

Although these were minor disagreements, and amounted
to honest differences of opinion, they demonstrated
the basic political nature of the two Conservative
leaders: Heydebrand was a type that spanned the
generations between Tivoli and *Volkspartei* with an
overwhelming desire for Conservative survival. Yet
he was bound to a certain degree of hesistancy, perhaps
out of a fear of things he could no longer understand:
Westarp was more "modern", less upset by change and
more willing to embrace thoughts not directly related
to things ultimately Conservative. Most importantly,
Westarp was not afraid to differ with Heydebrand and
the Conservatives were clearly not a one-man Party.

Like most of the other bourgeois parties, the
Conservatives were hardly consulted by the government
during the July crisis. Westarp met with Foreign
Office officials in the Wilhelmstrasse on a few occasions,[29]
but was not informed of events beyond a superficial stage.

As late as August 3, Heydebrand, beside the fact that
he was not even in Berlin, seemed totally unaware of
the diplomatic moves that had frantically been carried
out in an attempt to prevent military conflict.[30]
Although Heydebrand had expressed the view that war
would "strengthen the patriarchal order and spirit",[31]
at least one leading Conservative viewed the outbreak
of war as a disaster for Germany. On June 20, Mirbach-
Sorquitten drew up a memorandum[32] for the Committee of
Fifty which struck a totally pessimistic note: Germany
would be unable to defeat either Russia or England;
as a result of war, America would become the richest
nation in the world. Mirbach rejected Pan-German war
aims in the Near East as "utopic"; finally, he rejected
the size and duration of Germany's political aid to
Austria.

Despite Mirbach's reservations, the Conservatives
had much to gain from the outbreak of war, both in an
economic and political sense: the promise of increased
agricultural production and the hope of a unified
Germany. Certainly their *Reichstag* position could get
no worse; they had practically lost all hope of regaining
their former parliamentary influence:[33]

> Is such a *Reichstag* still viable for a
> system of state based upon a monarchy? From
> the Conservative point of view this question
> must be answered with a resounding no.

The July crisis paved the way for a realization of
Conservative promises and hopes. The increasing
"mismanagement" of the July events by the *Reich* (aided
in part by a diplomatically slow-moving Austria-Hungary)
forced Germany to abandon hopes for a localization of
the conflict between Austria and Serbia. Instead, it
became clear to Bethmann, and even more so to the
"radicals" in the military, that a global conflict was
imminent. Faced with such a decision, the small group
of men charged with Germany's policy formulation opted
for a war against the *Entente* powers, but especially
against Russia. For, it was believed, a war against
Russia would be popular with all political groups in
the German Empire. Using their most traditional weapon,
manipulation, conservative forces therefore assured
themselves of a national unity encompassing even the
SPD leadership.[34]

The German Conservative Party, faced with continued
political impotence and a murky economic future, joined
with other conservative forces in the so-called

145

Flucht nach vorn, granting a bit more time to a Prusso-German state deep in the grip of structural paralysis. In many ways this path held the potential of political and economic salvation, a road the *Junkers* had traveled before and were quite prepared to travel again.

ii. The hand of friendship is extended--albeit reluctantly

What had preoccupied the thoughts of conservative Germany for nearly three years now became a reality:[35]

> War! War! The people have arisen--as if
> they had not existed before and now suddenly are
> there, powerful and moving. Everyone crawls out
> of his corner, seemingly in the greatest confusion,
> and yet in the most purposeful order : Millions
> have already crossed the Rhine.

On August 4, Kaiser Wilhelm called into existence a *Burgfrieden*, the medieval term which, roughly translated, meant a "truce within the fortress." The *Burgfrieden* was a kind of political cease-fire, in which the weapons to be withdrawn included all of the demands for democratization which had become a permanent part of the pre-war political and social paralysis of the Prusso-German state. It also marked the legitimization of the SPD as a national Party. The outsider had become the insider at last.

The waves of national enthusiasm which swept over Germany in the first weeks and months of the war were extraordinary. Quite literally the whole nation responded as one voice to the Kaiser's pronouncements. And whereas such enthusiasm had found its beginnings in the period before August 1914, when Army League and Pan-German speakers had stirred the emotions of millions, new parts of German society now joined the cheering crowds, and socialist politician stood next to reactionary *Junker*. Mars had truly displaced Venus in the German sky.

Almost at once the German nation began to search for the true "sense" of the war in which it was engaged. Initially, it had been the idea of defense, a reaction to the ignominious attack of the Triple Entente. This was one reason why the SPD had thrown its last principle out the window and placed itself squarely behind the nation. But such a mood would soon disappear, replaced

146

by neo-Rankean concepts of Germany's push to world
equality. Guided by its academic elite, Germany
found the positive philosophy necessary to sustain
its spiritual reserves during the trying period of
armed conflict: [36]

> The general feeling at the beginning of the
> war was this : the day of the Germans had arrived;
> not in the sense of the Romans, French or English
> in antiquity--not through world conquest. Much
> more, the conviction that the day of the Germans
> meant a claim ot world equality for the German
> spirit.

The "Ideas of 1914", as this philosophy came to
be known, sought to contrast every aspect of German
life with that of its military enemies. With one
quick stroke, the "Ideas of 1914", would sever all
alien influences from the German people. What the
"Ideas of 1789" had done to make Germany morally and
philosophically impure, the new concept, with its
uniquely German vision, would readily undo. The
spirit of the French Revolution, with its accompanying
concepts of democracy and humanity, would finally be
broken in the "German" war. Ironically, the man who
introduced the term "Ideas of 1914" to Germany was
Rufolf Kjellen, a Swede.

The "Ideas of 1914" were devoid of almost all
realistic political thought. No aims save philosophic
ones were, at first, expressed. However, as the year
1914 drew to a close, various sections of German
society began to demand previously-formulated political
and economic aims designed to catapult Germany into
world power status. This had its effect on Germany's
philosophic guidelines. At the year's end, although
still covered in philosophic abstractions and expressing
no concrete political goals, the "Ideas of 1914"
sounded strangely like a mixture of German idealism
and power politics: [37]

> Without poetry and philosophy there can
> be no rebirth, no freedom from eighteenth-century
> foreign domination; but also without these there
> can be no fulfillment of the dreams of Kaiser
> and *Reich*, no experience of the reality of life
> and no realization of Germany's will in the world.

Among those sitting in the *Reichstag* chambers
listening to the Kaiser on August 4 was Count Westarp.
To Westarp, one of the bitterest parliamentary foes of

the SPD, the Kaiser's political truce must have seemed
confusing. Then to see the SPD delegation stand and
cheer the Kaiser must have drained Westarp of all emotion.
Yet he regained enough composure to offer his hand to
various SPD members, whose presence he would have
ignored the day before. Only later did Westarp inform
his own Party of the action: "I presented the
Conservative members with a *fait accompli*," he later
wrote Heydebrand, "Bieberstein and Boehlendorf and
others accepted my action under protest, Kreth and
Oertel supported me." But stirrings of national unity
were not foremost in Westarp's mind: "The golden bridge
that we have held out to the SPD will reap many
advantages later on. Of that I am certain. Therefore
I deem my action correct."[38] Heydebrand, who, as head
of the Party, could have easily rebuked Westarp for
his decision, congratulated him instead. He found
Westarp's behavior vis-a-vis the SPD to be correct.
He also found the actions of the Bethmann government
to be "first class."[39]

Despite Westarp's confidence and Heydebrand's
concurrence, many Party members or sympathizers put
no faith in the possibility of a national SPD:[40]

> The Conservative Party has to see to it
> that the government does not try to end the war
> too early. After the first few battles, the
> SPD will call for peace. In my view, the
> Conservative task is to influence the result
> of this war and then, with the aid of public
> opinion, beat down the SPD after the war.

Neither was much hope held out for a different *Reichstag*
once the war had ended:[41]

> Without a doubt, the so-called *Burgfrieden*
> that is now in effect will not last long after
> the war. Certain conflicts between the parties
> will once more become apparent.

Because Heydebrand was obligated to remain on his
Silesian estate at Tschunkawe (under threat of Russian
attack) he was unable to participate in much of the
Party's policy-making. Instead, the Executive
Committee in Berlin regularly transmitted its decisions
for his approval. With the conflict not yet a month
old, Heydebrand received, and presumably authorized,
the Executive Committee's recommendations for Conservative
strategy during the early part of the war: the Conservatives
were not to become conspicuous in defeat and were not to
be sold short in rewards if Germany were victorious.[42]

148

iii. The BdL on the attack...*Burgfrieden* or not

During the first weeks of war, the BdL was also
carefully considering its own position. The agrarians
wished to pursue a course based primarily upon the continuation of their pre-war strategy as participant in
and liaison between the *Kartell der schaffenden Staende*
and the National Opposition. Towards this aim, soon
after the outbreak of fighting, the BdL sent a letter
to its entire membership, declaring that "the unity
of our nation demands an understanding between the rural
and urban areas. Any differences between them must
disappear forever."[43]

There was, in fact, some basis for agrarian worry
about the war-time position of heavy industry. Soon
after the Kaiser's speech on August 4, the CDI and BdI
had begun negotiations to discuss the union of both
interest groups into a *Kriegsausschuss der deutschen
Industrie* (War Committee of German Industry). Such a
union was achieved on August 8, to the satisfaction
of both groups, but with the BdI being as Gustav
Stresemann admitted, "numerically too weak against
the CDI."[44]

In order to ascertain the mood of heavy industry,
and estimate the influence (if any) of the anti-agrarian
BdI, v. Wangenheim met with the CDI's Max Roetger. In
a subsequent letter to Roesicke, v. Wangenheim stressed
the common agreement by both men on the internal dangers
that faced the *Reich*:[45]

1. The danger of a hasty peace agreement and
    a slackness towards the SPD.
2. Both men agreed that an early peace with
    England was not advisable.
3. Both men feared that the government's
    attitude toward the SPD would create new
    domestic strife.

V. Wangenheim concluded his letter by advising Roesicke
that "we must arm against these possibilities."

The establishment of a *Burgfrieden* hardly lessened
the BdL's determination to struggle against its pre-war
foes. Although v. Wangenheim demonstrated a slightly
less hostile attitude toward the *Hansabund*,[46] there
was no let-up against the SPD or Bethmann and Delbrueck.
By the end of August, the *Bund* was beginning to think
in terms of renewing the struggle against the Chancellor,

149

especially after Roesicke was able to gather information
indicating that "Bethmann, Delbrueck and Loebell will
quite obviously give much consideration to our present
Voting Law in Prussia as soon as the war is over."[47]

Concerned by the *Burgfrieden's* apparently negative
effects on the struggle against the Left, the BdL
decided once more to become the gadfly of the Right.
On August 31, v. Wangenheim informed Roesicke that
"we must, in association with the ADV and very quietly,
point out the dangers which appear to threaten us and
prepare a movement which will make slackness towards
the SPD quite impossible."[48] In September, the BdL
met the representatives of trade, commerce, industry,
ADV and Conservative Party to discuss the government's
position on the SPD, "which seems to now have a free
reign." The fact that the government "allows and
supports this SPD domination," wrote Roesicke, "frankly
fills me with great worry."[49]

iv.   The ADV: war aims and the new Germany

The outbreak of war was the culmination of a
Pan-German dream. Although the ADV, too, was looking
to unify the German nation, it was hardly the *Burgfrieden*
kind, with its implied aim of a cessation of political
hostilities. In fact, Class and Gebsattel corresponded
with each other as though the Kaiser had never delivered
his August 4 speech. It was on the very same day as
Wilhelm's address to the *Reichstag* that Gebsattel
proposed a five-point programme for the survival of
the Prusso-German state:[50]

> The following must be achieved at all costs :
> 1. a solution to the Jewish question; 2. a solution
> to the Voting Right, both in Daniel F r y m a n n's
> sense; 3. an adjustment of the Prussian system;
> 4. a stabilization of the state's authority;
> 5. a return of the German nation to agriculture
> upon which we shall base our national might.

Gebsattel did not see an easy implementation of these
aims, since, unlike the more favorable pre-war climate,
"the Jews and Social Democrats are conducting themselves
in such an uncommonly loyal manner."

Two days later, Class answered his second-in-command
with proposals of a more general nature:[51]

> The aims of this war are two-fold : 1. the
> securing of our position in the world; our place
> in the sun and our freedom of movement; 2. removal
> of (as you mention) the poison from within the
> body of our nation...We simply must do this
> through Frymann's program without parliamentism
> and the German people must be placed once more
> upon the land.

On August 28, after consultations with the Krupp director,
Hugenberg, and the academician, Dietrich Schaefer, Class
was ready to present his war-aims' programme to an
assembled meeting of the ADV's Executive Committee.
Class's recommendations went beyond the wildest thoughts
of most of the assembled members. Yet such was his
confidence, that Class was able to inspire a motion
from the floor that he print his program for national
distribution.[52] Class informed the Executive Committee
that his aims incorporated both western and eastern
fronts. In the west, Class demanded the complete
annexation of Belgium, Germany's incorporation of all
French territories to the mouth of the Somme including
the ore-rich areas of Longwy-Briey and improved border
zones in Alsace. In the east, Class demanded land for
German settlement; the separation of Congress Poland
and the Ukraine from Russia. Most importantly, Class
demanded that these annexed areas should be "free of
people": after the annexations the native populations
would be resettled elsewhere. Abroad, Class called for
a great German colonial empire (Central Africa), created
at France and Belgium's expense.[53] Added to this was
a huge indemnity to be paid by the defeated nations.

For the next three weeks, Class labored over his
pamphlet. He consulted closely with Hugenberg and
Stinnes and received tentative support for his program
from Krupp v. Bohlen and Halbach. Finally, on
September 18, Class was finished.[54] Entitled *Zum
deutschen Kriegsziel (Concerning the German War-Aim)*,[55]
the pamphlet elaborated upon Class's presentation before
the Executive Committee. The tone of the pamphlet was
intensely social-darwinistic and reemphasized v. Bernhardi's
feelings that "self-preservation is the supreme law" cf
any nation and demanded outright annexation of foreign
territories if needed. Furthermore, Class made no
pretensions as to the type of conquests he was
advocating: he rejected "cultural" conquests for the
explicitness of "cold-blooded" demands for land. Finally,
Class proposed a German-dominated "Central European
Economic Association" which would include Austria-Hungary,

151

the Netherlands, Switzerland, Denmark, Sweden, Norway,
Finland, Italy, Belgium and Rumania as well as the
annexed territories. "There is no doubt," concluded
Class, "that as a result of this war there will occur
a completely new ordering of this earth."

The idea of a "new ordering"--whether of the world
or Europe--preoccupied a large part of the German nation
during the period of initial military victory. On the
evening of August 21, in the midst of one of the hottest
spells in memory, Bethmann and his chief confidant, Kurt
Riezler, were also considering the "new face" of
Europe:[56]

> This evening a long discussion about Poland
> (wrote Riezler-AJP) and the possibility of a
> loose association of other states to the *Reich*--a
> Central European system of differential tariffs;
> Greater Germany with Belgium, Holland, Poland as
> the closer protective states, Austria as the
> further one.

This initial discussion evolved into the now-famous
"September Programme" which Bethmann completed on September 9,
and described as "provisional notes on the direction of
our policy on the conclusion of peace."[57] Expecting
peace negotiations to begin at any time, Bethmann drafted
a set of objectives which, while more moderate than
Class's, still centered upon German expansion at the
expense of other nations. This included annexations
in both east and west, indemnities and the creation of
a Central African colonial empire. But the key aim
for Bethmann was the creation of a Central European
Tariff Union--under German leadership.[58] What is
important for an understanding of the varieties of
German imperialism formulated during the war,[59] is
that this programme was not "an isolated inspiration"
on the part of the Chancellor. It represented the
thinking of economic and political leaders who would
have shuddered at the thought of being compared to
the ADV.[60] Men such as Rathenau, v. Gwinner and
Salomonsohn were respected figures of business, possessed
with insight and restraint. But the form of their
war-aims could not disguise a substance which held
expansion and domination to be the very nature of its
being.

152

v. The Pan-German breakthrough and agrarian strategy

Sometime near the end of August, Westarp met with
v. Gebsattel. On August 30, the ADV second-in-command
reported the details of the meeting to Class.[61]

Westarp, it seemed, had badly misjudged the actions
of the Chancellor and the Foreign Office. Influenced
initially by Heydebrand's belief that Bethmann's policies
were "first class", Westarp had soon become convinced
of the folly of such an opinion. Now he felt that both
Bethmann and the Wilhelmstrasse were exhibiting signs
of "defeatism" and were prepared to conclude an
"indifferent" peace. He begged Gebsattel to consider
using the influence of the ADV on the nationalist press
and urge them to try and counter the actions of the
"defeatists." Furthermore, the Conservative Count
asked Gebsattel to support his party in the struggle
it would eventually have to face against the call for a
universal and direct Voting Law in Prussia. That such
a call (among others) was bound to arise at the war's
end was a feeling shared by certain conservatives as
early as 1914. Among the most illuminating statements
to this effect was made by the industrialist Alfred
Hugenberg in November:[62]

> The consequences of the war will in themselves
> be unfavorable for the employers and industry in
> many ways. There can be no doubt that the capacity
> and willingness of the workers returning from the
> front to produce will suffer considerably when they
> are subordinated to factory discipline. One
> will probably have to count on a very increased
> sense of power on the part of the workers and
> labor unions, which will also find expression in
> increased demands on the employers and for legis-
> lation.

Westarp was prepared to give much in return for
Pan-German aid. He agreed with the territorial annexations
demanded by the ADV and with their aim of defeating
England. When Gebsattel proposed that Germany annex
land "free of people", however, Westarp was "visibly
surprised." "This was something quite new for him,"
wrote Gebsattel, "and he felt that he had to think it
over." Finally, Westarp told Gebsattel about his
dealings with the SPD on August 4 in the name of national
unity. "I told him," related Gebsattel to Class, "that
he made a big mistake. The Sozis had to acquiesce to
everything if they did not want their party to break
apart. He admitted that perhaps I was right."

153

Sensing that he had taken a big step towards winning the support of the second most important member of the Conservative Party, v. Gebsattel quickly took the initiative. Only a few days after their meeting, he sent Westarp an 11-page letter outlining in full the extensive war aims of the ADV.[63] He stressed the themes of the struggle against Jewry and the SPD, the fact that Germany had to become a "nation of warriors", and reemphasized the concept of annexed territories "free of people."

To Gebsattel, the differences between economic and political aims were lost in the all-out drive towards world status. All aspects of the ADV programme seemed to blend into one enormous aim: Greater Germany. This was not the case with the Conservatives. Basing their whole war-time policy upon the tactical procedure of being in the right spot in both defeat and victory, the Party could not afford to support too extreme or controversial an aim, lest it bring further isolation upon itself. This is why Westarp supported Pan-German territorial aims, but was so hesitant about the populationless scheme proposed by Gebsattel. That there was a very definite feeling against political war aims was indicated by Kreth in a letter to Westarp:[64]

> Annexation in an economic relationship and the right to obtain property...is what we need. Our time of history, with its humane viewpoint, has no talent for colonization.

The next meeting between Conservatives and Pan-Germans on October 24 turned into another confrontation between Class and Heydebrand, as the Pan-German leader later recounted:[65]

> Discussion in the Prussian House of Deputies. Heydebrand was for our economic aims. But he would not listen to any of our political ones. These were all new thoughts to him. So he simply got up and left.

Yet, despite the ever-present Conservative irritant, the ADV was successful in persuading many segments of business, industry, economic-interest groups and the political parties to support its war-aims programme.

Of primary interest to the ADV was the support of this programme by the *Kartell der schaffenden Staende*. "This was a major preoccupation for Hugenberg and myself," wrote Class, "the necessity of winning the *Kartell* for our war aims..."[66] As already noted, the BdL considered the ADV as an essential part of any movement which would fight "slackness" towards the SPD. It was, therefore, not difficult to find a common ground between the organizations. On September 28, the *Kartell* met in Berlin to give its support to a programme of territorial expansion and to declare against an "indifferent peace."[67] This was followed in early October by a meeting between Class and Roesicke in which the agrarian leader informed Class that "the ADV is correct in its aims and we must work together for the rescue of the Fatherland from its internal dangers and from our incredibly incompetent diplomats."[68] Thus was formed the basis of the strategy which defined the activity of the German Right during the remainder of the First World War. It was to be a continuation of the *Schutz und Trutz* alliance created after the election of 1912 to secure the rescue of the Prusso-German state from parliamentism and democracy. In the midst of this alliance stood the German Conservative Party, by definition an important member, but in reality a very uncomfortable participant.

Officially, then, the BdL was among the first of the economic-interest groups to place itself solidly behind the Pan-German programme of territorial expansion. Privately, however, the *Bund* maintained its place as the patron saint of agrarian interests. In fact, part of its enthusiasm for Pan-German war aims was the extremely positive position taken by v. Gebsattel in the question of "inner colonization":[69]

> ...So we have to strive with all our
> strength for a new ordering in Germany; one
> which will create more favorable conditions
> for agriculture. And the manner in which we
> shall achieve this is through inner colonization.

2

Inner colonization, as a Pan-German aim, had never ruled out the possibility of a full-scale division of *Junker* estates into smaller plots of land for the benefit of colonizing agrarian workers. The fear of such an eventuality had been one of the reasons behind the *Bund's* cooperation with the ADV in 1913. V. Wangenheim had attempted to change the ADV's position on this matter.[70]

Now, with the introduction of the ADV's demands for
the acquisition of land in Germany's eastern borders,
the possibility of colonization increased, but the
chances of *Junker* estates being involved decreased.[71]
Such reasoning served as the basis for an urgent letter
from Roesicke to Westarp, arguing against the possibility
of a quick peace with Russia:[72]

> I would greatly regret the fact that we did
> not get a good piece of land, at least as much
> as we expected, from Russia. Germany is too
> small; it must expand, especially in its
> agriculture...The western war aims are good,
> but, through industrialization, they threaten
> the equality of development between industry
> and agriculture, so necessary for a healthy
> Germany.

The question of agrarian interests was also evident
in the controversy over price ceilings which developed
in the summer and autumn of 1914.

In May, as already noted,[73] the agrarians had met
with Delbrueck over the question of grain supplies in
case of war. At that time, v. Wangenheim had
suggested a reintroduction of the Kanitz Proposal
(nationalization of the grain trade and subsidies to
the agrarians) as well as the erection of warehouses
for the storage of grain. Delbrueck had promised to
attend to the matter as expeditiously as possible,
but, in fact, had ignored it in favor of other concerns.
Now, in September, with the hope of a quick German
victory more remote, the question of grain supplies
for the year 1915 became a predominant issue.

On September 6 and 7, v. Wangenheim met with
Delbrueck over the question of grain prices. Established
agrarian policy over the years had been, of course, to
sell grain at the highest prices possible. The protection
of their own interests over the needs of the nation had
been a long-standing criticism of agrarian policy. Yet
on these two days v. Wangenheim insisted that the
government had to establish fixed price ceilings--that
is to say, grains could not be sold above a certain
price level.[74] Later, price ceilings were to be demanded
upon flour and bread.[75]

There were several reasons for this type of agrarian
behavior. First, it was partially in response to the
demands of certain industrial interests (Hugenberg,
Stinnes) who favored pushing up the price of grains and,[76]

156

later, bread[77] in order to force reduced consumption
and insure that enough food would be available for
1915. The agrarians were against such schemes for at
least two reasons: 1. Left to an unrestricted market
in which prices would possess no limits, agriculture
would ultimately receive the blame for profiteering--an
image which it could ill afford during a period of
so-called national unity.[78] 2. Although industry
intended most of the price rises to affect the working
class, v. Wangenheim was certain that the worker would
remain unaffected:[79]

> The view of industry and parts of the government
> that one has to drive up prices in order to secure
> thriftiness, rests upon an erroneous assumption...
> The workers who it should affect will not be
> affected because they earn such high salaries.
> Instead, bureaucrats, officers, artisans, the
> real *Mittelstand*, will be affected.

As self-proclaimed "defenders" of the German *Mittelstand*,
who in actual fact served as the "cover" for agrarian
self-interests, the BdL was not about to allow such a
possibility.

There was a further reason, however, one which
showed the cunning of the BdL at its best.

Almost at the outset of the war, the government
had abolished duties and other restrictions on the
import of agricultural products. This was done because
of the critical shortage of domestic products and as
a gesture of national unity to the SPD.[80] Stripped
of the agricultural protection they so desperately
needed, the agrarians hit upon the idea of asking the
government to pay them the difference between the grains
they sold domestically at the fixed prices and the vastly
higher prices they had to pay for imported grains.[81] It
was not difficult to recognize the old Kanitz Proposal
as the basis of this demand.

vi. The gap widens: growing differences
between Pan-Germans and German Conservatives

The implementation of the *Burgfrieden* had made
little difference, initially, to Bethmann's basic
political outlook. He still sought the majority of
his support from the parties of the right[82] and
viewed the "national" position of the SPD as a temporary
necessity:[83]

As far as the SPD is concerned, one cannot
make any basic decisions about them, as far as
their future actions. As for now, the SPD must
be handled in the same manner in which they
respond to us; otherwise we will be unable to
survive this difficult period.

But, as the radical demands for annexation grew
among the conservative parties in the *Reichstag*,
Bethmann was no longer able to count on this segment
of the parliament. As a result, he soon sought his
support from the center parties and, after much deli-
beration, from the SPD.[84] In order, however, to secure
SPD support, more was needed than a *Burgfrieden*: for
as early as the last part of 1914, the national exultation
of the SPD had become dulled as the voices of the radical
Right grew in a unison call for the continued struggle
against the Social Democrats.[85] Bethmann's answer to
this dilemma was the "New Orientation", a further
development of the *Burgfrieden*, in which the newly-
legitimized SPD was to receive the promise of action
on its demands at the conclusion of hostilities.[86] On
November 6, Bethmann used this term for the first time.[87]

At the end of his talk with Gebsattel, Westarp had
re-examined his whole position on the question of the
SPD; if not in the Pan-German camp, he was obviously
influenced by the arguments put forth by the General.
This became apparent at the end of October when Westarp
met with Under Secretary of State Heinrichs. The Under
Secretary, whether on his own initiative or not, attempted
to argue the merits of the Prussian Voting Law with
Westarp. This occurred after Heinrichs and the Count
had already argued over Belgium--Westarp maintaining
that Germany had to have it and Heinrichs declaring it
would be difficult to hold the country. At any rate,
Heinrichs then asked Westarp to take some changes in
the Voting Law under consideration. "I represented the
Conservative viewpoint," Westarp wrote to Heydebrand,
"and let it be known that the Imperial government was
being too soft to the SPD."[88]

But the full impact of Gebsattel's warning about
the SPD came during the middle of November. For nearly
three hours, Westarp was witness to the incessant demands
of the SPD and Poles for changes in all *Ausnahmegesetze*
(exceptional laws) including the lifting of the ban on
Jesuits. This occurred during a scheduled meeting
between Delbrueck and the *Reichstag* parties. Throughout
the meeting, Westarp maintained that all demands had
to be placed aside until the war's end. Delbrueck then

brought up the "New Orientation" and stated that there would be a reexamination of all domestic politics at the end of the fighting. For the SPD, Scheidemann asked that the statement be published, a request which, Delbrueck said, needed Bethmann's agreement.[89]

At his estate in Silesia, Heydebrand began to show the effects of his forced separation from Berlin. In some of his actions, there was the hint of irrationality or perhaps of an individual growing further and further out of touch with political reality. When Westarp asked him for an endorsement of fixed price ceilings, Heydebrand's reply was that he "had no objections against fixed prices, since it is a sparkling refutation of agrarian greediness."[90] It was also Heydebrand who in 1913 had called for "force" to be used against Russia; in September of 1915, he felt a "collosal yearning for Russia", and hoped for a Russo-German understanding.[91]

But part of Heydebrand's actions may be explained by the influence of Professor Otto Hoetzsch of Berlin University. In 1913, Hoetzsch, a professor of East European history, had unsuccessfully attempted to form a German-Russian society, whose cultural exchanges, he hoped, would calm the animosity between the two nations.[92] Hoetzsch, however, was quite popular and influential among leading Conservatives and may have been responsible for a part of Mirbach-Sorquitten's pessimistic memorandum in June 1914--especially the section dealing with Germany's inability to defeat Russia.[93] Hoetzsch was convinced that Germany would never overcome Russia if the *Reichs'* war aims were also set for a destruction of England's supremacy of the sea. Instead, he suggested that German policy had to attempt an understanding with Russia, to draw it out of the enemy coalition, isolate it, while at the same time bringing Germany out of her own isolation.[94] This meant, in effect, that Germany had to give up any ideas of annexing parts of Russia, large parts of the Baltic, and could do nothing to change Poland's status quo situation. These actions would serve as the basis of a Russo-German understanding.[95]

In early September, Otto Hoetzsch became the new foreign affairs editor of the *Kreuzzeitung*, replacing Theodor Schiemann, a fanatically anti-Russian German of Baltic extraction, who had held the position for twenty-five years. Schiemann's downfall came as the result of an article advocating an early peace agreement with England. He had, in turn, been attacked by Ernst Graf v. Reventlow in the BdL-oriented *Deutsche Tageszeitung* and by v. Grumme-Douglas and forced to

resign.[96] Although Hoetzsch was, at first, publicly
silent about his pro-Russian orientation, he was more
open in his private comments. Inevitably, his opinions
reached the ears of v. Gebsattel who immediately sent
off letters to Westarp and Roesicke:[97]

> I have been told that Hoetzsch is an
> enemy of large annexations in the east. I
> hope he will make no mention of it in the
> *Kreuzzeitung;* otherwise I shall deeply
> regret that he ever took over from Professor
> Schiemann.

By the beginning of November, the ADV had gathered
a substantial number of forces and organized them into
a legitimate "war-aims movement." Included among the
"movement's" members were heavy industry (although Class
had lost Krupp v. Bohlen and Halbach),[98] the BdL and
the National Liberal Party, now united under Bassermann
and Stressmann.[99] These groups were fully in the Pan-
German camp. Partially represented were the Center
Party, the Free Conservatives, and the BdI. The great
enigma remained the Conservative Party.

During November, the Conservatives participated in
two meetings concerned with the war-aims issue. The
first, on November 7, was exploratory, and no firm
commitments were asked for or given. The second meeting
was scheduled for November 30 and, here, Class made
certain that Westarp was fully informed of the ADV
programme; the Conservative leader became the first
politician to receive a copy of Class's pamphlet,
describing, in full, the war aims of the Pan-German
League.[100]

Because Heydebrand was still isolated at
Tschunkawe,[101] Westarp led the Conservative delegation
in negotiations. Most probably under orders from
Heydebrand, Westarp remained evasive as to the extent
of his Party's commitments. Several days later,
Westarp received a letter from Gebsattel[102] expressing
his "bitter disappointment" over the Conservative
actions. In polite terms, he warned the Conservative
leader that the War and the politics of the government
could bring about a "democratic deluge." Shifting his
emphasis somewhat, Gebsattel attempted to appeal to the
real interests of the Party:

> If we can annex Suwalki, Grodno, Wilna and
> Minsk and get rid of all the non-German estate
> owners, what a chance for the Conservative
> Party. All those new colonists will flock to
> join the Party. I know you fear the decline
> of Prussianism; that can best be handled by
> inner colonization in the east.

Gebsattel had also sent off a letter of disappointment
to the BdL.[103] So that the Conservative position would
not reflect on the whole agrarian-industrial movement,
v. Wangenheim sought to assure the Pan-German that
"you can be certain that on the side of both the
Conservative and industrial leaders there exists a sincere
desire to work with you."[104]

The next scheduled meeting between the Conservative
and the war-aims groups was to be held on December 15.
Prior to that Heydebrand and Westarp met with a few of
the Party members to discuss strategy for the upcoming
negotiations. According to a letter from the ADV member
and Conservative deputy,[105] v. Grumme-Douglas, Heydebrand
maintained the position that Belgium, now under German
administration, had to be given up and that annexations
in the east were "harmful and unwelcome."

The tone of v. Grumme's letter was bitter and full
of outrage. He withdrew from the Conservative delegation
to the December 15 meeting and warned Westarp that he
not only feared for the unity of the Party (several of
whose members would cross over to the annexationist
National Liberals) but that the Conservatives would
lose "the excellent opportunity we now have for solid
ties with industry, which we have long desired."[106]
The first real cracks in the Conservative Party were
beginning to show.

On December 15, representatives from agriculture,
industry, the ADV and the Conservative Party met to
finalize the demands of the war-aims movement.[107]

For the most part, the meeting was a success.
Industry (heavy and light) as well as agriculture
accepted the basic demands as set forth by Class.[108]
There was general agreement on the western war aims
and, after difficult bargaining, it was agreed that
the annexation of industrial Belgium necessitated an
equal annexation of agricultural territory in the east.
All groups agreed that the removal of native populations
from the annexed territories and a denial of their
political rights was in order.[109]

161

Radicals and Reactionaries

The Conservatives, represented by Westarp and
Dietrich, proved to be far less intransigent than in
previous meetings; they agreed to land acquisitions
in both east and west and declared that their views
would not remain subject to change. They also accepted
the removal of native population from the annexed
territories.[110]

Although Class was generally satisfied with the
results of the meeting, the fact that the Conservatives
would still not commit themselves to membership in the
movement troubled him.[111] So did the attitude of many
members at the meeting. To a convinced *voelkisch* leader
such as Class, anything short of total agreement with
his own ideals was unsatisfactory:[112]

> With the exception of Hugenberg, who is
> ADV through and through, only v. Wangenheim
> and perhaps Roesicke have an understanding
> of our national-political strivings. The
> Conservatives and heavy industrialists spoke
> only of national policy but one can understand
> that they mean something else. What they are
> really describing is the protection and
> demands of their own interests.

It took Westarp nearly two weeks to inform Heydebrand
of the December 15 meeting.[113] And when he did, the
tone of his letter was apologetic: He informed Heydebrand
that "Roesicke, Dietrich and I could no longer avoid the
pressure put on us by the Pan-Germans to declare our
'peace' aims." Although the Conservatives were "extreme
in our demands for east and west", Westarp assured
Heydebrand that none of the declared war aims were final.
"In fact," concluded Westarp, "we asked all types of
questions about the practical meaning of these 'peace'
aims, how one would propogandize them and how we would
implement them. We will receive answers on January 7."
At the same time, Westarp was attempting to placate
Gebsattel by assuring him that "despite some disagreements,
we will in no way ignore the national goals when peace
finally comes."[114]

At the end of December, Class and Gebsattel once more
confronted Westarp at a scheduled meeting between
Conservatives and industrialists to which the Pan-Germans
had not, apparently, been invited. Heydebrand received
a report of the meeting at his estate.[115] According to
this, Class and Gebsattel expressed fears that the Party
would not remain firm against Russia; that the Conservatives

162

would reneg on their promise of eastern war aims. As
proof of this, the Pan-Germans pointed to Hoetzsch,
whom they described as an "enthusiastic friend of
Russia's" who now wrote the *Kreuzzeitung's* foreign
affairs column. The Conservative Executive Committee,
which issued the report, suggested that "perhaps Herr
Professor Hoetzsch should be made aware of these
accusations and asked to act with utmost caution."

Westarp next heard from Heydebrand on December 30.
Heydebrand's tone and the contents of his letter deserve
to be quoted in full, for they set the mood of events
which would confront the German Conservative Party
over many months and, at times, challenge its existence:[116]

> I received a letter from Class on December 28,
> about peace demands and one from Hugenberg over the
> agreement of December 15. I answered them both
> very politely, but firmly, that I hold their
> proposed ideas for far too wide-reaching and for
> the most part neither practical, realizable or
> necessary.
> I am ready to discuss them. But I would like
> to leave no doubt with you that under no circumstances
> can I engage these gentlemen in their schemes of
> utopia and political hot air. What I would really
> like to do would be to withdraw from the planned
> meeting. But I believe it would be more correct
> to express my thoughts out in the open. I'll
> therefore come.
> As for Hoetzsch, there is no hurry--he is
> doing very well.

CHAPTER VII

The Right Gathers: Reality and Illusion
in the German "War-Aims Movement" (1915)

i.   The continuing troubles
     of the German Conservative Party

     A student of events in Germany during the Great
War, should he turn his attention to the study of
domestic politics during this period, might note at
once the emergence, during 1915, of a seemingly
unified "war-aims movement."   Furthermore, most
historical accounts would trace the beginnings of this
movement from the creation of a "Conservative-Pan-
German" alliance.[1]   Our student could not, were he to
accept this analysis at face value, be more mistaken.
In fact, investigation of the original sources
provides evidence that states otherwise.   The year
1915 has been found to be a time of great tension among
the various elements that made up the Prusso-German
state at war.   The development of a radical-*voelkisch*
program of land acquisitions on both eastern and western
fronts (the so-called *Kriegszielen*) not only severely
tested the relationship between the ADV and the German
Conservative Party, but resulted in a divided Conservative
Party.   There were similar tensions between the
Conservatives and the BdL; within the BdL; between the
BdL and heavy industry; and finally, within the ADV.

                              1

     Early in 1915, the ADV convened the various members
of the "war-aims movement" (the BdL, CDI, BdI and
representatives of all the "national" parties including
the German Conservatives) for a final time.   They met
in order to draw up and sign a petition of demands to be
handed in to Bethmann.   The Pan-Germans expected the
meeting to be a mere formality, since all the organizations
had voiced agreement with the programme introduced on
December 15.   Class and v. Gebsattel were especially
looking forward to Westarp's signature, since they were
certain that their constant pressure upon the Count
had achieved its aim.   The Conservative's name on their
document would represent not only a moral victory, but a
full legitimization of the "movement."

     Heydebrand's influence, however, proved stronger.
Only days before the meeting of January 7, he had informed
Westarp that under no circumstances would Heydebrand
"become entangled in impossibilities for which I could
be blamed."[2]   Despite his own admission that "Heydebrand's
refusal to form a direct link with the ADV was much stronger

                              164

than mine," Westarp heeded the wishes of the Party
chairman and refused to sign.[3] He declared that he
was unable to accept the individual points of the
December 15 resolution because "in print such a
resolution looks much different than merely being
read out loud."[4] It is not certain if Heydebrand
himself was present at the meeting. Nevertheless,
v. Gebsattel and v. Grumme-Douglas both attacked the
decision and warned Westarp that such Conservative
"tactics" would lead to the "decline" and, perhaps,
the eventual disappearance of the Party.[5]

Bitterly disappointed over the "negative" results
of the meeting,[6] the Pan-Germans were able to take some
consolation in the fact that the agrarians of the BdL
and the heavy industrialists of the CDI had remained
faithful to the programme. And despite Hugenberg's
insistence that "nothing remains to be discussed with
the Conservatives",[7] Gebsattel and Class were cheered
by the fact that v. Wangenheim had not ceased to believe
that Heydebrand's opinion of the "movement" was only a
temporary aberration.[8]

The continuing reluctance of the Conservatives to
provide full support for the ADV programme was based
upon two factors, both of which involved Party Chairman
Heydebrand. The first of these, as noted, was
Heydebrand's insistence that he wished to remain aloof
from the war-aims movement rather than allow himself
to become involved in "impossibilities" and be held
responsible for them. Such tactics were designed not
only to maintain Heydebrand's anti-ADV orientation but
to insure that the Conservatives, just in case the war
went badly, would not suffer further damage to their
social and political credibility as the "scapegoats"
of an ignominious defeat.

A second factor, equally or more important, was
the growing influence of Professor Otto Hoetzsch. His
pro-Russian orientation not only affected Heydebrand's
outlook and brought the Conservatives into conflict with
annexationist goals, but his support of official censorship
policies during the early part of the war stamped him
as "governmental."[9] Furthermore, Hoetzsch's positive
feelings toward Russia brought him into direct conflict
with the large, anti-Russian Baltic German wing of the
Conservative Party. Led by Theodor Schiemann, the
deposed foreign affairs editor of the *Kreuzzeitung* whose
position Hoetzsch now occupied, the large group of "Balts"
within the Party had, for nearly three decades, helped
shape the Conservative view of Russia. Possessing their

own newspapers and other organs of mass propoganda,
the Baltic Germans had been instrumental in whipping
up the frenzied hatred that thad characterized Germany's
opinion of Russia just prior to the war.

Now in January 1915, their influence and opinion
within the Party discredited because of Schiemann's
removal, the Baltic Germans sought to recapture their
once-powerful role. They founded a journal entitled
Das Deutsche Reich whose foreign affairs editor would
be none other than Theodor Schiemann. The journal's
appearance prompted Hoetzsch to send Westarp a letter
expressing apprehension and fear over the consequences
of such an event.[10] The appearance of *Das Deutsche
Reich* was, according to Hoetzsch, "unwelcome", because
"there are, no doubt, numerous Conservatives who support
the Pan-German aim of Russian annexations and for whom
this journal and Schiemann's articles would serve as a
gathering point." "Really," continued Hoetzsch, "the
wishes of 165,000 Baltic Germans can no longer determine
the monumental questions of the east." He concluded
the letter on a rather ominous note: "It is impossible
that in one political party both of these opposing
points of view can find equal representation."

By the middle of April, the Conservatives had not
yet come to any decision about Belgium--one of the most
important of the territorial claims put forth by the
ADV. Contrary to Pan-German, CDI and BdL demands that
Belgium, as well as vital mining areas in northern
France, be annexed to Germany, Heydebrand continued
to reject both aims[11] and Westarp thought the latter
unnecessary.[12] Despite his more moderate view of the
Pan-Germans, Westarp too, came under Hoetzsch's
influence: Westarp felt it would be better to set
aside annexationist wishes in the east in order to
concentrate upon a full victory in the west.[13] The
Conservative leadership thus presented a viewpoint
completely contrary to the BdL's. As early as March,
v. Wangenheim began to lose hope of Heydebrand's
conversion to the nationalist cause. To Roesicke,[14]
he wrote that "Professor Hoetzsch is an editor on the
Kreuzzeitung who basically advocates a defeatist opinion
about Russia and is either influenced by or is
influencing Heydebrand." And for the first time since
1909, an outright split developed between party and
pressure group: a number of Conservatives under Hoesch
maintained that the Party had to develop its own political
programme even if it differed greatly from the BdL's.[15]
Reflecting the growing *voelkisch* orientation of *Bund*

policies, v. Wangenheim was of the opinion that the
Conservative leadership "missed the whole point of
the nationalist thrust" in their party politics.[16]
After months of defending Heydebrand against continued
attacks by the ADV (most notably v. Gebsattel), Roesicke
finally admitted to v. Wangenheim that "Heydebrand is
on the verge of becoming a very uncomfortable opponent
against us."[17]

It must have seemed particularly disturbing to
many within the German Conservative Party that the
actions of their leaders seemed so contrary to agrarian
interests. This was so at a time when the agrarian
cause seemed to have regained its national standing
and when concern with agriculture's position in the
overall economy was at its highest level since Caprivi.
Particularly responsible for this turn of events was
the ADV (and especially v. Gebsattel) which pictured
itself as uniquely equipped to restore agriculture to
its rightful place as the leading sector in German
national life. Moreover, the existence of eastern
and western war-aims propogated by a combined force of
agrarians and industrialists made economic parity an
almost inevitable consequence of *Kartell* strategy.

But not only the Pan-Germans and the *Kartell* were
concerned with agriculture and eastern and western war
aims. On Bethmann Hollweg's instructions, Friedrich
v. Schwerin, President of the Administrative Council
of Frankfurt on Oder and President of the *Gesellschaft
zur Forderung der inneren Kolonization* (Society for the
Promotion of Inner Colonization) was commissioned to
produce a memorandum on the creation of new areas for
settlement on Germany's eastern frontier. The long
memorandum[18] was sent to Bethmann on March 25. Schwerin's
most notable suggestion was that the annexation of Belgium,
with its obvious advantages for German industrial
expansion, had to be balanced by the settlement of
German small farmers in the east--where such a large
peasant population would keep German colonists from
decline.[19] This was a necessary measure to counter
the growth of the Polish population in the eastern
provinces. Included in Schwerin's remarks was a pointed
reference to the problem that had always remained at
the heart of the inner colonization question--the
possibility that the large *Junker* estates would have to
be divided for peasant colonization.[20]

A similar proposal was authored by Wolfgang Kapp,
an East Prussian and a leading spirit of the inner
colonization movement. Kapp's rather provocative

contribution to the question of eastern settlements
was to suggest that these soon-to-be annexed areas
be colonized by war veterans. His reasoning behind
the suggestion was based on the belief that such
battle-tested and brave warriors would quickly redress
the imbalance between city and country which resulted
from "*Landflucht* and depopulation of the rural areas,
the unhealthy growth of large cities and industrial
centers which have endangered the most vital interests
of our people."[21]

To the BdL, the eastern war aims were seen as
crucial to the continued existence of a sound agrarian
sector. The annexation of eastern territories would
serve to ease the land problem of a confined German
populace while at the same time allowing for the
revitalization of agriculture. It was for this reason
that the *Bund* sought to further the inner colonization
movement, although the agrarians took exception to many
of Schwerin's proposals.[22] By 1915, ADV ideology
(as formulated by v. Gebsattel) led the Pan-German view
of inner colonization to a most bizarre, yet prophetic,
conclusion. It stressed that Germany had to maintain
the annexed territories for at least 100 years. If
that were to occur, then Germany "would gain the
intellectual leadership of the world and the military
leadership of Europe against the Mongol storm (with
or without the Slavs)." In ADV eyes, the "free land,
free of people concept" lay at the core of any inner
colonization. And inner colonization was a movement
that superseded the concern for a colonial empire, for,
as v. Gebsattel wrote in early 1915, "without inner
colonization there will be no stop to the decline in our
birth rate and eventual racial death."[23]

With their annexationist demands in print since
the beginning of March,[24] the Pan-Germans began to take
account of their support:[25] "Here are the groups that
stand behind us: officially the BdL and the CDI,
semi-officially the Prussian Conservative Party and
the National Liberals; furthermore, I know that the Free
Conservatives and the *Mittelstand* Association share
my views." On April 22, various members of the war-
aims movement met to draw up plans for a petition to
be handed in to Bethmann-Hollweg. Then, on May 1, at
the urging of Hirsch (Essen), leader of the extreme
right-wing of the National Liberals, and Erzberger of
the Center, representatives of the bourgeois parties
and interest groups met to clarify further their position
vis-a-vis the Chancellor. It was also an opportunity
for the Pan-Germans to establish with some certainty

the extent of their political support. All the
economic-interest groups enthusiastically supported
the proposal that a Pan-German declaration of aims,
purporting to speak for all the assembled representatives,
be sent to Bethmann. The same was true with the National
Liberals, whose Chairman, Bassermann, had once led an
anti-CDI movement within the Party but now was "...arm
in arm with heavy industry--a grotesque sight for those
who know his previous position."[26] But in a surprising
declaration, the Center--upon Spahn's insistence--refused
to go along with the proposal and, not surprisingly,
was supported in this by the Conservative Party.[27]

In a letter to Class several days after the meeting,
v. Gebsattel expressed his "deep disappointment" at
the Conservative tactic:[28]

> The party that I feel closest to was the
> most obstructive. I am glad that in January
> I found the courage to tell the Conservatives
> that if they did not change their position,
> they would become the grave-diggers of the
> Party and the monarchy.

His critical view of the Conservative leaders, however,
did not stop v. Gebsattel from sending Heydebrand the
declaration of aims that had been adopted at the
meeting of May 1 with a request to reconsider the
Party's rejection. Heydebrand's answer was typically
vague and evasive:[29]

> If we Conservatives are not identified
> with all the individual aspects of the ADV,
> the traditions of our party, nevertheless,
> stand firm. We support everything that
> strengthens our German fatherland in the
> world within the range of the possible and
> reasonable.

Heydebrand's reply convinced Gebsattel that "Herr
Heydebrand has not overcome his mistrust of us. In
fact, his letter could just as easily have come from
Bethmann."[30] Class, too, finally came to realize that
Heydebrand was a "misfortune",[31] and a "failure as a
leader..."[32] Along with Hoetzsch, whose pro-Russian
views Gebsattel had already termed "intolerable",[33]
Heydebrand now became the focus of Pan-German scorn
and intrigue.[34]

Yet the growing strength of the annexationist forces was not altered by the failure of the Conservatives and large parts of the Center to wholly support their aims. In mid-1915, the *Hakatisten* and the Free Conservatives were added to the movement. From a meeting of May 20, there emerged the "petition of the Six", a set of demands, closely paralleling those of the ADV, sent to Bethmann and signed by the CDI, BdI, BdL, *Deutschen Bauernbund*, RDMV and the *Christliche deutsche Bauernvereine* (Association of Christian German Farmers)--in short, nearly the whole of the German economy. Later the *Hansabund* was added to these groups.[35] In July, another petition was handed to the Chancellor, the so-called Petition of the Intellectuals, again demanding the aims of the ADV programme. This petition and its forerunner, the so-called Proclamation of the 93, was signed by hundreds of university professors.[36] Also noteworthy was the petition of the leading west German industrialists (Hugenberg, Stinnes, Kirdorf, Thyssen) requesting the implementation of the Pan-German demands. As a means of coordinating the various war-aims committees and propagating both eastern and western aims, a group of politicians from the National Liberal Party created the *Auskunftstelle Vereinigte Verbaende* (Information Center of the United Associations).[37] At the center of this frenzied activity stood the ADV. In what was very much a continuation of its pre-war role as the "holding company of the Right", the Pan-Germans directed Germany's path to European hegemony:[38]

> Our task is to mobilize all the outstanding groups in the German Empire : business groups, political parties and the intellectuals. We want to insure that their petitions to the Chancellor all reflect a similar sense in terms of demands. In the meantime, we remain behind the scenes.

Writing to Bethmann Hollweg in June, the Deputy Commanding General of the 7th Army Corps in Muenster, General v. Gayl, commented upon a phenomenon that has already been noted in this study:[39] "It is characteristic for the changing viewpoints of our liberal circles that they now endorse the widespread use of expropriations." Beginning in 1915, there was a far-reaching consensus between both outright annexationists and the more "liberal" forces in the *Reich*. Although their methods differed, both elements shared a coveted position among Germany's ruling classes and by 1915 both had become more certain as to the final aim of their economic and political hopes.[40] Under the guise

170

of a "Central European Economic Association", dominated
by Germany, both groups were intent upon achieving an
imperialistic position in Europe. Whether it was in the
form of Paul Rohrbach's "ethical imperialism",[41]
Friedrich Naumann's "Central Europe" conception or the
widespread "cultural imperialism" view, there was little
to differentiate these "liberal" goals from the final
aims of the ADV. Hence, when the *Freie Vaterlaendische
Vereingung* (Free Fatherland Association) was founded
in February 1915 as the first significant propoganda
organization of the "liberal" elements, it was attacked
by the annexationists of the "war-aims movement" as
much from a feeling of disgust at this hypocritical
stance as for any other reason.[42] The "liberal"
disguise had long since been abandoned, or would soon
be, by politicians such as Bassermann and interest
groups like the *Hansabund* or the BdI. To the radical-
voelkisch forces, any further play at maintaining an
artificial difference between Class, Rohrbach or Naumann
would only impede the road to Germany's greatest hour.

ii. The BdL moves further to the right

The degree of commitment and intensity to their
annexationist policy, as evinced by the Pan-German
League and *Bund* members, resulted in a number of "moderate"
victims. Disagreement with policy led to the resignation
of Theodor Reismann-Grone, editor of the *Rheinisch-
Westfaelische Zeitung* and a long-time member of the ADV
Executive.[43] Within the BdL, too, there was friction
between v. Wangenheim and two editors of the *Deutsche
Tageszeitung*, a publication which reflected BdL opinion.
Dr. Georg Oertel, chief editor of the paper, maintained
an anti-ADV position and called Class a "dangerous
dreamer."[44] Count Ernst v. Reventlow, who in 1913 had
already been the focus of ADV criticism because of his
opinions as foreign affairs specialist, continued to
concentrate upon an anti-English theme to the disregard
of Russia and France.[45] Both men were soon stripped of
their editorial powers. But the main culprit remained
Hoetzsch, and he drew an increasing amount of criticism
for his pro-Russian attitude and for his influence
upon Heydebrand.

Throughout 1915 the cooperation between agrarians
and Pan-Germans, begun in 1913, was intensified in
several areas. These ranged from a combined scheme to
establish a total ban against all Polish Jews wishing

to enter the *Reich* (which would later become governmental policy) to a proposed struggle against the possibility of a national party to be founded by Count Hatzfeld and others whose slogan would be "Struggle against all *Ausnahmegesetze*" (exceptional laws most often directed against the SPD).[46] The result of such a blossoming relationship was the steady growth of ADV involvement in domestic affairs and of BdL concern with foreign relations. The BdL became not only the intermediary of the ADV in its dealings with the Conservatives, but its liaison to the *Reichstag* parties in the matter of war aims. Thus, on May 10, v. Wangenheim was able to report to Gebsattel that he had successfully convinced most of the party leaders--Bassermann as well as Oerter and Herold of the Center--to accept the Pan-German war aims. The only difficulty had been Heydebrand.[47]

One direct result of the ADV-BdL bond was a setback in the cooperation between agrarians and heavy industry and, consequently, a further erosion of the principles that once governed the semi-mythical *Kartell der schaffenden Staende*. This came about despite several indications of v. Wangenheim's concern for the continued function of the *Kartell*. In early 1915, for example, the BdL followed the lead of the CDI in trying to improve its relations with the BdI. In v. Wangenheim's view this was necessary for the "fulfillment" of the *Kartell*. And when the first rumors of the plan for the creation of a "National Party of the Right" began to circulate, the BdL Chairman rejected the proposal in favor of the "need for a *Kartell* of *staatserhaltenden* parties."[48]

Two factors weighed heavily against the smooth continuation of the relationship first formed between the two economic sectors in the summer of 1913. The first of these, which caused v. Wangenheim to comment on the "difficulty of cooperating with the gentlemen of industry",[49] was the continuation of the dispute over price ceilings. Industrialists such as Hugenberg and Stinnes continued to uphold the view that unrestricted high prices had to be implemented on such staple foods as bread--a step which was supposed to lead the masses towards thrift and "self-control."[50] More importantly, perhaps, the *Bund* had become a very willing slave of ADV ideology. Master Pan-German theoreticians such as v. Gebsattel and, to a lesser degree, Class had developed a *voelkisch* ideology which stressed that agriculture and inner colonization were the two single-most needs of the German nation. Eventually agrarians such as v. Wangenheim and Roesicke began to lose sight of the value inherent in an agricultural-industrial alliance--especially since it was an alliance based essentially on

172

DR. GUSTAV ROESICKE

(Photograph courtesy of
Ullstein Bilderdienst)

a defense of the status quo. Pan-German ideology, on
the other hand, was a curious blend of "modernization"
and reaction. While it sought to employ the politics
of mass mobilization under the banner of the *Volk*, it
simultaneously strove to reestablish a medieval atmosphere
in which agriculture provided the life blood of the
nation. Roesicke, for one, displayed the effect of his
relationship with the Pan-Germans:[51] "The future lies
in inner colonization. And this is more important than
the pure needs of industry and export. In fact, the
industrialists are alligned with us because they see in
agriculture the manner in which to stop the Sozis."
Finally, during 1915, the agrarians rejected in full
the "old" notion of *Weltpolitik*, a concept that had
never received their complete devotion and had been
the cause of agrarian-industrial conflict:[52] "If we
bind ourselves to the export interests of heavy industry
and the BdI, where is the *Heimatspolitik* that has
always been the basis of our policy? If we continue
along these lines we will have brought other interests
to their aims and forgotten our own."

iii. Anti-Semitism enters once more

       The internal squabblings of the Right, however,
were able to occupy center-stage only so long as the
perennial social and class conflicts of the Prusso-
German state remained quiescent. By 1915, however,
the brief flirtation with the *Burgfrieden*, which even
the BdL had respected until late spring,[53] as a means
of side-tracking the unresolved social issues of the
Reich was over. The renewed vigor of the SPD in
Reichstag matters, its unrelenting insistence upon the
destruction of the Prussian Voting Law and a "new
orientation" in post-war Germany forced the agrarians
of the BdL to consider means necessary to counteract
the renewed socialist threat. As a first step in this
direction, they reversed their economic position vis-a-vis
a nationalized grain market. The old Kanitz Proposal,
parts of which they now advocated, had been introduced
in a time of conservative stability and a *staatserhaltende
Reichstag*. But conditions were now different and
Roesicke, for instance, feared that a proposed
Reichs-Getreidemonopol (*Reich* Grain Monopoly) would
bring it under the control of the *Reichstag* and make
it a "mere plaything of democratic agitation...and
agriculture will be blamed even more than before for
every price increase."[54] As a further result of the

renewed tension between Left and Right, the agrarians
and heavy industrialists began to formulate long-range
policies toward the preservation of the status quo after
the war's end. This was the purpose of a meeting held
on August 24, 1915. Present at the meeting were
Roesicke, Hirsch (Essen), Hugenberg, Heydebrand and
Westarp. They decided that all the *staatserhaltende*
forces would attempt to demonstrate, during the course
of the war, that "other problems beside the Prussian
Voting Law...must be solved first." They suggested the
solution of the *Reich* finances and other "social"
problems.[55]

Among the unresolved social questions, the continuing
undercurrent of anti-Semitism, which had only briefly
ceased with the establishment of the *Burgfrieden*, once
more began to play a major role in domestic politics.

Like Social Democracy, that other favorite spectre
of the Right, anti-Semitism had enjoyed rather uneven
periods of popularity during the course of the Second
Empire. From a highpoint just before the turn of the
century, the anti-Semitic "wave" had been forced to
wait until the election of 1912 before again reaching
a national crest. In that year, it had become a major
force in German right-wing politics,[56] only to see its
growing impetus silenced by the Kaiser's speech on
August 4, 1914. German Jewry had rushed to the
Fatherland's defense, and in such numbers and enthusiasm
that the leading anti-Semitic voices of the *Reich* had
been all but stilled. Individual Jews such as Ernst
Lissauer, author of the widely-quoted *Hassgesang gegen
England* (Song of Hatred Against England), added to the
generally accepted view that German Jewry had joined
the patriotic effort.

But not all Germans shared this view. Fanatical
anti-Semites such as Baron F. Bodelschwingh-Schwarzenhasel,
a Conservative and BdL member, continued to attack the
"Jewish press" and the "Jewish-international spirit
which dominated the Social Democratic Party."[57] Although
few in number during the first months of the war, anti-
Semitic references increased sharply during 1915.
Because of strict press censorship, the anti-Semitic mood
was reflected mainly in private correspondence. Among
the Conservatives, for instance, the Deputy v. Bonin
(Neustettin) was outspokenly anti-Semitic. In a
privately printed[58] pamphlet to the voters of his district
in November, he bitterly criticized the government's
"new orientation" as leading to "an even greater democratization and judaization of our public situation." The

attack extended to his own party as he criticized the
Conservatives for not combatting the Jewish danger
"earlier and more sharply." He recommended that his
constituents learn the real threat of Jewry by reading
If I Were the Kaiser. Even so-called "moderates" on
the anti-Semitic question such as Count Westarp
demonstrated a new level of anti-Jewish feeling: to
v. Kries, Westarp suggested the possibility of an
Ausnahmegesetz to ban the freedom of *Ostjuden* to
travel to Germany.[59] And to v. Bonin, he wrote an
extremely revealing letter, one which demonstrated
that the term "moderate" did not exclude a decidedly
anti-Semitic nature:[60]

> I am certainly in full agreement with you
> in most of your basic ideas...I do, however,
> doubt that it will be possible at any given
> time after the War to further limit the size
> of the distribution of Jews in public office.
> It will be difficult enough to defend the
> present situation. In this respect it will
> be necessary to use material which will
> demonstrate the activities of the Jews during
> the War and their uncommon ability for profit
> in the War.

The Pan-German League, however, remained the prime
driving force behind the revitalized anti-Semitism. It
will be remembered that Gebsattel had maintained the
continuity of ADV goals even as the Kaiser was
pronouncing the *Burgfrieden*.[61] Foremost among these
had been a "solution to the Jewish question." That
this aim had remained unchanged nearly a year after
the War's start was evident in Gebsattel's letter to
another ADV member, the notorious *Englandfresser*
(fanatical enemy of England), Admiral Hans v. Thompsen:

> If Germany wishes to fulfill its mission
> in the world, it must become healthy again in
> every manner. This is only possible if the
> Jewish predominance in banking, property and
> publishing, its domination of cultural areas
> such as art, literature and theatre is broken.
> This can only be accomplished if the strength
> of the German people is once more based upon
> agriculture. Otherwise we face racial death.
> Thus we have to give people the opportunity
> to settle as rich farmers and we must provide
> land and earth at a cheap price and favorable
> conditions. Perhaps, then, they will leave
> the cities.

175

Gebsattel, for one, did not feel that the time was quite appropriate for the start of a national anti-Semitic campaign: "We must, out of technical considerations, avoid the appearance of conducting an anti-Semitic propoganda."[63] This opinion was shared by v. Vietinghoff-Scheel who was uncertain as to the depth of anti-Semitic feelings in the various ADV chapters. Yet v. Vietinghoff was definite as to the role anti-Semitism would play in the future plans of the Pan-German League:[64]

> I can assure you that the Pan-German League considers it one of its most important future tasks to support the propogation of racial questions and especially the elevation of German racial awareness in the *Volk*.

To avoid being openly identified with anti-Semitism, the ADV was willing to go to extreme lengths. This included a suggestion by v. Gebsattel that the League accept "decent" Jews into the ADV. "I believe, however," ventured v. Gebsattel, "that the application of a Jew for membership in the ADV remains a very remote possibility."[65]

Privately, Gebsattel was extremely active. At the end of October, he sponsored a meeting of the *Reich's* leading anti-Semites. It was here that Gebsattel met Theodor Fritsch for the first time and found that he liked him "beyond my expectations." The two agreed to begin a data-gathering project involving the "economic activities of the Jews in the War." Included in this report would be the percentage of enlisted Jews, "those hiding behind the front, those remaining at home, etc."[66]

But even while the ADV was shunning the anti-Semitic spotlight, events in the *Reich* ensured that it could not long remain so. A series of price rises upon staple foods and the forecast of another winter at war drove large portions of German society to express their anger and frustration in an all-too-typical manner. The *Preussische Jahrbuecher* first noted the phenomenon at the end of September when it reported "the growth of a new anti-Semitism--the anti-Semitism of the educated classes."[67] In November, Class was informed by the *voelkisch* publisher Lehmann[68] that "we can no longer avoid mentioning Jewry in our publications. The people's awareness of Jewish activity in the War has grown extraordinarily." This was due, according to Lehmann, "on the one hand, because of price usurers and, on the other, because of an incomplete yet steadily clarifying awareness that Jewry is the soul of defeatism." As concrete evidence, Lehmann offered the example of his own city, Munich:

176

> Here in Munich, I have asked numerous
> strangers who is to blame for the high cost
> of staples. The answer is always--"the usurers,
> the Jews." Also the members of the economic
> associations have told me that the awareness
> of the Jewish danger has risen dramatically,

iv. New moves against Bethmann

The end of the *Burgfrieden* was further reflected
in the growing number of attacks upon Bethmann Hollweg.
Instrumental in the publishing and distribution of these
anti-governmental tirades was Professor Hans v. Liebig,
a leading anti-Semite who, according to Westarp, "tended
to find in everything a connection between Bethmann
Hollweg and his dependence upon Jewry."[69] In the summer
of 1915, v. Liebig distributed a privately-published
periodical entitled *Zu Neuen Ufern (To New Shores)*. It
reflected both his pro-annexationist, anti-Bethmann
and anti-Semitic viewpoints. An article by Rudolf
Theuden, for example, supposedly sent from Italy, attacked
"the Jewish-led Freemasons who are clamouring here for
war against Germandom." And in his own column, v. Liebig
printed annexationist war aims and attacked Rohrbach's
view of Germany as a *Weltvolk*.[70] *Zu Neuen Ufern* managed
to appear twice before being suppressed by military
authorities. Its publication was paralleled by a sharp
increase in the number and intensity of pro-annexationist
speeches held throughout the nation. One of the earliest
and most militant of these was reported by the Police
President of Frankfurt am Main, whose agents had recorded
the words of one Kurd v. Strantz, a co-founder of the
Reichsverband gegen Sozialdemokratie and, like v. Liebig,
a member of the Pan-German League:[71]

> The speaker (v. Strantz-AJP) indulged in
> tactless utterances about the purpose and goal
> of the present war. Prince Bismarck's war
> had been a war of conquest and so was this
> one. It would be silly to try and deny this.
> He claimed that it made no difference if the
> war were to continue for a few more years; the
> main thing was that Germany would receive
> suitable gains.

Although Bethmann was unable to directly implicate
Class, v. Gebsattel or the ADV in the anti-government
attacks, the circumstantial evidence was overwhelming.
Not only were most of the known Bethmann-critics ADV

177

members or sympathizers,[72] but the Chancellor was by
this time fully aware of the existence of a "clique"
determined to drive him from office.

In April, Albrecht v. Graefe warned Westarp that
a government which was prepared to abandon Belgium, for
any reason except military defeat, ran the risk of losing
the support of the economic-interest groups and the
staatserhaltende parties. "Such a split between
government and these groups," he went on to add, "means
a severe danger for our domestic future and would drive
the government directly into the arms of democracy."[73]
V. Graefe's dire prediction was, in fact, based upon an
ex post facto analysis. Apparently unknown to him, at
least two groups had not only withdrawn their support
of Bethmann, but had already decided that his replacement
as Chancellor was an immediate necessity. Again Westarp
was the recipient of a letter, this time written by
v. Wangenheim at the end of March. The BdL leader informed
Westarp of a meeting he had attended, at which several
leading Bavarian officials expressed their concern and
pessimism over the political views of Bethmann and
Delbrueck. They had decided that "this situation can
no longer continue," and asked v. Wangenheim if the
Conservatives agreed with their position. "I told them,"
wrote v. Wangenheim, "that we, as well as the representatives
of the great economic associations, were fully convinced
that Germany faced total collapse if a change of personnel
were not made in the leading governmental positions."[74]
No doubt there was more than a little personal consideration
involved in v. Wangenheim's reply: for in February, the
BdL's annual conference at the Circus Busch had been forbidden by military decree and, in June, the publication
of the *Deutsche Tageszeitung* would be banned for several
days.[75]

Also in March, Gebsattel had written a secret
memorandum in which he not only outlined the aims of
the ADV but sharply criticized Bethmann: "We have had
no luck with the Federal Chancellor...for the time being
it is perhaps necessary to have a 'strong man' lead us
into the transition from war to peace (Graf Posadowsky?)."[76]
And two months later, Gebsattel directly attacked anti-
annexationist groups as being "the same circles that
were against an increase in the army; against the building
of the German fleet; against a protective tariff policy
and German agriculture; against a strong monarchy...and
for the unrestrained democratization of our entire public
life." "These same circles," he concluded, "are today
the only support and comrades-in-arms of the Federal

Chancellor."[77] In early May, Bethmann finally replied
to the war-aims petition that the ADV had sent to him.
In the letter,[78] he referred to a "threat" and to a
"small minority...who are attempting to force their
will upon the leader of the *Reich's* affairs, a man
chosen by the Kaiser."

Until that point in time, Bethmann had been only
vaguely aware of the forces opposing his policies. In
April, he was told by the National Liberal Deputy,
Hirsch, that all of the interest groups were opposed
to him and were actively discussing his dismissal.
Hirsch further informed Bethmann that the basis for
the opposition was the Chancellor's failure to pronounce
and seek to attain specific war aims. Bethmann was
affected by Hirsch's revelations, but was not, apparently,
fully convinced that Hirsch was being completely truthful.
Only days later, according to a letter from Westarp to
Heydebrand, "Bethmann told Theodor Schiemann that a
small clique was trying to purge him--and that I stood
at the very head of the conspiracy."[79]

Bethmann could not have been more mistaken. Of all
the right-wing groups in the Empire, the Conservatives
were the least able to lead such a purge. Westarp,
himself, understood this quite clearly, as he showed
in his memoirs:[80]

> In the struggle for Bethmann's dismissal,
> we Conservatives were restricted not only
> legally but by circumstances. Precisely
> because we opposed his policies, we did not
> have the Kaiser's ear; precisely because we
> set ourselves against the democratic trend
> of the time, we were in a minority and often
> isolated. We never expressed the demand that
> Bethmann be dismissed, nor did we speak out on
> the matter in the *Reichstag* or *Landtag*. This
> would have been contrary to the constitution.
> Every parliamentary attack by us would only
> have strengthened Bethmann's position.

It is clear that the Conservatives were afraid of the
consequences of an outright confrontation with the
Chancellor. Were Bethmann Hollweg to emerge victorious,
then the parliamentary doom of the Conservative Party
would have been complete.

In those same memoirs, Westarp also wrote the
following:[81] "The degrading attack upon one's person,
personal intrigue, the anonymous pamphlet--this was not

our style." It was the style, however, of the Pan-
German League. During 1915, Conservative participation
in such actions would have brought the Party to the
point of near-total identification with the ADV--a
situation that Heydebrand wished to avoid at all costs.

Instead, the Party leadership followed a strict
policy of rejecting all calls for Bethmann's purge.
These came amidst renewed, but unsuccessful, attempts
in April for a reconciliation between National Liberals
and Conservatives.[82] There was, however, more than
one attempt to directly influence Heydebrand and Westarp
against the Chancellor, most notably by Tirpitz through
his son-in-law, Ulrich v. Hassel.[83] Throughout the
spring and summer, in fact, Westarp grew more optimistic
about Bethmann's attitude towards the western war aims,
especially on the question of Belgium. Thus he was
able to tell Heydebrand, on May 13, that Bethmann "went
further today in positive war aims than was generally
expected."[84] And on August 7, he informed the Conservative
Deputy, v. Kessel, that "the Chancellor told the members
of another party this week that he endorsed a full
military, economic and political rule over Belgium.
He stressed, however, that he did not wish to make it
publicly known that he had endorsed these things."[85]

As the outcry against Bethmann's refusal to openly
discuss Germany's war aims increased, even Westarp and
Heydebrand were forced to consider the possibility of
his successor. At the end of July, Heydebrand made it
quite specific that he was far from happy with the
most widely-mentioned choices:[86]

> Buelow is unacceptable to us. So is
> Tirpitz without much serious consideration;
> Rheinbaben unfit; even more so than
> Bethmann...The thing is really not so
> simple.

By autumn, it was clear that Tirpitz had become the
definite choice of the Pan-Germans. Since Heydebrand
had played a leading role in unifying the conservative
parties in favor of the U-boat question earlier in the
year,[87] Tirpitz naturally considered this a plus in
his own favor; as State Secretary of the *Reich* Naval
Office, he, too, had been advocating the widespread
use of the submarine in Germany's war effort. Once
more, through v. Hassel, he attempted to influence
Heydebrand and discuss with him both the U-boat and
Chancellor questions.[88] But because Tirpitz was
favored by the ADV, Heydebrand refused to see the

Grand Admiral, claiming that their discussions might
bring about "new misunderstandings."[89]

v. German Conservatives and the "war-aims" question

"The demand for the most vigorous war effort
against England," wrote Westarp very early in his
memoirs, "was, in essence, the basis of Conservative
policy in the War."[90] During 1915, this aim took on
increased importance as the *Burgfrieden* disappeared
amidst renewed conflict between Left and Right. With
the petitions of the ADV and the economic-interest
groups in Bethmann's hands, Westarp attempted to explain
his own refusal to sign the war-aims demands:[91]

> I did not participate in the demands...
> because, basically, as Chairman of the *Reichstag*
> group, I did not feel it correct to give my
> approval to each individual demand.

What Westarp really meant to say was that he was opposed
to the ADV call for annexations in Russia. As early
as January, Gustav Stresemann noted that "especially
in conservative circles there is a growing desire for
a separate peace with Russia. They see this tie
between the two as a bulwark against the feared
democratization of Germany."[92]

This feeling, in fact, was more or less widespread
throughout the more traditional Conservative circles--to
which Heydebrand could certainly be counted. During
March, it became a conviction shared by Bethmann Hollweg,
who began actively to search for ways through which a
separate peace with Russia might be concluded.[93]
Conservative reluctance to join in the growing attacks
upon Bethmann, later that summer, may be partially
explained by their mutual interest in Russia.

Yet the question remains: why a separate peace
with Russia when, in 1913, the Conservatives had even
threatened to use violence against that nation in order
to forestall the loss of Russian grain markets?[94]

Part of the reason may lie in the fact that by late
1915 the Conservatives had realized that to struggle for
a continuation of the status quo would mean to remain
politically powerless. The status quo, in this instance,
meant the post-1912 political situation and the
accompanying isolation in the *Reichstag*, financial crises

and voter stagnation. Conservatives such as Heydebrand
and the traditionalists who made up the Conservative
delegation to the *Herrenhaus* began to appreciate that
only with the return to a pre-1912 political state of
affairs could the Party restore its power and
influence. And for the conservative Prusso-German
state to remain intact, its superiority over the
forces of democracy had to be shown.

An all-out conflict with the SPD or the left
Liberals was not possible, as long as the *Burgfrieden*
still carried meaning to millions of soldiers at the
front and millions more at home. Only by defeating the
liberal nations of the West, and especially England,
could such a blow for conservatism be struck. What
made this type of thinking so realistic was the
influence of the "Ideas of 1914", which had convinced
so many Germans that they were indeed involved in an
Armageddon between liberalism and conservatism for
the control of Germany's destiny. The annexation of
parts of Russia and Poland, therefore, would not only
introduce a large alien element into the Prussian state,
but damage a potential aristocratic ally--a move that
threatened to further weaken the *Junker* base in Germany.

Not all those associated with the Conservative
Party, however, held such a view. This was made evident
in November, when Westarp suggested that the Party make
an attempt to influence the other *staatserhaltende*
parties to adopt a similar anti-Russian annexations
point of view. "But before we do this," he wrote to
Heydebrand,[95] "it would be wise to discuss our relationship
to Russia with Roesicke and v. Wangenheim...We could
present the problem this way: do you want half-efforts
on both fronts or wouldn't you agree that it would
be wiser to drop the eastern aims as much as is necessary
and achieve a full victory in the west? Maltzahn feels
they are coming round to this point of view; I haven't
yet noticed it."

The BdL, through the person of Roesicke, filled
with grandiose Pan-German ideas about the primacy of
agriculture and aware of the enormous possibility of
agrarian profits in the east, found the Conservative
suggestion totally unacceptable:[96]

> I have heard that the leaders of the
> Conservative Party are willing to drop our
> expansion towards Russia in order to achieve
> a peace with the Russians. They wish to do
> this because they feel it is more important

that Belgium be annexed as well as the French
mining areas, the ports, free access to the
seas, etc.
I really fear the worst for the future.
The BdL cannot, in my opinion, follow this
path. Especially so, since heavy industry
wishes to obtain, through the annexation of
iron and coal areas, secure supplies of raw
materials and to eliminate Belgian and French
competition. Through its spheres of influence,
heavy industry wishes to become predominant
in these areas. I personally think so-called
"control" over these areas would suffice.

Roesicke's rejection of the Conservative position
on Russia was clear proof of the growing rift within
the German Conservative Party. The main difference
seemed to center upon the question of ideology and
the differing Conservative points of view: (1) a
traditional Conservative *Weltanschaauung*, ready to
accept some aspects of the *voelkisch*-nationalist
movement, but still viewing the aristocratic Estate
and its survival as its primary concern and (2) a
purely profit-oriented, agrarian-dominated view, which
had combined the most extreme points of BdL and ADV
ideology.

The latter viewpoint was predominant in the
Provinzialausschus der Provinz Ostpreussen, which
on October 19, called for annexations in Russia and
Poland.[97] Only a few days later, on October 24, Class
announced to a cheering group of Pan-Germans that the
Conservative Party had come out of its formerly
"hesitant position", and now fully backed the ADV
programme.[98] This was not altogether true. What
had occurred was an Executive Committee resolution of
mid-October,[99] which had attempted to walk a delicate
line between the two Conservative viewpoints. Although
the Conservative resolution endorsed "territorial
expansion", it made no mention of Russian annexations.
Instead it called for acquisitions in Poland, the
Ostsee provinces and Lithuania. Yet it had also called
for German hegemony over Belgium--a demand now
propogated by the anti-English Heydebrand-Hoetzsch
Conservatives. That the conflict between the two
divergent viewpoints had not been resolved in this
resolution was demonstrated by the interest Heydebrand
showed in a Pan-German charge in November that
Erzberger, Spahn and Trimborn of the Center had signed
anti-annexationist petitions. "I wonder if you know

more about the ideas of these gentlemen," inquired
v. Heydebrand of Westarp, "I really doubt, however,
that they agree with our specific point of view."[100]

At the same meeting in which Class announced
Conservative acceptance of the Pan-German war aims, a
Conservative speaker, Professor Lezius of Koenigsburg,
delivered a sharp attack upon Conservative policy in the
question of government censorship. Lezius explained
to the Pan-Germans that he, himself, was a Conservative
but was losing patience with the Party leadership,
which was doing nothing to change the censorship
situation.[101] This was not the first instance in which
a Conservative member had expressed unhappiness with
Party policy during the War, but it was the first time
it had been done in a non-Conservative environment.

Westarp, in fact, had received an extremely critical
letter from v. Graefe in June[102] in which the Conservative
Reichstag Deputy attacked the "feminine government" of
Bethmann Hollweg as well as Conservative support of the
Chancellor. "Something is rotten in the state of Denmark
of our Conservative Party," v. Graefe had written, "and
there is no more passion among our leadership." Yet in
September, another prominent Conservative, the *Herrenhaus*
member, Count Tiele-Winkler, sent an anti-annexations
petition with thirty signatures to Bethmann, in which the
Conservative had tried to show the Chancellor "that not
all Germany stands behind the annexationist propoganda
of the six economic associations."[103]

The unity which had once marked the German
Conservative Party was at an end by the year 1915.
Definite points of disagreement over war-aims, Bethmann
Hollweg, Pan-German influence and the direction of
German society separated two distinct camps within the
Party.

On the one side were a large number of *Herrenhaus*
Conservatives, whose opposition to any deviations from
the teachings of Stahl and v. Gerlach had been well-
documented from the time of Tivoli. Usually powerless,
their opposition this time took on a major significance.
Firmly behind Bethmann, they supported a separate peace
with Russia and held an aristocratic world-view to be
more important than Pan-German propoganda or BdL agrarian
ideology. Among them could be counted Tiele-Winkler,
Count Seidlitz-Sandreczki, Count Schulenberg, and v.
Heydebreck. In the Prussian House of Deputies there were
v. Kessel, v. Schuckmann, Count Groebern and v. d. Osten.
Finally, there was Heydebrand.[104]

184

Radicals and Reactionaries

On the other side, in what one might call the
voelkisch camp, were such ADV-oriented Conservatives
as v. Grumme-Douglas, Salm Horstmar, v. Hertzberg Lottin,
v. Somnitz and v. Graefe.[105] One could also count almost
the whole of the BdL, including Roesicke and v. Wangenheim.
Only Westarp was able, at this time, to avoid any
classification.

It was v. Graefe who distinguished himself as the
most persistent critic of the Party in 1915. *Voelkisch*-
oriented, anti-Semitic, in touch with key ADV members,
and a devotee of the "strong man" as leader theory,
v. Graefe was also a keen student of the moods of German
society. As a soldier in the trenches, he was strangely
prophetic in a letter to Westarp in April,[106] in which
v. Graefe analyzed the mood of those at the very heart
of Germany's defense: "From the attitudes of our field
grays I know that after the war, a leader that really
wishes to lead, will be able to implement his plans
much easier than ever before."

But it was in a letter to Hans v. Liebig, on the last
day of 1915, that v. Graefe gave an indication of just
how deeply the rift in the Conservative Party had gone
and just how much antipathy there existed toward the
traditional world of Conservative politics:[107]

> If we Conservatives ever tried to approach
> the National Liberals with a secret proposal
> of cooperation, within a short period of time
> the judaized National Liberal press would raise
> a furor against the Chancellor-purging Conservatives.
> This it would do in order to try and convince the
> naive German people, the "unpolitical of the world",
> of the loss of power of the ruling *Junker* caste.
> For, "naturally," Conservative opposition to the
> "B" system[108] stems "only" from their trembling
> fear of an end to their national might through
> Bethmann's desire to reform the Prussian Voting
> Law.
> This domestic delusion and confusion, for
> which we can thank the wretched use of lowly Party
> secretaries as our main political speakers, is a
> national misfortune...For not only the nation in
> a narrow sense, but the "intelligentsia" follows
> these lies...May the year 1916 gain many recruits
> for "our" struggle.

185

CHAPTER VIII

New Parties and Old Politics: The Further
Radicalization of the German Right (1916)

i.   Heydebrand loses control and Westarp responds

1

As the War entered its third year, Heydebrand wrote
a letter to Westarp in which he closed with the
following thought: "These times necessitate a closer
cooperation between you and me than ever before."[1]
Superficially read, perhaps, it was an indication of
Heydebrand's confidence and trust in his Conservative
associate.   Yet seen within the context of our study,
it sounded suspiciously like a statement written out
of desperation and fear.   For by the beginning of 1916,
Heydebrand's position as leader of the German Conservative
Party was in jeopardy.   Isolated, hundreds of kilometers
from Berlin, in his Silesisan estate at Tschunkawe, the
"uncrowned King of Prussia" and the embodiment of old
Prussian conservatism sat atop his throne, shorn of most
of the respect and support of the German Right.   It was
now Westarp who made the day-to-day decisions of
Conservative policy and who carried out the difficult
task of preserving the Party's waning influence in and
out of the *Reichstag*.   Heydebrand, no doubt, grasped
the significance of maintaining the closest possible
connections to his younger colleague.   As noted,
Westarp had enjoyed more than a nodding acquaintance
with the leaders of the ADV--and for the Count to turn
against Heydebrand would have entirely eroded the
Conservative Chairman's already shaky base of power.
It was fortunate for Heydebrand that Westarp still
possessed a half-hidden awe for his legendary political
leader.[2]

The fear of total political isolation within his
own party, it seems, lay behind the startling news that
Heydebrand now supported the annexation of two eastern
war aims--Courland and Lithuania.[3]   In his own
interpretation, Class had assumed that this had meant
full Conservative Party support for his programme and
the disposal of any "reluctancy" on its part.   It
was exactly the interpretation that Heydebrand had hoped
for, since it eliminated, temporarily, a major part of
the opposition that had built up against him.[4]   It
also allowed for the possibility of regaining the degree
of power within the Party and Prussia which had once
earned him the accolades of the Right and the grudging
recognition of the Left.

Radicals and Reactionaries

Confident that his acceptance of the two eastern
war aims had given him some time to consider strategy
without the pressure of Pan-German criticism, Heydebrand
went on the offensive. He let it be known that, after
a period of tactical "hesitancy",[5] he was joining the
growing conspiracy against Bethmann Hollweg, in which
Heydebrand had played such an important, if unsuccessful,
pre-war role: "The conspiracy against Bethmann...must
go forth."[6] Yet it would be a mistake to assume that
his reasons were in any manner related to the Pan-Germans
in their efforts to remove the Chancellor. Whereas the
ADV sought to get rid of Bethmann because he frustrated
their grandiose war-aims programme, Heydebrand admitted
privately that Conservative demands from Bethmann in
1916 "are no different than in 1909 or 1912/13."[7] In
other words, Heydebrand wanted Bethmann out because of the
continuing problem of direct property taxes[8] and the
Chancellor's apparently lax attitude toward the Social
Democrats. Furthermore, his opposition to Bethmann
remained covert--hidden as it was in the lines of
correspondence and the conversation of secret meetings.
In no way did the Conservative leader wish to have his
political party or his name linked to an anti-Bethmann
clique or to a common conspiracy with the Pan-German
League.

Because Heydebrand chose to spin his intrigues in
secret, the Conservative Party came under heavy political
fire from several quarters. Especially the Pan-German
leaders, v. Gebsattel and Class, and Pan-German
Conservatives, such as v. Grumme and Prince Salm, were
infuriated that v. Heydebrand took such a seemingly
conciliatory attitude toward Bethmann.[9] Little did
they realize that it was part of his tactical maneuvering
in an attempt to keep the Chancellor off his guard. And
on several other points, Heydebrand brought renewed
attacks upon himself. He continued to maintain the
closest of relations with Hoetzsch, who was now charged
by the ADV with being a "tool" of the government.[10]
Heydebrand, furthermore, scoffed at the idea of a
"national movement" to secure a "German" peace through
the use of unrestricted submarine warfare. Although
the idea was gaining an impressive number of recruits,
he thought that such a movement was "very premature"
and might have "bad side effects." When informed that
several of the extra-parliamentary associations were
suggesting the creation of a "great national party",
he commented that one always met a "certain naivete"
when dealing with such groups.[11]

Yet the "certain naivete" was displayed by
Heydebrand in thinking that his tactical approach to
politics would remain unnoticed. One after another,
attempts to recapture some of his and the Party's
old charisma with spectacular political feats came to
nought. An attempt by the Conservative Deputy,
v. Kessel, to seek a "meeting of reconciliation" with
Kaiser Wilhelm resulted, as v. Hindenburg informed
Bethmann, in the "Kaiser's attitude against the
Conservatives being more hostile than ever."[12]
Relatedly, Bethmann's suspicions and fears toward
Heydebrand increased. The Chancellor had immediately
assumed that v. Kessel had been sent to see Wilhelm
in order to stir up differences between the Kaiser and
Bethmann.[13] To make matters worse, *Bund der Landwirte*
resentment grew as Heydebrand and Westarp continued to
veto its request to allow Kapp to stand as a Conservative
candidate in a forth-coming by-election.[14] Moderate
conservatives, too, such as v. Valentini, saw Heydebrand's
anti-Bethmann stance as politically and ideologically
"suicidal."[15] Slowly, then, a sort of political impotence
was overtaking the "uncrowned King of Prussia"--brought
on by both "moderates" and "extremists."

In mid-1916, Heydebrand received one of the
periodic reports sent to him at Tschunkawe by the Central
Association of the German Conservative Party in Berlin.[16]
The news was not good. Dissension within the Party,
according to the report, was still widespread over the
question of Germany's main enemy: England or Russia;
the *Kreuzzeitung* was receiving increasing criticism of
its political "prevarication." The newspaper would
only hold the command of the majority of Party members,
the report went on, "when it becomes extreme...it is
impossible for it to continue a middle-line." The
report also indicated that the Conservatives had to
hold "some kind of progressive-looking rally if we are
not to be isolated." In addition, the financial situation
within the Party was disastrous and there was a desperate
need to "get close to heavy industry" in order to secure
much-needed funding. But it was the final point of
the report which must have caused Heydebrand excessive
grief: a large part of the *Herrenhaus* Conservatives
were defending Bethmann against any attacks; the Party
was fully split on the question of war-aims and, finally,
numerous reports had been coming in of deep-seated
differences of opinion between Heydebrand and Westarp
on questions concerning the Kaiser, Bethmann, the
Government and war aims.

188

Radicals and Reactionaries

Despite his worsening political position, Heydebrand chose to continue a series of speaking engagements. On August 13, he spoke in Frankfurt am Main. The setting and audience were neither agrarian nor Prussian Conservative. It is for this reason, perhaps, that Heydebrand delivered a speech much franker than any the politically-experienced Conservative might have given in Berlin or East Prussia. He began his comments by presenting a glowing description of industry:

> Where would Germany have been, my friends, if not for the glorious contribution of our industry? Do you seriously believe that we could have maintained this glorious war effort if it had not been for the great sacrifices made by our German industry?

These references were an obvious attempt to begin the process of "getting near" the huge coffers of industrial finance, so badly needed by the financially-troubled Conservative Party. Yet Heydebrand admitted to the audience that "we were not economically prepared for this war," a fact which the BdL membership was certain to view with much displeasure, since they had maintained all along, ever since their meeting with Delbrueck on May 25, 1914, that Germany would have more than adequate food supplies for the War's duration. Even more out of character was Heydebrand's admission that the Conservative Party was disunited and composed of both moderate and extremist elements. He also chose to single out England as Germany's main enemy, a position no doubt guaranteed to bring about the wrath of the Pan-Germans. If this were not enough, Heydebrand spoke of Russia in neutral, almost conciliatory tones:

> What we must do about Russia remains a very, very difficult question. In my view it would be very unreasonable to allow her borders to remain as they were. We owe at least that much to the border areas of Germany that have suffered so much in this war. I really can't see any other type of *arrangement* (italics mine-AJP) with Russia.

No mention was made of Russia as a "deadly enemy", a label which Heydebrand was quick to apply to both the French and English. Finally, the Conservative leader concluded his talk with a timid, almost positive, discussion of the SPD.[17]

Without knowing it, Heydebrand had finally committed
political suicide. A torrent of abuse came hurtling
down from the Party and it was directed more at the man
than at the contents of his speech. Heydebrand had
overstepped the boundaries of political ethics: he
had criticized his own party while hardly bothering to
attack the "internal and external" enemy, and in front
of a non-Conservative audience. Westarp tried to spare
Heydebrand from having to endure much of the criticism.
He wrote to tell him that he had heard good comments about
the speech from various sides of the Party.[18] In reality,
however, Westarp was receiving a majority of letters
like the one from the Conservative Deputy, Kresse:[19]

> Heydebrand is now leader in name only. He
> has, without a doubt, become old like Spahn of
> the Center and it would be a good thing if he
> resigned quite soon. As soon as Heydebrand
> goes, all the blame for what the Conservatives
> will do or miss will fall...upon you.

Westarp had no choice but to accept the burden of
Conservative leadership. His moderating influence was
the only factor which allowed the Party to remain united,
if only in appearance. In actual fact, Conservative
members were divided upon almost every issue ranging
from foreign affairs to the struggle against Bethmann.

A clear example of this disunity was in the question
of war aims. Although the Party had aligned itself more
closely to the demands of the ADV, Westarp, like Heydebrand,
continued to demonstrate a reluctance to commit the Party
to exorbitant territorial demands. This he did with
the full knowledge that the *Deutsche Zeitung* (a strongly
Pan-German newspaper-AJP) will most certainly attack
the Conservative Party as defeatist."[20] As late as
December 1916, Westarp insisted that "the Party is in no
position to demand war aims that involve the conquest of
territories not yet in our hands."[21] The Conservative
Party was able to propogate this view despite the fact
that radical Conservatives constantly proposed wildly
annexationist programmes[22] and the BdL continued to
demand large territorial conquests in the east as
counterweights to industrial "gains" in the west.[23]
Westarp even preferred "the acquisition of Briey to
Warsaw as a war aim."[24]

Unlike some of his contemporaries, Westarp was
realistic enough to understand that a decisive military
defeat of Germany's enemies "is not possible in the
foreseeable future."[25] Consequently, when Hoetzsch, in

September 1916, spoke of the Party's war aims, they
reflected the moderate realism set forth by Westarp:[26]

1. The security of Germany's borders against
   France and Russia; the guarantee of Austria's
   continued position as a Great Power; the
   guarantee that Bulgaria would maintain a
   port; Turkey's continued security.
2. A guarantee against future attack by England;
   Germany's possession of the coast of Flanders.
3. The guarantee of Germany's colonial and
   continental presence.
4. Germany's guaranteed place among the concert
   of nations.

A few months later this moderation went a step further.
In a *Kreuzzeitung* article, Hoetzsch speculated on the
possible consequences of an independent Poland (which
the Conservatives opposed), whose creation was sure to
effect Prussian policies towards its Polish population.
He admitted that Prussia had not governed her Poles
very effectively and that a "basic revision of Prussia's
Polish legislation is essential and cannot wait until
the War's end."[27]

Westarp's attempts to maintain Party unity were
hampered severely by the ever-increasing fragility of
the *Burgfrieden*, the monarchically-imposed political
truce which had been in effect since the start of war.
Since that time, however, Bethmann's attempts at a
middle course between left and right had achieved little
in cementing the Kaiser's stirring recognition of
Germans and not political parties. In a report written
at the end of 1915, Interior Minister v. Loebell noted
this failure:[28]

> The Government has not been able to support
> fully the aims of the Right because it would
> then sacrifice the absolutely necessary step
> of trying to incorporate the SPD into our
> national political life. Neither has it been
> able, quite obviously, to turn to the Left...

Bethmann's lack of success only aided in convincing
many political groups in the Empire that the Chancellor
had to go. The BdL chose to be devious about its
feelings and actions, as Roesicke related to Westarp:[29]

> We will have a much better chance to
> influence Bethmann if we assure him that we
> don't wish to purge him, only make him see
> the correctness of our ways.

191

The Pan-Germans, on the other hand, were totally
committed to ousting the Chancellor at any price;
according to Gebsattel,[30] the path to Germany's victory
was clouded by his continued presence: "I don't
know how all of this is going to end if we don't
remove him."

By August the framework for a conspiracy against
Bethmann had been completed. Its presence was no
secret and was investigated by the Chief State's
Attorney for the province of Berlin. He was able to
report that "the following people are working against
Bethmann Hollweg: v. Liebig, Lehmann, Heinrich Worms,
v. Bodelschwingh, Dr. Neumann and Dr. Heinrich Pudor."[31]
Additionally, in June, the ADV and elements of heavy
industry had created the *Unabhaengiger Ausschuss fuer
einen deutschen Frieden* (Independent Committee for a
German Peace) under the leadership of Dr. Dietrich
Schaefer.[32] The Independent Committee was formed
from the nucleus of academic and economic interest
groups that had been responsible for the various war-
aims petitions of 1914-15. It passed itself off as
an exponent of the "true" opinion of the *Volk*. In
its capacity as a "movement beyond the political parties",[33]
it was used as a vehicle to attack publicly the advocates
of a "rotten peace." In actual fact, by attacking the
Government and the *Reichstag* as well as the SPD and the
trade unions, it was admitting to the failure of the
Burgfrieden as a manipulated attempt at social harmony.

A large number of radical conservatives flocked to
join the new conspiracy. The files of the Independent
Committee listed the following *Bund* members: Roesicke,
v. Wangenheim, Schmitz-Huebsch, and Weilnboeck. And
notably, an even larger number of Conservative Party
members appeared on the membership lists: v. Grumme-
Douglas, Graef, Hoesch, Kapp, Reventlow, Count Roon,
v. Richthofen-Mertschuetz, Salm-Horstmar, Hertzberg-
Lottin, v. Graefe and Baecker.[34] In early August,
Reventlow publicly attacked the Chancellor in Munich.
His speech, which also criticized the *Reichstag* and
the political parties, was received with wild enthusiasm
from the audience.[35] Shocked by the sudden outburst of
anti-Bethmann feeling, the SPD politician, Ernst David,
noted in his diary the realization by the Left that the
brief period of Germany's domestic peace was over:[36]

> Anger over the blinding agitation of the
> Conservative and National Liberal annexationists;
> Heydebrand, Westarp, Fuhrmann, Gebsattel; the

naive belief in the omnipotence of force;...The
reactionaries believe in all seriousness that
their time has come.

Because the Conservative Party had so swelled
the ranks of the Independent Committee, it was assumed
that the entire Conservative leadership had lent its
support to the organization. In fact, quite the opposite
was true. Since June, the official Party policy had been
to restrict sharply its criticism of Bethmann both in
public speeches and in the columns of the *Kreuzzeitung*.
Such a policy had become necessary after Bethmann had
openly denounced several anti-Government publications
(especially those written by Kapp, v. Liebig and Franz
Sontag)[37] as the work of "pirates of public opinion."
According to a letter written to Westarp by Bruno
Schroeter, General Secretary of the Party, "many letters
have come in, especially from the battlefield, criticizing
our position against a Chancellor who gives such excellent
and energetic speeches...We have now been put on the
defensive and it would not be crucial if we abandoned
this part of our domestic agitation."[38] Nevertheless,
Westarp continued to be put under pressure by radical
Conservatives who demanded that the Party join the
anti-Bethmann conspiracy.[39]

Yet Westarp was also under pressure of a different
sort. During 1916 various articles had been written
by moderate conservatives, demanding that the German
working-class become the object of wide-ranging reform
in Germany's employment laws. This was moderate
conservatism's solution to the defeat of the SPD and
the integration of the working-class into the national
State. As Dietrich v. Oertzen observed:[40]

> Now is the time, if ever, when a new
> employment law must be created. In this
> manner will it be possible to change the
> old, unfruitful revolutionary workers'
> movement into a fruitful reform party.

Even more strident was the continuing call, brought forth
by other moderates, for the Conservative Party to open
its ranks to the *Volk*. In an article printed in the
Konservative Monatschrift, Dr. Friedrich Thimme ended
such a call by warning the Party that "the Conservatives
can be nothing without the *Volk* and must exist only for
the *Volk*."[41]

Obviously worried by such demands, Westarp was
forced to take some sort of action. In September he
wrote to a representative of the Hamburg shipbuilding

193

industry, assuring him that "I am in the position of
now understanding, with the greatest amount of
sympathy, the position of the shipbuilders'
associations."[42] Two months later, Westarp declared
that the Conservatives "now see the necessity of
creating a 'yellow' (nationalist workers' trade-union-AJP)
seat in the *Reichstag*. We Conservatives are ready to
make available such a seat in one of our secure voting
districts."[43]

Yet Westarp's difficulties remained minimal in
comparison to those faced by the Chancellor. Beset by
attacks from the *voelkisch* camp and growing calls for
his replacement by a "strong man",[44] Bethmann decided
to go on the offensive. In addition to his "pirates of
public opinion speech", he directed that rebuttals to
the Bethmann *fronde* be written and made public.[45] He
also sought to split the conspiracy by removing the
opposition of the Conservatives to his political presence.
As a result, he allowed the Prussian *Landtag* to introduce,
in early 1917, a bill calling for the restructuring of
the *Fideikommis* (entail) law. The passage of this
legislation would have meant an increase in the economic
privileges of the *Junkers*.[46]

Bethmann's strategy, however, was based on a misreading
of the political situation. He, like many others, had
been deceived into believing that the attacks of radical
Conservatives had been a part of the official Conservative
Party policy. In fact, the growing demands that Bethmann
be replaced either by General v. Falkenhayn,[47] Chief of
the General Staff, or by Tirpitz[48] were the actions of
individual members of the Bethmann *fronde*. Moreover,
when the incompetent v. Falkenhayn was finally replaced
by Generals Hindenburg and Ludendorff in August, Bethmann
seemed totally unaware that the radical Right now believed
it had gone a long way in finding Germany's saviors.
In fact, as Gerald Feldman has noted, "Bethmann *wanted*
(italics Feldman's-AJP) to believe that Germany could be
saved by Hindenburg and Ludendorff."[49]

As the power of the two Generals began to assert
itself in late 1916, and as their early reluctance to
oppose Bethmann[50] turned into an active participation
in the conspiracy,[51] Westarp once more faced a crucial
decision: in what manner should the Party deal with
Hindenburg and Ludendorff? Again, Westarp took the
initiative in policy formation, and once more he took
a position based more on tactical considerations than
on an active desire to be included in political conspiracy.
To Heydebrand he wrote that "meeting with Hindenburg and

Ludendorff, or more rightly with the latter, will do
us no harm. But we must not be the Party that attempts
to grab the initiative in order to politically influence
both men."[52] His meeting with the two on November 14
apparently followed precisely this strategy.[53] But
Bethmann's meeting with them, at the end of December,
had other results, as he explained to v. Valentini:[54]

> I now understand that the essential
> characteristic of their (Hindenburg and
> Ludendorff-AJP) goals remains dictatorial
> rule and its consequent aim--the complete
> militarization of our way of life.

At the end of 1916 it was not the Conservative Party
that made the difference in Imperial politics. That
period of history had given way to the rise of the
voelkisch agitator and the growing might of two
military leaders.

ii. The BdL faces realities

For the BdL, the events within the Conservative
Party only reaffirmed its growing doubt as to that
party's continued political viability. If, in 1915,
Hugenberg could have written to Class that "a full
cooperation (by the ADV-AJP) with the BdL is not
possible until there is unity in the Conservative Party",[55]
the circumstances that lay behind that statement no
longer applied in 1916. Firstly, the cooperation between
the *Bund der Landwirte* and the Conservatives on economic
policy (price ceilings) no longer existed.[56] There was,
furthermore, no longer any unity within the BdL, itself,
on the matter. V. Wangenheim had changed his viewpoint
and now agreed with Kapp on the principle of "economic
freedom",[57] whereas Roesicke maintained the earlier
agrarian point of view.[58] As a result, v. Wangenheim
solidified his relations with heavy industry (Hugenberg
and Stinnes), whereas, in 1914/15, he had bitterly
opposed the industrialists' scheme to obtain the highest
prices possible for their products.[59] Secondly, the
BdL was no longer confident of the Conservatives' ability
to provide adequate leadership of the parliamentary Right.
Such doubt had begun in 1913, when the Conservatives had
emerged from the tax debates in an isolated and semi-
powerless position. Despite *Bund* attempts to aid that
isolation, the Party remained weak and without influence.
By 1916, this situation remained largely unchanged.

Towards the end of 1916, v. Wangenheim addressed himself precisely to this problem. Uppermost in his mind was the growing storm of criticism leveled at the *Reichstag*, but especially at the parties of the Right:[60]

> I must talk to the Conservatives about the life and death struggle we are in. If they lose this opportunity they are finished in the country for good. There's a growing opinion in Germany that regards political parties as unimportant. I have just recently told Heydebrand that the Party which wishes to have the future in its hands is that which becomes the mouthpiece and leader of the real *nationalgesinnte* cirlces within Germany.

V. Wangenheim, in fact, was concerned about more than just the future of the Conservatives. The *Bund* itself had lost much of its former influence. It was no longer an equal in its coalition with the ADV. In March, Class had called for a *Kartell* of organizations to form the basis of a "national opposition" to Bethmann Hollweg.[61] The *Bund* found itself no longer the driving force behind the *Kartell* idea, but one of the many organizations under the "holding company" direction of the ADV.

Shortly thereafter, v. Wangenheim wrote to Roesicke that "there now exists a tendency to shunt our organization to one side. We should take our group and initiate a merger with other large organizations as a 'firm necessity of the times'."[62] But by August, the *Bund* had achieved little success.[63] With the Conservatives in near-total disarray and their own *Sammlung* plans thwarted, the *Bund* was left with little choice if it wished to continue to protect agrarian interests and remain involved with the new direction of Imperial politics. Indeed, v. Wangenheim was forced to admit that:[64]

> If the Conservatives... and other ecomomic groups, as such, have failed, then there remains nothing left for us than to participate in the dealings of the (ADV-created-AJP) Independent Committee for a German Peace and lend our name to it.

iii. The ADV: from conspiracy to anti-Semitism

1

   At about the same time, the ADV made several
strategic moves in order to improve its position of
strength and influence in German politics.[65] It, first
of all, sought to further its relations with heavy
industry and, especially, with Krupp von Bohlen and
Halbach, with whom it had been at odds over war aims
and Bethmann since early in the War.[66] This positive
step resulted in a contribution of 25,000 Marks to the
ADV in early January.[67] The initiator of this planned
overture to industry was O. H. Hopfen, an aide to Class.
Hopfen had very good reasons for such a course of action.
In June 1915, he had suggested to Class that the ADV
should become the foundation of a "great national Party"
of the Right to be called the "German Society of Might
(Battlefield Grey)." His plan had not been successful
for two reasons: Hopfen had sought support for the
Party in more liberal south German industrial circles
and had failed and, too, Class was reluctant to found
such a movement lest he alienate the Conservatives, whose
full support he (at that time) still hoped to obtain.[68]

   But now, at the end of 1916, Hopfen had planned
his strategy somewhat differently. He arranged for a
meeting between the coal and iron magnates of western
Germany and Salm-Horstmar, the ADV Conservative. As
moderator of the meeting, Hopfen began by declaring
that none of the early groups created for the purpose
of influencing governmental and public opinion in the
matter of Pan-German war aims had been successful. He
suggested that what was really needed was an organization
that had the ADV as its foundation. For this, both
the membership of the ADV (16,500 at the end of 1915)
and its finances, to the tune of 500,000 Marks, had to
be increased. Class made only one contirbution to
the meeting--that Bethmann had to be "fought at any
cost" for his domestic and foreign failures. As a
result of the meeting, the drive for ADV funds, known
as the *Sammlung Salm*, had collected nearly 150,000
Marks by the end of 1916.[69]

   Class, however, was still not firmly convinced
that a "national party" would be the answer to the
growing foreign and domestic difficulties of the nation.
He continued to maintain his focus upon Bethmann and
held him, as mentioned, fully responsible for the failure
of the ADV programme (partly because of censorship) to
influence little more than a fraction of German society

and for the renewed political threat of the SPD. As
a result, he decided to attempt, personally, to replace
the Chancellor with someone who would fit the Class
image of the "strong man" in the *Reich* leadership. His
final choice was Tirpitz. But in March 1916, Class was
unable to convince Hindenburg and Ludendorff, by then
the most influential of military leaders, of the
necessity to replace Bethmann. To complicate matters
further, Tirpitz refused to have any association with
the scheme. To save political face, Class dismissed
Tirpitz as being "just as bad" as Bethmann.[70]

Convinced that such attempts would remain unsuccessful,
Class decided that only a movement that could influence
public opinion to remove Bethmann would succeed. On
March 25, he ordered that a "national opposition" to
Bethmann be organized by the following groups: ADV, BdL,
Eastern Marches Association, Army League and the Independent
Committee for a German Peace under Professor Dietrich
Schaefer.[71]

While Class was experiencing frustration in his
attempts to remove Bethmann, his second-in command,
v. Gebsattel, was giving the problems of war aims and
the future of the Prusso-German state his utmost
consideration. In a letter to Georg Schiele, a
Conservative and close friend of Kapp, he expressed
his concern:[72]

> I am worried over our returning veterans
> and the question they will ask : "What have
> we sacrificed for?" And what if they find
> nothing? Therein lies the great danger.

Externally, v. Gebsattel was convinced that Germany
had to become the leading power on the European continent.
This was to be achieved through the creation of a Central
European Economic Community with Germany as the dominant
nation. In addition, Germany had to obtain a large enough
colonial empire so that she could maintain an autarchic
economy through needed goods imported from abroad.[73]

Domestically, however, v. Gebsattel was at a loss
for solutions. Outside of the limited success of inner
colonization as a rallying point of the Right,[74] nothing
else had been effective. As he told Graf Roon, v. Gebsattel
had lost all confidence in Heydebrand and Westarp.[75] And
since the Tirpitz failure, he had ruled out the idea of a
coup, for "who would the strong man be?"[76] In May,
however, during a discussion with ADV member, Berthold
Koerting, v. Gebsattel believed he had found the solution.

198

Koerting had suggested, along the same lines as Hopfen, that the ADV found a "new party" which would incorporate all *staatserhaltende* elements. V. Gebsattel immediately brought the suggestion to Class, who promised to consider it. In correspondnece with his chairman, v. Gebsattel urged Class to found such a party "because the battle against the Jews and traders must be taken up before it is too late."[77]

To Class, the soundness of such a plan was unmistakable. Despite his continuing hope of convincing the Conservatives to support his aims, a close reading of the events told Class that the Conservatives were a political party on the decline, whose support he no longer needed. Furthermore, the ideological mentor, Houston Stewart Chamberlain, by now a German citizen and ADV member,[78] had been developing a line of reasoning that could not help but influence the ADV head. In a letter to the ADV member and *voelkisch* publisher, J. H. Lehmann of Munich, Chamberlain wrote of his concept: the creation of a new German political system in which there would be "a destruction of the present parties, a throwing out of all professional politicians and their replacement with men of real interests."[79] And the radical Conservative Deputy, Albrecht v. Graefe, closer, perhaps, than most to the real "spirit of 1914", wrote from the battlefield that he saw "the voices of the trenches growing against all parties--especially against the Right."[80] None of this was particularly new. We have seen it on various occasions when the Conservative system felt itself threatened by Social Democracy and a general "democratizing" spirit. But it was now a time of "total" war where passions remained at a fever pitch. In such a situation, where values were constantly being revalued,[81] what had failed in the past could, in such an atmosphere, succeed in the present.

Although Kapp, Schiele and, even, v. Wangenheim worked throughout the summer to coordinate all *nationalgesinnte* groups under the general command of the ADV, the results were, at best, moderate.[82] Books and pamphlets by Hans v. Liebig, Junius Alter (Franz Sontag), and Kapp, attacking Bethmann's politics, had barely influenced public opinion:[83] an ADV report of August stated that there was hardly any real opposition to Bethmann except by the Pan-Germans.[84] The turning point seems to have come in September. From Chemnitz came a report that the city's largest industrialists "who previously did not care about the ADV are all now coming over to our side."[85]

The decision to form a new party was up to Class.
He surveyed the various names that has already been
suggested: from Koerting came the name "The German
Party";[86] Count Hoensbroech suggested "The Party of
Action";[87] most importantly, Schiele led a group of
radical Conservatives who advocated the founding of a
new Conservative Party which would be known as the
"Conservative *Mittelstand* Party."[88] The latter
suggestion must have intrigued Class, for it meant that
Heydebrand's hold on Conservative Party personnel had
been considerably weakened, and that the basis for a
more *voelkisch*-oriented conservatism was now possible.
Finally, reports began to come in from East Prussia,
Mecklenburg and Pomerania that the ADV had, at long
last, set up district and local branches.[89] Heinrich
Class, no doubt, returned in thought to that day in 1910
when Heydebrand had vowed that the ADV would never penetrate
"our still uncontaminated East." Now, it seemed, both
Heydebrand and his impenetrable political territory
were broken. Class agreed that it was time to found
a "great national party."[90]

2

With the onset of war, the *Burgfrieden*, accompanied
by stringent censorship laws, had effectively silenced
the voice of organized anti-Semitism. By 1914, the
anti-Semitic movement, formerly represented by small
parliamentary groups, had finally yielded to the
extraparliamentary agitation of the ADV and its
affiliated groups:[91]

> ...there no longer existed a conventional
> parliamentary brand of anti-Semitism that could
> withstand the appeal of the revolutionaries.
> The failure of the anti-Semitic parties left
> the field open to Fritsch, Class and their
> friends.

Yet the Pan-Germans considered it unwise, at first, to
carry on the mission which Gebsattel had outlined when
he listed the "Jewish Problem" among the most important
questions of the War. For nearly two years, little
was heard from the *voelkisch* camp.

In the meantime, Jews had succeeded in distinguishing
themselves on the battlefield and off, demonstrating an
enthusiasm for the *Vaterland* motivated, in part, by the
need to prove once and for all their claim to be both
Germans and Jews. Another motivating factor, no doubt,
was the opportunity to prove it.

200

Radicals and Reactionaries

By 1916, this enthusiasm had been translated into
a newly-found self-confidence. Hermann Goldschmitt,
for instance, could claim that both Jews and Germans
had been chosen to "fulfill a great cultural mission
during the War." He went on to state that:[92]

> The prophets regarded the Jews as the
> people of God, Fichte regarded the Germans
> as the source of all humanity. Now both
> peoples have chosen themselves for this task.

So little thought was given to the problem of German
anti-Semitism that the Jewish financier, Max Warburg,
was more concerned for the plight of the Jews in Poland.
Warburg was convinced that if captured Poland were given
over fully to Austria-Hungary, then "the outbreak of
a strong anti-Semitic wave" would surely occur.[93]

Such confidence, however, was short-lived. At
about the same time that attacks against Bethmann and
the *Reichstag* began to tear apart further the nearly
twenty-four months of domestic harmony, noticeable
signs of a renewed round of vicious anti-Semitism
began to appear. As could be expected, the ADV lay
behind the initial action of 1916, circulating a
petition in February which would have "prohibited
foreigners" from entering Germany. The move was directed
against the *Ostjuden* (eastern Jews) who were arriving
in the *Reich* to fill vital manpower needs.[94] During the
same month, the *voelkisch* writer, Kurd v. Strantz,
declared that "it is extremely painful to watch the
Imperial Chancellor being protected by the Jew
newspapers."[95] In March, this alleged connection was
made the subject of an attack by the prominent anti-
Semite, F. v. Bodelschwingh, who (besides attacking
the Conservative Party for its laxity on the "Jewish
Question") stated that "the Chancellor, as everyone
can plainly see, is completely tied to Jewry."[96]

During the summer months of 1916, at the same time
that the *fronde* against Bethmann was nearing completion,
several *voelkisch* newspapers, silent for nearly two
years, began to emerge from their obscurity.[97] In
addition, many German cities were the scenes of anti-
Jewish sloganeering.[98] The anti-Bethmann conspiracy
was clearly demonstrating the direction of its politics:
it was engaging once more in the defence of the Prusso-
German state, this time with the vanguard of a
revolutionary conservatism leading the way by attacking
socialism and Jewry to get at Bethmann.

201

The intensity of public opinion began, during the middle and end of 1916, to focus upon the Jew. He began to replace the agrarian as the "usurer" in the public image[99] and his whole contribution to the war effort was put into question. Once more it was the ADV and its associates that set the standard for anti-Semitic propaganda. Beginning in the autumn of 1916, the ADV decreed that comprehensive sets of "Jewish statistics" be kept to judge the quantity and quality of the Jewish "contributions" to the war effort.[100] On October 11, the effectiveness of the ADV campaign was demonstrated in a meeting of the Budget Committee of the War Office. Aided by their link to the OHL, Colonel Max Bauer, the Pan-Germans introduced the questionability of Jewish participation in the War and caused that particular topic to emerge as a major area of discussion among the military. At the meeting, anti-Semitic officers demanded to know government statistics showing how many Jews had entered military service voluntarily, how many had fallen at the front or had received the Iron Cross, Class I or II. A week later, on October 19, during a meeting of the Committee on Food Questions, the leading politicians of the *Reich*, among them Erzberger, demanded to know similar sorts of answers. The search for a political scapegoat had begun.[101]

Part of the Pan-German tactic was to aid in the creation of a united and *voelkisch* anti-Semitic organization, created from the numerous *voelkisch* groups then in existence. Yet the ADV still thought it "dangerous" to associate openly with such a movement.[102] Instead, Gebsattel suggested that the various associations join the ranks of the ADV as full members. "This will be no problem," he wrote to the editor of the anti-Semitic *Political-Anthropological Journal* at the beginning of 1917, "for the ADV is led by a spirit of acute anti-Semitism. Our support is the first step in order to advance on the path that we both wish to travel."[103] That path, Gebsattel assured his nephew Theodor, would soon lead *voelkisch* Germany to the "most dangerous battle faced by the German *Reich*. It will only come after peace has been achieved--and it will be waged against the Jews."[104]

CHAPTER IX

Between Fatherland and *Volk:* Increasing Democratization
and the Last Gasp of the Prusso-German State (1917)

i. For the German Conservatives the situation worsens.

By early 1917 it had become apparent that Heydebrand
had lost control of the German Conservative Party. His
most spectacular failure had occurred at the end of 1916
when he attempted to intercede, without success, in a
conflict between *Herrenhaus* Conservatives and the Party
leadership. A main factor in *Herrenhaus* resentment
was a feeling of neglect in major policy decisions
concerning the direction of Conservative aims. Deeper,
still, was their conviction that Conservative principles
had been sacrificed for the sake of political appearance.[1]

Heydebrand and Westarp were forced to bear the
enormous burden of a divided Party. On February 18,
every conceivable resentment that had developed over a
period of three years was openly and bitterly expressed.
The occasion was a meeting of the Party's General
Executive Committee. To begin with, Pan-German
Conservatives cited several "failings" on the part of
both v. Heydebrand and Westarp. Among the most severe
charges were that: neither leader had been energetic
enough in important "national" questions, primarily the
issue of war aims; neither man had endorsed meetings
that dealt specifically with war aims; they had continually
denied Kapp the opportunity to stand as a Conservative
candidate in East Prussia; they had taken no part (!) in
the national opposition against Bethmann. *Herrenhaus*
Conservatives, on the other hand, led by Count Seidlitz,
took an opposing view. They praised the two leaders for
not having participated, in Seidlitz's words, "in the
cheap fireworks of a *Fronde*" against the Chancellor.
Seidlitz then reminded the assembled Conservatives that
the Party "must be directed by principles and not by
opinion."[2]

But Conservative principles would not bail the
Party out of its growing financial crisis;[3] nor would
they bring it back into an influential position in the
Reichstag or stop the daily demand by the SPD for
reforms in the Prussian Voting Law. Throughout the
early months of 1917, these problems, and not the
concern over principles, dominated Conservative thought
and action. Yet, despite increasing pressure from the
BdL to alter their negative opinion on the acquisition
of Russian territory, both Heydebrand and Westarp
managed to retain such views as well as other points of
Conservative policy. They also continued to reject Kapp's
candidacy and ruled out Party participation in any anti-
Bethmann scheme led by the ADV.[4]

203

Radicals and Reactionaries

While the internal problems of the Party seemed
most compelling, its external difficulties refused to
disappear from sight. In early February, Westarp was
invited to a meeting of anti-Bethmann forces at the
Hotel Adlon in Berlin.[5] The meeting was to be chaired
by Count Hoensbroech, a former Progressive Party member
and now a fringe character in the anti-Bethmann movement.
Despite Westarp's low opinion of Hoensbroech, whom he
called a "not quite respectable personality",[6] the
Conservatives could ill-afford yet another controversy
over their position towards Bethmann. Westarp thus
accepted the invitation--but with great reluctance.[7]
Shortly before the meeting was to be held, however,
Westarp discovered its real purpose: Hoensbroech was
prepared to take a petition to the Kaiser, demanding
Bethmann's ouster and his replacement by General
Hindenburg, who would combine the duties of OHL head
and Chancellor of the *Reich*.[8] Appalled at the plan
and its possible consequences, Westarp, along with
several other politicians, cancelled his acceptances.
The "Adlon Action", as it was known, resulted in a
dismal failure.[9] In his search for a source of the
Adlon collapse, Hoensbroech centered his resentment
upon Westarp and the Party--at a time when the Conservatives'
national image had reached a depressing low.[10]

In April, Heydebrand summarized the Conservative
position in the bleakest of terms: "Now we are quite
alone." In a letter to Westarp,[11] he stressed his
concern over the *Herrenhaus* situation and the fact that
its position "as one of our factors of power" had become
considerably weaker. In actual fact, much more had
been damaged, most of it as a result of the Conservatives'
own actions. As already mentioned, the whole concept of
the *Reichstag* and political parties had come under
severe criticism from *voelkisch* quarters. The mood
spread from extraparliamentary sources into parts of
the Conservative Party. Among the most radical
Conservatives, there was a growing feeling that to
remain in the *Reichstag* was tantamount to political
suicide. Conservative Deputies such as Kresse urged
Westarp to organize a large Conservative *Volkspartei*
and to stop pursuing "tactical" politics and take the
offensive.[12] Another variant of this dissatisfaction
with Party politics came from Alfred v. Gossler. The
Conservative Deputy initiated talks with the Free
Conservative Deputy, v. Halem, about the possibility of
an association between the two Conservative parties and
an eventual political union.[13]

No doubt these Conservatives had caught the mood of a nation searching for new solutions to ancient problems. In nationalist circles this was translated into a call for the "strong man" to rescue the Prusso-German state from both military defeat and political collapse. In these circles the feeling existed that the *Reichstag* had ceased to express a positive function (if it ever had) and thus was to be replaced. In addition, Pan-German pressure upon Westarp continued to increase. Heydebrand, of course, had been written off as a mediocre politician unable to comprehend fully the meaning and purpose of the *voelkisch*-nationalist spirit. And yet, as we have seen, Westarp had not significantly altered Heydebrand's policies. His only saving grace lay in the fact that he had never antagonized Class and was always on very cordial terms with the ADV leadership.[14] But even this relationship began to fade in 1917. At one point, Westarp went to great lengths to avoid any sort of communication with v. Liebig.[15] Furthermore, he frustrated attempts by the Pan-German writer, Franz Sontag, to pressure the *Kreuzzeitung* into adopting a more radical line.[16] And Westarp would not leave the *Reichstag*. In a letter to v. Breitenbach, he discussed the hopelessness of the Conservative position. The Party, he maintained, had to remain "parliamentary"--for to leave the *Reichstag* "would serve no purpose." It was the duty of the Conservatives to voice their interests there "even if, at present, there is no success in sight."[17]

With their influence in the *Reichstag* completely gone, the Conservatives began to focus most of their attention upon Prussia. By July, it had become evident that the "national opposition" was about to achieve its aim. On July 6, the Center Deputy, Erzberger, presented the *Reichstag* with a very pessimistic picture of the military situation. The subsequent shock of his pronouncement helped to remove Bethmann and opened the way for a peace resolution supported by the "majority" parties in the *Reichstag*. The Conservatives had little to do with the frantic behind-the-scenes negotiations that highlighted Bethmann's departure.[18] To be sure, they denounced Bethmann in terms that left no doubt as to their opposition,[19] but Conservative interests, as already mentioned, were even then moving away from national affairs toward a final struggle over the Prussian Voting Law.

In the Westarp Nachlass, there is a memorandum written by a Conservative member of the Prussian *Abgeordnetenhaus*, v.d. Osten-Warnitz, and dated

Radicals and Reactionaries

August 6, 1917.[20] It is what today would be called a
"scenario", that is, an attempt to predict the possible
aftermath of some momentous event based upon a
reconstructed model of that event. In this case, it
was a "scenario" that dealt with the future of Prussia
after the "radicalization" of the Prussian Voting Law.
After speculating on the results of an election to the
Abgeordnetenhaus under such circumstances, the report
listed the following conclusions: the SPD would receive
increased representation from 9 seats to between 120
and 140; all other parties of the Left would also gain
sharply; on the other hand, all parties of the Right
would lose large numbers of seats and the Conservative
Party would decline from 147 seats to perhaps 70. The
concluding section of the report went on to state that
"Prussia will thus have the fate of being ruled by
Social Democracy with the aid of Poles, left Liberals
and the trade unions." The memorandum, furthermore,
pointed out that such a majority would exercise "an
improper influence" on Prussia's further development in
the following areas:

1. Railways, workers and bureaucracy;
2. Taxes; the decision over taxes would
    go into the hands of the propertyless
    and there would be "a good chance of
    the complete destruction of private
    property";
3. Internal administration;
4. Cultural tasks;
5. Inner colonization would be brought
    "onto the false path of a destruction
    of large estates";
6. German policies in the Eastern Marches
    would be destroyed and the Marches
    would become fully Polish within two
    years;
7. The new majority would also push
    Reichstag politics in a "radical"
    direction.

So disturbing was this information that the
Conservatives were even unable to comprehend fully the
momentous significance and aims of the Deutsche
Vaterlandspartei (German Fatherland Party) founded in
September. Their total involvement with Prussia
allowed the founding of the Fatherland Party to
practically pass them by--with hardly a dent in their
myopic concentration upon the Voting Law.[21] The
Conservatives had lost so much influence and were,
therefore, so far on the periphery of political affairs

that v. Klitzing, in an incredibly naive letter to
Westarp, was able to state that "the aim of the
Fatherland Party is more propaganda; our aims are
more economic and political."[22] In fact, it appears
that there was only one realist among all the
Conservatives--Heydebrand. In November he complained
bitterly that "v. Schwerin seems to have taken the
reigns of the Party leadership."[23] The recognition of
his own political impotency was further illustrated
at the very end of 1917 when he wrote to Westarp that
"the German people, on the whole, deserved a better
fate. Bethmann will triumph."[24] No doubt he meant
this statement to apply equally to his own desperate
situation and to that of the German Conservative Party.

ii. The BdL and a return to basics.

But 1917 was a different sort of year for the BdL.
Whereas the Conservatives had begun the War in a semi-
powerless position, the BdL had seen its political
situation decline gradually until it had become little
more than a small cog in the much larger ADV wheel. In
1916, the _Bund_ had desperately tried to revive its
influence among the economic interest groups--but to
no avail. At that time the hold of the Pan-German
League upon these groups had been too strong.[25] By
the end of 1916, however, the BdL had succeeded in
reestablishing some degree of political independence.
V. Wangenheim, influenced by Roesicke, had refused to
allow the _Bund_ to participate in a visit to the Kaiser
that had been planned by Class. The _Bund_ forced the
CDI to follow suit and ultimately both groups refused
to sign the petition that Class would present to the
Emperor.[26] Furthermore, at the beginning of 1917, the
Bund demonstrated an even greater degree of self-
expression by refusing to follow the ADV in its attacks
upon the government,[27] while at the same time strengthening
its ties with heavy industry.[28]

Why did the _Bund_ decide to no longer accept fully
the ADV whip? For one thing, there was the simple desire
of the agrarians to maintain a degree of independent
leadership among the various economic interest groups
within the Empire. Also important was the increasingly
bad image of agriculture that began to dominate big
city opinion. This was one result of the agrarian
decision to abandon price ceilings. Agricultural products
began to increase in price--when they could be obtained.
"Usurer" became, during the winter of 1916, a word almost

synonymous with farmer. The *Bund* thus needed time and
freedom--both obtainable away from the ADV sphere of
influence--to change such an image. Luckily for the
BdL, the image of the "usurer" in German society had,
by the beginning of 1917, been transferred from agrarian
to Jew.[29]

A further concern for the *Bund der Landwirte* was
the degree of alienation that had developed between
the *Junkers* and elements comprising middle-and small
range farmers.[30] Traditionally the backbone of *Bund*
support, and willing recipients of BdL ideology, these
groups had felt a keen sense of neglect during the
period of close cooperation between agrarians and
Pan-Germans. It was primarily for these reasons that
the *Bund* wished, once again, to head up a national
movement of economic groups which would exercise an
independent and influential role in the politics of the
Reich.[31]

To do this, however, the BdL needed the assistance
of Wolfgang Kapp.[32] Ostensibly a *Bund* man, Kapp was
instrumental in developing the idea of an integrative,
extraparliamentary movement, whose creation, however,
he offered to Hansa interests rather than the BdL.[33]
As Roesicke explained it to Wangenheim in August:[34]
"Kapp does not seem to want to put himself in the service
of our scheme (unsere *Sache*)." But as circumstances
developed, Kapp was, eventually able to join with the
agrarians who, thus, had a role in the creation of the
German Fatherland Party. Nevertheless, the *Bund's* own
drive for power did not cease to be the primary concern
of the agrarians. On September 12, for example,
v. Wangenheim informed Roesicke that the *Bund's* aim
was to "get in at all levels of the Fatherland Party."[35]

iii. Continuity and action: the German
      Fatherland Party and Wolfgang Kapp.

Wolfgang Kapp had always been a man of action.
From his earliest involvement with the inner colonization
movement to his position as *Generallandschaftsdirektor*
of East Prussia, he had never hesitated in pursuing an
objective to its ultimate success.[36] For many years,
Kapp, along with his assistant, Georg Schiele, was a
vital part of the many political triumphs gained by
the BdL. As a result, he was held in the highest
esteem by both v. Wangenheim and Roesicke and was a
key consultant to the group in both economic and political

affairs. But Kapp had always maintained a degree of
independence, never allowing himself to become a mere
functionary within the *Bund*.[37] His ability for action
and results was matched only by a passion for personal
power.

As well as a practical side, however, there was
also a theoretical part to Kapp. It was not far
removed, however, from Kapp's mania for action. Since
the beginning of the War, Kapp had been witness to the
steady growth of a "new orientation" psychology, spawned
by the political pronouncements of Bethmann and Delbrueck.
It had manifested itself in the *Reichstag* through the
"majority" parties and in the nation through the renewal
of SPD demands for a "peace without annexations" and
attacks upon the Prussian Voting Law. These events led
Kapp to a pair of very significant conclusions: that
the "new orientation" could only be stopped by eliminating
the *Reichstag* "majority"; and that the SPD could not
maintain its political initiative if it found the majority
of its supporters, from the ranks of the working class,
against it.[38] Armed with such conclusions, Kapp decided
to act.

It is, therefore, hardly surprising to see Kapp
emerge in 1917 as a major figure in the ultimate attempt
to provide a vehicle for the rescue of the Prusso-German
state during the War. Kapp preceded this rise to power
with the publication, in 1916, of a damning attack upon
Bethmann's foreign and domestic policies. Bethmann
had responded with his "Pirates of Public Opinion"
speech against Kapp, to which the East Prussian replied
with an unsuccessful challenge to a duel. Kapp's standing
among the anti-Bethmann forces increased ten-fold as a
result of these events and gave him the necessary confidence
to pursue his greatest objectives to date--the removal of
Bethmann and the elimination of the "new orientation."
Ultimately, however, Kapp was prepared to pursue the
objective of creating a mass-movement of the Right, not
only as a means of stopping the SPD but as a stepping-
stone toward the creation of a military dictatorship
bolstered by big agriculture and heavy industry.

As a background to our understanding of Kapp's view
of domestic politics during the War, two pamphlets of
his, written in 1915 and 1917, are of value. The first
was a rather obscure little piece entitled *A Chapter on
Organization* and subtitled *The Conquest of the Masses
Through Embrace*. The rather odd-sounding title and
subtitle belie the very important contents of the work--
which is no more and no less than a primer on the successful

uses of propaganda to win the masses. Among the key
points mentioned by Kapp, the following were most
significant: "The masses, who are to be won through
propaganda, must have the feeling that their own
thoughts are being expressed...the trick is to use sales
techniques to win the masses...Politics and propaganda
are or should be one and the same thing...," and, finally,
"Propaganda can also be effective if lies, slander and
immorality are its basis."[39] As shall be demonstrated,
these were concepts implemented by Kapp in 1917 as the
foundation points for the incredible success of the
German Fatherland Party in becoming, within months of
its founding, a mass organization with over a million
members and a "pre-fascist" political and social appeal.

In January 1917, Kapp wrote another piece in which
he clearly outlined the type of organization necessary
to achieve the objectives already described. The work
was extremely important because it signified the end
of any hopes that Kapp might have entertained for the
Conservative Party as the standard-bearer of the Right.
Among the numerous points raised by Kapp was the
suggestion that a committee be built that would be
extraparliamentary in nature (although supported by
the parties and members of the *Reichstag*): "...a great
movement, led for the purpose of convincing the will
of the German people to achieve our war aims."[40] According
to Kapp, there would be public gatherings in all the
large cities which would discuss the theme of "Germany
can and Germany will." Presumably this committee was
to be the nucleus of the German Fatherland Party and
would employ the propaganda techniques developed and
refined by Wolfgang Kapp.

As a first step in the direction of such a scheme,
Kapp convinced the unfortunate Count Hoensbroech of
the need for a "complete change in our political system."
According to Kapp, this aim was only possible through
the intervention of the Supreme Military Command (OHL)
and, especially, General Ludendorff.[41] The Adlon
Conference demonstrated the folly of such a notion in
early 1917 as a means of uniting the Right. Fortunately,
for Kapp, Hoensbroech was almost singularly associated
with the Adlon debacle. In fact, from February until
June, the Government's "new orientation" policy seemed
to be gaining the upper hand in its popularity struggle
with the "national opposition" movement. Yet Kapp was
convinced that deep within the German nation another
kind of longing lay dormant, far removed from liberalism
and democratic change. On July 11, he expressed these
sentiments to Ludendorff in an impassioned note:[42]

> It is not true that the will of the
> people thinks with the *Reichstag* majority.
> It is not true that revolution threatens
> if the Crown does not give in. The *Volk*
> longs for a solid hand, for the strong
> leader, he who can deal with our enemies
> and the neutrals and is filled with a
> will to victory and strong nerves. The
> only savior possible is v. Hindenburg in
> association with yourself. You must meet
> with the Kaiser in case Bethmann does
> not resign...

By mid-July, however, Bethmann was gone. Kapp saw
this as the perfect opportunity to deliver a "knock-out"
blow against the "majority" parties in the *Reichstag*.
As he noted on July 15, 1917, "...a party must now be
founded which will stand against the *Reichstag* majority."[43]
For Kapp, the most obvious step would have been the
creation of a political party with its strength in East
Prussia, an area where Kapp could have drawn upon the
resources of the BdL and other agrarian groups. But
Kapp was mindful of agriculture's extremely sensitive
position vis-a-vis large urban areas. There, criticism
had continued unabated against agrarian profiteering
and the hoarding of foodstuffs. Furthermore, in late
June, Kapp had been informed by v. Wangenheim that the
harvest in East Prussia would be a bad one--an issue
sure to add to the already ugly mood of the cities.[44]

It was for these reasons that Kapp chose the Hanseatic
cities of Hamburg and Bremen as the centers for his new
organization.[45] Yet even this was not enough to prevent
resentment at the fact that the creation of a Hansa-based
organization was directed by an East Prussian.[46] Kapp
was forced to take his movement back to East Prussia.
In order to maintain a sense of unity between the various
conservative groups that he was recruiting, and to
avoid exactly this type of sectional strife, Kapp proposed
that the new organization would not become involved in
domestic problems or religious differences.[47]

The German Fatherland Party had its first public
expression on September 2, 1917 in Koenigsberg, provincial
capital of East Prussia. It was the anniversary of the
battle of Sedan, commemorating the great German victory
over France nearly a half-century earlier. The final
choice for a name had evolved from *Bismarckbund* to
Bismarckpartei to *Hindenburgpartei* to, finally, *Deutsche
Vaterlandspartei*. There had been some initial controversy
over naming the organization. Would it be a *bund* or

partei? Advocates of the former had felt that *partei*
was inappropriate since:[48]

> Parties have always been interest groups
> who fought for power in the nation. These have
> been either for ideal or material purposes. But
> now the struggle is for the nation itself--for
> the retention or loss of our power--which goes
> far beyond party interests. In fact, the special
> interests that parties have must disappear.

But advocates of the latter overcame these objections
with arguments that were obviously more convincing:[49]

> A loosely-coordinated *bund* is an extremely
> impractical thing...The organization must be
> merged into a *partei*. Only in this manner will
> we have a politically significant coordination.
> *Partei* has a completely different appeal to the
> public than does *bund*. It is, in fact, the only
> manner in which we can make an impression on the
> *Reichstag* parties.

At its constituent assembly on August 22, the following
interest groups were represented: BdL, CDI, RDMV,
Independent Committee for a German Peace and the
Deutsche Vereinigung. The Honorary Chairman was the
Duke v. Mecklenburg; First Chairman was v. Tirpitz
and the Second Chairman, Heinrich Class. Members of
the "inner council" were Koerte, v. Wangenheim, Schaefer
and v. Below.[50]

By the end of September, the Fatherland Party had
amassed over one and a quarter million members. Its
Speakers' Bureau listed over three hundred available
speakers and the list read like a "Who's Who" of the
German Right (e.g., Paul Fuhrmann, Andreas Gildemeister,
v. Wangenheim, Dietrich Hahn, Otto Hoetzsch (!), v. Tirpitz,
Schaefer, v. Bodelschwingh, Ludwig Thoma, Schifferer).[51]
These Party members travelled far and wide preaching the
Fatherland Party line about their involvement with "only"
Germany's foreign affairs.[52] They represented a diverse
cross-section of political and economic Germany-left
Liberals, National Liberals, Centrists, industry, labor,
agriculture, anti-Semites, trade and commerce. What
united them was a common feeling that here was a movement
capable of achieving more than trite political slogans.[53]
They also felt liberated from the entrenched *Reichstag*,
where a democratic monster ruled the day.[54] The Party
seemed to be a united front encompassing all sections
of German society. In actual fact, it was not. Using

212

his theory that "propaganda can also be effective if
lies, slander and immorality are its basis", Kapp sought
to disguise the fact that the German Fatherland Party
was actually manipulated by powers long familiar to
the *Sammlung* game.[55] As he wrote to Bendixen on August 22,
the Fatherland Party was "based on the combination Hi-Wa
(Hirsch-Wangenheim)." Kapp further admitted that, in
fact, it was "the *Kartell der schaffenden Staende* which
forms the invisible backbone of our group."[56] The
conservative system, all but dormant since the beginning
of war, was once again on the move--in its most ambitious
venture to date. The lines of continuity, which stretched
from 1913, remained "unbroken."[57]

iv. Pan-German aims: from the conquest
     of land to the conquest of soul.

1

     Although the ADV had managed to remain a powerful
group throughout the War, this power was reflected more
in terms of influence than in membership size. In the
early years of its political activity, moreover, size
had meant little in relation to the visibility of its
members, who managed to infiltrate the broad spectrum
of *Reichstag* parties, interest groups and nationalist
associations that made up an important part of the
Reich's "public opinion." Yet the ADV had always faced
the problem of economic and political "self-interest"
among the groups it attempted to dominate and this
obstacle had remained the chief stumbling block to the
"Pan-Germanization" of Imperial politics.

     The year 1916 had been no different. Aware of the
growing national revulsion to the "majority *Reichstag*",
the Pan-Germans looked to 1916 as the year in which their
aim of a truly "national" opposition would be achieved.
For this task, however, influence would not be enough.
What was needed were sheer numbers of Germans prepared
to bring about a national dictatorship. This would be
achieved, according to ADV strategy, in a two-stage
programme: stage one would be the creation of a *Volksrat*
(National Council) to be comprised of the largest national-
voelkisch associations and regional anti-Semitic groups
and, relatedly, a complete organization of the economic
associations, which Class described to v. Gebsattel as
the "connection between the true democratic and aristocratic
elements";[58] stage two would see the *Volksrat* function
as an "association of associations", replacing the *Reichstag*
once a dictatorship had been created.[59]

213

Radicals and Reactionaries

As with its previous creation, the largely ineffectual Independent Committee, the ADV would allow the *Volksrat* to function independently, but would control all policy-making. To ensure ADV anonymity, a leader of national recognition had to head the *Volksrat*. First choice was Duke Johann Albrecht v. Mecklenburg, a co-founder of the ADV, but no longer a member. But the Duke had resigned from the ADV in 1909 as a direct result of a disagreement with Class, and the issue had remained unresolved and the animosity between the two unsettled. The Duke's refusal forced Class to approach v. Tirpitz, but the Grand Admiral rejected the offer with a great deal of bitterness. In September, Class decided to proceed to the next step, the organization of the economic associations. Dietrich Schaefer, head of the Independent Committee was assigned the task. But, as we have seen, the economic groups, and especially the BdL, were no longer willing to accept full subservience to the ADV and the anti-Semitic groups and were now more concerned with political and economic survival. The *Volksrat* died a quiet death at the beginning of 1917.[60]

Class, however, was by no means finished. During the early months of 1917 he moved from scheme to scheme, each time meeting rejection. Among other things, he approached the Commanding Generals with the idea of a military dictatorship but found little enthusiasm. He then turned to the search for a "strong man" dictator but found both candidates, the ADV's own v. Vietinghoff-Scheel and General Bernhardi of "preventative war" fame, to be lacking in various qualities essential to the position.[61]

In February 1917, with their plans all but frustrated, the ADV looked on as Hoensbroech attempted to organize his Adlon "action." Neither Class nor v. Gebsattel thought much of Hoensbroech,[62] but v. Gebsattel felt that Adlon, at least, would be "a further energetic action toward the removal of Bethmann. Thus it is necessary for a representative of the ADV to be there."[63] Class, however, prevented his aide from attending the meeting, explaining to v. Gebsattel that Hoensbroech "was not the man to represent such a good thing."[64] Nevertheless, the intensity of feeling against Bethmann demonstrated by those coming to Adlon convinced Gebsattel that "now is the time to lead a mighty blow against Bethmann."[65]

Toward this end, the ADV turned, once more, to the Conservative Party. Pressure was put upon the newest member of the *Reichstag* Conservatives, the Saxon

214

industrialist, Wildgrube, to aid the Pan-German cause.[66]
Despite ADV articles attacking Heydebrand and attempting
to isolate him fully from the Party,[67] the Conservatives
were not to be won. As Keim reported to v. Gebsattel,
"the Conservatives do not want to act against Bethmann-
Hollweg since one does not know how long he might remain.
The Conservatives are, after all, receptive to *Liebesgaben*
of every kind."[68] At long last, in March, v. Gebsattel
completely gave up on the Conservatives: "With the
forfeit of the Conservatives in the *Reichstag*, there is
no way for them to change. Heydebrand and his colleagues
can brag that they are the "gravediggers" of the
Conservative Party."[69] In a letter to Schmidt-Gibichenfels,
Gebsattel pledged to maintain his opposition to a change
in the Prussian Voting Law. But, unlike earlier letters,
he no longer viewed it in terms of a simple defence of
Prussianism. He now saw it as a struggle to stop the
Jewish "conspiracy" from gaining the political and
economic domination of the Prusso-German state.[70]

This final failure to engage Conservative support
marked the beginning of a notable shift in Pan-German
strategy. For three long years, the ADV had carefully
constructed a programme designed to consolidate the German
nation behind it in a frontal attack upon Bethmann and
the "new orientation" as well as a covert attempt to
create a *voelkisch* dictatorship. The war-aims programme
had been the key element in this strategy and its success
was measured by the diverse political orientation of its
supporters. But to the ADV, this support had not
demonstrated a conversion in terms of *voelkisch* awareness
nor a real desire to bring about the glory of a "Greater
Germany." Instead, as has been noted, economic aid and
political "self-interest" had ruled the hearts and minds
of most politicians and pressure-group members.[71] The
Conservative attitude had been, more or less, the last
straw.

Furthermore, even after the censorship on public
debate of the war-aims issue had been lifted in late
1916,[72] grave military and economic problems had forced
the war-aims question to occupy a relatively low position
on the list of national priorities.[73] To the ADV, war
aims no longer seemed so profitable a cause. Because of
its massive involvement in the foreign political direction
of the Empire, it had developed a special sensitivity to
shifts in the population regarding optimism and defeat.
Call it criminal cunning (which the Allies considered
the ADV to possess) or political insight, this "canary
in the coal mine" sensitivity was at work in early 1917.
It told the ADV that, for instance, the attacks against

the agrarian "usurers" were only a foreshadowing of the
potential wrath of a nation on its way to a military
defeat. Long before the political parties and interest
groups were aware of it, the ADV had quietly dropped
its insistence upon war aims in favor of an emphasis
upon anti-Semitism.[74] As one historian has put it:[75]

> So that the nation would not turn against
> those who had led the nation and were responsible
> for the defeat, another enemy had to be shown
> them, on whom they could vent their aggressions.

Unable to penetrate the political consciousness of
Germany, the ADV sought converts to the *voelkisch* movement
in previously uncharted waters. Through the use of
publications such as *Panther, Sueddeutsche Monatshefte,
Die Wirklichkeit* and, especially, *Deutschlands Erneuerung,*[76]
Germany's famous "unpolitical" types were to be introduced
to the world of *voelksich* ideology, but in terms familiar
to them, as Wilhelm Kiefer told J. H. Lehmann:[77]

> It is a fact that the least amount of our
> readers belong to the ADV or to the German
> Conservative Party or to any German-*voelkisch*
> organization. These, above all others, must be
> strategically drawn in. Our movement is more
> of a purely intellectual nature. There are
> people who have not become interested in the
> political relations of the time, but in its
> intellectual life; in art, in the soullessness
> and nihilism of our culture. People to whom
> the terms national and *voelkisch* are quite
> strange are also part of our intended group:
> they will become our best troops. For these
> people are internally alive while our German
> *voelkisch* types are often corpses. The adult
> *Wandervogel* will also join our movement and
> we should not underestimate the importance of
> the Youth Movement.

We have already seen the importance of anti-Semitism
in the pre-war programme of the ADV. At the beginning
of the conflict, however, anti-Semitism had all but
disappeared from public discussion--a victim of the
government censor and the *Burgfrieden*. The ADV had used
it sparingly after that. V. Liebig, for instance, had
called Bethmann the "Chancellor of German Jewry" and
had also proclaimed the war-aims programme as the struggle
between Jewish and German aims.[78] Other anti-Semites
such as Albrecht v. Graefe viewed Bethmann's "new
orientation" as a plot to aid the "unGerman" Jews in
creating a "new orientalism."[79]

216

In March and April, the ADV-owned *Deutsche Zeitung*
began openly to attack German Jewry. This culminated
on June 18 with an article written by Class but signed
by v. Gebsattel. It was entitled "Pan-German--Perhaps
Pan-Jewish?"[80] In it, Class/Gebsattel charged that the
Jews "had given millions to certain political parties."
Quite obviously, the "certain political parties" were
the SPD and the left Liberals. The article urged that
it was once again time to take up the investigation of
Jewish ownership and domination in art, commerce, science
and theatre. A week later, a two-part article appeared
in the *DZ* entitled "Germandom and Jewry."[81] Both parts
of the article were devoted to non-German Jewry. Instead
they attempted to demonstrate the extent of the unGerman
influences exerted by "Eastern" and "International" Jewry.

On July 8, the Executive Committee of the ADV met
to discuss the "Jewish Question." Several voices were
raised expressing reservations about making too great an
issue of anti-Semitism.[82] Class, however, carried the
day when he declared that "although we have said little
about the Jews, they remain our most dangerous enemy.
We can only fight them through an awakening of national
interests." In September, the ADV viewed the creation
of the Fatherland Party[83] with an eye towards spreading
the anti-Semitic agitation within its ranks. On
September 21, v. Gebsattel published an article entitled
"Jewish Vote, Jewish Peace",[84] in which he stated that
the "Jewish-elected majority *Reichstag*" could only conclude
a peace that would benefit the Jews. He also threw out
a challenge to the Fatherland Party concerning the use
of anti-Semitism as a political weapon:[85] "Here lies an
important and urgent task which, I feel, the Fatherland
Party will be unable to avoid." Admiral Tirpitz, however,
refused to accept the challenge.[86] Accordingly, Class
ordered v. Gebsattel to open a full-scale anti-Semitic
campaign and to utilize groups such as the Independent
Committee towards that purpose. By the end of 1917, Class
had fully redefined the purpose of the ADV. It was now
"the anti-Semitic voice of the national political movement."
"For the Jews," warned the ADV head, "the struggle for
existence has begun."[87]

2

On September 2, the day of the Fatherland Party's
founding, Class received a message from Wolfgang Kapp,
inviting him for political discussions. Deeply involved
at the time in the creation of a major anti-Semitic
movement, Class, nevertheless, went to see the founder
of the German Fatherland Party.[88]

It was the first time that the two of them had met
and Class's impression of the East Prussian was none
too favorable. Reflecting back on their meeting, Class
later wrote about Kapp that "at least it could be said
of him that he was, if not to be taken seriously
politically, at least a proper person."[89] This was
hardly Kapp's impression of himself. Boasting of his
political creation, he proudly informed Class that even
left Liberals were joining the Fatherland Party. Continuing
to exude confidence, Kapp informed the Pan-German leader
that he had named Class to be Second Chairman of the Party.
The shrewd Class replied that Kapp would have been
better off taking the Party into his own hands. Kapp
replied that he had done just that: Duke v. Mecklenburg
was a mere figurehead and the aging v. Tirpitz had
assigned all his work to Kapp. Thus the party that
he had created was, after all, in his own hands.[90]

Class was now aware that his own appointment had
not been meant to give him or the ADV any influence
within the Fatherland Party. He refused to cooperate
with the Party except as part of an "absolute national
opposition" with a full integration of the two groups.
It took his trusted friend Hugenberg to convince Class
that this was not possible. On October 6, a month after
their first meeting, Class pledged to Kapp ADV support
in the building of local Fatherland Party committees.[91]
On October 16, Class attended a meeting of the Fatherland
Party Executive Committee. When the time had come for
v. Tirpitz to speak, the Grand Admiral launched into a
tirade against the Pan-Germans: "It is in the interest
of our scheme if we could avoid giving the appearance
of being another form of the ADV." Although v. Wangenheim
and Kapp publicly rebuked the v. Tirpitz speech, the
damage had been done.[92] Class attended only one other
meeting of the Fatherland Party (where v. Tirpitz attacked
Kapp for usurping his role as head of the Party).[93]
Thereafter, he received no further invitations and concluded
that this action was intended to get rid of the "uncomfortable
Pan-Germans." Even the small amount of work done by
the ADV on behalf of the Fatherland Party was, in Class's
words, "not exactly appreciated."[94] By December, there
was, as v. Liebig reported to Class, "no hope in the
Fatherland Party" on anti-Semitism or any other questions.[95]
Class summed up his feeling about the German Fatherland
Party in the following manner: "I was convinced that the
whole creation--its goals and leadership--was not suited
for the most necessary task in the nation--the fight
against a weak and aimless government."[96]

On the eve of 1918 no trace could be found of the old war-aims movement. Instead, one found the economic-interest associations and the expansion-oriented politicians merged into the German Fatherland Party: a vast collection of over a million Germans, supported by the "invisible backbone" of the *Kartell der schaffenden Staende*, or rather, those groups who were associated with its name. For them, there lay ahead the promise of new territory and added material wealth. Here the *Sammlung* schemes of nearly a half-century of German history had found their ultimate achievement: for from Bismarck to Miquel to Tirpitz to Kapp, the dream had been and remained financial profit and political and social status quo. Yet the fulfillment of this dream was hampered by the continued opposition of the political enemy--now divided into a majority and minority SPD.

Apart from these groups stood the Pan-German League, frustrated by the very obstacles that united the Fatherland Party. No longer flush with the fever of an expected *voelkisch* triumph or even the appearance of the "strong man", the Pan-Germans were content merely to save themselves from the disaster that they knew was bound to come; and there were others like them. On October 17, Class met General Ludendorff for the first time and found that they "agreed on everything," especially that the hapless Kaiser was "an even greater danger than we assumed."[97] Aware that Germany could not win at the front and, most likely, would have a hard time doing so domestically, these elements sought to cover their political tracks through the anti-Semitic scapegoat. Some, like v. Gebsattel, had only recently seen the light of a *voelkisch* future at the end of the democratic tunnel. Now the "canary in the coal mine" told them of a different fate, as v. Gebsattel confided to Class: "Do you have any kind of hope? If not, it is best to leave this world."[98]

"The revolution from above has to be openly threatened," urged a letter[99] to Westarp at the end of 1917. "I see no other possibility of stopping the growing evil of parliamentarism." It was a classic recommendation, in line with the traditional method of nipping-in-the-bud any challenge to the dominance of the conservative system. Yet what had happened to German parliamentary politics between June and December 1917 had been more than a challenge. The Majority Parties had succeeded in creating at least the illusion of a revolution of the Left--thus rendering the "revolution from above" completely harmless. In reaction to the conversion of the *Reichstag* into a parliamentary institution, the agrarian-industrial interests that ruled Germany created the German Fatherland Party,

and in so doing "embarked upon the attempt to mobilize
every effort for the retention of the social, political
and economic *status quo*."[100] To many on Germany's
political right, the creation of a thoroughly modern
and mass-based organization like the Fatherland Party
appeared as "the last chance to deal with this evil
Reichstag in a constitutional manner, perhaps even to do
away with it."[101] Thus while the long-term goal of the
conservative system was to maintain itself with the aid
of a military dictatorship,[102] the short-term aim was
to destroy the parliamentary powers of the Majority
Parties. Toward this end, the mobilization of Germany's
famous "unpolitical" types was a chief concern, since,
as George Mosse has pointed out, this vast segment of the
population was hardly "unpolitical":[103]

> Unpolitical must be understood as applying
> to those men and women who thought political
> parties divisive, who were uninterested in
> democratic machinery because it did not have
> any relevancy to life.

Among the members of the Pan-German League there
was little desire to save the status quo. While the
agrarian-industrial interests of the Fatherland Party
moved ahead with grandiose aims for the conquest of new
territories and added material enrichment, the ADV
looked on in disgust and frustration. Unable to conquer
the "soul" of the German nation and eliminate its
obsession with purely material self-interests, the ADV
now sought to maximize its efforts to win the struggle
for a *voelkisch* Germany by shifting its concentration
from war-aims to anti-Semitism. The struggle against
the Jew would serve two distinct functions: it would
protect the Pan-Germans against the eventual wrath of a
defeated Germany and shift all blame upon the Jews;[104]
it would serve as the basis for the renewed ADV onslaught
against a democratic post-war Germany.

The creation of the German Fatherland Party and
the ADV's declaration of war upon German Jewry had
profound effects upon the ideology of traditional
conservatism. These events clearly demonstrated that
"anti-Semitism, racism and imperialism had been mixed
together in a new integrative ideology which sought to
win not only the middle classes but the lower ones as
well."[105] Traditional conservatism had no place in the
new "pre-faschism" (Stegmann) of late 1917. Like the
Conservative Party, it was too exclusive and apprehensive
to meet adequately the threat of democratization.

The end of 1917 found the German Conservative Party wrapped in a cloak of "splendid isolation."[106] Heydebrand, surrounded by a few reactionary friends, had long ago lost the reigns of power; Westarp had chosen to stay in the *Reichstag* and avoid the excesses of the ADV. These actions had stamped the Party as wishing to take its chances in a system that had outlived its usefulness in a time of total war and democratic revolution; of pledging its allegiance to a monarchy that no longer had any authority;[107] and of refusing to leave a political institution that was earmarked for destruction. In short, the Conservatives waited.

Were they waiting for the military victory that would return them to a pre-1912 position of power in *Reich* affairs? If, indeed, waiting was the key to their actions, then this policy was directly in opposition to the plans of the men of action like Kapp or the cunning manipulators of the ADV. The political reality of 1917 was that traditional conservatism and the party system were now in conflict with charismatic mass politics. If waiting was the Party's answer to the "capitalistic-bourgeois counterrevolution", then waiting might prove to be a very unpleasant, even fatal, experience.

CHAPTER X

The Politics of Preservation and Decline (1918)

i.   The lesson is learned too late

     In January 1918, Otto Hoetzsch's articles in the
Kreuzzeitung had irritated the BdL to the point of
outrage. Especially upsetting was his attitude towards
the eastern war aims, an area still considered essential
by the agrarians to their economic and political survival.
"Hoetzsch's articles," wrote Roesicke in a note[1] to
Westarp, "are a step towards the SPD point of view."
Westarp's reply (and in this he was joined by Heydebrand),
promptly written and extremely conciliatory, marked a
major shift in Conservative policy: *"We agree with you*
(italics mine-AJP). We had a serious talk with Hoetzsch
and gave him an ultimatum that he accepted at once."[2]
As both leaders had been, up to that point, in almost
total agreement with Hoetzsch's approach toward Russia
and the eastern war aims, this new attitude toward the
BdL reflected a growing concern about the future of
Prussia and the German Conservative Party. Yet there
was little that the Conservatives could do to maintain
Hoetzsch's opinions about eastern aims--the negotiations
at Brest-Litovsk between the OHL and the new Marxist
leaders of Russia made the imminent annexation of vast
Russian territories a near-*fait accompli*.[3] Afraid to
alienate the BdL any further, a group whose strength it
desperately needed in the struggle against voting reform,
the Party leadership dropped another of its previously
intransigent positions when it allowed Kapp to stand
as a successful Conservative candidate in a February
by-election.

     Why concessions such as these? During the early
months of 1918, a badly disunited Conservative Party
faced a variety of dangers to its continued existence
in Prussia and the *Reich*. Chief among these was the
growing threat to the three-class voting system in
Prussia. The Conservatives had been forced, in 1917,
to concede that they, too, foresaw the necessity for
some changes, but in a manner which they termed "organic
development"--and certainly not before the War's end.
In this manner, they hoped that some kind of miracle
would produce a German victory and, in the ensuing
delirium, when the Party had resumed its prestige and
influence, they would salvage much of what they were
to have conceded. Isolated in *Reichstag* affairs, the
Conservatives saw the thrust of their defence coming
from the BdL and the Fatherland Party, both with an
ability to appear "above the parties" and thus able
to gather a wide-ranging group of defenders.

Radicals and Reactionaries

Neither Heydebrand nor Westarp contributed much in terms of time or advice to the Fatherland Party. There is, furthermore, little in the Westarp *Nachlass* which gives any indication of the degree of cooperation between the two organizations. Neither Westarp nor Heydebrand were on the Speakers' List of the Fatherland Party although, significantly, Hoetzsch was. What is certain is that the *Kreuzzeitung* vigorously endorsed the Fatherland Party throughout its existence. What is also certain is that the Fatherland Party was much more in line with Conservative thinking on war aims (western-oriented, hence Hoetzsch's participation) and in the struggle against the *Reichstag* "majority" than was the ADV.

In a sense, the Conservatives were able to find a refuge of sorts in the antagonism between Class and the Fatherland Party. It lessened ADV concern with the course of Conservative politics and reduced their unhappiness with Heydebrand. It did not, however, lessen the plans of the Pan-German Conservatives in their efforts to destroy the existing Conservative Party, as Class informed v. Gebsattel:[4] "Our friends (Salm, v. Grumme, Hertzberg, v. Kleist) want to build a new party," or efforts to alter it significantly, as the estate owner, Pretzel, told Class: "The Conservative Party must give up its name and become a great national party on a national-*voelkisch* basis, including workers and the lower bureaucracy."[5]

During this period of Conservative apprehension and general organizational disarray, Westarp maintained a remarkably coherent view of Conservative policies. It showed him to be only slightly less inflexible than Heydebrand in a situation where such inflexibility was leading to political oblivion. Thus, a number of Westarp's letters from May, June and August give an indication of his reluctance to become "extreme": "I do not see any Jewish or business influences in the Wolf Telegraphic Bureau reports (this to an ADV charge-AJP).[6] We must... oppose war aims that are unrealistic;[7] the Conservatives should come out directly for reparations and 'guarantees' in Belgium although the ADV will consider us *Flaumacher* (defeatists-AJP) because of this."[8]

But a too close identification with the Fatherland Party was also to be avoided. The ability of this mass organization to gather to it a wide variety of social groups badly exposed the narrow basis of Conservative membership. As the Conservatives on the strength of

223

some *Mittelstand* ties, had claimed, ever since 1913, to be a *Volkspartei*, the "pre-fascist" politics of Kapp's creation tended only to illuminate further the reality of Conservative exclusivity.

In a January speech[9] to the Hamburg Conservative Association, Westarp warned of the dangerous situation that would arise once "our millions of troops come home and find a huge tax bill or a ruined economic life...then we will face democratization." One cannot be certain whether Westarp was more concerned about the state of the German economy or the mood of the returning veteran as a cause of "democratization." But one thing was clear: the Conservatives feared the battlefield soldier and his possible impact on a post-war Prusso-German state. Especially frightening was a new kind of social equality which had developed at the front and threatened to carry back to Germany, as Paul Meyer related to Westarp: "In our army there is no more room for differences between Estates or wealth."[10]

Just who were the "warriors" that would be coming home after years of trench warfare and what threat did they pose to the Conservatives? Firstly, they were the millions of Germans who had marched off to war in the belief that a truly classless society had been proclaimed by the Kaiser on August 4, 1914. They had fought alongside one another as Germans and as "comrades" and not as merchants, farmers and working-class men. They had died similar deaths in a war in which a bullet had made no distinction between classes. Secondly, they had been subjected to the "patriotic instruction" of the OHL, in which their nationalistic spirit had been lifted to xenophobic heights.[11] They were warned about the "unpatriotic" seductiveness of the "internationalist" SPD. Yet, on the other hand, many of them had been SPD members or sympathizers and had continued to keep abreast of Party speeches and meetings. They were aware of the Independent Socialist line characterizing them as cannon fodder for the "imperialistic ruling classes." Their confused state, at the War's end, would leave them open to the demagoguery of the Left and Right. But one thing would remain clear: they would not come home as they had left, full of an idealized sense of duty. They would expect something for their valor and it could only come from those with something to give. This is what frightened the Conservatives so much at the start of 1918--for they had among the most in terms of tangible possessions. Always having managed to avoid giving any of it up, whether in the form of direct taxes, land, or support for the national *Weltpolitik*, they were now certain to be among the first asked.

Radicals and Reactionaries

By the middle of the year, this kind of thinking
had led to a panic situation within the Party. The
situation was further exacerbated by reports that
Russia's returning soldiers had deserted the battlefield
for the promise of expropriated land. Westarp was
besieged with letters expressing a fear of the front-
line soldier. Among these was a letter from Limburg-
Stirum,[12] a veteran Conservative politician, who wrote
to Westarp of his fear that "upon the return of the
troops, some two million of them, the call for (land-AJP)
expropriation will grow loud. We large-estate owners
should give up small parts (of our estate) for settlement."
Much the same theme was voiced by v. Kleist,[13] who took
the opportunity to remind Heydebrand of an old Daniel
Frymann/Class demand: "The large-estate owner must be
ready to give up some of his property to maintain a
healthy Estate of farmers. This the German Conservative
Party must do." Other Conservatives suggested promoting
to a higher voting class all those who had served at
the front. Ironically, while some individual Conservatives
were beginning to demonstrate a sense of *Lernfaehigkeit*,
or learning capability, in regard to adapting to these
new dangers, the Conservative Party remained stubbornly
opposed to any changes in the three-class system. Yet
even those who attempted to forestall the dangers now
threatening the conservative system were unable to introduce
proposals far-reaching enough to act as a "safety-valve"
in this situation. In June, the historian, Fritz Hartung,
wrote of the feeling among many conservatives that the
German Conservative Party's opposition to voting reform
was no longer based on any perception of reality:[14]

> The leaders of the German Conservative
> Party seem not to have noticed that there is
> more to the voting reform than merely the
> number of seats; namely its relation to
> the new times that have been brought about
> by nearly four years of unheard of application
> of all our national strengths. As if their
> belief in the power of conservatism is missing,
> they allow themselves to be led only by the
> view of their momentary material position--
> but they are actually endangering not only the
> existence of the Party, but of the whole nation...

From July until mid-October, the opposition to the
Voting Law reform dominated the politics of the Party.
Quite subtly, however, without arousing the attention
of either Westarp or Heydebrand, positive steps were
being taken by those long-opposed to a virtual two-man

dictatorial grip over decision-making. At the end of
July or the beginning of August, a proposal in the
form of a memorandum began to circulate among Party
members.[15] It asked the following question: "How can
we build a more purposeful and fruitful organization
in the German Conservative Party?" The answer was
"through the organization of a General Staff; for we
have two Generals but no General Staff." The memorandum
proposed the following Conservative members: v. Graefe,
Kreth, Graef-Anklam, Schiele, Block v. Blettnitz. Each
of the candidates had, throughout the War, pushed the
Party in "radical" directions, most notably v. Graefe
and Schiele. Now they attempted to usurp a share of
Party control.

No action was taken on the memorandum because
Conservative opposition to voting reform was running
into the dilemma of a worsening military situation.
In July, the Prussian *Herrenhaus* rejected a bill for
reform and proposed, instead, a system based upon a
plural vote. Although significantly different from
the three-class vote, neither this suggestion nor a
later one that foresaw a system based upon age were
enough to satisfy socialist demands. However, the
increasingly gloomy military reports seemed to have
an effect on several Conservatives sitting on the
Herrenhaus Voting Law Commission.[16] By the end of
September, Westarp was able to tell Heydebrand that
a "compromise seems likely as many Conservatives drop
their intransigence to an equal Voting Law proposal."[17]

Yet this was not accomplished without a great
degree of friction between the differing Party factions.
At the beginning of October, Westarp was predicting a
"crisis" situation in the Party over acceptance or
rejection of reform.[18] This was confirmed on October 15:
"I am assuming that in any case there is a split in
the Party and a 'Heydebrand crisis' is possible."[19]
Finally, on October 18, v. Klassing informed Westarp
that:[20]

> The opposition in the Party against
> v. Heydebrand appears to be v. d. Osten.
> There is a lively opposition to v. Heydebrand's
> leadership in the *Abgeordnetenhaus* as well as
> a desire to rewrite the Party programme and
> do away with the old name.

By mid-October, both the *Herrenhaus* and *Abgeordnetenhaus*
had accepted compromise reform proposals. This was done
in a "no-choice" spirit, reflecting the reality of

Octoberparlamentarisierung, in which the Majority Parties entered (for the first time) the Chancellor's cabinet.[21] Faced with an internal political rift which threatened to tear the Party to pieces and a shift of power to the Left, the Conservatives attempted one final desperate act of salvation. At the beginning of October, Kapp announced to the Hamburg Conservative Association that the Party was prepared to participate in a "Coalition Ministry of National Defense."[22] Kapp's proposal carried with it an attempt to bring the Conservatives out of their total *Reichstag* isolation and into the cabinet of Chancellor Max v. Baden. The Party was determined to have some say over governmental matters. More important to Conservative politics, however, was the self-pronounced *Burgfrieden*, which was the attempt to form a truce between the various factions within the Party. For nearly three weeks, the Conservatives pursued this aim and actually believed that they would accomplish their objective. Even Westarp seems to have entertained the idea: on October 21-22, in correspondence with the New Stettin Conservatives, he expressly forbade the consideration of Heinrich Class (!) as a substitute candidate for the resigned deputy, v. Bonin. In Westarp's words, "no candidate is to be put in v. Bonin's place that would endanger the *Burgfrieden*."[23]

Quite obviously both Kapp's and the Party's attempts failed. The Conservatives were superfluous to *Reichstag* matters in the first instance, and too-far ruptured ideologically in the second instance. Yet the Conservatives did miss a genuine opportunity to bolster their almost non-existent support outside of East Prussia and increase their membership ranks. On October 17, Westarp received a letter from Wahl of the Bremen Committee for a German Workers' Peace.[24] Wahl represented thousands of "yellow" trade unionists, a militantly nationalistic segment of the working class. Wahl turned to the Conservatives after having failed to interest the National Liberal Party. He informed Westarp that the Conservative Party had a "holy duty to gather all national-thinking workers against the internationalists. If the Party does this, then large numbers of workers will follow the German Conservative Party." Westarp, however, left both of Wahl's letters unanswered.[25] But after the failure of the "Coalition Ministry" plan and the internal *Burgfrieden*, matters took on a more extreme appearance. Survival as a political entity became the new Conservative concern. Consequently, Westarp sent a letter to Wahl assuring him that he saw the necessity of a "yellow" seat in the *Reichstag*. But, continued

Westarp, the "economic peace movement should not settle
its hopes on one party but should look for pressure
group influence."[26] Almost at once, Kapp and the
Fatherland Party were able to organize these "yellow"
workers into the *Deutsche Arbeiter und Angestellte
Partei* (German Workers and Employees Party) whose
significance cannot be overlooked in the rise of
National Socialism.[27]

The missed opportunity was the last for the
Conservative Party. Without support, except for a
few Party stalwarts, Westarp and v. Heydebrand were
besieged with letters condemning their lackluster
leadership throughout the War.[28] If Westarp had not
shown enough *Lernfaehigkeit* to recruit the nationalist
workers, at least he and v. Heydebrand possessed
enough political foresight to form a commission whose
task it was to study the feasibility of revising the
Tivoli Programme of 1892. The creation of such a
committee was partially inspired by a letter from
Hoetzsch to Westarp on October 6. The letter was
pessimistic to the point of despair and presented an
argument that, apparently, was fully convincing:[29]

> I am of the opinion that the present
> turn in our domestic politics is permanent
> and that the Conservatives must accept it.
> If not, there will certainly arise a new
> Conservative Party and, without a doubt,
> it will be directed against the old Prussian
> aristocracy. In my opinion, the Party needs
> 1. a new programme and 2. another organizational
> and propaganda plan that will allow elements of
> property, right-wing National Liberals, Free
> Conservatives and right-wing elements in general
> to be drawn in...

By the end of October, both suggestions had been
acted upon: negotiations had gotten underway with the
right-wing and anti-Semitic *Deutsche Partei* (German Party)
for the development of a new Party programme. In early
November, the unrest within the Conservative Party
continued. A group of Conservatives under Dietrich
were pushing ahead for a complete change of the
Conservative programme.[30] Albrecht v. Graefe, on the
other hand, tried to move the Party toward the Christian-
Social camp, which was both *voelkisch* and extremely
anti-Semitic, and also clamored for a change in the
Party name.[31] At the same time, in an effort to gain
credulity among the troops who were soon to return now

that the War was lost, the Party announced that it
advocated a doubling of salary for troops and officers
and that both officers and enlisted men should receive
equal room and board.[32]

In the fading hours of the Empire, it became clear
that the German Conservative Party had reached a point
of no return. It had either to cease all operations
or emerge with a completely new image. This was known
to a great many members, some of whom had advocated
such drastic measures as early as 1916.[33] On November 5,
Westarp received three memoranda. Singularly, they
advocated significant changes in both the structure
and operation of the Party. Collectively, they sought
to destroy the basis of Conservative existence for nearly
half a century and prepare the Party for life in the
now inevitable Republic.

The first memorandum was from Dr. Richard Fuss.[34]
He informed Westarp that the Conservative Party "must
retain what is retainable." He suggested giving up
the basic fight against the SPD and called for a
"people's monarchy" and a "reconciliation between
country and city." Finally, he suggested to Westarp
that the Conservatives "cannot maintain our opposition
to a property tax." The second memorandum came from
Baron v. Hammerstein[35] and expressed the almost-paranoid
fear of the *Junkers* about the returning soldiers: "the
aristocracy must give up some of its land to the returning
war veterans." The third, and most comprehensive blueprint
for Conservative change, came from Hoetzsch[36] who sent
it to a number of Conservatives including Westarp. It
is difficult to know the intimacy of their relationship
since 1917. Hoetzsch had been a speaker for the
Fatherland Party and several of his suggestions to
Westarp bear the imprint of Fatherland Party ideology.
The Hoetzsch memorandum is especially significant
because it was the first time a Conservative theoretician
had suggested the idea of a Conservative *Volkspartei* not
based on agrarian demagogy.[37] Instead, Hoetzsch accepted
the fundamental idea that the Conservative Party would
have to function within a Germany that was politically
and constitutionally dissimilar to the Empire. He
appealed to Conservative members to abandon their economic-
interest orientation and nationalistic foreign policy.
The Party was to become, instead, a right-wing alternative
to the SPD and draw its support from landed farmers
(whose numbers would increase through inner colonization),
the bureaucracy and a small section of the independent
Mittelstand. Most revolutionary of all was his contention
that the Party would pick up industry and "high" finance

with such a membership composition. The Party was
also to give up its *Mittelstand* policy because, no
doubt, the *Mittelstand* would be anti-Semitic after
the War. Finally, there would be a need for the
Party to create a strong political relationship to
the western and eastern Slavic world.

Westarp left this letter from Hoetzsch unanswered.
It is unknown whether this was because of the rapidity
with which the Empire collapsed or because Hoetzsch's
proposals were too "left-wing" for Westarp's tastes.
At any rate, the Conservative Commission working on
suggestions for change, at a much slower and deliberate
pace than even Westarp could tolerate, announced on
November 7 that it had decided to build a committee
for the purpose of forming a "working community" with
other right-wing groups and to prepare for the reworking
of the Party programme.[38] On November 8, most likely
at the prodding of influential Conservatives, the
commission issued another statement, in what must have
been the speediest meeting ever held in Conservative
history: it announced that a union of all right-wing
parties was an "immediate necessity" and that the Party
programme had been changed so that "we will try to bring
in more national circles than ever before. We want
to secure a place for the Party in the future of Germany."[39]

The "future of Germany" was only a day away. On
November 9, the Empire ceased to be and became a part
of the mythology that would surround the "good old
times" discussions of future beer evenings. The last
Conservative speech in the *Reichstag* had been made on
October 27 (and significantly, it was delivered by
v. Graefe).[40] On November 11, Westarp wrote to Heydebrand
that "as a result of the news I've received, I am going
on vacation for a while. There is nothing that the
Conservative Party can do."[41] Indeed, there was little
that any of the German Right could do. With the Kaiser
in exile and the Empire at an end, both Heydebrand and
Westarp remained away from Berlin for several days:
v. Heydebrand at Tschunkawe and Westarp at a friend's
estate in Mecklenburg.[42]

Upon his return to Berlin on November 19, Westarp
found a totally new social and political situation.
The "hour of the little man" had come to Germany and
Junkers and Pan-Germans--indeed the Right in general--were
discredited.[43] He soon realized that the only possibility
for the Conservatives lay in cooperation with the newly-
formed German National Peoples' Party (DNVP) and to try
to insure as much Conservative influence in the new party

230

as possible.[44] As a result, Westarp entered into
negotiations with the DNVP and agreed to keep a low
profile along with most of the discredited pre-Republic
Right.[45] Opposition to Westarp's tactics came from
v. Heydebrand, who was furious at what he considered
Westarp's docility during the DNVP-Conservative talks.

The question of Conservative participation in the
DNVP came up at a Party meeting in Breslau at the end
of November. There the anti-Heydebrand resentment
exploded in full force, as Liegnitz reported to Tiele-
Winkler:[46]

> There were many battles with the Heydebrand
> people, including Richthofen and Count Sedlitz.
> They called the DNVP a sort of German Fatherland
> Party that we could support, but the German
> Conservative Party had to be maintained. Proposals
> to this effect were rejected. There were also
> battles between Heydebrand and the Breslau
> Conservative Association, which demanded that
> Heydebrand resign. But he remains stubborn.

Westarp was untainted by the conflict between old
and new. His special talent for political survival
allowed him to remain a force, albeit, like all
Conservatives, a minor one, for some time.[47] The new
DNVP bore a striking resemblance to the old Conservative
Party in some ways[48] and hardly at all in others.
Heydebrand, like the Conservative Party, remained in
name only--but he had "died" politically long before.[49]
In fact, the "new" Conservative no longer thought of
himself as a member of the German Conservative Party,
as this letter to Westarp reflected:[50]

> The idea of a Conservative Party is fully
> discredited. It is silly for the Conservatives
> to try and get a new programme, for we no longer
> represent the monarchy. Now we represent the
> christian-conservative ideals of the Republic.

Some things, however, never changed. As Count
Carmer indicated to Westarp, *Lernfaehigkeit* had finally
come to the Conservative Party, although much too
limited and much too late:[51]

> We must take a clear position to the
> Ebert-Scheidemann wing (of the SPD-AJP).
> This wing is just as *staatserhaltend* as
> the bourgeois parties. We will have to

> fight against the Independent Socialists
> and Spartacus. I therefore deem it possible
> to reach an understanding with the right-wing
> of the SPD and also quite necessary. I am
> convinced that the SPD is ready to reach an
> agreement with us and the other bourgeois
> parties.

But the time for such manipulative schemes had not yet
come. More indicative of the reality of the moment
and the decline of the "small but powerful" Conservative
Party was a letter sent by Party Secretary Bruno Schroeter
to the Workers' and Soldiers' Council for Berlin:[52]

> Would you please return Count Westarp's
> desk, typewriter and papers from his *Reichstag*
> office. We demand to know when it will be
> possible to obtain this private property and
> place it in our possession.

ii. Adapt and survive

Concern over the collapse of the Conservative Party
was evident in BdL Circles. As 1918 stretched into
spring and summer, the major concern of the agrarians
no longer centered upon war aims. Although it continued
to maintain a voice in the frenzied, last-gasp propaganda
drive of the Fatherland Party during the summer military
offensive, it was clear that the *Bund* did not wish to go
the way of the Conservatives. Rather, it chose to
concentrate upon solidifying its own interests at the
expense of aiding the war effort or the German Conservative
Party. For most of early 1918, the BdL had centered its
activities in a drive against the restrictive war-time
economy imposed by the government.[53] The *Bund* argued
that such a governmental policy "would lead the German
farmer directly into socialism."[54] Translated into
practical politics, this meant that the agrarians were
worried over the amount of governmental interference
in the ability of all segments of the agrarian sector
to produce financial profits. From the advocacy of
price ceilings and governmental committees to regulate
the distribution of foodstuffs, the agrarians came full
circle to demand their abolition.[55] At stake was the
continued ideological domination by the *Bund* of unhappy
middle and small farmers. And, for the first time in
its history, the BdL concerned itself with the situation
of the farm laborer, a badly misused and long-neglected
part of the agrarian community.[56]

232

This was hardly done out of a real concern for the welfare of these groups. Rather, as it became clearer that the Prusso-German state was in mortal danger from the Left, the *Bund* began to erect long-range measures to counter an expected SPD initiative among farm laborers and smaller land owners and farmers. In July, the BdL announced the creation of farmers' associations to meet the demands of the unhappy farmers.[57] Within months of the Empire's end, the *Bund* was able to build up its political base in this area. In conjunction with its traditional *Mittelstand* policies, the *Bund* strengthened its ideological influence over most segments of the agrarian community.[58] This was done by the propagation of a comprehensive "trade union" idea: by creating farmer and farm laborer councils, the *Bund* was thus able to block any attempts by the SPD to organize the farm workers and was able to maintain its dominant political and social position in the agricultural sector.[59]

These developments were symptomatic of the consequences of an almost certain military defeat and the bankruptcy of domestic and foreign aims. In a matter of a few weeks before the War's end, the *Kartell* groups demonstrated an incredible political flexibility and pragmatism.[60] Their sense of political survival gave them an edge in cunning that the Conservatives did not possess. In October, therefore, the CDI entered into negotiations with the radical trade unions.[61] At the same time, the Fatherland Party continued to base its final hopes on the establishment of a military dictatorship. But with military defeat so close, Bauer and Ludendorff held such a move to be unwise. Instead they hoped to saddle the Majority parties with the responsibility for the Peace Resolution of 1917 and, therefore, with Germany's defeat.[62] This action would be used as the basis for the systematic struggle of the Right against the now almost-inevitable democratic regime.

iii. The dream is realized

While the *Kartell* groups were on the path to political compromise for the sake of social and economic continuity, voices within the ADV were calling for a revolution. Among them, Theodor Fritsch, now fanatically *voelkisch* and calling himself Thorwalt, wrote the following plea to Gebsattel in July:[63]

233

> If we don't make the revolution, the
> rabble, led by the Jews, will. Let's prepare
> the revolution in a national and moral sense.
> The minute we threaten revolution, it will
> be noted above; for above (the Kaiser-AJP)
> there reigns fear and cowardice.

But Gebsattel who, along with Class, was aware of
the national mood, counseled otherwise:[64]

> It would be a terrible mistake to threaten
> revolution. We'd get nowhere--for those who
> rule would never believe revolution made by the
> good German bourgeois. You would have your
> revolution move against Jewry. They lead the
> extreme Left. They have more experience than
> we in revolutionary practice. We would be
> working for the purpose of our bitterest foe.
> We shouldn't try a revolution because we could
> achieve nothing but our own destruction.

Gebsattel's alternative idea, as expressed to Class in
early October, was much less extreme, but showed an
ability to perceive an essentially hopeless present:[65]
"We must first lie low and then build a political
Fatherland Party for the next election."

But what would be the glue that would hold this
"political Fatherland Party" together? By the beginning
of October, this had become evident to the ADV. Anti-
Semitic racism would be used in a new integrative ideology
to win not only the bourgeoisie but the lower classes
of society as well.[66] By October, in fact, both the CDI
and the BdL had begun to voice strongly anti-Semitic
propaganda.[67] The *Kartell*, more or less, dissolved the
Fatherland Party in order to jump aboard the anti-Semitic
wave;[68] since early 1918, anti-Semitism had become a
sort of *leitmotiv* among social groups ranging from the
officer corps to university professors.[69] Such was
this intense spread of Jewish hatred that Class was
able to tell an ADV conference on October 20 that "we
stand on the viewpoint that Kirdorf...is anti-Semitic
as are all the people in heavy industry. I also believe
that the army and the Prussian bureaucracy are vehemently
so!"[70]

On October 21, Gebsattel spelled out to Lehmann
the predominant task of the Pan-German future:[71] "The
most important thing to do is to fight against Jewry.
The time is more favorable than ever. We must devote

ourselves to this battle and not the fruitless struggle
for a better peace." Gebsattel's confident tone had
been decided by the ADV conference of the previous day,
in which the decision had been made to march against
German Jewry and to put all blame for the impending
defeat upon them. As Gebsattel told the cheering
members,[72] "the Jews will be used as a lightning rod
for all that seems to us unjust." Class, not to be
outdone, then closed the meeting with an eerily prophetic
pronouncement about the Jews: "Kill them all! The
rest of the world, in judging these actions, will not
ask for your reasons."[73]

EPILOGUE

1

As the clock struck midnight for the Prusso-German state, Hans Delbrueck bade it farewell with an appropriate observation. "The old no longer believes in itself, the new has made its entrance without opposition."[1] So it had, sweeping away the vestiges of a discredited political system. Amidst the debris were the remnants of the German Conservative Party. It, too, was a part of the old, lumped together with other relics of an Imperial age. In its place stood the German National People's Party (DNVP), a party created out of five formerly independent groupings (German Conservative Party, Free Conservatives, Christian Socials, German Socials, Reform Party) and a number of *Mittelstand* adherents represented by organizations such as the DNHV.[2]

Yet the German Conservative Party still felt the old longing, still wanted a voice of influence in the new constellation of parties opposed to the republic. As a result, it continued to keep its Executive Committee functioning, urging its members to join the DNVP, but at the same time refusing to abandon the old ways:[3]

> But of our revered and good conservative principles that form the basis of our monarchial-constitutional tradition, we will give up nothing. We will remain true to the old colors.

Its line of attack was similarly unchanged:[4] "We declare war upon this revolutionary government."

Events, however, had not been as decisive for the BdL and the ADV. Both groups had withstood the batterings of the Empire's collapse and had emerged politically strengthened. The BdL eventually changed its name to the *Reichslandbund*, but maintained its manipulative skills to a point where it was able to "stabilize its dominant political and social role in the agricultural sector."[5] The Pan-German League, too, found that its presence in a "criminal" republic did not mean a diminished political role. By 1920, its Membership had risen to 300,000 members in various local groups. Its pre-war and war-time message—the death-struggle with Jewry—was accepted by many "legitimate" circles, like the industrialist Stinnes, who told Class a year after the War's end that the "struggle against Jewry was the correct one."[6]

236

Radicals and Reactionaries

The post-war path to political power for the ADV was, indeed, a smooth one. The Pan-German strategy to create a "scapegoat" for Germany's defeat had succeeded beyond its wildest expectations. As early as December 1918, the Jews had been blamed for destroying the monarchy and for being the "new kings of our time."[7] Even earlier, in September 1918, the viciously anti-Semitic *Auf Vorposten* had issued a *Deutsche Judenordnung*, calling for the disenfranchisement of all Jews among its 31 anti-Semitic demands.[8] Every Jew was soon charged with being a "voluntary agent of the *Entente*" and Jewish "Bolschevists" were held responsible for "stabbing Germany in the back."[9] After the creation of the Weimar Republic, antipathy to this democratic institution was expressed by referring to it as a "Jew Republic", by condemning its constitution as a "Jew constitution" and by deriding its flag as a "Jew flag." Golo Mann has correctly assessed the temper of those early Weimar years:[10]

> Never was the anti-Semitic passion in Germany more rabid than in the years 1919 to 1923. It was more rabid than 1930 until 1933 or 1933 until 1945.

By 1922, it was common in *voelkisch* meetings to hear demands made urging the placement of all Jews in concentration camps as an immediate step before eventual expulsion.[11]

In February 1919, during a meeting in Bamberg, the ADV declared that the *Judenfrage* would be the chief concern of its existence. As Class put it:[12]

> The *Judenfrage* would now be placed even more strongly in the forefront of activities. Its solution was our most pertinent task.

To implement this aim, the ADV formed the *Deutschvoelkischer Schutz und Trutzbund* (German *voelkisch* Defensive League). It was led by Gebsattel and ADV functionary v. Hertzberg-Lottin. From 1919 to 1922, the *Schutz und Trutzbund* carried out an extraordinary campaign of terror (albeit mostly agitational) against German Jewry.[13] The *Schutz und Trutzbund*, whose symbol was the swastika, reached its highpoint, according to Class, with the assassination of Jewish Finance Minister Walter Rathenau on June 24, 1922.[14] Shortly thereafter, the organization was banned by governmental decree. It immediately disbanded, with Gebsattel and v. Hertzberg leading their members *en masse* into the National Socialist Workers' Party (NSDAP) headed by Adolf Hitler.[15]

237

2

In the midst of such an anti-Semitic atmosphere,
Oskar Hergt, strongly conservative but unburdened by
affiliation with any political party, was elected
chairman of the DNVP on December 19, 1918. Such a
type, colorless and without political experience, was
needed to lead the Party; professionals such as Westarp
and other conservative politicians were a discredited
lot, representing failure and defeat. It was also important
to Party stability that Hergt enjoyed excellent relations
with the anti-Semitic Christian Socials and the DNHV,
because, from the very outset of its existence, the
DNVP was beset by differences over the place of the
Judenfrage in Party politics. In the heart of this
debate stood former members of the German Conservative
Party, both "traditionalists" and "modernizers."

Collectively discredited, many individual Conservatives
chose to join the DNVP. Both "left" and "right-" wings of
the Party, in the person of Otto Hoetzsch and Albrecht
v. Graefe, brought their views on anti-Semitism with
them. Almost from the moment of its creation, the
DNVP was under attack for its "softness" on the *Judenfrage*.
Auf Vorposten launched the first tirade almost before
Hergt had time to celebrate his election as first chairman:[16]

> One receives the impression that the
> DNVP is only a new version of the Fatherland
> Party.[17] Symbolic of the DNVP's tactics
> is the fear of opening up the *Judenfrage*...
> In many local chapters, Jews are involved in
> party operations.

In this connection, the Conservative Party, too, came
under attack by *Auf Vorposten*[18] for the allegedly
"unsavory" ideological influence left by "that baptized
Jew", Friedrich Stahl. His writings, according to
Auf Vorposten, "did not represent a German conservative
but rather a talmudic conservative *Weltanschauung*." The
publication concluded that:

> Whoever has followed the history of
> the Conservative Party finds it quite easy
> to distinguish between two wings: the real
> German Conservatives, for whom the Jew is
> the natural enemy of our *Volk* and those
> close to the Party leadership, who tend to
> defend the Jew.

238

Outrageous as part of these charges may have been, they did bear some semblance of reality. By 1920, two clear points of view did emerge concerning the *Judenfrage*: Albrecht v. Graefe and those close to the Christian Social Party were slowly pushing the DNVP toward an active and official anti-Semitic policy while moderates such as Hoetzsch and Hergt attempted to keep the Party from adopting such a move. By the summer of 1922, Graefe and the other extremists had succeeded in turning many of the local DNVP chapters into covert anti-Semitic organizations.[19] A worried Hoetzsch wrote that "a battle exists in the Party between proper and improper people. There is a danger that the proper ones will be pushed into the background."[20]

By the end of the year, however, it was the "improper" ones, in the guise of Henning, Reinhold Wulle and v. Graefe, who were pushed out of the Party—only to form the German *Voelkisch* Freedom Party and establish links with the National Socialists.[21] Within local DNVP organizations, a great amount of active anti-Semitism remained hidden from Party officials.

The bitterness over the *Judenfrage* all but obliterated Hergt's chances of establishing a firm basis for effective leadership. Beyond anti-Semitism, the Kapp Putsch of 1920, when many moderate elements left the Party, and the DNVP's split in 1924 over acceptance or rejection of the Dawes Plan finished the unfortunate Hergt. He resigned a short time later.[22]

In November 1924, Ernst Heydebrand und der Lasa died, bitter to the end over the events that led to his political demise during the War. The *Berliner Tageblatt*,[23] commenting on his death, stated that for the "Little One's" passing "history need not turn a page. His death has no political meaning." It was not the most fitting of obituaries for the hero of East Prussia. What political meaning, then, could be derived from the startling news that Hergt's successor would be Count Cuno Westarp?

Westarp's assumption of power in 1924 was filled with political nostalgia. Taking over from Hergt was a politician of the old school, not close to the new direction of German politics nor a man who had lost his identity, ideal, or prestige, even during the years of political obscurity after 1918.[24]

Westarp, as Annelise Thimme has suggested, was not the "strong man" that the Party sought to close the gaping wounds caused by the internal conflicts of its early years.[25] Instead, he was a remnant of the "good old times", close to the principles of a discredited ideology. Westarp's election was a victory for the "restoration" policies of moderates within the DNVP: for no matter how much the Party viewed itself as a *Massenpartei*, neither its programme nor its policies reflected anything more than a "weimarized" German Conservative Party. Indeed, the DNVP, after 1924, found itself a member of the government, sitting in a cabinet with politicians it despised. Yet Westarp's conservatism, his love of order and his belief in the principle of "first the state and then the *Volk*", pushed him, and consequently the DNVP, toward a *regierungsfromm* stance. The DNVP eventually wound up vowing to defend a republic it hated.[26]

From 1924 until 1928, Westarp tried to guide the DNVP along traditional conservative lines. His election sloganeering spoke of his belief in a *Volksgemeinschaft*, but his heart was never in it. With the unfortunate results of the 1928 election, in which the DNVP suffered heavy losses, Westarp saw his grip on the reigns of power slip and then disappear. Heinrich Class and the ADV, through their DNVP representative, Alfred Hugenberg, forced Westarp out of the DNVP.[27] The reason was quite simple: Westarp's policies had not changed drastically in the years since 1918. Yet Class's policies, too, had remained constant, as he had written in 1922:[28]

> When I spoke to the *Grossgrundbesitzer*,
> I told them that our plan was not to produce
> a so-called restoration, the simple reestablishment
> of the political situation before the collapse.
> I told them our plan called for a new Germany.

By 1928, Class was convinced that the time for a "new Germany" had, indeed, come. Hugenberg, as the new chairman of the DNVP, was to use the Party to aid in the establishment of a Pan-German dictatorship over Germany.[29]

Despite his ouster from the DNVP, Westarp was not quite finished. He proceeded to create the *Konservative Volkspartei*,[30] once more demonstrating that his *Lernfaehigkeit* was of the kind that was too little and came too late. Westarp was an "old-fashioned man" who no longer had a place in the right-wing politics of Weimar Germany. This was amptly demonstrated by the manner in which the *voelkisch* and para-military *Stahlhelm* attacked--or, better, laughed at--the *Konservative Volkspartei* in the election of 1930.[31]

240

Radicals and Reactionaries

The German Conservative Party, or at least its
spirit, had been given one final chance to demonstrate
the "eternal truth" of its beliefs. For one more
moment in time, the *Junkers* had had the opportunity
to be the "small but powerful party" of a by-gone era.
But like Heydebrand's epitaph in the *Berliner Tageblatt*
of 1924, its death "had no political meaning." Time
had moved on, and the "conservative revolution" of the
twenties did not refer to a Prussian-based band of
Herrenmenschen, as Dr. Rudolf Fischer pointed out in
1929:[32]

> The sense of true Conservative policy
> must be centered in a new aristocracy. But
> not in the traditional one--this group is
> degenerate. The "freeborn" that I refer to
> come from all segments of the *Volk*. They
> are the *avant garde* of the attack against
> civilization.

The formal epitaph for the Conservative Party was
written in 1928 by Georg Decker. Writing in *Die
Gesellschaft*, Decker entitled his article, "The Death
of a Party."[33] "The split between the DNVP and the
German Conservative Party," he wrote, "is of no earth-
shattering consequence." It was more symbolic, for it
highlighted the "no-compromise" policy of the Conservatives
versus the compromise and unprincipled aims of the German
Nationalists. Too much had changed in Germany, Decker
felt, for men like Westarp to deserve power and leadership:

> When Westarp took over the DNVP, he tried
> to move backward to an intransigent, basic
> opposition. This meant suicide for the
> Conservatives. The DNVP was looking for
> further participation in the political
> consolidation of the bourgeoisie and the
> continuation of the struggle for power in
> the Republic.

The DNVP wanted power, he concluded, "but if that goal
cannot be achieved in a constitutional fashion, then
one needs other means, other ways to get it. This is
what is now evident in the DNVP's will to power, whose
victim the German Conservative Party has become."

It had taken the ADV two decades since 1910 to
destroy the elitism and Prussian-based *hubris* of the
German Conservative Party. Now the script was played
out and the final curtain had fallen. For Westarp and

241

the German Conservative Party, indeed for traditional
conservatism as a whole, there would be no more encores.
What followed for German history was a tragedy of
immense proportions acted out by a different cast of
characters. The roles they created as well as their
dramatic performances would become immortalized in infamy.

NOTES

Chapter I

1. Fritz Stern, *The Failure of Illiberalism*, London
1972, p. 57. See also Geoffrey Barraclough, "A
New View of German History," Part III, *The New
York Review of Books* Volume XIX, 8, November 16,
1972, p. 25.

2. Helmut Boehme, "Big Business, Pressure Groups and
Bismarck's Turn to Protectionism, 1873-1879," in
The Historical Journal X (2) 1967, p. 219.

3. Fritz Stern, "Money, Morals and the Pillars of
Society," in *The Failure of Illiberalism*, pp. 27-57.

4. Hans Rosenberg, "Political and Social Consequences
of the Great Depression of 1873-1896 in Central
Europe," in *The Economic History Review*, Vol. 13,
1943, p. 59.

5. There were, in fact, within the period of the
"Great Depression" three "mini-depressions"
(1873-1878, 1882-1886, 1890-1894) as well as
two slight positive rises in 1879-1882 and
1886-1889. After 1894 another more permanent
economic rise took place which was to last until
1913. See Hans Rosenberg, *Grosse Depression und
Bismarckzeit*, Berlin (West) 1967, p. 53.
  The whole question of the effects of the
"Great Depression" upon Britain as well as the
validity of the term itself have recently been
questioned by Professor S. B. Saul in *The Myth
of the Great Depression*, London 1969. Professor
Michael Balfour, in the "Afterward" to his
American edition of *The Kaiser and His Times*,
New York 1972, p. 526, wonders whether "...German
economic historians may not be tending to over-
emphasize the Depression just at the moment when
British ones are beginning to play it down." The
present author's feelings are somewhat more in
sympathy with the view of Professor Hans Rosenberg
who attempts to emphasize not only the economic
consequences, but also the social-psychological
effects.
  Professor Saul's figures in terms of the
percentage of annual increase in manufacture per
head of population (p. 39 Table V) are impressive
in showing the effects of the Depression to have
been more serious in Britain than in Germany in
this particular area. Equally noteworthy are the
figures in W. G. Hoffmann and J. H. Mueller, *Das
Deutsche Volkseinkommen 1851-1957*, Tuebingen 1959,

pp. 14, 35-40. These show figures of employment
rising and real wages on the increase. Rosenberg
in *Grosse Depression*, p. 47, takes this latter
point into consideration and, in fact, feels that
in a socio-historical sense this is "...one of the
most meaningful results of the Great Depression..."
No trend period, according to Rosenberg, was as
influential in the wage rises of the working class
as the so-called Great Depression. It solved their
material complaints and allowed them to focus on
social and political issues, throwing them into
a direct confrontation with the ruling classes and
thus sharpening an already developing class conflict.
    The effects of the "Depression" upon east
German grain exports and the decline in inland grain
prices made the economic situation very much an
agricultural depression. The fear of economic
disaster forced the agrarians to resort to tactics
which would be a basis for their "political style"
throughout the Second *Reich*. These two reasons
more than suitably support the preservation of the
term "Great Depression" in the German context whatever
the feeling towards its desirability in Britain.
For a favorable and similar view on the depression
as essentially an agricultural one, see Hans-Juergen
Puhle, *Von der Agrarkrise zum Praefaschismus*,
Wiesbaden 1972, pp. 17-18.
    An American view has been represented by Professor
Alexander Gerschenkron in a review of *Grosse Depression*
in Alexander Gerschenkron, *Continuity in History
and Other Essays,* Cambridge, Mass. 1968, pp. 405-408
(first published in *Journal of Economic History*,
March 1968). Professor Gerschenkron also points out
the positive growth rate of labor and attributes
the agricultural problem to one of structure rather
than cycle (p. 48), "...resulting from the expansion
of grain output overseas in conjunction with the
cost-reducing technological progress in ocean
transportation." This is, undoubtedly, true. But
Professor Gerschenkron, an advocate of the "spurt"
theory of economic growth, does not take advantage
of the possibilities of his theoretical position.
He fails to see that the "spurt" theory may also
be said to possess a negative factor. In the case
of the "Great Depression" the collapse of the
Gruenderzeit was the "spurt" necessary to speed
up the structural crisis of German agriculture.
This event plus the additional cyclical crisis produced
profound changes in agricultural thought and action.

6. Stern, "Money, Morals..." p. 46; P. G. J. Pulzer,
   *The Rise of Political Anti-Semitism in Germany and
   Austria*, London, 1964, p.88. Klaus Epstein,
   Geschichte und Wissenschaft im 20 Jahrhundert,
   edited by E. P. Kart, D. Junker, G. Hufnagel,
   Frankfurt am Main 1972, p.25.

7. Quoted in Rosenberg, *Grosse Depression*, p.61 (present
   author's translation as are all others in this work
   not quoted directly in the German or otherwise noted).

8. Rosenberg, "Political and Social..." p.63.

9. Personal financial considerations on Bismarck's
   part may have also played a role. Hence, it is
   known that Bismarck, too, suffered from losses
   in speculative land purchases. See Rosenberg,
   "Political and Social Consequences...", p.67 and
   Dieter Groh, "Negative Integration und Revolutionaerer
   Attentismus" in *International Wissenschaftliche
   Korrespondenz zur Geschichte der Deutschen Arbeiterbewegung*,
   April 15, 1972, pp.1-17.

10. See J. C. G. Roehl, *From Bismarck to Hitler*, London
    1970; Klaus Hildebrand, *Deutsche Aussenpolitik 1933-45
    Kalkuel oder Dogma?*, Stuttgart, West Berlin 1971,
    and Andreas Hillgruber, *Kontinuitaet und Diskontinuitaet
    in der deutschen Aussenpolitik von Bismarck bis
    Hitler*, Duesseldorf 1969.

11. Wolfgang Sauer, "Das Problem der deutschen Nationalstaates,"
    in Hans-Ulrich Wehler, *Moderne deutsche Sozialgeschichte*,
    Koeln, West Berlin 1970, 3rd edition, p.409. This was
    true, for instance, in the Stein-Hardenberg reforms and
    the constitutional concessions of 1848. See also
    Leonard Krieger, *The German Idea of Freedom*, Boston 1957.

12. For the early history of Conservatism in Germany to
    1815 see the excellent study by Klaus Epstein, *The
    Genesis of German Conservatism*. Princeton 1966.

13. Andreas Dorpalen, "The German Conservatives and the
    Parliamentarization of Imperial Germany," in *The
    Journal of Central European Affairs*, 1951. Vol. XI,
    pp. 184-199; Lothar Wallraf "Deutschkonservativepartei
    (DKP) 1876-1918" in D. Fricke (ed.) *Die Buergerlichen
    Parteien in Deutschland 1830-1945*, 2 Vols. Leipzig
    1970, Vol. I, pp.674-675; Erich Jordan, *Die Enstehung
    der Konservative Partei und die preussischen Agrarverhaeltnisse
    von 1848*, Muenchen 1914. See the soon-to-be completed thesis
    by Richard Schult "Die Grundung einer konservative Partei
    in Preussen," University of Hamburg.

14. Dorpalen, "The German Conservatives...," p.148;
    Robert Berdahl, "Conservative Politics and Aristocratic
    Landholders in Bismarckian Germany," in *Journal of
    Modern History*, No. 1, Vol. 144, March 1972, p.1.
    The Party centered around the newspaper, the *Preussische
    (Kreuz) zeitung* (first appeared July 1, 1848) which
    served as the official organ of Conservative thought
    and opinion.

15. Wallraf, "Deutschkonservative Partei...," p.675.

16. Berdahl, "Conservative Politics...," p.3.

17. Dorpalen, "The German Conservatives...," p.184.

18. Berdahl, "Conservative Politics...," p.12.

19. Ibid.

20. For a detailed account of the *Kreisordnung* and its
    effects upon the Conservatives, see the unpublished
    doctoral dissertation of Robert M. Berdahl, "*The
    Transformation of the Prussian Conservative Party*,"
    1866-1876, Ph.D. thesis, University of Minnesota,
    1965. For an older account of the Conservative
    change from a purely particularist party to an east-
    Elbian-based "national" party see Gerhard Ritter,
    *Die preussischen konservativen und Bismarcks Politik
    1858-1876*, Heidelberg 1913.

21. The concept was to be a continuous factor in German
    anti-parliamentary thinking, reflecting widespread
    nationalist opinion prior to and during the First
    World War. See R. H. Bowen, *German Theories of the
    Corporate State with a Special Reference to the
    Period 1870-1919*, New York 1947.

22. The Prussian Landtag Conservatives dropped from 116
    members to 32, only four of whom could have been
    considered "Old Conservatives." In the federal
    Reichstag the Party dropped from fifty members to
    twenty-one. See Berdahl "Conservative Politics...,"
    p.7; also, Hans Booms, *Die Deutschkonservative
    Partei,* Duesseldorf 1954, p.5.

23. See page 5.

24. David Yeling Allen, "*From Romanticism to Realpolitik.
    Studies in Nineteenth Century German Conservatism.*"
    Ph.D. thesis, Columbia University, 1971, p.436.

25. W. Zorn, "Wirtschaftliche und Sozialgeschichtliche Zusammenhaenge der Deutschen Reichsgruendungszeit (1850-1879)," in *Historische Zeitschrift*, Vol. 197, 1963, pp.318-342; Alexander Gerschenkron, *Bread and Democracy in Germany*, New York 1943, 1966, p.42; M. Balfour, *The Kaiser...*, p.525.

26. Boehme, "Big Business, Pressure Groups...," p. 225.

27. Ibid.

28. Helmut Boehme, *Deutschlands Weg zur Grossmacht*, West Berlin 1966, p.225.

29. Ivo N. Lambi, "Die Organisation der industriellen Schutzzollinteressen" in Karl Erich Born (ed.) *Moderne deutsche Wirtschaftgeschichte*, Koeln, West Berlin 1966, p.308.

30. Helmut Boehme, "Big Business, Pressure Groups...," pp.228-230. Delbrueck eventually "retired" from office in 1877.

31. Helmut Boehme, "Politik und Oekonomie in der Reichsgruendung und spaeten Bismarckzeit" in M. Stuermer (ed.) *Das Kaiserliche Deutschland*, Duesseldorf 1970, p.40.

32. Boehme, "Big Business, Pressure Groups...," pp.231,232.

33. Berdahl, "Conservative Politics...," p.13.

34. Literally, "Lord of the manor"--a term from the middle ages which maintained the conservative conception of a link with the feudal past. For an explanation of land-owning terms, see S. R. Tirrell, *German Agrarian Politics after Bismarck's Fall*, New York 1951, pp.16-18.

35. Rosenberg, *Grosse Depression*, p.162.

36. Quoted in Tirrell, *German Agrarian Politics*, p.32.

37. Boehme, "Big Business, Pressure Groups...," pp.235-236.

38. Ibid; also see Michael Stuermer, "Konservatismus und Revolution in Bismarck's Politik," in Stuermer, *Das Kaiserliche Deutschland*, p.157.

39. Berdahl, "Conservative Politics...," p.19 and see point 1 of the German Conservative Party Program in Wilhelm Mommsen, *Deutsche Parteiprogramme*, Muenchen 1960, p.67.

40. Berdahl, ibid., p.19.

41. The term "illiberalism," while neither new nor limited
    to Fritz Stern's latest publication, *The Failure of
    Illiberalism*, perhaps more than any other, best
    describes the politics of Germany's ruling classes
    from 1871 until 1918; Booms, *Die Deutschkonservative
    Partei*, p.5; see also Max Weber's Freiburg University
    Inauguration speech of May, 1895, in Max Weber,
    Gesammelte Politische Schriften, Muenchen 1921, p.24,
    and Rosenberg, *Grosse Depression*, p.73.

42. Rosenberg, *Grosse Depression*, p.72. Friedrich Naumann
    judged the number to be about 24,000 individuals.
    See Friedrich Naumann, *Demokratic und Kaisertum*,
    Berlin 1904, p.91.

43. Hans Rosenberg, "Die Pseudodemokratisierung der
    Rittergutsbesitzerklasse" in Hans-Ulrich Wehler
    (ed.), *Moderne Deutsche Socialgeschichte*, Koeln,
    West Berlin 1970, 3rd edition, p.288 (first appeared
    in *Zur Geschichte und Problematik der Demokratie*.
    Festgabe für Hans Herzfeld, West Berlin 1958). Otto
    Stolberg-Wernigerode fails to consider the elements
    constituting Conservative "modernity." He states
    that: "Es kann noch weitgehender behauptet werden,
    dass sie keine moderne Partei geworden ist..." and
    he allows only that "...sie bei Wahlen die ueblichen
    propagandistischen Methoden zur Gewinnung von
    Waehlern anwandte..." See Otto Graf zu Stolberg-
    Wernigerode, *Die Unentschiedene Generation*, Muenchen
    1968, p.211.

44. See Naumann, *Demokratie und Kaisertum*.

45. Manfred Messerschmidt, "Reich und Nation in Bewusstsein
    der Wilhelminischen Gesellschaft," in Wilhelm Deist
    and Herbert Schottelius (eds.), *Marine und Marinepolitik
    in Kaiserlichen Deutschland 1871-1914*, Duesseldorf
    1972, pp.11-33.

46. Boehme, *Deutschlands Weg zur Grossmacht*, p.400; Dirk
    Stegmann, *Die Erben Bismarcks*, Koeln, West Berlin
    1970, pp.20-22.

47. Rosenberg, *Grosse Depression und Bismarckzeit*, p.49.

48. Stern, "Money, Morals...," p.48.

49. See Eckart Kehr, "Zur Genesis des Königlich Preussischen Reserve Offiziers," in Hans-Ulrich Wehler (ed.), *Der Primat der Innenpolitik*, West Berlin 1965, pp.53-63.

50. Kehr, "Das Soziale System der Reaktion in Preussen unter dem Ministerium Puttkamer," in *Primat der Innenpolitik*, pp.64-86.

51. Boehme, "Politik und Oekonomie...," pp.36-37. It is interesting to note that Ludwig von Gerlach expressed the same sentiments in 1848: "Vergessen wir nicht dass es der hohe Beruf des Adels ist, die ganze Nation zu adeln." Quoted in Oskar Stillich, *Die politischen Parteien in Deutschland,* Vol. I: *Die Konservativen.* Leipzig 1908, p.211.

52. Rosenberg, *Grosse Depression und Bismarckzeit,* pp.146, 153; Booms, *Die Deutschkonservative Partei,* pp.39, 41-42; J. C. G. Roehl, *Germany without Bismarck,* London 1967, pp.18-19.

53. Ibid.

54. Booms, *Die Deutschkonservative Partei,* p.21.

55. The *Berliner Bewegung* was anti-Semitic, anti-Socialist, and anti-Liberal. Stoecker's Party (the *Christlichsoziale Partei*) was part of this wider movement. For Stoecker and the *Berliner Bewegung* see, among others, Walter Mohrmann, *Antisemitismus,* Berlin 1972; P. G. J. Pulzer, *The Rise of Political Anti-Semitism in Germany and Austria,* London 1964. Dieter Fricke, "Christlichsoziale Partei (CSP)," in *Die Buergerlichen Parteien,* Vol. I, pp.245-255; Paul W. Massing, *Vorgeschichte des Politischen Antisemitismus* (English title: *Rehearsal for Destruction),* Frankfurt a. M. 1959; Walter Frank, *Hofprediger Adolf Stoecker und die Christlichsoziale Bewegung,* Hamburg 1935, 2nd edition.

56. Wallraf, "Deutschkonservative Partei...," p.681.

57. Ibid. See also Pulzer, *The Rise of Political Anti-Semitism,* p.118, and Dieter Dueding, *Der Nationalsoziale Verein 1896-1903,* Muenchen, Wien 1972, p.17.

58. Hans-Ulrich Wehler, *Bismarck und der Imperialismus,* pp.454, 486; Koeln, West Berlin 1969; Stuermer, "Konservatismus und Revolution...," p.158.

59. For a dissenting, although theoretically uncritical,
     thesis see P. M. Kennedy, "German Colonial Expansion:
     Has the 'Manipulated Social Imperialism' been Ante-
     Dated?" in *Past and Present*, 54, February 1972,
     pp.134-141.

60. Wehler, *Bismarck und der Imperialismus*, p.481; Stegmann,
     Die Erben Bismarcks, p.106.

61. Pogge von Strandmann, "Domestic Origins...," p.143.

62. Roehl, *Germany without Bismarck*, p.46. For a specialized
     examination of the end of the *Kartell*, see J. C. G.
     Roehl, "The Disintegration of the Kartell and the
     Politics of Bismarck's Fall from Power 1887-1890," in
     The Historical Journal, IX, 1966, pp.60-89.

63. Hartmut Pogge v. Strandmann, "Domestic Origins of
     Germany's Colonial Expansion under Bismarck," in
     Past and Present, Number 42, February 1969, pp.152, 156.

64. Michael Stuermer, "Bismarck in Perspective," in
     Central European History 4, 1971, p.296.

65. Geoffrey Barraclough, *New York Review of Books*,
     November 16, 1972, p.26. This article as well as two
     others under the general theme of "Rethinking Germany"
     is an attempt by Professor Barraclough to indict
     the so-called "liberal historians" (Hajo Holborn, etc.)
     and their traditional views of German history and
     to plead for the acceptance of a "radicalized" approach
     based on the research of younger German historians.

66. Dirk Stegmann, "Wirtschaft und Politik nach Bismarck's
     Sturz. Zur Genesis der Miquelischen Sammlungspolitik,"
     in Imanuel Geiss and Bernd Juergen Wendt, (eds.),
     Deutschland in der Weltpolitik des 19 und 20 Jahrhunderts,
     Duesseldorf 1973, pp.161, 162.

67. Stuermer, "Bismarck in Perspective," p.297.

68. Rosenberg, *Grosse Depression und Bismarckzeit*, p.201.

69. Stuermer, "Bismarck in Perspective," pp.327, 328; Michael
     Stuermer, "Staatsstreichgedanken in Bismarckreich," in
     Historische Zeitschrift 209, 3, 1969, p.611; Rosenberg,
     Grosse Depression und Bismarckzeit, p.128.

70. Stuermer, "Konservatismus und Revolution...," p.163.

Chapter II

1. The Conservatives' *Reichstag Mandatzahl* dropped from
    80 to 73 seats; the *Reichspartei*-Free Conservative
    total from 41 to 20 seats, and the National Liberals
    from 99 to 42 seats. Bismarck was dismissed from
    office by William II on March 18, 1890.

2. See pp. 7ff..

3. Even the well-known Conservative Party leader, Heydebrand,
    in reflecting over the course of Conservative Party
    history, characterized v. Helldorff-Breda as "weak."
    Ernst Heydebrand und der Lasa, "Beitrage zu einer
    Geschichte der Konservativen Partei in den letzten
    30 Jahren 1888 bis 1919," in *Konservative Monatschrift*
    77, 1920, p.499; see also Georg v. Below, "Otto
    Heinrich von Helldorff-*Breda*," in Hans v. Arnim and
    Georg v. Below, *Deutscher Aufstieg*, Berlin, Leipzig
    1920, p.245.

4. While this error was not responsible for the defeat
    of the Bill-tactical considerations allowed it to
    expire without a decisive vote--it was a further factor
    in the destruction of the *Kartell*. Animosity within
    the Conservative Party between *Kreuzzeitungspartei*
    politicians and the *gouvernemental* groups was a decisive
    factor in allowing Bismarck to proceed with his plans
    for the *Kartell's* dissolution. When seen in this light,
    von Helldorff-*Breda's* misinterpretation of Bismarck's
    strategy does not altogether appear as politically
    inept, since part of that strategy seems to have been
    a planned effort to mislead the Conservatives. See
    Roehl, "Disintegration of the Kartell...," pp.60-89
    and Roehl, *Germany without Bismarck*, pp.48, 49.

5. James J. Sheehan, "Political Leadership in the German
    Reichstag 1871-1918," in *American Historical Review*
    LXVIV, 1968, p.512.

6. Massing, *Rehearsal for Destruction*, p.63; Nipperdey,
    Die Organisation der deutschen Parteien vor 1918,
    p.264; Hans-Juergen Puhle, "Der Bund der Landwirte
    im Wilhelminischen Reich-Struktur, Ideologie und
    politische Wirksamkeit eines Interressenverbandes in
    der Konstitutionellen Monarchie 1893-1914," in Walter
    Rüegg and Otto Neuloh (eds.), *Zur soziologischen Theorie
    und Analyse des 19. Jahrhunderts*, Goettingen 1971,
    pp.146,147.

7. Massing, *Rehearsal for Destruction*, p.61.

8. Ibid, p.49.

9. Among these forces, the National Liberal minister Johannes von Miquel. See Roehl, *Germany Without Bismarck*, p.278.

10. Massing, *Rehearsal for Destruction*, p.60, and see also Hans Leuss, *Wilhelm Freiherr von Hammerstein*, Berlin 1905, p.90.

11. Among the major countries involved in treaty negotiations with Germany were Austria-Hungary, Italy, Belgium, Switzerland, Serbia, Rumania, Spain, and Russia.

12. See Chapter I.

13. Herman Lebovics, "Agrarians versus Industrializers," in *International Review of Social History,* Vol.12, 1967, p.39.

14. Kenneth D. Barkin, *The Controversy over German Industrialization, 1890-1902*, Chicago 1970, pp.41, 42.

15. Ibid, p.42.

16. This was a concept first elaborated by Professor Fritz Fischer in *Krieg der Illusionen*, Duesseldorf 1969, pp.24,25. It has also been briefly discussed by Stegmann in *Die Erben Bismarcks*, p.60. The theme was recently reiterated by Fischer and leading West German historians in a combined West German-Soviet Union historians' conference held in the *Bundesrepublik* in October 1973. An interesting result of the conference was a call for a review and reinvestigation of the whole Caprivi era and an intense dissatisfaction with the results of available research.

17. This concerned a Conservative proposal which would have allowed strengthened church control over Prussian education. It was subsequently defeated. See Roehl, *Germany Without Bismarck*, p.79.

18. Ibid., p.278.

19. As Andreas Dorpalen has commented: "The Conservatives held the key position in both houses of the Prussian Landtag. No chancellor could ignore this fact. Since he depended on the Conservatives for the enactment of his Prussian legislation, he could not afford to disregard their wishes in the Reich." Dorpalen, "Parliamentarization

of Imperial Germany," p.195. Caprivi insisted on
having nothing to do with affairs in either House.
Directly or indirectly, then, he was effectively cutting
off agrarian abilities to influence national matters.

20. Hans-Juergen Puhle, *Agrarische Interessenpolitik und
preussischer Konservatismus im Wilhelminischen Reich
(1893-1914), Ein Beitrag zur Analyse des Nationalismus
am Beispiel des Bundes der Landwirte und der Deutsch-
Konservativen Partei,* Hannover 1967, p.32.

21. See pp.17f.

22. V. Below, "Otto von Helldorff-Breda," p.244.

23. Massing, *Rehearsal for Destruction,* p.63.

24. Tirrell, *German Agrarian Politics after Bismarck's
Fall,* p.146.

25. The anti-Helldorff leader of the Westphalian Conservatives,
v.d. Rech, complained that the aristocratic and Berlin-
centered "Committee of Eleven" *(Elfer Ausschuss)* was
unresponsive to provincial needs and that provincial
leaders did not wish to be ruled "...by such a parliamentary
organ (von so einen parliamentarischen Organ nicht
reagiert sein)." This eventually led to the creation
of the Committee of Fifty *(Fuenfziger Ausschuss)* which
reflected a fairer representation of provincial Conservatives
but in no way diminished the decision-making powers of the
Berlin group. See Nipperdey, *Die Organisation der deutsche
Parteien vor 1918,* p.253.

26. Tirrell, *Agrarian Politics after Bismarck's Fall,* pp.146,
147; v. Below, "Otto von Helldorff-Breda," pp.243,244.

27. Von Manteuffel was in 1887 one of the founders of the
Conservative group in the first Prussian Chamber and
also served as Chairman of the *Reichstag* and *Herrenhaus*
factions.

28. See the article by Dieter Fricke, "Christlichsoziale
Partei (CSP)," in *Die Buergerlichen Parteien in Deutschland
1830-1945,* I, pp.245-255.

29. See pp.12f..

30. V. Below, "Otto von Helldorff-Breda," p.248.

31. See later sections of this chapter.

32. D. Fricke, "Christlichsoziale Partei," pp.248, 249;
     Alexander Burger, *Die deutsch-konservative Partei
     und Reichspartei,* n.p. 1911, pp.19,20.

33. See the article by Dieter Fricke, "Anti-Semitische
     Parteien," in *Die Buergerlichen Parteien in Deutschland
     1830-1945,* I, pp.36-40, and Massing, *Rehearsal for
     Destruction,* p.65, and, most recently, Richard S.
     Levy, *The Downfall of the Anti-Semitic Parties in
     Imperial Germany,* New Haven, 1975. Anti-Semitic
     groups had elected five members in 1890 and sent
     sixteen members to the *Reichstag* in 1893.

34. This was a term used by the "Radau" anti-Semites to
     denote their hatred of both Jewish finance and
     Conservative *Grossgrundbesitzer* and to signify that
     no appreciable differences existed between them.

35. Massing, *Rehearsal for Destruction,* p.65.

36. Ibid.

37. A copy of the programme is to be found in Wallraf,
     "Deutschkonservative Partei," pp.682, 683, and
     Mommsen, *Deutsche Parteiprogramme,* pp.78ff. Points
     1 and 2 reflected the *Kreuzzeitung* emphasis upon
     Christian piety and the anti-Semitism of the Stoecker
     and "Radau" groups; point 10 called for a continuation
     of high agricultural tariffs; point 11 presumed to
     speak for industrial needs by demanding high industrial
     tariffs and also indirectly attempted to point out
     the equal basis upon which both agriculture and industry
     were situated; point 12 showed Conservative support for
     the *Mittelstand;* point 13 reflected the anti-capital
     position of agrarians; and points 14 and 15 were anti-
     Social Democratic in content. See also the *Kreuzzeitung*
     article, "Der Konservative Parteitag," December 9, 1892 (A.A.)

38. The extent of Conservative need and, at the same time,
     fear of the "Radau" anti-Semites was expressed by v.
     Manteuffel who, several months after Tivoli, commented on
     the inclusion of the radicals in the Party Day in the
     following manner: "We could not avoid the Jewish
     question unless we wanted to leave to the demagogic
     anti-Semites the full wind of a movement in which they
     just would have sailed by us," quoted in Massing,
     Rehearsal for Destruction, p.65, and see Puhle,
     *Agrarische Interessenpolitik und preussischer Konservatismus
     im Wilhelminischen Reich (1893-1914),* p.123, 137, 138;
     and also see his article, "Der Bund der Landwirte in
     Wilhelminischen Reich...," p.155 in which he states:

"Der Antisemistismus wurde dabei aus einer anti
Konservativen Rebellion zu einem Anhaengsel des
Konservatismus..." See also Levy, in *The Downfall
of the Anti-Semitic Political Parties in Imperial
Germany*, Chapter 3.

39. See later sections of this chapter,

40. See Lothar Wallraf,"*Zur Politik der Deutschkonservativen
Partei in den letzten Jahrzehnten Ihres Bestehens (1898-
1918) unter den Bedingungen der Imperialistischen Epoche,*"
Diss. phil. Friedrich Schiller Universitaet, Jena, 1970,
p.46; and Fritz Klein, *Deutschland 1897/98-1917*, Berlin 1972,
p.51. In Dr. Klein's opinion: "In wenigen Jahren war unter
der Kanzlerschaft Caprivi's das System der herrschenden Klasse
empfindliche gestoert worden. Sein Versuch, die Arbeiterbewegung durch zugestaendnisse aufzuweichen, war gescheitert.
Seine Handelspolitik hatte die Grossgrundbesitzer zu wilden
Agitation gegen die Regierung getrieben. Seine Aussenpolitik
hatte die Kolonisten und die hinter ihnen stehenden Monopole
empoert und zur Gruendung des Alldeutschen Verbandes gefuehrt
Das Buendnis zwischen Rittergut und Hochhofen war ins Wanken
geraten." Marxist historians, whose picture of Bismarckian
and Wilhelminian Germany leaves previous little room for
positive comment about German chancellors, see in the Caprivi
chancellorship a certain amount of opportunity for reform
and redistribution of power. Whether that reform and power
were available to the working class is a question yet to
be fully rejected or accepted. Bourgeois historians have
more or less neglected this extremely important line of
inquiry. Even John Roehl in *Germany without Bismarck* is
much too preoccupied in tracing the development of the
Kaiser's "personal rule" to evaluate the Caprivi period
in this manner. It has, however, received some mention
by Dirk Stegmann in his article for the Fritz Fischer
Festschrift. Stegmann attributes the change in the
societal power distribution to Caprivi's readiness to
involve the left Liberals and the Center in his
government in order to assure his policies. See Dirk
Stegmann, "Wirtschaft und Politik...," pp.167-170.

41. This was particularly true in the reaction against the
working class and the Social Democratic Party. V.
Hammerstein was quoted at the Tivoli meeting as
explaining that, "There is no other method against
Social Democracy than to provoke the workers and let
them be shot." ("...es gibt kein anderes Mittel gegen
die Sozialdemokratie, als man die Arbeiter provoziert und
schiessen laesst.") Quoted in Helga Grebing, *Geschichte
der Deutschen Parteien*, Wiesbaden 1962, p.65, and Hans
Leuss, *Wilhelm Freiherr von Hammerstein*, p.108. See also
Born, "Strukturwandel...," p.279.

42. Stillich, *Die politischen Parteien in Deutschland*,
Vol. I: *Die Konservativen*, p. vi. Otto Hintze
too, found much the same situation when, writing
some three years later, he observed that, "By us
the parties are not really political, but more
economic, social or religious..." Quoted in
Eberhard Pikart, "Die Rolle der Parteien in
deutschen Konstitutionellen System vor 1914," in
Ernst-Wolfgang Boeckenfoerde, *Moderne deutsche
Verfassungsgeschichte (1815-1918)*, Koeln 1972, p.271.

43. Thomas Nipperdey, "Uber einige Gruendzuege der
deutschen Parteigeschichte," in Boeckenfoerde,
Moderne deutsche Verfassungsgeschichte (1815-1918), p.241.

44. Ruprecht-Ransern, writing in the *Bunzlauer Provinzblatt
fuer Bauern*, December 21, 1892, quoted in Puhle,
*Agrarische Interessenpolitik und preussischer
Konservatismus im Wilhelminischen Reich (1890-1914)*,
p.33. See also the *Kreuzzeitung* article, "Wollen wirklich
die Landwirte sich aufrassen," January 26, 1893 (A.A.)

45. Conrad Freiherr v. Wangenheim to Hans Freiherr v. Wangenheim,
December 24, 1893, in H. Freiherr v. Wangenheim (ed.),
Conrad Freiherr v. Wangenheim-Klein Spiegel, Berlin 1934,
pp.20, 21. See also the *Kreuzzeitung* articles, "Zum 'Bund
der Landwirte'," February 14, 1893 (A.A.), and "Der 'Bund
der Landwirte'," February 20, 1893 (A.A.).

46. Among published monographs on the *Bund* the most important
is the previously quoted Hans-Juergen Puhle, *Agrarische
Interessenpolitik und preussischer Konservatismus im
Wilhelminischen Reich (1893-1914)*. Dr. Puhle has
subsequently produced four other analyses of agrarian
pressure groups with emphasis upon the *Bund der
Landwirte*: Hans-Juergen Puhle, "Parliament, Parteien
und Interessenverbaende 1890-1914," in Michael Stuermer,
Das Kaiserliche Deutschland, Duesseldorf 1970, pp.340-377;
"Der Bund der Landwirte im Wilhelminischen Reich--Struktur,
Ideologie und politische Wirksamkeit eines Interessenverbandes in der Konstitutionellen Monarchie 1893-1914,"
in Walter Ruegg, Otto Neuloh (eds.), *Zur Soziologischen
Theorie und Analyse des 19 Jahrhunderts*, Goettingen
1971, pp.145-162; *Von der Agrarkrise zum Praefaschismus*
(Thesen zum Stellenwert der Agrarischen Interessenverbaende
in der Deutschen Politik am Ende des 19 Jahrhunderts),
Wiesbaden 1972; "Radikalisierung und Wandel des
deutschen Konservatismus vor dem Ersten Weltkrieg,"
in Gerhard Albert Ritter (ed.) *Die deutschen Parteien
vor 1918*, Koeln 1973, pp.165-186. Dr. Puhle's
methodological approach has emphasized an overwhelmingly

ideological critique of the *Bund* and its function.
In this he has been criticized by Dr. Dirk Stegmann
for being unable to broaden the methodology to allow
more emphasis upon a socio-economic analysis, and
relatedly, for providing an insufficient source basis
for important periods of the *Bund's* political activities.
See Stegmann, *Die Erben Bismarcks,* p.16. Other works
dealing with the *Bund* are two Marxist analyses:
Eduard David, *"Der Bund der Landwirte als Machtinstrument
der ostelbischen Junker tums 1893-1920,"* Diss. phil,
Martin-Luther Universitaet, Halle-Wittenberg 1967;
and Dieter Fricke (ed.), "Bund der Landwirte," in
Die Buergerlichen Parteien in Deutschland 1830-1945,
2 Vols, Leipzig 1970, pp.129-149. Both are somewhat
better than Puhle at analyzing the function of the
BdL as a representative of the ruling class, but
because of heavy emphasis on doctrinal approaches also
suffer from an inadequate number of sources. Other
bourgeois works dealing specifically or substantially
with the BdL are: Ursula Lindig, *"Der Einfluss der
Bundes der Landwirte auf die Politik des Wilhelminischen
Zeitalters 1893-1914,"* Diss. phil. Hamburg 1953; Hannelore
Horn, *Der Kampf um den Bau des Mittelland Kanals,* Koeln
and Opladen 1964; Hanne-Lore Land, *Die Konservativen und
die Preussische Polenpolitik (1886-1912),* Diss. phil.,
Free University of Berlin (West) 1963. Works before
1918 on the *Bund* include Curt Buerger, *Die Agrardemagogie
in Deutschland,* Berlin 1911, and the two anniversary
editions by the BdL official Otto von Kiesenwetter,
Zehn Jahre Wirtschaftlichen Kampfes, Berlin 1903, and
Fuenfundzwanzig Jahre wirtschaftspolitischen Kampfes,
Berlin 1918.

47. Other groups founded or reorganized that year were
     the German National League of Commercial Employees
     (Deutsch-Nationaler Handlungsgehilfenverband) and the
     Pan-German League *(Alldeutscher Verband)* in 1893/4.
     See Karl Dietrich Bracher, *The German Dictatorship,*
     (tr. Jean Steinberg) Penguin edition, 1973, p.63.
     Eberhard Pikart has described this tendency to view
     all parties in an unfavorable and powerless role:
     "...die Parteien wurden nicht als etwas Notwendiges
     und Elementares angesehen; sie waren einfach da;
     sie waren uebungsgemaessig vorhanden, sie wurden
     'extra konstitutionell hingenommen;' Die spielten
     im politischen leben ihre Rolle, aber die Verfassung
     beruecksichtigte sie nicht und erkannte sie nicht."
     Eberhard Pikart, "Die Rolle der Parteien im deutschen
     konstitutionellen System...," p.265.

257

48. Among the most serious of the economic and structural
     crises was a continuing loss of landworkers. This
     Landflucht--estimated by Born to have been 100,000
     in 1893 and to have reached two million by 1914--was
     primarily an internal resettlement to the big industrial
     centers and the promise of higher wages. To the
     agrarians, it was the clearest symbol of the change
     from an "agrarian state" to an "industrial state,"
     See Born, "Struktur und Wandel," pp.272, 273,

49. Puhle, "Der Bund der Landwirte im Wilhelminischen
     Reich...," p.152; and Puhle, *Agrarischen Interessenpolitik
     und Preussischer Konservatismus im Wilhelminischen
     Reich (1893-1914)*, p.92,

50. Ibid., p.34.

51. Puhle, *Von der Agrarkrise zum Praefaschismus*, p.60.

52. This is especially stressed by Hans Rosenberg in
     several of his essays on the problem of the social
     function of agrarian politics in the *Wilhelmine Reich*.
     See especially, "Zur sozialen Funktion der Agrarpolitik
     im Zweiten Reich," in Hans Rosenberg, *Probleme der
     deutschen Sozialgeschichte* (edition Suhrkampf),
     Frankfurt am Main 1969, pp.51-80, and especially page
     61 where Rosenberg states, "Was die deutschen Grosslandwirte
     aus dem Gleichgewicht warf, jedoch nicht so sehr der
     ueberseeische und osteuropaeische Weltbewerb an sich, als
     vielmehr die hohen Erzeugrungskosten der Getreidewirtschaft
     und die ueberhoehten Gueterwerte; ...Aus dieser Lage
     erwuchs nach Angfaenglichen Zoegern die unabsehbare
     Ausnutzung ihrer exquisitem politischen Macht und
     Gesellschaftsrangstellung soweit wie moeglich das
     Einfrieren und daher die Mobilisierung des *Kollektiven*
     (italics Rosenberg) Grundbesitzstandes der Landaristokratie
     zu erzwingen sowie ihr *auf Kosten anderen* (italics mine-AJP)
     eine bevorzugte wirtschaftliche Stellung und eintraegliche
     Bondenrente zu sichern." See also Puhle, *Von der
     Agrarkrise zum Praefaschismus*, pp.16, 17; and Peter-
     Christian Witt, "Der preussische Landrat als Steurbeamter
     1891-1918, Bemerkungen zur politischen und sozialen
     Funktion des deutschen Beamtentums," in Imanuel Geiss
     and Bernd Juergen Wendt (eds.) *Deutschland in der
     Weltpolitik des 19 und 20 Jahrhunderts*, Duesseldorf
     1973, p.218.

53. Stegmann, *Die Erben Bismarcks*, p.20; Puhle states that:
     "Der Bund der Landwirte hat die Konservative Partei
     verformt. Er hat sie nicht nur organisatorische
     veraendert ihr Basis im Lande geschaffen und durch

258

die Hilfestellung seines Apparat und seine Wahlhilfe
den Grund gelegt fuer die inner parteiliche Koalition...
also die Ideologie den Konservativen wesentlich veraendert."
Puhle, *Agrarische Interessenpolitik und preussischer
Konservatismus im Wilhelminischen Reich (1893-1914)*,
p.274.

54. The economic aims of the *Bund* were a mixture of the
politics of the possible and impossible. It was centered
on the agrarian wish for a complete reliance on domestic
grains (a form of state autarky). The agrarians felt
that this was possible only with the greatest amount
of state intervention and subsidy. This demand came
in the form of the Kanitz Motion (*Antrag* Kanitz) which
called for the nationalization of the grain trade as
a basis for saving agrarians from economic collapse.
This, a form of state socialism theoretically antithetical
to Conservative beliefs, was merely a ploy. Agrarians
knew that it could never be accepted by either the
government or the other bourgeois parties and used it only
as a pretense to force through other aspects of their
programme. Primary among these were the *Grosse Mittel*
which included, apart from the Kanitz motion, a demand for
bi-metallism (as a form of creating "soft" money to
alleviate the payment of agrarian debts) and a reform
of the stock exchange. The program also called for
a *Kleine Mittel*--demands which ranged from agrarian
influence in schools to the types of benches on trains
to tariff and tax protection measures. Relatedly,
the agrarians wanted the *BdL* to become a *Sammelpunkt*
for agrarians of all parties to create a united economic
front. The *Bund* was able to achieve several important
concessions, notably a reform of the stock exchange,
the lifting of the so-called *Identitaetsnachweise*
and the granting of subsidies, *(Liebesgaben)* at great
cost to the rest of the population. See Puhle,
*Agrarische Interessenpolitik und preussischer Konservatismus
im Wilhelminischen Reich (1890-1914)*, pp.30, 35, 52, 179,
180; Puhle, "Der Bund der Landwirte im Wilhelminischen
Reich...," pp.151, 152; Puhle, *Von der Agrarkrise zum
Praefaschismus*, pp.43, 44; D. Fricke, "Bund der Landwirte,"
pp.129, 139-142. For the *Antrag* Kanitz see Gerschenkron,
Bread and Democracy in Germany, pp.53, 58; Wallraf,
"Zur Politik der Deutschkonservativen Partei," p.28; and
the Reichstag speech of Count Schwerin-Loewitz on the
Antrag Kanitz, January 16, 1896, in Glans Graf von
Schwerin-Loewitz, *Aufsaetze und Reden*, Berlin 1911,
pp. 160-167.

55. The ideological basis of the *BdL* can best be
    understood by viewing the group as an organization
    that wanted, "...land, economic autarky, and to
    maintain their position in Prussia,..they fought
    the cities and Liberalism, which symbolized free
    trade, capitalism, democracy, possible emancipation
    and *Zersetzung*." Puhle, *Von der Agrarkrise zum
    Praefaschismus,* pp.44, 45. Also the aim of the
    Bund was to make use of parliament as a platform
    from which it could influence decisions concerning
    agriculture and to confront voters in a direct
    face-to-face manner. See Puhle, *Agrarische Interessenpolitik
    und preussischer Konservatismus im Wilhelminischen Reich
    (1893-1914),* p.36.

56. In 1922 Hermann Schwalenbach introduced the term *Bund*
    as an additional aspect to the sociological dichotomy
    originated by F. Toennies. This dichotomy consisted
    of the terms *Gemeinschaft* which was a sense of wholeness
    or community and was countered by the atomized society
    of the *Gesellschaft*. The dichotomy itself originated
    as a pessimistic reaction to the break-up of human
    interaction and a community spirit which supposedly
    had given way to the rise of the metropolis. Schwalenbach
    saw the *Bund* concept as a means of restoring the
    Gemeinschaft along the lines of an "organic" sense of
    cohesiveness, much in line with the thinking of the
    Bund der Landwirte. See Puhle, *Agrarische Interessenpolitik
    und preussischer Konservatismus im Wilhelminischen
    Reich (1893-1914),* p.84. For a good explanation of
    the *Gemeinschaft-Gesellschaft* duality and its relation
    to German society, see Arthur Mitzman, "Toennies
    and German Society, 1887-1914: From Cultural
    Pessimism to Celebration of the Volksgemeinschaft,"
    in *Journal of the History of Ideas*, VXXXII, 4, 1971,
    pp.507-524.

57. Puhle sees this combination as the essence of the *Bund's*
    view of society; "...it was corporate-*(staendisch)*-
    patrimonially oriented." It was an ideology which
    combined a particular view of the agrarian *Staende*
    with a plebiscitarian orientation. As such, it contained
    the belief that "the best defense was the attack,"
    (Die beste Deckung der Hieb sei). Puhle, *Agrarische
    Interessenpolitik und preussischer Konservatismus im
    Wilhelminischen Reich (1893-1914),* pp.78, 105, 240,
    and Puhle, "Der Bund der Landwirte im Wilhelminischen
    Reich...," p. 157.

58. The anti-Semitism of the *BdL* was "...Konservativ
und rassischnational orientiert." It was also economically
motivated since Judaism was identified with liberalism
and free trade. Never a spontaneous, deeply imbedded
aspect of Conservative belief, it was used by the *BdL*
as a "rationally calculated and technically perfected"
approach toward a sense of solidarity with *Kleinbuerger*
and *Mittelstand* leading to integration. Under the
leadership of Dr. Diederich Hahn, the *Bund* became,
after the steady decline of the "Radau" anti-Semites,
"the most influential and at the same time the...
mightiest anti-Semitic organization in the Kaiserreich."
See Puhle, "Der Bund der Landwirte im Wilhelminischen
Reich...," p. 154, and Puhle, *Agrarische Interessenpolitik
und preussischer Konservatismus im Wilhelminischen
Reich (1893-1914)*, pp.111, 125.

59. The *Bund* was a professionally-organized, tightly-run
association with control resting in the hands of a
small group of *Rittergutsbesitzer*. In their own views,
however, the agrarians were a *Mittelstandsbewegung*
(a class estimated at about half of the German population).
Their aim was to solidify relations with smaller
farmers and to draw in as many members as possible
(excluding Jews and Social Democrats) in an attempt
to influence government policy from an extra-parliamentary
position. The *BdL* was the first political organization
to concern itself with the politics of the *Mittelstand*.
Later *Mittelstand* movements (which did not really
come into their own until the turn of the century)
clearly reflected *BdL* propaganda and ideology. Puhle,
"Der Bund der Landwirte in Wilhelminischen Reich...,"
p. 157, and Puhle, *Agrarische Interessenpolitik und
preussischer Konservatismus im Wilhelminischen Reich
(1893-1914)*, pp.105, 178, 180.

60. The particular brand of Social Darwinism espoused by
the *Bund* can only be regarded as "vulgar." Its
notion of the "survival" of the fittest was based
upon a belief that all political events were aspects
of biological selection. Especially the biological
relation of agrarians to "Mother Earth," their fitness
as a group and the racial anti-Semitic view that
they were involved in a death-struggle with Judaism had
an enormous influence upon Conservative beliefs. (The
1894 Conservative Handbook saw the Jewish question
strictly in terms of an economic, national, or
juristic argument. With the influence of the *BdL*
the 1911 edition reflected a clear Social Darwinistic
point of view.) See Puhle, *Agrarische Interessenpolitik
und preussischer Konservatismus im Wilhelminischen Reich*

(1893-1914), pp.92, 138, 139, and Puhle, "Der Bund
der Landwirte im Wilhelminischen Reich...," p.153.
For Social Darwinism in Germany, see Hans-Guenter
Zmarzlik, "Der Sozialdarwinismus in Deutschland als
Geschlichtliches Problem," in *Vierteljahresheft fuer
Zeitgeschichte* 11, 1963, pp.246-273; H.W. Koch, "Die
Rolle des Sozialdarwinismus als Faktor im Zeitalter des
neuen Imperialismus um die Jahrhundertwende," in
Zeitschrift fuer Politik 17, 1970, pp.51-70 (now
published in English as "Social Darwinism in the
New Imperialism," in H.W. Koch (ed.), *The Origins of
the First World War,* London 1972, pp.329-354.

61. The *BdL* was, in principle, anti-industrial. In 1894
the *Kreuzzeitung* stated that, "Agriculture represents
the strongest and because of its social significance,
the most important force against the radical transformation
of the existing social and economic order. We see in
Germany's development into an industrial nation a great
danger which threatens our fatherland and our monarch."
This view was maintained in the 1898 *Konservatives
Handbuch* in which agriculture was called the "core
of the German people." The campaign against industry
was, in actual fact, a struggle against big-city
finance, dominated by international and German Jewry.
Also, the corrupt and decadent atmosphere of the big
city was especiably emphasized to any of the landworkers
who might have envisaged a move to an industrial
center. The level of conflict between agrarians and
heavy and middle industrialists was never so high as
to deter both sections from maintaining a solid
defense against the emancipation tactics of the German
working class. For the *Kreuzzeitung* article, see the
quote in Herman Lebovics, "Agrarians versus Industrializers,"
pp.43, 44; the *Handbuch* quote is in *Konservatives Handbuch,*
1898, third edition, p.199. See also, Dieter Fricke,
"Bund der Landwirte," p.137, and Puhle, *Agrarische
Interessenpolitik und preussischer Konservatismus im
Wilhelminischen Reich (1893-1914)* pp.79, 80.

62. Puhle, "Parliament, Parteien...," p.358.

63. Ibid., p.354. Puhle has also viewed this problem
in the following manner: "Insbesondere die Verbindung
staendischer, radikal demokratischer und plebiszitaerer
Komponenten in der Buendischen Mittelstandes Ideologie
unter Umgebung ja Negation von Parliament und Parteien
hat angesichts der wirksamen Massenagitation des
Bundes mit dazu beigetragen das im deutschen politischen
Denken der Gedanke der Representation nicht tiefere
Wurzeln geschlagen hat." See Puhle, "Der Bund der Landwirte
im Wilhelminischen Reich...," p.154.

64. Puhle, in "Radikalisierung und Wandel des deutschen
    Konservatismus vor dem ersten Weltkrieg," in Gerhard
    Albert Ritter (ed.), *Die deutschen Parteien vor 1918*,
    Koeln 1973, pp.166ff. and also for the smaller, less
    significant divisions within the Party. Nevertheless,
    Eckart Kehr, never far off the mark, was not totally
    in error when he claimed it was characteristic
    for the Conservatives that "...in ihm die verschiedenen
    Schichten so verklammert selbst in ein und demselben
    Abgeordneten liegen, dass ihre reinliche Differenzierung
    kaum moeglich ist." Eckart Kehr, *Schlachtflottenbau
    und Parteipolitik, 1094-1901*, Berlin 1930, p.323.
    Especially in a character as complex as von Heydebrand
    these different strains of old and new conservatism
    were constantly at odds. His commentary on the history
    of the Conservatives 1888-1919 includes the statement
    that he was an "ueberzeugter Anhaenger des BdL."
    Difficult as that is to ascertain, due to the loss
    of the Heydebrand *Nachlass*, one can see that position
    steadily deteriorate as the *BdL* increased its political
    horizons by steadily adopting a Pan-German position.
    See Heydebrand, *Beitrage zu einer Geschichte*, p.544
    and succeeding chapters of this book.

65. Puhle, "Radikalisierung und Wandel," p.171: "...an
    die Stelle der alten, zentralen Kategorien des Konservatismus:
    Persoenlichkeit (im Stand, nicht Individualitaet),
    Eigentum (nicht Sache), Freiheit (nicht Gleichheit),
    leben (nicht Begriff) und Autoritaet treten neue:
    Mittelstand, nationale Arbeit, Volksgemeinschaft,
    Kampf ums Dasein." See also Puhle, "Parlament,
    Parteien...", p.157 and *Agrarische Interessenpolitik
    und preussischer Konservatismus im Wilhelminischen
    Reich (1893-1914)*, pp.274 ff. Puhle feels that the
    voelkisch-radical-democratic ideology was the fourth
    and final step in the different stages of Conservatism
    (romantic, liberal and realistic) analyzed by Sigmund
    Naumann in *Die Stufen des preussischen Konservatismus*,
    Berlin 1930, Vaduz 1965. I shall attempt in succeeding
    chapters to subject Puhle's assertion to analysis
    against the backdrop of the internal conflict and
    structural changes of a society engulfed by "total war,"
    1914-1918.

66. Fritz Klein, *Deutschland 1897/98-1914*, Berlin 1972, p.48.

67. "Negative integration," was first used by Guenther Roth,
    *The Social Democrats in Imperial Germany--A Study in
    Isolation and National Integration*, Totowa, N.J. 1963
    and has been accepted and improved as a heuristic tool
    by Dieter Groh who defines it as the "...zunehmende

oekonomische Besserstellung und Tendenzen zur rechtlichen
und faktischen Gleichberechtigung einerseits, bei
gleichzeitiger grundsaetzlicher Vorweigerung der
Gleichberectigung in Staat und Gesellschaft und
Fortdauern der Ausbeutung und der unterdrueckungsmassnahmen
andereseits." See Dieter Groh, *Negative Integration und
revolutionaerer Attentismus*, Frankfurt/Main, Berlin
(West) 1973, p.36,

68. Caprivi's motives, however, cannot be judged solely
on the basis of this analysis, and await more intensive
research. Groh's contention that Caprivi's strengthening
of industry was for the purpose of achieving the passage
of the Army Bill of 1893 sheds little light on his
overall strategy. Ibid., p.66.

69. The number of strikes declined from a high of 226 at
the beginning of Caprivi's appointment, to a low of 73
in 1892. There was only a slight increase in 1893, but
by 1894 they had risen to 131. See the table in Klein,
Deutschland, 1897/98-1917, p.84.

70. Real earnings, on the contrary, had been constantly
rising since 1885. See the table in Groh, *Negative
Integration und revolutionaerer Attentismus*, p.40,
and also in Klein, *Deutschland 1897/98-1917*, p.85,
which, however, divides real earnings into those of
the workers' aristocracy (which grew at a significantly
faster rate) and the "great mass" of the workers.

71. The political leadership of the Social Democratic
Party was, in fact, struggling to resolve its own
ideological dilemma between revolutionary self-
understanding and revisionist moderation. The highly
revisionist "Eldorado" speech by the Bavarian Social
Democrat Georg v. Vollmar in June of 1891 served
as a political basis for these events.

72. Klein, *Deutschland, 1897/98-1917*, pp.42, 43.

73. Annelise Thimme, *Hans Delbrueck als Kritiker der
Wilhelminischen Epoche*, Duesseldorf 1955, p.154.

74. Notation of March 4, 1894, quoted in Stegmann,
Die Erben Bismarcks, p.61.

75. Cited in Volker R. Berghahn, *Der Tirpitz-Plan*,
Duesseldorf 1971, p.234.

76. Stegmann, "Wirtschaft und Politik...," p.171.

77. W. v. Kardorff to his wife, March 10, 1891, printed
    in Siegfried v. Kardorff, *Wilhelm von Kardorff.*
    Ein Nationaler Parlamentarier in Zeitalter Bismarcks
    und Wilhelms II, Berlin 1935, p.237, and see
    Stegmann, "Wirtschaft und Politik..." p.167.

78. Stegmann, *Die Erben Bismarcks*, p.106f, and "Wirtschaft
    und Politik...," p.167.

79. Ibid., p.63 and pp.172, 173.

80. Karl Erich Born, *Staat und Sozialpolitik seit Bismarck's*
    Sturz-Ein Beitrag zur Geschichte der innenpolitischen
    Entwicklung des Deutschen Reiches 1890-1914, Wiesbaden
    1957, p.112ff; Stegmann, *Die Erben Bismarcks*, p.131;
    "Politik und Wirtschaft...," p.173; Roehl, *Germany*
    without Bismarck, pp.210ff, 276, 277; Berghahn, *Der*
    Tirpitz-Plan, pp.146, 147. The question of the
    Kaiser's "personal rule," a thesis which has been
    accepted by Berghahn, Roehl, and Stuermer among others,
    has been rejected by Stegmann on the grounds that
    decision-making was actually carried out by Miquel,
    Posadowsky-Wehner, Buelow and a small circle around
    them. Quoting the Bible, in the form of Eckart Kehr,
    who Stegmann feels gave a much greater role to the
    idea of a ruling system, Stegmann cites the lack of
    evidence ("Wirtschaft und Politik...," p.183, F.N.135)
    for such a conclusion. Yet, he offers very little
    evidence to objectively deflate the thesis, aside
    from a vague reference to the unsuitability of analyzing
    history through "individual carriers of political
    responsibility." (An attempt to discredit Roehl
    and Berghahn as adherents of the "great men make
    history" school?) It seems to the author, at any
    rate, that the Kaiser had achieved the coordination
    of the Ministry of State in 1897 and with that, the
    appearance of a "personal rule" through the selection
    of ministers with similar aims as himself. It also
    seems that this power was steadily eroded by the
    forceful personalities of men like Tirpitz and Buelow
    and finally consolidated in the hands of the ruling
    agrarian-industrial elites.

81. Roehl, *Germany without Bismarck,* pp.220, 221; Berghahn,
    Der Tirpitz-Plan, p.97, and also, "Der Tirpitz-Plan und
    die Krisis des preussisch-deutschen Herrschafts systems,"
    in Wilhelm Deist and Herbert Schottelius (eds.), *Marine*
    und Marinepolitik im Kaiserlichen Deutschland 1871-1914,
    Duesseldorf 1972, p.91; Klein, *Deutschland 1897/98-1917*,
    pp.53, 54; Born, *Staat und Sozialpolitik nach Bismarcks*
    Sturz, pp.136, 137.

82. Stegmann, "Wirtschaft und Politik...," p.170.

83. Letter of June 8, 1896, quoted in Roehl, *Germany without Bismarck,* p.191, and Berghahn, *Der Tirpitz-Plan,* p.235.

84. Stegmann, "Wirtschaft und Politik...," pp.173, 174, 178, 179.

85. Puhle, *Agrarische Interessenpolitik und Preussischer Konservatismus im Wilhelminischen Reich (1893-1914),* P.235.

86. The most recent and best analyzed account of the Miquel *Sammlungspolitik* has been presented by Dirk Stegmann in *Die Erben Bismarcks* and his essay in the Fritz Fischer *Festschrift,* "Wirtschaft und Politik...," pp.161-184.

87. The authoritative account is Volker R. Berghahn, *Der Tirpitz-Plan.* See also several other works by Berghahn relating to the fleet: Volker R. Berghahn, "Zu den Zielen des deutschen Flottenbaus unter Wilhelm II," in *Historische Zeitschrift* (hereafter referred to as *HZ*), 210, 1970, pp.34-100; "Flottenruestung und Machtgefuege," in Michael Stuermer (ed.), *Das Kaiserliche Deutschland. Politik und Gesellschaft 1870-1918,* Duesseldorf 1970, pp.378-396; "Der Tirpitz-Plan und die Krisis des preussischdeutschen Herrschaftssystems," in H. Schottelius und W. Deist, *Marine und Marinepolitik im Kaiserlichen Deutschland 1871-1914,* Duesseldorf 1972, pp.89-115. See also, *Ruestung und Machtpolitik. Zur Anatomie des "Kalten Krieges" vor 1914,* Duesseldorf 1973.

88. Stegmann, "Wirtschaft und Politik...," pp.172, 173.

89. Tirpitz to Stosch, December 21, 1895, quoted in Stegmann, "Wirtschaft und Politik...," p.174; Buelow to Eulenberg, December 26, 1897, in Bundesarchiv (hereafter referred to as BA), Nachlass Eulenberg 49, quoted in Roehl, *Germany without Bismarck,* p.252, and Stegmann, "Wirtschaft und Politik...," pp.180, 181.

90. Eckart Kehr, "Englandhass und Weltpolitik," in Wehler, *Primat der Innenpolitik,* pp.164, 166.

91. Stegmann, "Wirtschaft und Politik...," p.181.

92. Stegmann, *Die Erben Bismarcks,* p.67; Puhle, *Agrarische Interessenpolitik und preussischer Konservatismus im Wilhelminischen Reich (1893-1914),* pp.329-31.

93. Stegmann, "Wirtschaft und Politik... " p.180.

94. Berghahn, *Der Tirpitz-Plan,* p.16.

95. Quoted in Hans-Ulrich Wehler, "Sozialimperialismus,"
    in H. U. Wehler (ed.), *Imperialismus*, Koeln, Berlin
    (West) 1970, p.86 and Berghahn, *Der Tirpitz-Plan*,
    p.116.

96. Berghahn, *Der Tirpitz-Plan*, pp.15, 146f, 157, 552,
    590, 591, 592ff.

97. Ekkehard Boehm, *"Ueberseehandel und Flottenbau;
    Hanseatische Kaufmannschaft und deutsche Seeruestung
    1879-1902."* Diss. phil., Universitaet Hamburg 1971,
    p.196ff. According to Boehm, the Kaiser was also
    looked upon as an opponent of agriculture by Hanseatic
    interests (1899) also on page 196. See also Stegmann,
    "Wirtschaft und Politik...," p.181. See also Elsabea
    Rohrmann, *Max Schinckel, Hanseatischer Bankmann im
    wilhelminischen Deutschland*, Hamburg, n.d., p.171.

98. Stegmann, "Wirtschaft und Politik...," p.178.

99. Berghahn has defined this as the difference between
    the fleet as a "large" concentration or gathering
    and Miquel's programme as a "small" one. Berghahn,
    Der Tirpitz-Plan, p.152, F.N. 162 and in "Das Kaiserreich
    in der Sackgasse," in *Neue Politische Literatur* (NPL)
    4, 1971, pp.498ff.

100. Stegmann, *Die Erben Bismarcks*, p.67.

101. I am indebted to Dr. Geoff Eley of Cambridge University
    for pointing out the importance of the following two
    factors and for kind permission to incorporate them
    into my own study. They form part of a critique
    of the Tirpitz plan and Miquel's *Sammlungspolitik*
    which Dr. Eley hopes to publish in the near future. See
    also Geoff Eley, "Sammlungspolitik, Social Imperialism
    and the Navy Law of 1898," in *Militaergeschichtliche
    Mitteilungen (MGM)* 1, 1974, pp.29-63.

102. Dueding, *Der Nationalsoziale Verein*, pp.51, 111-113 and
    Thomas Nipperdey's review of *Die Erben Bismarcks* in *HZ*
    (275) 7, August 1972, p.168.

103. This in fact did occur after 1905 when sections of
    the left-Liberals replaced the Center in the so-called
    "Grosse Sammlung." Berghahn interprets this as being
    an indication of the left Liberals' support of the
    conservative system. But could such a radically
    opposed stance to *Junker* politics really have so
    radically changed without the promise of certain
    structural changes within the state? See Berghahn,
    Der Tirpitz-Plan, p.544.

104. Stegmann, "Wirtschaft und Politik...," p.179. See also Elizabeth Fehrenbach, *Wandlungen des deutschen Kaisergedankens 1871-1918*, Muenchen, Wien 1969, esp. pp.158-183.

105. Stegmann, "Wirtschaft und Politik...," p.183.

106. Berghahn, *Der Tirpitz-Plan*, p.125; Stegmann, "Wirtschaft und Politik...," p.181.

107. Berghahn, *Der Tirpitz-Plan*, p.203. On this last point, for example, the Naumann view in Dueding, *Der Nationalsoziale Verein*, p.27.

108. See F.N. 82.

109. See Dueding, *Der Nationalsoziale Verein*, p.27.

110. Quoted in Stegmann, "Wirtschaft und Politik...," p.183, F.N. 133.

111. Ibid., p.179.

112. Capelle to Tirpitz, August 7, 1897, quoted in Boehm, *Ueberseehandel und Flottenbau*, p.246, and Stegmann, "Wirtschaft und Politik...," p.180.

113. See page 13.

114. Boehm, *Ueberseehandel und Flottenbau*, p.246; Roehl, *Germany without Bismarck*, p.254.

115. Stegmann, "Wirtschaft und Politik...," p.181. See also Amandus Wulf, *"Die Rolle der Flottenbewegung bei der Durchsetzung einer imperialistischen Politik in Deutschland 1897 bis 1900,"* Diss. phil., Rostock Universitaet, 1965, and the Ph.D. thesis on the *Flottenverein* by Dr. Geoff Eley (University of Sussex, 1974).

116. Stegmann, *Die Erben Bismarcks*, p.74.

117. Ibid, and "Wirtschaft und Politik...," p.181.

118. Ibid.

119. This is particularly well worked out by Eley in his critique of *Sammlungspolitik*.

120. This resulted in the creation of the *Centralstelle zur Vorbereitung von Handelsvertraegen* in 1897 and the *Handelsvertragsverein* in 1900. See Stegmann, *Die Erben Bismarcks*, pp.75ff.

121. Puhle, *Agrarische Interessenpolitik und preussischer Konservatismus im Wilhelminischen Reich (1893-1914)*, p.104.

122. See F.N.54 of this chapter.

123. Quoted in Fricke, "Bund der Landwirte," p.141.

124. Quoted in Buerger, *Die Agrardemagogie in Deutschland*, p.32.

125. V. Kardorff, *Wilhelm v. Kardorff*, p.305; Fricke, "Bund der Landwirte," p.142; Kehr, *Schlachtflottenbau und Parteipolitik*, P.50; Boehm, *Ueberseehandel und Flottenbau*, p.78.

126. Stegmann, "Wirtschaft und Politik...," p.180; Fricke, "Bund der Landwirte," p.142.

127. See page 40.

128. Buerger, *Die Agrardemagogie in Deutschland*, pp.29, 30.

129. Barkin, *The Controversy over German Industrialization, 1890-1902*, p.215; Puhle, *Agrarische Interessenpolitik und preussischer Konservatismus im Wilhelminischen Reich, (1890-1914)*, p.242.

130. Horn, *Der Kampf um den Bau des Mittelland Kanals*, pp.52ff; Roehl, *Germany without Bismarck*, pp.264, 265.

131. Roehl, *Germany without Bismarck*, pp.262ff.

132. Speech by Graf Schwerin-Loewitz in the Reichstag, February 10, 1900, in Schwerin-Loewitz, *Aufsaetze und Reden*, 365ff., and Kehr, *Schlacht-flottenbau und Parteipolitik*, pp.199,200.

133. Boehm, *Ueberseehandel und Flottenbau*, p.248.

134. Miquel resigned in the spring of 1901 after again introducing and failing to secure the passage of the Middleland Canal Proposal. He died shortly thereafter. See Barkin, *The Controversy over German Industrialization, 1890-1902*, p.217.

135. Boehm, *Ueberseehandel und Flottenbau*, p.230; Berghahn, *Der Tirpitz-Plan*, p.239.

136. Barkin, *The Controversy over German Industrialization, 1890-1902*, p.223.

137. Stegmann, *Die Erben Bismarcks*, pp.83, 84; v. Kardorff, *Wilhelm v. Kardorff*, pp.344, 345.

138. Barkin, *The Controversy over German Industrialization, 1890-1902*, p.217; Kardorff, *Wilhelm v. Kardorff*, p.345; Stegmann, *Die Erben Bismarcks*, p.84. The proposal was finally accepted and passed in 1904 with a minority of Conservatives voting for its acceptance.

139. *Deutsche Zeitung* (German Daily), no.290, June 24, 1901, quoted in Barkin, *The Controversy over German Industrialization, 1890-1902*, p.218. See also the full and excellent discussion of the tariff negotiations and their consequences both within Germany and for German-Russian relations in Barbara Vogel, *Deutsche Russlandpolitik. Die Scheitern der deutschen Weltpolitik unter Buelow, 1900-1906*, Hamburg 1973, pp.27-43.

140. The following table reflects the state of tariff proposals in October 1902:

		Rye	Wheat	Barley	Oats
Caprivi rate		3.50	3.50	3.50	3.50
Government	minimum	5.0	5.50	3.00	5.00
proposal	maximum	6.0	6.50	4.00	6.00
Tariff	mimimum	5.5	6.00	5.50	5.50
Commission	maximum	7.0	7.50	7.00	7.00
Proposal					
(dominated by					
Conservatives, Free					
Conservatives, and					
agrarian wing of					
Center)					
Wangenheim	minimum	7.50	7.50	7.50	7.50
Proposal (BdL)	maximum	9.00	9.00	9.00	9.00

Source: Vogel, *Deutsche Russlandpolitik*, F.N.35, p.243.

141. Stegmann, *Die Erben Bismarcks*, p.86; Fricke, "Bund der Landwirte," p.143.

142. Boehm, *Ueberseehandlung und Flottenbau*, p.257.

143. Kardorff's compromise plan was as follows:

Minimum

Rye	5.00
Wheat	5.50
Barley	4.00
Oats	5.00

144. Stegmann, *Die Erben Bismarcks,* p.89; Barkin, *The Controversy over German Industrialization, 1890-1902,* p.241.

145. Stegmann, *Die Erben Bismarcks,* p.90.

146. Ibid.

147. See the letter of v. Wangenheim to his wife, December 16, 1902: ",..Der gestrige Tag war ziemlich geistig anstrengend: in der Fraktion ist eine, wenn auch Kleine Clique welche den Bund und mich wuetend hasst und jetzt hofft, es sei der Moment gekommen, mich zu erschlagen und aus der Fraktion herauszuwerfen... Kommt spaeter eine Trennung, so wuerden wir eine Gruppe von 25 bis 30 Herren haben, welche dann den Ausgangspunkt fuer eine neue Partei geben wuerden." Printed in y. Wangenheim, *Conrad Freiherr v. Wangenheim-Klein Spiegel,* pp.76, 77.

148. See the letter from v. Kardorff to Hermann Arnim, December 31, 1902: "Mein Entschluss der Absage an den *Bund der Landwirte* wurde hervorgerufen durch die wiederholte Erklaerung Wangenheim in Koenigsberg, die Reichspartei muesse ausgerottet werden und durch das vollstaendige Schweigen der Konservativen zu dieser Kriegserklaerung." Printed in v. Kardorff, *Wilhelm v. Kardorff,* p.355.

149. Stegmann, *Die Erben Bismarcks,* p.91.

150. Ibid. The Free Conservatives were, in a sense, the truest representatives of the spirit of *Sammlungspolitik.* The Party consisted of ennobled industrialists as well as agrarians who were actively involved in capitalistic undertakings. The Free Conservative Party's chief drawback was that it contained many "generals" but no "soldiers."

151. V. Kardorff to Hermann v. Arnim, December 31, 1902, printed in v. Kardorff, *Wilhelm v. Kardorff,* p.355 and Stegmann, *Die Erben Bismarcks,* pp.140, 141.

152. Elard von Oldenburg-Januschau, *Erinnerungen*,
     Leipzig 1936, p.70.

Chapter III

1. Kehr, *Schlachtflottenbau und Parteipolitik*, p.205.

2. Stegmann, "Wirtschaft und Politik...," p.184; Peter-
   Christian Witt, *Die Finanzpolitik des Deutschen Reiches
   von 1903 bis 1913*, Luebeck and Hamburg 1970, p.62.

3. Kehr, *Schlachtflottenbau und Parteipolitik*, pp.262f..

4. See Chapter II, p.45.

5. Berghahn, *Der Tirpitz-Plan*, pp.236, 237 F.N.73.

6. Barkin, *The Controversy over German Industrialization,
   1890-1902*, p.202. Compare this with Professor Klein
   who feels that in the union between "monopoly
   bourgeoisie" and *Junkers* it was the bourgeoisie that
   maintained the dominant position. It is our contention
   that this became a fact only after 1912, when the
   added impetus of the *voelkisch* movement and the
   diminished status of the agrarians plus Conservative
   isolation in the *Reichstag* brought about a situation
   similar to Klein's theory. See Klein, *Deutschland
   1897/98-1917*, p.67 and Stegmann, *Die Erben Bismarcks*,
   pp.128f.

7. Ibid.

8. Puhle, *Von der Agrarkrise zum Praefaschismus*, pp.49-51.

9. Stegmann, *Die Erben Bismarcks*, p.132.

10. Groh, *Negative Integration und revolutionaerer Attentismus*,
    p.54f.

11. Stegmann, *Die Erben Bismarcks*, p.128.

12. Wangenheim in a letter to his wife of December 16, 1902
    named Oertel, Oldenburg-Januschau, Schrempf, Hilgendorf,
    Dewitz-Schoenhagen, Weitzel, Queis, Treuenfels and
    Maltzahn as among those Conservatives willing to leave
    the Party, in v. Wangenheim, *Conrad Freiherr v. Wangenheim-
    Klein Spiegel*, p.76.

13. Ibid. Wangenheim to his wife, January 21, 1904, p.77 and see Stegmann, *Die Erben Bismarcks*, p.142 as well as Puhle, *Agrarische Interessenpolitik und preussischer Konservatismus im Wilhelminischen Reich (1893-1914)*, pp.224, 232f..

14. Wangenheim, *Conrad Freiherr v. Wangenheim-Klein Spiegel*, p.79.

15. Wallraf, "Zur Politik der Deutschkonservativen Partei," p.71.

16. Stillich, *Die Konservativen*, p.212.

17. Fricke, "Bund der Landwirte," pp.143f.

18. Puhle, *Agrarische Interessenpolitik und preussischer Konservatismus im Wilhelminischen Reich (1893-1914)*, p.240.

19. Quoted in Lindig, "Der Einfluss der Bund der Landwirte auf die Politik des Wilhelminischen Zeitalters 1893-1914," p.220 and Anlage 5; Fricke, "Bund der Landwirte," p.144.

20. Groh, *Negative Integration und revolutionaerer Attentismus*, p.31.

21. Kehr, "Englandhass," p.153.

22. Ibid., p.174.

23. Berghahn, *Der Tirpitz-Plan*, p.447.

24. Vogel, *Deutsche Russlandpolitik*, p.232; George W. F. Hallgarten, *Imperialismus vor 1914*, Munich 1963, I, pp.638ff.

25. Hallgarten, *Imperialismus vor 1914*, I, pp.664ff.

26. Vogel, *Deutsche Russlandpolitik*, p.233.

27. Konrad Schilling, *Beitraege zu einer Geschichte des radikalen Nationalismus in der Wilhelminischen Ara, 1890-1909*," Diss. phil., Koeln 1968, p.287.

28. Heinrich Class, *Wider den Strom. Vom Werden und Wachsen der nationalen Opposition*, Leipzig 1932, pp.115f.

29. Ibid. p.529.

30. An English translation may be found in George Dunlop Crothers, *The German Elections of 1907*, New York 1941, 1968, pp.249-253.

31. Keim would also play an important role in the Pan-German League, especially 1914-1918.

32. Klein, *Deutschland 1897/98-1917*, p.183.

33. See Dieter Fricke, "Der Reichsverband gegen die Sozialdemokratie von seiner Gruendung bis zu den Reichstagswahlen von 1907," in *Zeitschrift fuer Geschichtswissenschaft* (hereafter *ZFG*) H. February 1959, p.273 F.N.172 where Professor Fricke documents the difficulty in getting the Pan-German leader, Professor Hasse, elected to a seat in Doebeln because of the lack of BdL and Conservative support. See also pp.274f. F.N.183; Fricke, "Bund der Landwirte," pp.54f.

34. Schilling, *Beitraege zu einer Geschichte des radikalen Nationalismus*, p.291 F.N.24; Eschenburg, *Das Kaiserreich am Scheideweg*, pp.54f.

35. Witt, *Die Finanzpolitik des Deutschen Reiches von 1903 bis 1913*, p.160.

36. Historisches Archiv, Koeln, NL Bachem Nr. 267 Protokoll der Moenchen Gladbacher Besprechung, July 22/23, 1907, quoted in Witt, *Die Finanzpolitik des Deutschen Reiches von 1903 bis 1913*, p.163.

37. Ibid.

38. Kapp to Buelow, September 25, 1907, in Zentrales Staatsarchiv, Merseburg (formerly Deutsches Zentralarchiv, Merseburg, hereafter referred to as ZStA II), Nachlass (hereafter NL) Kapp, CV III Nr. 1.

39. Oldenburg-Januschau, *Erinnerungen*, pp.88f.

40. Land, *Die Konservativen und die Preussische Polenpolitik (1886-1912)*, p.17 and see also Richard Wonser Tims, *Germanizing Prussian Poland*, New York 1941.

41. Ibid. p.26; see also Weber, *Gesammelte Politische Schriften*, pp.10f.

42. Ibid. pp.28f.

43. After the first initial of each of the surnames of
    its founders: Ferdinand v. Hansemann, Hermann Kennemann
    and Heinrich v. Tiedemann.

44. Land, *Die Konservativen und die Preussische Polenpolitik*
    (1886-1912), p.37. In May of 1894, Professor Haase
    of the Pan-German League sent a memorandum to leading
    public figures. In it the Pan-German leader emphasized
    that what the Poles would not give to the Prussian
    state, i.e., land, should be taken from them. See
    also Johannes Nichtweiss, *Die auslaendisch Saisonarbeiter*
    in der Landwirtschaft der oestlichen und mittleren
    Gebiete des Deutschen Reiches 1890-1914, Berlin (West) 1959.

45. Adam Galos et al., *Die Hakatisten. Der Deutsche*
    Ostmarkenverein (1894-1934), Berlin 1966, pp.78, 103f;
    Land, *Die Konservativen und die Preussische Polenpolitik*
    (1886-1912), p.46; David, *"Der Bund der Landwirte als*
    Machtinstrument," p.123.

46. Land, *Die Konservativen und die Preussische Polenpolitik*
    (1886-1912), pp.46f.

47. Stegmann, *Die Erben Bismarcks,* p.339.

48. The Danzig shipbuilder, Carl H. Ziese in the article
    "Arbeitslosversicherung" in *Deutsche Wirtschafts-*
    Zeitung (German Economic Newspaper) Nr. 4, February 15,
    1914, Sp. 155, quoted in Stegmann, *Die Erben Bismarcks,*
    p.339.

49. Zentrales Staatsarchiv, Potsdam (formerly Deutsches Zentral-
    archiv, hereafter referred to as ZStA I) 1391/5 Bd.1 Fol. 102.
    See also Wallraf, *"Zur Politik der Deutschkonservativen*
    Partei," pp.129f.

50. Puhle, *Agrarische Interessenpolitik und Preussischer*
    Konservatismus im Wilhelminischen Reich (1893-1914),
    p.256f. Count Westarp, later to achieve a prominent
    role in Conservative politics, based his successful
    1908 election to the Reichstag on the Ostmarken issue:
    "Politisch am wichtigsten war mir die Gelegenheit, meine
    besondere Aufgabe als Ostmarker...," in Kuno Graf
    Westarp, *Konservative Politik im letzten Jahrzehnt*
    des Kaiserreiches, Berlin 1935, I, p.33.

51. Ibid. pp.259f.

52. See the pamphlet "innere Kolonisation und Selbstverwaltung"
    in ZStA II, Rep 92 NL Kapp, CII Nr. 10, where the
    avoidance of importing Slavic workers was viewed as
    being in the "national interest."

53. See the pamphlet "Zur Frage der Zweckmaessigen Organisation der inneren Kolonisation in der Provinz Ostpreussen," January 1909, in ZStA II, Rep 92 NL Kapp, CII Nr. 11.

54. Edgar Jaffe in *Archiv fuer Sozialwissenschaft und Sozialpolitik* Band 2, Heft 5, 1909, pp.649f.

55. Krupp v. Bohlen und Halbach to v. Wangenheim, May 1, 1909, in ZStA II, Rep 92 NL Kapp, CII Nr. 23.

56. Wangenheim sought to recruit Kapp as a candidate (presumably as a Conservative) for the Reichstag in order to aid the *Bund* in forthcoming tariff debates and to place Kapp on the *DLR*. Letters of May 26, 1910 and July 28, 1910 in ZStA II, Rep 92, Kapp, CII Nr. 23.

57. Puhle, *Agrarische Interessenpolitik und preussischer Konservatismus im Wilhelminischen Reich (1893-1914)*, p.260; Galos, *Die Hakatisten*, p.225f.; Land, *Die Konservativen und die Preussische Polenpolitik (1886-1912)*, p.96.

58. Speech before the Landes-Oekonomie-Kollegium, February 11, 1910, in Schwerin-Loewitz, *Aufsaetze und Reden*, pp.79f.

59. Berghahn, *NPL*, 4, pp.499f.

60. Lujo Brentano to F. Naumann February 7, 1907, in ZStA I, NL Naumann, Nr. 133, quoted in Witt, *Die Finanzpolitik des Deutschen Reiches von 1903 bis 1913*, p.160.

61. For a much fuller discussion of these problems see Witt as well as the older work by Wilhelm Gerloff, *Die Finanz und Zollpolitik des Deutschen Reiches*, Jena 1913, esp. pp.408ff. For the problem of dualism in the German Reich see Hans Goldschmidt, *Das Reich und Preussen im Kampf um die Fuehrung von Bismarck bis 1918*, Berlin 1931.

62. Witt, *Die Finanzpolitik des Deutschen Reiches von 1903 bis 1913*, pp.7ff, 101 F.N.305; Manfred Rauh, *Foederalismus und Parlamentarismus im Wilhelminischen Reich*, Duesseldorf 1973, p.263; Lindig, *Der Einfluss des Bundes der Landwirte auf die Politik des Wilhelminischen Zeitalters 1893-1914*," p.180. The so-called Franckenstein Clause provided that any intake of the Reich of over 130 millions was to be transferred to the Reich states, thus serving as the basis for a continuous deficit in the Reich budget.

63. Berghahn, *Ruestung und Machtpolitik*, p.22.

64. Ibid. p.65 and Berghahn in the following: *NPL*, 4, 502, *Der Tirpitz-Plan*, pp.271ff., and "Educated and Less Educated Guesses; Kritischen Kommentar zu den Ruestungswettlauf und Eskalationsstudien," in Klaus Juergen Gantzel et al., *Konflikt-Eskalation-Krise, Sozialwissenschaftlichen Studien zum Ausbruch des Ersten Weltkrieges*, Duesseldorf 1972, pp.250f..

65. Groh, *Negative Integration und revolutionaerer Attentismus*, pp.90f.

66. Ibid., p.89; Otto Pommer, *Die Konservativen*, Berlin 1912, pp.36ff..

67. Groh, *Negative Integration und revolutionaerer Attentismus*, pp. 90f..

68. Rauh, *Foederalismus und Parlamentarismus*, p.329,

69. Witt, *Die Finanzpolitik des Deutschen Reiches von 1903 bis 1913*, p.98f; Rauh, *Federalismus und Parlamentarismus*, pp.278f.

70. Von Oldenburg-Januschau, *Erinnerungen*, pp.102f, and see the article "Erbzuwachssteuer" by Hans Delbrueck in *Preussische Jahrbuecher*, July 24, 1912.

71. Westarp, *Konservative Politik*, I, p.67.

72. Rauh, *Foederalismus und Parlamentarismus*, p.288,

73. See Chapter I, p.10,

74. Von Oldenburg-Januschau, *Erinnerungen*, pp.102f; Westarp, *Konservative Politik*, I, p.67.

75. Thus it was a well-known fact that Bismarck rarely paid taxes upon his income and then in a sum bearing no relation to the actual amount of his earnings, See Hellmut von Gerlach, *Von Rechts nach Links*, Zuerich 1937, pp.96ff.. Gerlach further states that as far as he knew v. Wangenheim paid no income tax, p.319. See also Peter-Christian Witt, "Der preussische Landrat als Steuerbeamter," pp.205-219,

76. Witt, *Die Finanzpolitik*, pp.163, 167.

77. Ibid., pp.190, 214f.

78. Ibid. p.215.

79. Ibid. p.225. The result of the Voelkisch-nationalist
    entrance into the reform matter must be seen as one
    of the earliest attempts by these organizations to
    influence national policy. This was a direct consequence
    of their growing power and the experience they had
    gained during the "Hottentot" election. It is interesting
    to note that a committee set up under the initiative of
    Ludwig Sevin, who had earlier aided Buelow in the 1907
    election contained (among others) the names of v. Liebert
    and Professor Dietrich Schaefer who later featured
    prominently in nationalist movements.

80. Berghahn, *Ruestung und Machtpolitik*, pp.66f.

81. Speaker at the general meeting of the BdL February 17, 1908,
    quoted in Puhle, *Agrarische Interessenpolitik und
    preussischer Konservatismus im Wilhelminischen Reich
    (1893-1914)*, p.264.

82. Ibid. and Witt, *Die Finanzpolitik*, pp.238f..

83. Witt, Die Finanzpolitik, pp.232f.

84. See p.57.

85. A report by Eisendecher, November 23, 1909, in ZStA I
    RdI 16501, quoted in Rauh, *Foederalismus und
    Parlamentarismus*, p.346. The Conservatives also lost
    15 seats in the Landtag elections in Saxony, Stegmann,
    Die Erben Bismarcks, p.197, F.N.122.

86. See the article "Der Blockgedanke" by Dr. M. in
    Die Grenzboten, August 26, 1909.

87. Stegmann, *Die Erben Bismarcks*, pp.176ff; Rauh,
    Foederalismus und Parlamentarismus, p.345; Witt,
    Die Finanzpolitik, p.308f..

88. Quoted in Stegmann, *Die Erben Bismarcks*, p.177. See
    also Berghahn, *NPL 4*, p.502.

89. See pp.61ff..

90. Wallraf, "Zur Politik der Deutschkonservativen Partei," p.154.

91. Stegmann, *Die Erben Bismarcks*, p.196f· Wallraf, "Zur
    Politik der Deutschkonservativen Partei," pp.154ff; Witt,
    *Die Finanzpolitik des Deutschen Reiches von 1903 bis
    1913*, p.306; Juergen Bertram, *Die Wahlen zum Deutschen
    Reichstag vom Jahre 1912*, Duesseldorf 1964, p.17;

Der Allgemeine Deligiertentag der Deutsch-Konservativen Partei, Berlin, am 11. Dezember 1909, Stenographic report; *Deutsch-Konservative Handbuch,* 1911, p.93.

92. Thus Theodor Eschenburg in the title of his work, *Das Kaiserreich am Scheideweg. Buelow, Basserman und der Block,* Berlin 1929. See also Dieter Grosser, *Vom monarchischen Konstitutionalismus zur parlamentarischen Demokratie,* Den Haag 1970 and Gert Udo Schiedler, "Parlament, Parteien und Regierung im Wilhelminischen Reich 1890-1914," in *Aus Politik und Zeitgeschichte* (Beilage to *Das Parlament*), 12, 1971, pp.16-24.

93. Witt, *Die Finanzpolitik des Deutschen Reiches von 1903 bis 1913,* p.304.

94. Ibid.

95. Among them the Conservatives seemed best represented by the candidacy of Rheinbaben and the future Minister of Agriculture Schorlemer-Lieser, suggested by Bethmann Hollweg. See Konrad H. Jarausch, *The Enigmatic Chancellor. Bethmann Hollweg and the Hubris of Imperial Germany.* New Haven and London 1973, pp.67f.

96. Jarausch, *The Enigmatic Chancellor,* p.67.

97. Wolfgang J. Mommsen, "Die Latente Krise des Deutschen Reiches 1909-1914," in *Handbuch der Deutschen Geschichte* (ed. Leo Just), Frankfurt am Main 1973, p.10f; Grosser, *Vom monarchischen Konstitutionalismus,* p.9.

98. Mommsen, "Die Latente Krise des Deutschen Reiches," p.10.

99. Jarausch, *The Enigmatic Chancellor,* p.73.

100. Grosser, *Vom monarchischen Konstitutionalismus,* p.9.

101. Hans-Guenter Zmarzlik, *Bethmann Hollweg als Reichskanzler 1909-1914,* Duesseldorf 1957, p.76; Jarausch, *The Enigmatic Chancellor,* p.84.

102. Stegmann, *Die Erben Bismarcks,* pp.218f..

103. Quoted in Zmarzlik, *Bethmann Hollweg als Reichskanzler,* p.44.

104. The Bill proposed minor increases in the numbers eligible to vote in the first and second classes. The first class total was to increase from 3.8% to 7% and the second class from 13.8% to 17%. The Bill

also contained the so-called "carriers of culture"
paragraph which would have allowed academics,
magistrates and soldiers, after appropriate service
to the State, to achieve promotion to second class
voting rights. See Mommsen, "Die Latente Krise des
Deutschen Reiches," pp.12f. and Stegmann, *Die Erben
Bismarcks*, pp.199f.

105. Westarp blamed the failure of the reform upon the
inability of the Center and National Liberals to work
together and upon Bethmann's refusal to accept the Law
without the approval of the National Liberals. See
Westarp, *Konservative Politik*, I, p.110 and Jarausch,
The Enigmatic Chancellor, p.79.

106. Jarausch, *The Enigmatic Chancellor*, pp.82, 79.

107. 1851-1924. Estate Owner and Member of the Prussian
House of Representatives since 1888; 1905-1918
Chairman of the House of Representatives Party;
1912-1918 Party Chairman.

108. For an example of Heydebrand's grasp of Conservative
principles see his address to the Leipzig Freistudentenschaft,
"Ueber Konservative Gedanken und Ziele," undated speech
in BA (Kleine Erwerbungen) Nr. 536, Heydebrand und der
Lasa, Bl.1-13, and Puhle, *Agrarische Interessenpolitik
und preussischer Konservatismus im Wilhelminischen
Reich (1893-1914)*, p.338.

109. Westarp in v. Buelow, *Deutscher Aufstieg*, p.349.

110. Stegmann, *Die Erben Bismarcks*, pp.176ff; Fischer,
Krieg der Illusionen, pp.56ff; Mommsen, "Die Latente
Krise des Deutschen Reiches," p.10; Witt, *Die
Finanzpolitik des Deutschen Reiches von 1903 bis 1913*,
p.308.

111. Hutten-Czapski to Bethmann Hollweg, September 26, 1910,
in ZStA I, NL Hutten-Czapski, Nr. 8 Bl.49.

112. This extended to attacking the Free Conservative
leader, v. Kardorff for his part in bringing about
the tariff compromise of 1902. See v. Kardorff to
his wife December 31, 1902: "Der Kleine Heydebrand...
stimmte dann mit Fanatismus (of the BdL-AJP)..."
printed in v. Kardorff, *Wilhelm v. Kardorff*, p.355.

113. Stegmann, *Die Erben Bismarcks*, p. 53, F.N. 188 and
see Konrad H. Jarausch, "Die Alldeutschen und die
Regierung Bethmann Hollweg. Ein Denkschrift Kurt

Riezlers vom Herbst 1916," in *Vierteljahrshefte
fuer Zeitgeschichte* (VZG), 4, 1973 p,441, Among
Conservative members of the ADV were v, Brockhausen
(1898-1918), zu Dohna-Schlodien (1893-1905), Giese,
v. Graefe (1912-1918), v. Helldorff-Breda,
Liebermann v. Sonnenberg (Wirtschaftliche Vereinigung),
Mehnert, v. Michaelis (1903-1918), Arnim-Muskau
(until 1900), v. Mirbach-Sorquitten, v. Staudy,
Stolberg-Wernigerode (until 1900), Wagener, Wildgrube,
and Zeidler (1898-1903), listed in Schilling,ᴬBeitrage
*zu einer Geschichte des radikalen Nationalismus,*ᴮ p,409,
as well as Prince Salm. Horstmar and Admiral v. Grumme-
Douglas. See also Fischer, *Krieg der Illusionen,* p.353,

114. Class, *Wider den Strom,* pp.268ff.,

115. Witt, *Die Finanzpolitik des Deutschen Reiches von
1903 bis 1913,* p.308,

116. Ibid. p.309.

117. Stegmann, *Die Erben Bismarcks,* p.216,

118. Ibid.

119. Hartmut Kaelble, *Industrielle Interessenpolitik in
der Wilhelminischen Gesellschaft, (Centralverband
Deutscher Industrieller 1895-1914),* Berlin (West)
1967, pp.143ff..

120. Fritz Blaich, *Kartell-und Monopolpolitik im Kaiserlichen
Deutschland,* Duesseldorf 1973, p,227f. and Puhle,
*Agrarischen Interessenpolitik und preussischer
Konservatismus im Wilhelminischen Reich (1893-1914),*
passim.

121. Stegmann, *Die Erben Bismarcks,* pp.209, 199f..

122. Ibid., p,203.

123. Witt, *Die Finanzpolitik des Deutschen Reiches von
1903 bis 1913,* p.309,

124. Ballin in a letter to Maximillian Harden, June 29, 1909,
in BA NL Harden, Nr. 4 quoted in Ibid. p.309. For
Ballin and the Hansabund, see the brief and unsatisfactory
details in Lamar Cecil, *Albert Ballin. Business and
Politics in Imperial Germany, 1898-1918,* Princeton
1967, p.113,

125. See pp. 69f..

126. Fischer, *Krieg der Illusionen*, p.77; Mommsen, "Die Latente Krise des Deutschen Reiches," p.24; Jarausch, *The Enigmatic Chancellor*, pp.112ff..

127. Gutsche, *Aufstieg und Fall*, p.82.

128. Gutsche, *Aufstieg und Fall*, p.84. Wolfgang J. Mommsen, "Domestic Factors in German Foreign Policy before 1914," in *Central European History* I (March 1973) pp.23f..

129. Class, *Wider den Strom*, p.206.

130. Quoted in Fischer, *Krieg der Illusionen,* p.140 and see Jarausch, *The Enigmatic Chancellor*, p.124.

131. Jarausch, *The Enigmatic Chancellor*, p.125. Bethmann was also afraid that Heydebrand's speech would lead Britain and France to believe that there existed in Germany a war party "sans phrase." See the letter from Bethmann to the Kaiser, November 11, 1911, in ZStA II, Rep. 89H 1 Gen. Nr. 6, vol. 1,   in Witt, *Die Finanzpolitik des Deutschen Reiches von 1903 bis 1913*, p.342.

132. Karl Dietrich Erdmann (ed.) *Kurt Riezler Tagebuecher-Aufsaetze-Dokumente* (hereafter Riezler, *Tagebuecher*), Goettingen 1973, entry of January 20, 1911, pp.168f..

133. Hartmut Pogge v. Strandmann, "Nationale Verbaende zwischen Weltpolitik und Kontinentalpolitik," in H. Schottelius und W. Deist (eds.), *Marine und Marine-politik im Kaiserlichen Deutschland,* Duesseldorf 1972, p.315.

134. Bethmann to W. Oettingen, December 17, 1911, in BA (Kleine Erwerbungen) Nr. 517-2, quoted in Gutsche, *Aufstieg und Fall*, pp.89f..

Chapter IV

1. Bertram, *Die Wahlen zum Deutschen Reichstag vom Jahre 1912*, pp.18, 30, 251.

2. Ibid., pp.15, 31, 38f.

3. Fischer, *Krieg der Illusionen*, p.148.

4. Groh, *Negative Integration und revolutionaerer Attentismus*, p.269.

5. Stegmann, *Die Erben Bismarcks*, p.246.

6. Witt, *Die Finanzpolitik des Deutschen Reiches von 1903 bis 1913*, p.338.

7. Mommsen, "Die Latente Krise des Deutschen Reiches," P.35.

8. Fischer, *Krieg der Illusionen*, p.147; Mommsen, "Die Latente Krise des Deutschen Reiches," pp.35f.

9. Bertram, *Die Wahlen zum Deutschen Reichstag vom Jahre 1912*, p.254; Stegmann, *Die Erben Bismarcks*, p.257.

10. Count Kuno Fred. Vik. Westarp, 1864-1945, MdR 1908-1918; Chairman of Reichstag Party 1912/13-1918.

11. See the election materials in ZStA I, NL Westarp 1.

12. Stegmann, *Die Erben Bismarcks*, p.257 and ZStA I, NL Westarp 1.

13. See the figures in Bertram, *Die Wahlen zum Deutschen Reichstag vom Jahre 1912*, pp.206f.

14. Ibid., pp.257ff. and Fischer, *Krieg der Illusionen*, p.145.

15. V. Wangenheim to Major Endell, August 3, 1912, in ZStA I, Nachlass Roesicke, Nr. 35f, Bl.179-180. Printed in Puhle, *Agrarische Interessenpolitik und preussischer Konservatismus im Wilhelminischen Reich (1893-1914)*, p.323, Anlage 13.

16. See Chapter I, pp.2ff..

17. Dieter Groh, "Waiting For and Avoiding Revolution: Social Democracy and the Reich," in *Laurentian University Review* (Aspects of Imperial Germany), vol. 5, No. 3, June 1973, p.101; Kenneth D. Barkin, "Germany's Path to Industrial Maturity," in *Laurentian University Review*, June 1973, p.30.

18. See Kurt Wawrzinek, *Die Entstehung des deutschen Antisemitismus (1873-1890)*, Berlin 1927.

19. Quoted in Dieter Fricke, "Deutschsoziale Reformpartei, (DSRP)" in *Die buergerlichen Parteien*, I, p.760.

20. *Norddeutsche Allgemeine Zeitung*, 189, May 10, 1897, "Parteibewegung."

21. Quoted in *Vorwaerts*, 185, August 12, 1898, "Freiherr v. Wangenheim."

22. Ibid.

23. Staatsarchiv Hamburg (hereafter St. A. Hbg.), Politische Polizei 55915, Bund der Landwirte; Fricke, "DSRP," p.762.

24. Dieter Fricke, "Deutschsoziale Partei (DSP)" in *Die buergerlichen Parteien*, I, p.754.

25. Fricke, "BdL," p.139.

26. Uwe Lohalm, *Voelkischer Radikalismus*, Hamburg 1970, p.30.

27. George L. Mosse, *Germans and Jews*, New York 1970, p.8.

28. See Fritz Stern, *The Politics of Cultural Despair*, Garden City, New York, 1965, (Anchor Edition).

29. George L. Mosse, *The Crisis of German Ideology*, New York, 1964, pp.127ff.

30. Ibid., p.90.

31. Ibid., p.132f.

32. Ibid., p.9.

33. See Chapter II, P.24.

34. 290,000 of 330,000 BdL members. See *Konservatives Handbuch*, Berlin 1911, p.229. This is not to deny the existence of actual peasant aims and interests which were often demonstrated in their electoral behavior.

35. Mosse, *The Crisis of German Ideology*, p.134.

36. Ibid.

37. Heinrich August Winkler, *Pluralismus oder Protektionismus?*, Weisbaden 1972, p.30.

38. Mosse, *The Crisis of German Ideology*, p.92.

39. Ibid., pp.98, 99.

40. ZStA II, Rep. 90 a Abt. B. Tit. III, 2 b Nr. 6, Vol. 161, Staatsministerial Sitzungsprotokolle 1912 (Sitting of January 11, 1912).

41. Lohalm, *Voelkischer Radikalismus*, p.30.

42. Koch, "Social Darwinism as a Factor...," pp.346, 348.

43. Ibid.

44. See Chapter III, p.58.

45. See Chapter III, pp.58ff..

46. *Auf Vorposten* Jg. 4, Heft 6, 1919, "Staatserhaltende Parteien: Die Konservative Parteien," pp.91f. During the Delegiertentage of the Conservative Party on November 30, 1906, the Central Association of Teltow-Beeskow-Storkow-Charlottenburg attempted to introduce a resolution for a clear Conservative position against Jewry. Among the proposals was a call for a stop to the immigration of foreign races. Hahn also made such a proposal in 1906.

47. *Kreuzzeitung*, September 25, 1910, (evening edition).

48. *Konservatives Handbuch*, pp.5ff.

49. *Kreuzzeitung*, January 7, 1912, (evening edition).

50. *Kreuzzeitung*, January 31, 1912, (morning edition).

51. Quoted in Fischer, *Krieg der Illusionen*, pp.151f. Also see Moritz Goldstein, "German Jewry's Dilemma. The Story of a Provocative Essay," in *Leo Baeck Yearbook II*, 1957, pp.236-254 and my unpublushed M.A. thesis: Abraham J. Peck, "Crisis and Identity: Studies in German-Jewish Society, 1870-1933," The American University 1970, pp.70ff.

52. V. Wangenheim at the BdL convention, February 19, 1912, in v. Wangenheim, *Conrad Freiherr v. Wangenheim-Kleinspiegel*, p.92 and also *Hamburger Nachrichten* (hereafter *HN*) 83, February 19, 1912, "Die Tagung des BdL."

53. Lohalm, *Voelkischer Radikalismus*, p.30 and Norman Cohn, *Warrant for Genocide. The Myth of the Jewish World Conspiracy and the Protocols of the Elders of Zion*, Hammondsworth, England 1967. The head of the Association was Ludwig Miller v. Hausen (Gottfried

zur Beek), a former editor of the *Konservative Kalendar* and later (1919) responsible for introducing the *Protocols of the Elders of Zion* into Germany.

54. V. Wangenheim to Major Endell, August 3, 1912, in Puhle, *Agrarische Interessenpolitik und preussischer Konservatismus im Wilhelminischen Reich (1893-1914)*, p.323, Anlage 13.

55. Quoted in Reinhard Behrens, *Die Deutschnationalen in Hamburg, 1918-1933.* Diss. Phil. Hamburg 1970, p.29.

56. Fischer, *Krieg der Illusionen*, p.152.

57. Stegmann, *Die Erben Bismarcks*, pp.293ff.

58. *Konservative Monatschrift*, "Judenfrage und Antisemitismus," December 1912, pp.197ff; also see Stegmann, *Die Erben Bismarcks*, p.258. F.N. 10 for examples of Conservative unhappiness with the outbreak of racial anti-Semitism.

59. See Chapter III, pp.58ff..

60. Zmarzlik, *Bethmann Hollweg als Reichskanzler*, p.60.

61. Ibid., p.53, F.N. 5.

62. *HN*, Nr. 84, December 20, 1912, "Hauptversammlung der BdL."

63. ZStA II, Rep. 90a, Abt.B, Tit III, 2b Nr. 6, vol. 161, Staatsministerial Sitzungsprotokolle 1912 (Sitting of March 4, 1912), Bl.27, 42.

64. Witt, Die Finanzpolitik des Deutschen Reiches von 1903 bis 1913, p.351f.; Jarausch, *The Enigmatic Chancellor*, p.95.

65. Ibid.

66. Fischer, *Krieg der Illusionen*, pp.168, 384f..

67. Heydebrand und der Lasa, "Beitrage zu einer Geschichte der Konservativen Partei...," pp.608ff.; Westarp, *Konservative Politik*, I, p.194.

68. Fischer, *Krieg der Illusionen*, p.251.

69. Groh, *Negative Integration und revolutionaerer Attentismus,* p.356.

286

70. Witt, *Die Finanzpolitik des Deutschen Reiches von 1903 bis 1913*, pp.358f..

71. Volker R. Berghahn, *Germany and the Approach of War in 1914*, London and Basingstoke 1973, p.155.

72. ZStA II, Rep. 90a, Abt.B, Tit. III, 2b Nr. 6, vol. 162, Staatsministerial Sitzungsprotokolle 1913 (sitting of January 7, 1913).

73. Berghahn, *Germany and the Approach of War in 1914*, p.154.

74. Ibid., p.156.

75. Fischer, *Krieg der Illusionen*, p.262.

76. Ibid., p.263.

77. Ibid.

78. Ibid., pp.267ff..

79. Berghahn, *Germany and the Approach of War in 1914*, p.157.

80. Fischer, *Krieg der Illusionen*, p.266; Witt, *Die Finanzpolitik des Deutschen Reiches von 1903 bis 1913*, p.369.

81. Fischer, *Krieg der Illusionen*, p.267.

82. Witt, *Die Finanzpolitik des Deutschen Reiches von 1903 bis 1913*, p.371ff..

83. Quoted in Zmarzlik, *Bethmann Hollweg als Reichkanzler*, p.75.

84. Heydebrand to Westarp, July 5, 1913, in ZStA I, NL Westarp, Nr. 1, Bl.162-163, Fischer, *Krieg der Illusionen*, p.269.

85. Hans Delbrueck in *Die Prussische Jahrbuecher*, December 23, 1913, (v.156), p.193.

86. Gustav Schmidt, "Innenpolitische Blockbildungen in Deutschland am Vorabend des Ersten Weltkrieges," in *Das Parlament* (Beilage), May 13, 1972, pp.3ff..

87. Wolfgang J. Mommsen, "Die Latente Krise des Deutschen Reiches," in *Militaergeschichtliche Mitteilungen (MGM)*, 1/74, p.21.

88. See Chapter II, pp.37ff. of this work and Gustav
    Schmidt, "Deutschland am Abend des Ersten Weltkrieges,"
    in Stuermer, *Das Kaiserliche Deutschland*, p.405.

89. Schmidt, "Innenpolitische Blockbildungen," pp.11f..

90. Ibid., pp.25ff..

91. Ibid., p.30.

92. Berghahn, *Germany and the Approach of War in 1914*, p.162.

93. Ibid.

94. Mommsen, "Die Latente Krise," in *MGM*, p.23.

Chapter V

1. Erich v. Oettingen was a Latvian German who achieved
   prominence during the First World War as one of a
   number of Baltic Germans (among them Professor Axel
   Baron Freytag-Loringheven) who agitated for the annexation
   of Latvia by the German Reich and its elevation to
   a Prussian province. See Fritz Fischer, *Griff nach der
   Weltmacht*, Duesseldorf 1961, p.610.

2. Fischer mistakenly attributes this role to the ADV
   functionary, v. Vietinghoff-Scheel, see *Krieg der
   Illusionen*, p.399.

3. Daniel Frymann (Heinrich Class), *Wenn Ich der Kaiser
   Waere*, (1925 ed.), p.155.

4. E. v. Oettingen to Class, April 15, 1913, in ZStA I,
   ADV 246, Bl.128. See also ADV 1417/2, Bl.127f and
   for the following quotes.

5. V. Wangenheim to Roesicke, June 27, 1913, in ZStA I,
   NL Wangenheim, Nr. 8, Bl.51ff.; Fischer, *Krieg der
   Illusionen*, p.352.

6. Quoted in Fischer, *Krieg der Illusionen*, p.399.

7. Report of Senator Neumann to C. C. Eiffe, July 6, 1913,
   in ZStA I, ADV246, and for the following quote.

8. Fischer, *Krieg der Illusionen*, p.400.

9. Wangenheim to Class, July 30, 1913, in ZStA I, ADV 246, Bl.164.

10. Quoted in Fischer, *Krieg der Illusionen*, p.400.

11. Ibid. and see Frymann (Class), *Wenn Ich der Kaiser Waere*, p.155: "...the BdL is too close to the Center. It must advocate more of a national policy."

12. Fischer, *Krieg der Illusionen*, p.400; Class to ADV membership, in ZStA I, ADV 246, Bl.164.

13. No mention of the meeting with Class can be found in the NL Roesicke, located in the ZStA I and there is only specific reference to it in the aforementioned letter from v. Wangenheim to Roesicke, June 27, 1913.

14. For this see later sections of this chapter.

15. Quoted in Fischer, *Krieg der Illusionen*, p.400.

16. Frymann (Class), *Wenn Ich der Kaiser Waere*, p.149; Alfred Kruck, *Geschichte des Alldeutschen Verbandes 1890-1939*, Wiesbaden 1954, p.62.

17. Fischer, *Krieg der Illusionen*, p.401; *Berliner Neueste Nachrichten*, April 20, 1914, "Tagung des ADV;" *Die Post* (Berlin), Nr. 182, April 20, 1914.

18. See Chapter II, pp.74f.

19. Fischer, *Krieg der Illusionen*, p.399.

20. Frymann (Class), *Wenn Ich der Kaiser Waere*, p.147 and for the following quotes.

21. Ibid., p.151.

22. Ibid., p.147.

23. Kruck, *Geschichte des Alldeutschen Verbandes 1890-1939*, p.62. Class, *Wider den Strom*, p.267.

24. Class to Gebsattel, June 16, 1913, in ZStA I, NL Gebsattel, Nr. 1, Bl.18 and Stegmann, *Die Erben Bismarcks*, p.403, F.N.246.

25. *Kreuzzeitung*, Nr. 324, July 14, 1913 (evening edition), "Konservative und Alldeutschen."

26. Class to v. Klitzing, July 29, 1913, in ZStA I, ADV 246, Bl.139 and see also ADV 1417/2, Bl.139 for following quotes.

27. Heydebrand at Hereford (Westphalia) *Parteitag* of the Conservative Party, November 23, 1910, quoted in *Konservative Monatschrift,* October 25, 1913. See also Fischer, *Krieg der Illusionen*, p.386.

28. Quoted in Stegmann, *Die Erben Bismarcks*, p.352; *Berliner Neueste Nachrichten*, Nr. 87, February 17, 1913 (evening edition); *HN*, Nr. 84, February 20, 1913.

29. Quoted in Stegmann, *Die Erben Bismarcks*, p.353.

30. Ibid., pp.355f. and see Chapter III, p.76f.

31. V. Wangenheim to Roesicke, May 27, 1913, in ZStA I, NL Wangenheim, Nr. 8, Bl.33 and see David,"*Der Bund der Landwirte als Machtinstrument*,"p.126.

32. Quoted in Stegmann, *Die Erben Bismarcks,* p.358.

33. See Chapter IV, pp.93-100 of this book and the quote in Stegmann, *Die Erben Bismarcks*, p.360.

34. Quoted in Stegmann, *Die Erben Bismarcks*, pp.355f.

35. Quoted in ibid., p.363.

36. Quoted in ibid., p.365.

37. V. Wangenheim to Roesicke, August 14, 1913, in ZStA I, NL Wangenheim, Nr.8, Bl.88.

38. *Deutsche Wirtschafts-Zeitung*, Nr. 16/17, September 1, 1913, Sp.705ff., quoted in Stegmann, *Die Erben Bismarcks,* p.370.

39. Stegmann, *Die Erben Bismarcks*, p.440.

40. Ibid., p.283 and see Heinrich August Winkler, *Pluralismus oder Protektionismus?,* Wiesbaden 1972, pp.25f.

41. Stegmann, *Die Erben Bismarcks*, p.367, F.N.73; Groh, *Negative Integration und revolutionaerer Attentismus*, p.511.

42. Stegmann, *Die Erben Bismarcks*, pp.367ff.: Fischer, *Krieg der Illusionen*, pp.396f. The latter proposal included a reactivation of the National Economic Council proposed by Bismarck in 1881.

43. Stegmann, ibid.

44. Ibid. pp.378f.; Johannes Unold, *Kultur und Fortschritt*, np. 1913, pp.27ff.

45. V. Wangenheim to Class, July 30, 1913, in ZStA I, ADV 246, Bl.243.

46. For the economic aspects of the *Kartell*, see the next section of this chapter.

47. Stegmann, *Die Erben Bismarcks*, pp.392ff.

48. V. Wangenheim to Class, September 30, 1913, in ZStA I, ADV 246, Bl.168.

49. See Chapter II, pp.45f. of this book.

50. *Hamburger Correspondent* (hereafter *HC*), August 26, 1913, Nr. 433, "Industrie und Bund der Landwirte."

51. Fischer, *Krieg der Illusionen*, p.391 and see Gebsattel to Class, March 9, 1914, in ZStA I, ADV 355, Bl.95, "There is much antipathy in Munich circles to the BdL."

52. *Kreuzzeitung*, October 11, 1913, Nr. 477 (ev. ed.), "Zur handelspolitischen Lage."

53. Fischer, *Krieg der Illusionen*, p.523.

54. Ibid., pp.516ff. and Klein, *Deutschland 1897/98-1917*, pp.224f. For overproduction and price declines in the agrarian sector, see Puhle charts in *Agrarische Interessenpolitik und preussischer Konservatismus im Wilhelminischen Reich (1893-1914)*, p.319, Anlage 10 and Dr. Carl Ballard, "Deutsche Volksernaehrung im Kriege," in *Preussische Jahrbuecher*, v. 157 (1914), pp.116f.

55. Klein, *Deutschland 1897/98-1917*, p.249.

56. Groh, *Negative Integration und revolutionaerer Attentismus*, pp.456ff.

57. Quoted in Berghahn, *Germany and the Approach of War in 1914*, p.161. Translation is Berghahn's.

58. Groh, *Negative Integration und revolutionaerer Attentismus*, pp.459ff.

59. Ibid.

60. Fischer, *Krieg der Illusionen*, pp.530f.

61. Berghahn, *Germany and the Approach of War in 1914*, p.160.

62. Quoted in *HC*, March 18, 1912, "Konservativer Parteitag."

63. Berghahn, *Germany and the Approach of War in 1914*, pp.182f.

64. Roesicke to v. Wangenheim, March 22, 1913, in ZStA I, NL Wangenheim 8, Bl.16.

65. Wolfgang J. Mommsen, "Domestic Factors in German Foreign Policy before 1914," in *Central European History*, Volume VI, Number 1, March 1973, p.25.

66. Fischer, *Krieg der Illusionen*, pp.528f.

67. Berghahn, *Germany and the Approach of War in 1914*, p.183.

68. Ibid., p.184.

69. Fischer, *Krieg der Illusionen*, p.534. *Kreuzzeitung*, April 9, 1914, Nr. 168 (ev. ed.) "Ein deutsch-russischer Handels-Krieg."

70. Quoted in *Deutsche Tageszeitung*, July 2, 1914, Nr. 328 "Der Abgeordnete Heydebrand uber die politische Lage," and see Berghahn, *Germany and the Approach of War in 1914*, pp.184f.

71. Fischer, *Krieg der Illusionen*, pp.277 and 542f.

72. ZStA II, Rep. 90a, Abt. B Tit III, 2b Nr. 6 vol. 162, Staatsministerial Sitzungsprotokolle 1913 (Sitting of November 31, 1913) and Stegmann, *Die Erben Bismarcks*, p.418.

73. Thomas Nipperdey, review of *Die Erben Bismarcks* in *Historische Zeitschrift*, Band 275, Heft 7, (August 1972), p.168.

74. Thus Stegmann in his chapter IX of *Die Erben Bismarcks*.

75. Nipperdey in *Historische Zeitschrift*, pp.169ff.

76. Quoted in Stegmann, *Die Erben Bismarcks*, p.388.

77. Wangenheim to Roesicke, June 20, 1913, in ZStA I, NL Wangenheim I; v. Wangenheim at BdL meeting in Cologne, November 16, 1913, quoted in *HC*, November 18, 1913, Nr. 589.

78. Roesicke in 1913 in Kleine Erwerbung Roesicke
    (hereafter KE Roesicke) 230-32 in BA, Bl.37-40.

79. See the letter from v. Wangenheim to Prof. Dr. Curschmann
    of Greifswald University, March 10, 1924 in *Conrad
    Freiherr v. Wangenheim-Kleinspiegel*, pp.168.

80. Berghahn, *Germany and the Approach of War in 1914*,
    p.182, Fischer, *Krieg der Illusionen*, p.286.

81. Roesicke to Kaiser Wilhelm, February 12, 1913, in
    Lindig, *"Der Einfluss der Bund der Landwirte,"* Anlage 0
    and also in KE Roesicke, 230-32 in BA, Bl.10.

82. Ibid.

83. *Korrespondenz der BdL* (hereafter *KdBdL*), January 29,
    1914, Nr. 7., "Viehhaendler ueber die Fleischversorgung
    Deutschlands," p.25.

84. V. Wangenheim to Dr. Curschmann, in *Conrad Freiherr
    v. Wangenheim*, March 10, 1924, p.168; Fischer, *Krieg
    der Illusionen*, p.639; Westarp, *Konservative Politik*
    II, p.374; *KdBdL*, June 11, 1914, "Volksernaehrung
    im Kriegsfall," p.154.

85. V. Wangenheim to Roesicke, May 27, 1914, in ZStA I,
    NL v. Wangenheim Bl.43f.

86. The Government was to pay the agrarians the difference
    between their domestic prices and the world prices for
    grain.

87. Nipperdey review, p.168.

88. Kruck, *Geschichte des Alldeutschen Verbandes, 1890-1939*,
    pp.81ff.

89. See Chapter V, pp.102ff. of this work.

90. Gutsche, *Bethmann Hollweg*, p.103; ADV 355, in ZStA I,
    Bl.350.

91. Hartmut Pogge v. Strandmann, "Staatsstreichplaene,
    Alldeutsche, und Bethmann Hollweg," in v. Strandmann
    and Geiss (eds.) *Die Erforderlichkeit des Unmoeglichen*,
    Frankfurt am Main, 1965, p.14.

92. See Chapter V, pp.101ff.

93. Quoted in Pogge, "Staatsstreichplaene...," pp.14f.

94. Stegmann, *Die Erben Bismarcks,* p.396, F.N. 212.

95. Ibid., p.397.

96. Class to Gebsattel August 28, 1913, in ZStA I,
    NL Gebsattel I, Bl.37f.

97. Pogge, "Staatsstreichplaene...," pp.16ff.

98. See the following sections of this chapter.

99. Gutsche, *Bethmann Hollweg,* p.103; Pogge, "Staatsstreich-
    plaene..." pp.18ff.; Berghahn, *Germany and the Approach
    of War in 1914,* pp.163f.

100. Gebsattel to v. Liebert, June 26, 1914, in ZStA I,
     NL Gebsattel I, Bl.147-148.

101. Gebsattel to v. Liebert, February 12, 1914, in ZStA I,
     NL Gebsattel I, Bl.16.

102. We will see this dilemma arise frequently in our
     discussion of the Conservatives in subsequent chapters.

103. V. Liebert to Gebsattel, July 21, 1914, in ZStA I,
     NL Gebsattel I, Bl.158.

104. Gebsattel to v. Oldenburg-Januschau, January 20, 1914,
     in ZStA I, NL Gebsattel I, Bl.91.

105. Gebsattel to v. Liebert, June 26, 1914, in ZStA I,
     NL Gebsattel I, Bl.147-48; Class to Gebsattel,
     May 16, 1914, in ZStA I, NL Gebsattel I, Bl.141.

106. Class to Gebsattel, July 27, 1914, in ZStA I,
     NL Gebsattel I, Bl.168. Class had in fact formulated
     these aims as early as September 1911 in a speech at
     Duesseldorf, see Fischer, *Krieg der Illusionen,* p.657.

107. Quoted in Kruck, *Geschichte des Alldeutschen Verbandes,
     1890-1939,* p.69.

108. Quoted in Klaus Wernecke, *Der Wille zur Weltgeltung.
     Aussenpolitik und Offentlichkeit im Kaiserreich am
     Vorabend des Ersten Weltkrieges,* Duesseldorf 1970,
     pp.213f.

109. Quoted in Kruck, *Geschichte des Alldeutschen Verbandes,
     1890-1939,* p.63.

Chapter VI

1. See chapter II, *passim*.

2. Quoted in *HN*, April 3, 1912, 158.

3. Quoted in *Hamburger Fremdenblatt* (hereafter *HFr*), March 11, 1912, Nr. 59, "Aufruf der Hamburg Konservative Vereinigung."

4. Quoted in *HN*, August 24, 1912.

5. Quoted in *HN*, January 15, 1914.

6. In *HFr*, March 7, 1914, Nr. 56, "Ein konservativen Vorstoss gegen Hamburg."

7. Copy of a letter, June 23, 1914, in ZStA I, NL Westarp, Nr. 2, Bl.72.

8. Quoted in *National Liberale Zeitung*, August 22, 1912.

9. Quoted in *Berliner Tageblatt*, December 18, 1909.

10. Ernst Deetjen, *Freikonservativ! Die Nationale Mittelpartei*, Ratibor 1913, pp.29ff; Stegmann, *Die Erben Bismarcks*, pp.319ff.

11. Otto v. Pfister, *Deutsch-Konservativ*, Berlin 1913, p.18.

12. *KZ*, May 11, 1914, *Beilage* Nr. 218.

13. See chapter V. pp.102f.

14. Berghahn, *Germany and the Approach of War in 1914*, pp.149f; v. Wangenheim in *DT*, September 2, 1913, Nr. 444 (evening edition); Max Sering in *DT*, February 13, 1913, Nr 73 (morning edition); Georg Cleinow, *Die Grenzboten*, July 15, 1914, "Nationalpolitik und Staatspolitik," p.145 and June 30, 1913, "Das polnische Problem und die preussische Ostmarkenpolitik," pp.519ff; v. Wangenheim in *DT*, September 2, 1913, Nr. 444 (evening edition).

15. Mirbach-Sorquitten to Westarp, April 6, 1914, in ZStA I, NL Westarp, Nr. 2, Bl.14.

16. Limburg-Stirum in *KZ*, January 26, 1914, Nr. 42 (evening edition).

17. For a history of the Preussenbund, see the article
    by Robert Ullrich, "Preussenbund," in *Die Buergerliche
    Parteien* II, pp.470-472. Co-founder of the Preussenbund
    was Wolfgang Eisenhart. Other leading figures were
    Dr. Paul Rocke, Major General D. W. Rogge.

18. See Hahn's speech in *KdBdL*, February 16, 1914, Nr. 2;
    KZ, February 16, 1914, Nr. 78 (evening edition).

19. Vereinigung der Steuer und Wirtschaftsreformer,
    February 16, 1914, in ZStA II, Rep. 92, DIII5, NL Kapp.

20. Wolfgang Eisenhart, "Ein Wort ueber die Liberalisierung
    Preussens," in *KZ*, May 1, 1914, Nr. 201 (morning edition).

21. General v. Kleist, in *KZ*, July 14, 1914, Nr. 324.

22. Westarp to Heydebrand, December 18, 1913, in ZStA I,
    NL Westarp Nr. I, Bl.190.

23. Heydebrand to Westarp, December 20, 1913, in ZStA I,
    NL Westarp Nr. I, Bl.200-201.

24. Members of the Young Conservatives' Main Directorate
    were F. Koner, R. Baumann, H. Mueller, W. Funke,
    G. Siegesmund.

25. Westarp to Heydebrand, August 8, 1914 and Heydebrand
    to Westarp, August 4, 1914, in Heydebrand-Westarp
    correspondence (hereafter H-W).

26. Quoted in *Leipziger Blatt* and reported in *KZ*,
    August 26, 1914, Beilage to Nr. 345.

27. Heydebrand to Westarp, July 4, 1914 in H-W. I am
    indebted to Freiherr Hiller v. Gaertringen for making
    available to me a copy of this correspondence from
    his private archives covering the years 1914-1918.
    Freiherr Hiller v. Gaertringen is a grandson of Count
    Westarp.

28. Westarp to Heydebrand, July 15, 1914, in H-W.

29. Westarp, *Konservative Politik* I, p.407.

30. Heydebrand to Westarp, August 3, 1914, in H-W. See
    also Mommsen, "Domestic Factors...," P.42, F.N.76.

31. Jarausch, *Enigmatic Chancellor*, p.155; Riezler
    Tagebuecher, entrance of July 7, 1914, pp.181ff.

32. Memorandum by Mirbach-Sorquitten, dated June 20, 1914, in ZStA I, NL Westarp Nr. 2, Bl.71 and see Fischer, *Krieg der Illusionen*, p.747.

33. Quoted in *Konservative Monatschrift*, June 1914, p.955.

34. For a good analysis of the attempt at management of the July crisis see Berghahn *Germany and the Approach of War in 1914*, chapter 10.

35. Quoted in Jarausch, *Enigmatic Chancellor*, Chapter 7.

36. Dr. Paul Lorentz, "Der Weltkrieg und die deutsche Weltanschaaung" in *Preussische Jahrbuecher*, v. 158 (October-December 1914).

37. Ibid.

38. Heydebrand to Westarp, August 9, 1914, in H-W.

39. Westarp to Heydebrand, August 6, 1914, in H-W.

40. Artur Kresse to Westarp, August 6, 1914, in ZStA I, NL Westarp, Nr. 3.

41. Report of the Executive Committee of the German Conservative Party to Heydebrand, August 26, 1914, in ZStA I, NL Westarp, Nr. 98.

42. Report of the Executive Council to Westarp, August 26, 1914, in ZStA I, NL Westarp, Nr. 98, Bl.37.

43. Letter of August 1914, in ZStA I, NL Wangenheim 9, Bl.76; *Deutschland im Ersten Weltkrieg* I, pp.405ff.

44. Stegmann, *Die Erben Bismarcks*, p.451.

45. Wangenheim to Roesicke, September 9, 1914, in ZStA I, NL Wangenheim 9, Bl.117.

46. Wangenheim to Roesicke, October 13, 1914, in ZStA I, NL Wangenheim 9, Bl.166.

47. Roesicke to Wangenheim, August 28, 1914, in ZStA I, NL Wangenheim 9, Bl.93.

48. Wangenheim to Roesicke, August 31, 1914, in ZStA I, NL Wangenheim 9, Bl.96.

49. Roesicke to Wangenheim, September 20, 1914, in ZStA I, NL Wangenheim 9, Bl.125-126.

50. Gebsattel to Class, August 4, 1914, in ZStA I, NL Gebsattel I, Bl.175ff.

51. Class to Gebsattel, August 6, 1914, in ZStA I, NL Gebsattel I, Bl.185.

52. Stegmann, *Die Erben Bismarcks*, p.441.

53. Fischer, *Krieg der Illusionen*, pp.740f..

54. Stegmann, *Die Erben Bismarcks*, p.449.

55. Heinrich Class, *Zum deutschen Kriegsziel*, n.p. n.d. I have taken the quotations from the 1917 edition published by J. F. Lehmann Verlag, Munich; Fischer, *Krieg der Illusionen*, p.741.

56. Quoted in Fischer, *Krieg der Illusionen*, p.761.

57. Fritz Fischer, *Griff nach der Weltmacht*, Duesseldorf, 1961, p.116. For individual points of Bethmann's programme see ibid., pp.117f..

58. Ibid., p.113.

59. Among other programmes of expansion created during the early weeks of the War were those by the Center politician, Matthias Erzberger, the industrialist August Thyssen and, later, a *Mitteleuropa* association of states as formulated by Friedrich Naumann. His plan sought to make annexations superfluous and expected to create a German world power in a peaceful manner. Naumann also maintained his decades-long desire for a social people's state, enhanced by the "spirit of 1914" and the Kaiser's August 4 speech. For Naumann see Klaus Schwabe, *Wissenschaft und Kriegsmoral*, Goettingen, 1969, p.125 and "Zur politischen Haltung der deutschen Professoren im Ersten Weltkrieg," in *HZ* CSCIII (1961). Also, see Fischer, *Griff nach der Weltmacht*, pp.121ff..

60. Fischer, *Griff nach der Weltmacht*, p.119.

61. Gebsattel to Class, August 30, 1914, in ZStA I, NL Gebsattel I, Bl.200f..

62. Quoted in Gerald Feldman, *Army, Industry and Labor in Germany, 1914-1918*, Princeton, 1966, p.136.

63. Gebsattel to Westarp, September 4, 1914, in ZStA I, NL Westarp, Nr. 3, Bl.10ff..

64. Kreth to Westarp, September 15, 1914, in ZStA I, NL Westarp, Nr. 3, Bl.18. Herman Kreth (1860-?) was the Conservative Reichstag Deputy for Gumbinnen (electoral district 4).

65. Quoted in Stegmann, *Die Erben Bismarcks*, p.449.

66. Quoted in Class, *Wider den Strom*, p.330.

67. Stegmann, *Die Erben Bismarcks*, p.449; Class, *Wider den Strom*, p.342.

68. Class to Gebsattel, October 10, 1914, in ZStA I, NL Gebsattel I, Bl.242.

69. Gebsattel to Boettreich, December 4, 1914, in ZStA I, NL Gebsattel I, Bl.315.

70. See chapter V, p. 107f.

71. Fischer, *Krieg der Illusionen*, p.780.

72. Roesicke to Westarp, December 17, 1914, in ZStA I, NL Westarp, Nr. 4, Bl.135.

73. See Chapter V, pp.117ff..

74. V. Wangenheim to Roesicke, September 8, 1914, in ZStA I, NL Wangenheim 9, Bl.113 and same to same, September 14, 1914, Bl.123.

75. Letter from *Deutscher Landwirtschaftsrat* to Roesicke, October 7, 1914, in ZStA I, NL Wangenheim 9, Bl.164.

76. Feldman, *Army, Industry and Labor*, p.100.

77. Roesicke to v. Wangenheim, November 26, 1914, in ZStA I, NL Wangenheim 9, Bl.231.

78. Feldman, *Army, Industry and Labor*, pp.100f..

79. V. Wangenheim to Roesicke, December 21, 1914, in ZStA I, NL Wangenheim 9, Bl.253.

80. Gerschenkron, *Bread and Democracy in Germany*, p.87.

81. Roesicke to v. Wangenheim, October 9, 1914, in ZStA I, NL Wangenheim 9, Bl.145; memorandum to Bethmann, December 6, 1914, in ZStA I, NL Westarp, Nr. 4, Bl.19. Although price ceilings were initiated by the government, they were so high as to confuse most

299

agrarians and cause v. Wangenheim to proclaim that "it is as if Caprivi were ruling the German Empire once more," see v. Wangenheim to Roesicke, in ZStA I, NL Wangenheim 9, Bl.235.

82. *Deutschland im Ersten Weltkrieg* I, p.213.

83. Bethmann at a meeting of the Prussian Ministry of State, ZStA II, Rep 90a Abt. B, Tit III, 4c, Nr. 10, vol. 163, Staatsministerial Sitzungsprotokolle 1914 (Sitting of August 15, 1914).

84. *Deutschland im Ersten Weltkrieg* I, p.213.

85. This extended to Bethmann's own ministers in the Prussian Ministry of State as evidenced by a meeting of December 31, 1914 in which Minister of the Interior Dallwitz called for a "splitting up of the Party", and Agriculture Minister v. Schorlemer felt that "now is the time to take direct action against the SPD," ZStA II, Rep 90a Abt. B, Tit III, 4c, Nr. 10, vol. 163, Staatsministerial Sitzungsprotokolle 1914.

86. *Deutschland im Ersten Weltkrieg* I, p.213.

87. Reinhard Patemann, *Der Kampf um die preussische Wahlreform im Ersten Weltkrieg*, Duesseldorf, 1964, p.20.

88. Westarp to Heydebrand, November 1, 1914, in H-W.

89. Westarp to Heydebrand, November 18, 1914, in H-W.

90. Quoted in Westarp, *Konservative Politik* II, p.382.

91. Quoted in Riezler, *Tagebuecher*, notation of September 27, 1915.

92. Fischer, *Krieg der Illusionen*, p.542.

93. I base this on the fact that Mirbach had spoken with Hoetzsch about this matter as early as March 1913. See Fischer, *Krieg der Illusionen*, p.542, F.N. 1.

94. Schwabe, *Wissenschaft und Kriegsmoral*, p.58.

95. Schwabe, "Ursprung..." p.121.

96. See the report of the Conservative Executive Committee to Heydebrand, September 4, 1914, in ZStA I, NL Westarp, Nr. 98, Bl.47-48; Westarp, *Konservative Politik* II, p.35.

97. Gebsattel to Roesicke and Westarp, December 3, 1914, in ZStA I, NL Westarp, Nr. 4, Bl.5.

98. Class, *Wider den Strom*, pp.326ff.; Class to Gebsattel, December 3, 1914, in ZStA I, NL Gebsattel I, Bl.292.

99. Fischer, *Krieg der Illusionen*, p.749.

100. Class sent his *Denkschrift* to Westarp on November 20, 1914, See ZStA I, NL Westarp, Nr. 3, On December 22, 1914, Class sent nearly 2000 copies to prominent Germans.

101. Heydebrand to Westarp, November 22, 1914, in H-W: "The Russians are only six miles away,"

102. Gebsattel to Westarp, December 3, 1914, in ZStA I, NL Westarp, Nr. 4, Bl.43.

103. Gebsattel to Roesicke, December 3, 1914, in ZStA I, NL Westarp, Nr. 4, Bl.5.

104. V. Wangenheim to Gebsattel, December 6, 1914, in ZStA I, NL Gebsattel I, Bl.310-311.

105. V. Grumme-Douglas to Westarp, December 12, 1914, in ZStA I, NL Westarp, Nr, 4, Bl.20f.. Wangenheim felt later that v. Grumme had misunderstood Heydebrand's position; that it was the case of a party leader who was still awaiting proof of military success and of the ADV aims. V. Wangenheim to Roesicke, December 21, 1914, in ZStA I, NL Wangenheim 9, Bl.253.

106. As examples of closer industrial-Conservative ties are the discussions held by the Party in September 1914 about the possibility of Roetger of the CDI replacing Deputy Bauer, recently deceased, as the Conservative candidate for Bitterfeld-Delitzsch. See the report of the Executive Committee, September 25, 1914, in ZStA I, NL Westarp, Nr. 98, Bl.51f..

107. Among industrialists present were Hugenberg, Kirdorf, Stinnes, Reusch, Beukenberg, Roetger, Schweighoffer, Hirsch (Essen); from the BdL, Wangenheim and Roesicke; Westarp and Dietrich from the Conservatives and Class from the ADV. See Class to Gebsattel, December 17, 1914, in ZStA I, NL Gebsattel I, Bl.203ff.. Heydebrand was unable to come; see Heydebrand to Westarp, December 11, 1914, in H-W: "I will have to excuse myself from the meeting on December 15, because things are bad here at Tschunkawe and train connections are still uncertain."

108. Class to Gebsattel, December 17, 1914, in ZStA I,
     ADV 355, Bl.203ff..

109. Class to Gebsattel, December 16, 1914, in ZStA I,
     NL Gebsattel I, Bl.332.

110. Ibid.

111. Ibid: "The Conservatives still refuse to link
     themselves to us."

112. Class to Gebsattel, December 17, 1914, in ZStA I,
     ADV 355, Bl.204.

113. Westarp to Heydebrand, December 28, 1914, printed
     in Westarp, *Konservative Politik* II, p.42.

114. Westarp to Gebsattel, December 28, 1914, in ZStA I,
     NL Gebsattel I, Bl.313. Roesicke also wrote Gebsattel
     a letter expressing similar thoughts. Roesicke to
     Gebsattel, December 27, 1914, in ZStA I, NL Gebsattel I,
     Bl.317.

115. Report of December 29, 1914, in ZStA I, NL Westarp,
     Nr. 98, Bl.76.

116. Heydebrand to Westarp, December 30, 1914, in H-W.

Chapter VII

1. This is especially the case with numerous older
   studies of the period.

2. Heydebrand to Westarp, January 1, 1915, in H-W.

3. Quoted in Westarp, *Konservative Politik*, II, P.44.

4. Gebsattel to Lehmann, January 11, 1915, in ZStA I,
   NL Gebsattel I, Bl.364.

5. Westarp, *Konservative Politik*, II, p.44 and Gebsattel
   to v. Wangenheim, February 2, 1915, in ZStA I,
   NL Gebsattel I, Bl.462.

6. Gebsattel to Lehmann, January 11, 1915, in ZStA I,
   NL Gebsattel I, Bl.364.

7. Hugenberg to Kapp, January 11, 1915, in ZStA II,
   Rep. 92, DV4, NL Kapp.

8. V. Wangenheim to Gebsattel, January 14, 1915, in ZStA I, NL Gebsattel I, Bl.372f.: "There is a difference in Heydebrand's basic viewpoint, which one has to change. I, therefore, believe that our dealings with the Conservatives do not have to cease,"

9. Schwabe, *Wissenschaft und Kriegsmoral*, pp.126f.

10. Hoetzsche to Westarp, January 21, 1915, in ZStA I, NL Westarp, Nr. 5, Bl.15ff.

11. Heydebrand to Westarp, April 25, 1915, in H-W.

12. Westarp to v. Heydebrand, April 25, 1915, in H-W. Westarp also rejected an economic or political link with Belgium; rather, he advocated military control over Belgium's defenses and the North Sea coast. Westarp to Bethmann Hollweg, April 17, 1915, in ZStA I, NL Westarp, Nr. 6, Bl,12.

13. Westarp to Heydebrand, November 9, 1915, in H-W.

14. V. Wangenheim to Roesicke, March 20, 1915, in ZStA I, NL v. Wangenheim 10, Bl.70.

15. Hoesch to Westarp, April 20, 1915, in ZStA I, NL Westarp, Nr. 6, Bl.31f.; Roesicke to v. Wangenheim, October 25, 1915, in ZStA I, NL v. Wangenheim 10, Bl,264f.

16. V. Wangenheim to Roesicke, November 30, 1915, in ZStA, NL v. Wangenheim 10, Bl.291.

17. Roesicke to v. Wangenheim, October 27, 1915, in ZStA I, NL Wangenheim 10, Bl.273.

18. A copy of Schwerin's memorandum, which Westarp received on June 14, 1915, can be found in ZStA I, NL Westarp, Nr. 6. See also, *Die Hakatisten*, p.275 and Fischer, *Griff*, p.193ff.

19. *Die Hakatisten*, p.275.

20. Ibid.

21. Quoted in "Eigene Denkschrift zur Frage der Ansiedlung frueheren Kriegsteilnehmer," (1915) in ZStA II, Rep.92, DIX7, NL Kapp, Bl.53ff.; also Kapp to v. Wangenheim, October 11, 1915, in ZStA II, Rep 92, DIX8, NL Kapp, Bl.7.

22. Roesicke to v. Wangenheim, April 23, 1915, in ZStA I, NL v. Wangenheim 10, Bl.111.

303

23. Gebsattel to Cetto, January 14, 1915, and same to Graf
    Podewils, January 18, 1915, in ZStA I, NL Gebsattel I,
    Bl.382 and 392. See also Hugenberg's memorandum to
    the Prussian Minister of the Interior of February 2,
    1915, dealing with the creation of "closed" (German)
    language and racial areas in the Eastern Marches of
    Poland which would exclude Polish seasonal workers
    and their language. Galos, *Die Hakatisten*, pp.273f.

24. The memorandum was printed on March 10, and a copy
    may be found in ZStA II, Rep 77, tit 885, Nr. 4, Bd.I.

25. Gebsattel to Class, March 23, 1915, in ZStA I, ADV 356,
    Bl.42.

26. *Deutschland im Ersten Weltkrieg*, II, pp.149f.; Kruck,
    Geschichte des Alldeutschen Verbandes, p.278; quoted
    in Stegmann, *Die Erben Bismarcks*, p.455.

27. Kruck, *Geschichte des Alldeutschen Verbandes*, p.78;
    Deutschland im Ersten Weltkrieg, II, p.168. One of
    the chief factors militating against Conservative
    acceptance of the declaration was its criticism of
    a special peace with Russia. See Fischer, *Griff nach
    der Weltmacht*, p.200.

28. Gebsattel to Class, May 12, 1915, in ZStA I, ADV 356,
    Bl.75.

29. Heydebrand to Gebsattel, May 12, 1915, in ZStA I,
    NL Gebsattel I, Bl.626; Gebsattel to v. Heydebrand,
    May 9, 1915, in ZStA I, ADV 356, Bl.82.

30. Gebsattel to Class, May 15, 1915, in ZStA I,
    NL Gebsattel I, Bl.645.

31. Class to Gebsattel, May 14, 1915, in ZStA I,
    NL Gebsattel I, Bl.641.

32. Class to Gebsattel, May 18, 1915, in ZStA I,
    NL Gebsattel I, Bl.649.

33. Gebsattel to Class, February 12, 1915, in ZStA I,
    NL Gebsattel I, Bl.477.

34. See the letter from Gebsattel to v. Grumme Douglas,
    May 30, 1915: "You have so many connections to
    Conservative members. History will show that Heydebrand
    became the grave-digger of his party--hopefully not
    of the monarchy. We must enlighten the Conservatives,"
    in ZStA I, NL Gebsattel I, Bl.709.

35. Stegmann, *Die Erben Bismarcks*, p.451; Kruck, *Geschichte des Alldeutschen Verbandes*, p.77; Fischer, *Griff nach der Weltmacht*, p.200.

36. Fischer, *Griff nach der Weltmacht*, pp.197ff; Schwabe, "Ursprung," p.109.

37. Fischer, *Griff nach der Weltmacht*, p.201; Stegmann, *Die Erben Bismarcks*, pp.457f.

38. Gebsattel to Count Luxburg-Speyer, December 3, 1915, in ZStA I, NL Gebsattel 2, Bl.326.

39. General v. Gayl to Bethmann Hollweg, June 23, 1915, entry #105 in Wilhelm Deist (ed.), *Militaer und Innenpolitik im Weltkrieg, 1914-1918*, I, Duesseldorf 1970, pp.244ff.

40. *Deutschland im Ersten Weltkrieg*, II, pp.189ff.

41. For Rohrbach see Walter Mogk, *Paul Rohrbach und das "Groessere Deutschland." Ethischer Imperialismus im Wilhelminischen Zeitalter*, Munich 1972.

42. Stegmann, *Die Erben Bismarcks*, p.464. For the proclamation of the "Freie Vaterlaendische Vereinigung," see the *Preussische Jahrbuecher*, (Jan.-June 1915), v. 158, pp.182ff. Among its most prominent members were Eugen Schiffer, Carl Bachem, Hans Delbrueck, Arthur v. Gwinner, Ernst Jaeckh, Heinrich Rippler, Paul Rohrbach, Arthur Salomonsohn, Max Sering (!) and Adolf Wagner (!).

43. Reismann-Grone to Bethmann Hollweg, July 6, 1915, in ZStA I, 1422/24, Bl.5; Class to Hoensbroech, October 9, 1915, in ZStA I, ADV 453, Bl.47.

44. Roesicke to v. Wangenheim, March 17, 1915, in ZStA I, NL v. Wangenheim 10, Bl.68.

45. Ibid; Roesicke to Reventlow, April 5, 1915, in ZStA I, NL v. Wangenheim 10, Bl.84.

46. V. Wangenheim to Gebsattel, January 25, 1915, in ZStA I, NL Gebsattel I, Bl.439f.; Westarp to Count Hatzfeld, January 19, 1915, in ZStA I, NL Westarp, Nr. 5, Bl.8f.; v. Wangenheim to Roesicke, February 3, 1915, in ZStA I, NL v. Wangenheim 10.

47. V. Wangenheim to Gebsattel, May 10, 1915, in ZStA I, ADV 356, Bl.76.

48. Roesicke to v. Wangenheim, April 18, 1915, in ZStA I, NL v. Wangenheim 10, Bl.103.

49. V. Wangenheim to Roesicke, January 17, 1915, in ZStA I, NL v. Wangenheim 10, Bl.19f.

50. For the beginnings of the conflict, see Chapter VI, pp.149ff; see also Hugenberg to Gebsattel, in ZStA I, NL Gebsattel I, Bl.463; v. Wangenheim to Roesicke, January 23, 1915, in ZStA I, NL v. Wangenheim 10, Bl.25; v. Wangenheim to Westarp, n.d. (but presumably at the end of March 1915), in ZStA I, NL Westarp, Nr. 5, Bl.93. In early 1915, the agrarians demanded to get their own price ceilings. See *Deutschland im Ersten Weltkrieg*, II, p.249.

51. Roesicke to v. Wangenheim, November 24, 1915, in ZStA I, NL v. Wangenheim 10, Bl.287.

52. Ibid., Bl.288.

53. Roesicke to Westarp, April 22, 1915, in ZStA I, NL Westarp, Nr. 6, Bl.43: "Perhaps we could get the SPD into talks with the economic associations. I would rather not...but the *Burgfrieden* is on and it would be awkward."

54. Roesicke to v. Wangenheim, August 9, 1915, in ZStA I, NL v. Wangenheim 10, Bl.195f.

55. Roesicke to v. Wangenheim, August 24, 1915, in ZStA I, NL v. Wangenheim 10, Bl.204.

56. See Chapter IV, pp.91ff.

57. See the letters from Bodelschwingh to the Ullstein Press, December 3, 1914, and to v. Kessel, Supreme Commander in the Marches. in ZStA I, ADV 415, Bl.112 and 136ff.

58. Pamphlet of November 25, 1915, in ZStA I, NL Westarp, Nr. 10.

59. Westarp to v. Kries, July 6, 1915, in ZStA I, NL Westarp, Nr. 7, Bl.8.

60. Westarp to v. Bonin, April 21, 1915, in ZStA I, NL Westarp, Nr. 6, Bl.33ff.

61. See Chapter VI, pp.144f.

62. Gebsattel to v. Thompsen, July 3, 1915, in ZStA I,
    NL Gebsattel 2, Bl.78.

63. Gebsattel to Graf Luxburg, July 23, 1915, in ZStA I,
    NL Gebsattel 2, Bl.140 and Gebsattel to Lehmann,
    November 17, 1915, in NL Gebsattel 2, Bl.286.

64. V. Vietinghoff-Scheel to ?, August 26, 1915, in ZStA I,
    ADV 508/1, Bl.39.

65. Gebsattel to Class, May 28, 1915, in ZStA I, ADV 356,
    Bl.99.

66. Gebsattel to Class, October 31, 1915, in ZStA I,
    NL Gebsattel 2, Bl.268.

67. Paphnutius, "Die Judenfrage nach dem Kriege," in the
    Preussische Jahrbuecher, September 29, 1915, v. 158,
    p.395.

68. Lehmann to Class, November 12, 1915, in ZStA I, ADV 1418,
    Bl.30.

69. Westarp in *Konservative Politik*, II, pp.167f.

70. See copies of *Zum Neuen Ufern* in ZStA I, ADV 1416.

71. Letter from Police President v. Ries to the Commanding
    General of the XVIII Army Corps about a meeting of
    the Frankfurt branch of the *Wehrverein*, July 1915,
    in ZStA I, ADV 1416, Bl.31 and the letter from
    v. Strantz to v. Ries, August 1, 1915, in same, Bl.33.

72. See, for instance, the letter from Dr. Oskar Karstedt
    to Bethmann Hollweg, August 28, 1915, in ZStA I,
    ADV 1416, Bl.18: "I have the honor of sending you
    a copy of demands that I have just received from
    Leipzig. The author, who shall remain nameless, is
    very sympathetic to Class and anti-Semitism."

73. V. Graefe to Westarp, April 1915, in ZStA I, NL
    Westarp, Nr. 6, Bl.17f.

74. V. Wangenheim to Westarp, March 28, 1915, in ZStA I,
    NL Westarp, Nr. 5, Bl.91f.

75. See *Hamburger Echo (HE)*, January 16, 1915, Nr. 13,
    "Die Heerschau der Agrarier verboten," and v.
    Wangenheim to Roesicke, June 23, 1915, in BA (Kl.
    Erw.Roesicke) Nr. 230-1.

76. See the 14-page memorandum marked "very secret"
    written by Gebsattel, March 1915, in ZStA I,
    NL Gebsattel 6, Bl.149ff.

77. Memorandum of May 5, 1915, in Hamburg Forschungsstelle
    fuer die Geschichte des Nationalsozialismus in
    Hamburg (hereafter HFs) Nr. 412, ADV.

78. Published in the *Alldeutsche Blaetter* (hereafter *ADB*)
    May, 13, 1915.

79. Westarp to Heydebrand, April 6, 1915, in H-W.

80. Westarp in *Konservative Politik*, II, p.302.

81. Ibid.

82. Heydebrand to Westarp, April 15, 1915; Heydebrand to
    Westarp, April 19, 1915; Heydebrand to Westarp,
    April 21, 1915; Westarp to Heydebrand, April 22, 1915,
    all in H-W.

83. V. Hassel to Heydebrand, March 17, 1915, in H-W.

84. Westarp to Heydebrand, May 13, 1915, in H-W.

85. Westarp to v. Kessel, August 7, 1915, in ZStA I,
    NL Westarp, Nr. 7, Bl.47ff.

86. Heydebrand to Westarp, July 30, 1915, in H-W.

87. V. Wangenheim to Roesicke, June 23, 1915, in ZStA I,
    NL v. Wangenheim 10, Bl.181.

88. Westarp to v. Heydebrand, October 1, 1915, in H-W.

89. V. Heydebrand to Westarp, October 6, 1915, in H-W.

90. Westarp, in *Konservative Politik*, II, p.31.

91. Westarp to ?, June 17, 1915, in ZStA I, NL Westarp,
    Nr. 6, Bl.112.

92. Stresemann to Friedrich Uebel, January 16, 1915
    quoted in *Deutschland im Ersten Weltkrieg*, II, p.175.

93. See Fischer, *Griff nach der Weltmacht*, pp.253ff.

94. See Chapter V, pp.115f.

95. Westarp to v. Heydebrand, November 9, 1915, in H-W.

96. Roesicke to v. Wangenheim, November 24, 1915, in ZStA I, NL v. Wangenheim 10, Bl.287.

97. Letter of Provincial *Ausschuss* of East Prussia to Bethmann Hollweg, October 19, 1915, in ZStA II, Rep 77, 885, Nr. 4, 1.

98. Class at ADV meeting of October 24, 1915, in ZStA I, ADV 1416.

99. Fischer, *Griff nach der Weltmacht*, p.209.

100. Heydebrand to Westarp, November 6, 1915, in H-W.

101. Lezius at ADV meeting of October 24, 1915, in ZStA I, ADV 1416.

102. V. Graefe to Westarp, June 15, 1915, printed in Westarp, *Konservative Politik*, II, p.325.

103. Tiele-Winkler to Bethmann Hollweg, September 19, 1915, in ZStA I, NL Westarp, Nr. 100, Bl.3.

104. Westarp in *Konservative Politik*, II, p.313.

105. Ibid., p.305.

106. V. Graefe to Westarp, April 24, 1915, in ZStA I, NL Westarp, Nr. 6, Bl.51.

107. V. Graefe to v. Liebig, December 31, 1915, in ZStA I, ADV 1417, Bl.163f.

108. A term devised by v. Liebig to describe the politics of Bethmann Hollweg.

Chapter VIII

1. Heydebrand to Westarp, January 4, 1916, in H-W.

2. Westarp to Heydebrand, January 5, 1916, in H-W.

3. Westarp to Meseritz, April 14, 1916, in ZStA I, NL Westarp, Nr. 12, Bl.226.

4. V. Grumme, for one, gave up his opposition (temporarily) in June. See the report from Schroeter to Westarp, June 23, 1916, in ZStA I, NL Westarp, Nr. 12, Bl.107 : "Herr v. Grumme has forgotten his earlier animosity

and come back fully into the Party ranks." See also
the tactical letter of Heydebrand to v. Bonin,
endorsing a "closer cooperation between the ADV
and the Conservative Party." Heydebrand was of
the opinion that some kind of tie should have united
the "aristocracy and those numerous elements of the
bourgeoisie who are anti-big capitalist and anti-
democratic. Thus, I would welcome it, if numerous
members of the Conservative Party would join the ADV."
Heydebrand to v. Bonin, April 2, 1916, in ZStA I,
NL Westarp, Nr. 10, Bl.125. In the short run these
tactics modified the increasing demands of the ADV
upon the Conservatives. The ADV chapter of Cologne,
for instance, asked the Conservative Party to support
an inheritance tax! ADV chapter of Cologne to
Conservative Party, December 7, 1916, in ZStA I,
NL Westarp, Nr. 9, Bl.23. That Heydebrand's tactics
did little to improve either his or the Party's long-
term situation will be demonstrated in subsequent
chapters.

5. See letters from Westarp to Heydebrand, August 12, 1916;
Heydebrand to Westarp, August 13, 1916; Westarp to
Heydebrand, August 18, 1916, in H-W. See also
Westarp to v. Flottwell, September 21, 1916, in ZStA I,
NL v. Wangenheim 10, Bl.88.

6. Heydebrand to Westarp, December 30, 1916 in H-W.

7. Ibid.

8. For agrarian fear of direct taxation, see Roesicke
to v. Wangenheim, March 5, 1916 and v. Wangenheim
to Roesicke, March 7, 1916, in ZStA I, NL v. Wangenheim II,
Bl.16ff.

9. Class to Gebsattel, February 28, 1916, in ZStA I,
NL Gebsattel 2, Bl.585f. According to Westarp,
v. Graefe threatened to resign from the *Reichstag*
but was calmed by Westarp and others. See Westarp,
Konservative Politik II, p.130 and the letter from
v. Graefe to Westarp, January 28, 1916, printed in
Konservative Politik II, p.326.

10. This was the term used to describe Hoetzsch by
Prof. Johannes Haller of Tuebingen, a Baltic German.
See the report of a meeting of the Independent
Committee for a German Peace (Unabhaengiger Ausschuss
f.e. deutschen Frieden), August 21, 1916, in ZStA I,
1422, Bl.128f. See also Mehnert to Westarp,
September 19, 1916, in ZStA I, NL Westarp, Nr. 13, Bl.64.

11. Heydebrand to Westarp, December 30, 1916 in H-W.

12. See Westarp, *Konservative Politik* II, pp.312, 328ff.;
    Westarp to Heydebrand (n.d. but presumably December
    1916) in H-W. Heydebrand claimed to have been against
    the visit of reconciliation from the start. See
    Heydebrand to Westarp, December 26, 1916, in H-W
    and Westarp, *Konservative Politik* II, p.313. See,
    furthermore, v. Hindenburg to Bethmann, October 23, 1916,
    in ZStA I, 1392 and v. Valentini to Bethmann, July 6, 1916,
    printed in Westarp, *Konservative Politik* II, p.331.

13. Bethmann to v. Valentini, July 4, 1916, in ZStA I,
    1392, Bl.65. Bethmann claimed that Heydebrand had
    told him of these plans "in an impudent manner."
    Westarp, however, claimed that Heydebrand was incapable
    of such an action. Westarp, *Konservative Politik* II,
    p.303.

14. Report of the Main Association of the Conservative Party
    (Berlin) to Heydebrand, August 1, 1916, in ZStA I,
    NL Westarp, Nr. 98; Westarp to Heydebrand, August 3, 1916,
    in H-W; Mehnert to Westarp, September 19, 1916, in
    ZStA I, NL Westarp, Nr. 13, Bl.64.

15. V. Valentini to Loebell, June 30, 1916, in ZStA I,
    1392 Nr. 2, Bl.59.

16. Report of the Main Association of the German Conservative
    Party to Heydebrand, June 12, 1916, in ZStA I,
    NL Westarp, Nr. 98, Bl.177ff; a further report of
    June 23, 1916 and July 1, 1916 reconfirmed *Herrenhaus*
    unhappiness with Heydebrand's position against Bethmann.

17. The speech was reprinted in *Mitteilungen aus der
    Konservative Partei*, August 26, 1916, Nr. 35, pp.54ff.

18. Westarp to Heydebrand, August 19, 1916 and August 22, 1916,
    in H-W.

19. Oskar Kresse to Westarp, August 31, 1916, in ZStA I,
    NL Westarp, Nr. 12, Bl.142. See also v. Bodelschwingh
    to Heydebrand, September 21, 1916, in ZStA I, NL Westarp,
    Nr. 10, Bl.33.

20. Westarp to v. Berg, August 5, 1916, in ZStA I,
    NL Westarp, Nr. 10, Bl.63.

21. Westarp to v. Schwartz, November 19, 1916, in ZStA I,
    NL Westarp, Nr. 15, Bl.121.

22. See the programme presented to Westarp by Dr. Beutler
    for consideration by the Committee of Twelve,
    Dr. Beutler to Westarp, August 1, 1916, in ZStA I,
    NL Westarp, Nr. 100, Bl.20ff.

23. David, *Der BdL als Machtinstrument*, p.138.

24. Westarp to Heydebrand, December 27, 1916, in H-W.

25. Westarp to v. Berg, August 15, 1916, in ZStA I,
    NL Westarp, Nr. 25, Bl.60ff.

26. Otto Hoetzsch, "Wo stehen wir? Wohin streben wir?"
    Speech delivered to Hamburg Conservative Association,
    August 4, 1916, reported in *HN*, September 4, 1916,
    Nr. 450.

27. Galos, *Die Hakatisten*, p.286.

28. Quoted in *Deutschland im Ersten Weltkrieg*, vol. II,
    p.215.

29. Roesicke to Westarp, April 12, 1916, in ZStA I,
    NL Westarp, Nr. 14, Bl.25.

30. Gebsattel to General Keim, March 1, 1916, in ZStA I,
    NL Gebsattel 3, Bl.588-589.

31. Report of the Chief States' Attorney for the province
    of Berlin, August 18, 1916, in ZStA I, 1417/2, Bl.90f.

32. See Karl-Heinz Schaedlich, "Der 'Unabhaengigen
    Ausschuss fuer einen Deutschen Frieden' als ein
    Zentrum der Annexionspropaganda des deutschen
    Imperialismus im ersten Weltkrieg," in *Politik im
    Krieg, 1914-1918*, edited by Fritz Klein, Berlin,
    1964 and Dietrich Schaefer, *Mein Leben*.

33. Stegmann, "Zwischen Repression und Manipulation,"
    p.381. Westarp refused to join the Independent
    Committee ostensibly because it conflicted with his
    role as chairman of the *Reichstag* Conservatives. See
    Westarp's notation of August 7, 1916, in ZStA I,
    NL Westarp, Nr. 16, Bl.3.

34. See the memorandum of June 9, 1916, in ZStA II,
    Rep 92, NL Kapp DVI.

35. Weilnboeck to Roesicke, August 3, 1916, in ZStA I,
    NL v. Wangenheim 11, Bl.108-109.

36. See the notation of August 15, 1916, in *Das Kriegstagbuch des Reichstagsabgeordneter Eduard David 1914-1918*, edited by Erich Matthias, Duesseldorf, 1966,

37. Wolfgang Kapp, *Die nationalen Kreisen und der Reichskanzler*, Koenigsberg, 1916; Hans v. Liebig, *Die Politik von Bethmann Hollweg*, Muenchen, 1916; Junius Alter (pseud, for Franz Sontag), *Das deutsche Reich auf dem Wege zur geschichtlichen Episode*, Muenchen, 1916,

30. Schroeter to Westarp, June 23, 1916, in ZStA I, NL Westarp, Nr, 12, Bl.110. See also Kurt Koszyk, *Deutsche Presspolitik im Ersten Weltkrieg*, Duesseldorf, 1968, p.157, and Riezler's entry of June 12, 1916, in *Tagebuecher*, p.357.

39. Dr. Oestreicher to Westarp, October 10, 1916, in ZStA I, NL Westarp, Nr. 15, Bl.84.

40. Dietrich v. Oertzen, "Die Konservative Partei und der soziale Staat," in *Vom inneren Frieden des deutschen Volkes*, edited by Friedrich Thimme, Leipzig, 1916, p.384.

41. Friedrich Thimme, "Konservatismus und innerer Frieden," in *Konservative Monatschrift*, 1916, p.235.

42. Westarp to Woermann, September 8, 1916, in ZStA I, NL Westarp, Nr. 16, Bl.54.

43. Stegmann, *Die Erben Bismarcks*, p.480 and in "Zwischen Repression und Manipulation," p.380,

44. *Deutschland im Ersten Weltkrieg*, vol. II, P.369.

45. Leading the struggle against the ADV conspiracy was Bethmann's closest advisor, Kurt Riezler, See Riezler *Tagebuecher*, passim. Bethmann also authorized the creation of the *National Ausschuss zur Erreichung eines ehrenvollen Friedens* (National Committee for the Secural of an Honorable Peace) under Prince Wedel. See attacks against this organization in the *ADB*, 5.8. 1916 and in the *Korrespondenz des BdL*, August 10, 1916.

46. *Deutschland im Ersten Weltkrieg*, vol. II, p.723.

47. See the notes of Lieutenant General Wild v. Hohenborn dated March 9, 1916, in *Militaer und Innenpolitik im Weltkrieg 1914-1918*, 2 vols., edited by Wilhelm Deist, Duesseldorf, 1970, vol. 2, #142.

48. See Kapp's pamphlet entitled *Denkschrift zur Lage* (September 1916) and Kapp to Ludendorff, October 4, 1916, in ZStA II, Rep 92, NL Kapp, D IV 31.

49. Feldman, *Army, Industry and Labor*, p.145.

50. Ludendorff to Kapp, September 21, 1916, in ZStA II, Rep. 92, NL Kapp, D IV 19.

51. The conspiracy on the part of the *OHL* (Supreme Command) was directed by Col. Max Bauer, a chief aide to Ludendorff. See the NL Bauer in the BA and *Militaer und Innenpolitik*, vol. 2, #246. See also Feldman, *Army, Industry and Labor, passim.*

52. Westarp to Heydebrand, November 7, 1916, in H-W.

53. Westarp first met with Hindenburg and Ludendorff on November 14, 1916. See Westarp, *Konservative Politik* II, p.18.

54. Bethmann to v. Valentini, December 31, 1916, in ZStA II, Rep 92, NL v. Valentini, Nr. 2, Bl.42-43.

55. Hugenberg to Class, ??1915, in ZStA I, ADV 1418.

56. Georg Lisske to Westarp, August 7, 1916, in ZStA I, NL Westarp, Nr. 12, Bl.248.

57. V. Wangenheim to Roesicke, June 8, 1916, in ZStA I, NL v. Wangenheim 11, Bl.64. Kapp had written in *Die Nationale Kreisen und der Reichskanzler* that "the elimination of price ceilings would act as the liberator of our economic life and allow the producing classes to produce."

58. Roesicke to v. Wangenheim, June 2, 1916, in ZStA I, NL v. Wangenheim 11, Bl.62.

59. V. Wangenheim to Roesicke, August 7, 1916, in ZStA I, NL v. Wangenheim 11, Bl.103.

60. V. Wangenheim to Roesicke, September 29, 1916, in ZStA I, NL v. Wangenheim 11, Bl.155.

61. See the following section of this chapter for Class and the *Kartell*.

62. V. Wangenheim to Roesicke, August 4, 1916, in ZStA I, NL v. Wangenheim 11, Bl.91-92.

63. Since April, in fact, the BdL had been proposing the candidacy of Roetger, chairman of the CDI, as a Conservative candidate. See Roesicke to v. Wangenheim, April 18, 1916, in ZStA I, NL v. Wangenheim 11, Bl.40.

64. V. Wangenheim to Roesicke, August 1916, in ZStA I, NL Roesicke 2A, Bl.293.

65. See the interesting letter from M. Hobohm to Paul Rohrbach, May 24, 1916, in ZStA I, ADV 1417, Bl.184: "The basis of the ADV's might is the political enthusiasm of its members. This political movement works with a very strong organization and unlimited resources."

66. See Chapter VII.

67. See the letter from Gebsattel to Class, January 3, 1916, in ZStA I, ADV 356, Bl.223.

68. Stegmann, *Die Erben Bismarcks*, p.489.

69. Ibid., p.490.

70. See HFs, II/C2, p.66f.

71. Stegmann, *Die Erben Bismarcks*, p.493.

72. Gebsattel to Georg Schiele, February 1916, in ZStA I, NL Gebsattel 2. During the early months of 1916, Gebsattel was preoccupied with this question. See also his letters to v. Liebig, February 12, 1916, in ZStA I, NL Gebsattel 2, Bl.492-493 and to Class, March 21, 1916, in same, ADV 356, Bl.290-291. Other conservatives, too, began to voice similar fears. See the letter from Gustav Zeller to Dietrich Schaefer, printed in Schaedlich, "Der Unabhaengige Ausschuss," p.61 and J. Kruschwitz, *Das Kapitalabfindungsgesetz und die deutschen Bundesstaaten*, Dresden, 1916, p.1212.

73. Gebsattel to Georg Schiele, February 14, 1916, in ZStA I, NL Gebsattel 2, Bl.522.

74. Several books and articles dealing with the positive results of inner colonization appeared in 1916, e.g., Fr. v. Schwerin, "Die Bedeutung des Kapitalabfindungs- gesetzes fuer die innere Kolonisation," in *Der Panther* 10 (October 1916); Carl Blank, *Innere Kolonisation oder landwirtschaftliche Grosbetrieb nach dem Weltkriege?*, Berlin, 1916, Prof. Kranz, *Aus Preussens Ostmark*, n.p., 1916.

75. Gebsattel to Graf v. Roon, April 17, 1916, in ZStA I, NL Gebsattel 3, Bl.69.

76. Gebsattel to Class, May 25, 1916, in ZStA I, NL Gebsattel 3, Bl.229.

77. Gebsattel to Class, May 19, 1916, in ZStA I, ADV 356, Bl.314.

78. Class to Gebsattel, August 12, 1916, in ZStA I, NL Gebsattel 3, Bl.335.

79. Chamberlain to Lehmann, September 7, 1916, in ZStA II, Rep 92, NL Kapp, D VIII 5, Bl.86-87.

80. V. Graefe to the Central Committee of the German Conservative Party, November 28, 1916, in ZStA II, Rep 92, NL Kapp, D IV 12, Bl.8. The ADV found v. Graefe to be among the most outstanding members of the Conservative Party. See *ADB*, March 10, 1916.

81. See Pastor Petras, "Bauerntum oder laendlichen Proletariat," in *Preussische Jahrbuecher*, vol. 163 (1916), p.448: "The War has awakened a strong conviction in us...It means the beginning of a new time for us--the consequences of the revaluation of all values."

82. Stegmann, *Die Erben Bismarcks*, p.494.

83. See page 177.

84. See the report of J. Iversen over "Die Stimmung in Muenchen," August 2, 1916, in ZStA I, ADV 1417/2, Bl.7ff.

85. Quoted in Stegmann, *Die Erben Bismarcks*, p.493.

86. Ibid., p.495 and see the report of May 25, 1916, in ZStA I, NL Gebsattel III, Bl.229.

87. Hoensbroech to Kapp, June 22, 1916, in ZStA II, Rep 90, NL Kapp, D IV 26, The programme is in same. See also Stegmann, *Die Erben Bismarcks*, p.494.

88. Gebsattel to Lehmann, April 23, 1916, in ZStA I, NL Gebsattel 3, Bl.182 and see Stegmann, *Die Erben Bismarcks*, p.495. It is interesting to note that calls for the creation of new parties were also coming from the *Mittelstand* camp. See the call for the creation of a *konservative-fortschrittliche Partei*

316

issued by one G. Fraass of Hamburg. His aim was to
gain representation for the *Kaufmann*. His letter
is in Bestand E15 ICII, Nr. 237 of the Hauptstaatsarchiv
Stuttgart. I am indebted to the Hauptstaatsarchiv
for making available to me a copy of this letter.

89. Stegmann, *Die Erben Bismarcks*, p.494.

90. Quoted in ibid., F.N. 310.

91. Richard S. Levy, *The Downfall of the Anti-Semitic
Political Parties in Imperial Germany*, New Haven,
1975, p.261.

92. Hermann Goldschmidt, "Von Deutschen und Juden,"
Preussiche Jahrbuecher, vol. 163 (1916), pp.274-275.

93. Max Warburg to Wolfgang Kapp, April 18, 1916, in
ZStA II, Rep 92, NL Kapp, D II 10.

94. See the ADV petition of February 1916, in ZStA I,
NL Westarp, Nr. 9, Bl.2-9 and the *ADB*, June 19, 1916,
pp.41-42.

95. K. v. Stranz to Wahnschaffe, February 18, 1916, in
ZStA I, ADV 1417, Bl.67-68.

96. F. v. Bodelschwingh, March 15, 1916, in ZStA I,
NL Westarp, Nr. 10, Bl.99f.

97. Among the most outspoken were the following: *Auf
Vorposten, Deutsche Wille, Das Vaterland, Konservative
Zeitschrift fuer das saechsische Volk, Deutsch-voelkischen
Blaetter* and the *ADB*.

98. See the report in the *Hamburg-Israelitische Familienblatt*
of July 31, 1916.

99. Egmont Zechlin, *Die Deutsche Politik und die Juden
im Ersten Welt-Krieg*, Goettingen, 1969, p.521; Juergen
Kocka, *Klassengesellschaft im Krieg 1914-1918*,
Goettingen, 1973, p.104.

100. Gebsattel to nephew Theodor, November 30, 1916, in
ZStA I, NL Gebsattel 3, Bl.444 and the momo marked
vertraulich (1916) in same, ADV 1418, Bl.133. Even
Westarp began to question Jewish "contributions."
See Westarp to v. Bonin, August 24, 1916, in ZStA I,
NL Westarp, Nr. 10, Bl.89.

317

101. Zechlin, *Die Deutsche Politik und die Juden*, p.527f.

102. Gebsattel to Class, December 23, 1916, in ZStA I, ADV 489, Bl.3-4.

103. Gebsattel to Schmidt-Gibichenfels, January 4, 1917, in ZStA I, NL Gebsattel 3, Bl.489. Among the groups mentioned were the *Germanen Ordnen, Hammerbund, Der Verband gegen die Ueberhebung des Judentums*, etc.. See also Gebsattel to Fritsch, December 16, 1916, in same.

104. Gebsattel to nephew Theodor, November 30, 1916, in ZStA I, NL Gebsattel 3, Bl.444.

Chapter IX

1. See the report to Heydebrand from Schroeter, January, 11, 1917, in ZStA I, NL Westarp, Nr. 98, Bl.243-244.

2. See the report of the Executive Committee of the German Conservative Party, February 18, 1917, in ZStA I, NL Westarp, Nr. 98, Bl.250ff..

3. Schroeter to Heydebrand, June 6, 1917, in ibid., Bl.272 and the letter from Westarp to the German National Association of Retail Clerks (DNHV), complaining of a lack of Conservative Party funds, January 19, 1917, in ibid., NL Westarp, Nr. 19, Bl.25.

4. Westarp to Kalkstein, June 12, 1917, in ZStA I, NL Westarp, Nr. 20, Bl.80 and Schroeter's report to Heydebrand in ibid., NL Westarp, Nr. 98, Bl.299.

5. The meeting was strongly influenced by Kapp, who seems to have been the driving force behind it. See the memorandum dated "Beginning of 1917," in ZStA II, Rep. 92, NL Kapp, D IV 22-24, and Hoensbroech to Kapp, February 14, 1917, in same, Rep. 92, NL Kapp, D IV 17.

6. Westarp to Hoetzsch, December 11, 1916, in ZStA I, NL Westarp, Nr. 12, Bl.61.

7. Westarp to Hoensbroech, November 20, 1916, in ibid., Bl.63.

8. Hoensbroech to Kapp, n.d. (but before February 25, 1916), in ZStA II, Rep. 92, NL Kapp, D IV 17, and Hoensbroech

to Ludendorff, January 24, 1917, in ibid., Rep. 92,
NL Kapp, D IV 22-24.

9. Deutelmoser to Wahnschaffe, February 25, 1917, in
    ZStA II, 1392 #2, Bl.98-100.

10. Hoensbroech to Westarp, March 21, 1917, in ZStA II,
    Rep. 92, NL Kapp, D IV 22-24.

11. Heydebrand to Westarp, April 4, 1917, in H-W. In
    fact, as Deutelmoser related to Wahnschaffe, Heydebrand,
    too, was on the verge of being quite alone: "Herr
    Heydebrand is in a difficult position in the Conservative
    Party. In East Prussia and Pomerania he is viewed
    as being too meek, while others think he is too
    aggressive." Deutelmoser to Wahnschaffe, February 25,
    1917, in ZStA I. During June, this dual attack was
    highlighted by a series of articles written by
    Dr. Friedrich Thimme, a moderate conservative, and
    entitled "Drei Offener Brief an Herrn von Heydebrand
    und der Lasa," in which Thimme criticized Heydebrand
    for the perversion of Prussian conservatism into
    an aggressive, pro-annexationist policy. See *Die
    Grenzboten*, 1917, numbers 23-25. See also Schroeter's
    report to Heydebrand, June 20, 1917, in ZStA I,
    NL Westarp, Nr. 98, Bl.291, in which strategy for
    a reply to Thimme is discussed. A brief reference
    to the article is made in Annelise Thimme, *Flucht in
    den Mythos*, Goettingen, 1969, p.10f..

12. Oskar Kresse to Westarp, April 28, 1917, in ZStA I,
    NL Westarp, Nr. 20, Bl.50-51.

13. V. Gossler to v. Halem, June 6, 1917, in ZStA I,
    NL Westarp, Nr. 18, Bl.138-141. The Conservative
    leadership was against the possibility of such a
    political union. See the notes by Westarp of a
    discussion with v. Gossler in same, Bl.196. See
    also the v. Halem memorandums of April 13 and
    May 13, 1917, in same, NL Westarp, Nr. 19, Bl.120-136,
    and Westarp to v. Halem in same, Bl.144. Also
    Heydebrand to Westarp, November 10, 1917, in H-W.
    Ideas for a united Party of the Right had been
    advocated as early as December 1914. See the article
    by the Conservative Deputy, H. v. Dewitz, "Die
    politischen Parteien im Spiegel der Gegenwart," in
    Das neue Deutschland, December 22, 1914, p.59.

14. See Westarp's defence of the ADV and Gebsattel
    against charges of an involvement in the anti-
    Bethmann conspiracy in the *Kreuzzeitung* (evening edition),
    May 27, 1917, "Die innere Politik der Woche."

15. Westarp to Heydebrand, June 11, 1917, in H-W.

16. Schroeter to Westarp, June 8, 1917, in ZStA I,
     NL Westarp, Nr. 20, Bl.77.

17. Westarp to v. Breitenbach, May 24, 1917, in ZStA I,
     NL Westarp, Nr. 19, Bl.91.

18. As late as February, Westarp still refused to join
     the Pan-Germans in their anti-Bethmann efforts, as
     he wrote to Kurd v. Strantz: "...At this time, I
     see no reason why I should take a position against the
     Chancellor's policies. I see no useful purpose being
     served by a universal criticism of the man." Westarp
     to v. Strantz, February 21, 1917, in ZStA I,
     NL Westarp, Nr. 22, Bl.108.

19. On July 13, Heydebrand sent v. Maltzahn, a Conservative
     deputy in the Prussian House of Deputies, the following
     note: "The Federal Chancellor no longer has the
     confidence of the Conservative Party group in the
     Reichstag. Such a circumstance makes it impossible
     for us to work with him in the best interests of the
     nation." Heydebrand to v. Maltzahn, July 13, 1917,
     in ZStA I, NL Westarp, Nr. 21, Bl.99.

20. The memorandum may be found in ZStA I, NL Westarp, Nr. 73.

21. This concentration was made all the more necessary
     by the Kaiser's acceptance, in principle, of equal
     franchise for Prussia on July 11, 1917. For details
     see Fischer, *Griff nach der Weltmacht*, pp.521ff.;
     Reinhard Patemann, *Der Kampf um die Preussische Wahlreform
     im Ersten Weltkrieg*, Deusseldorf, 1964; Hellmuth
     Weber, "Zum Problem der Wahlrechtsreform in Prussen
     waehrend der Jahre 1917-1918," in *Deutsche Politik im
     Krieg 1914-1918*. The contemporary literature is
     enormous. See, for example, H. Schrader, *Gedanken
     zur preussischen Wahlrechtsvorlage*, n.p. 1917; Freien
     Vaterlaendischen Vereinigung, *Zur Reform des preussischen
     Wahlrechts*, n.p. 1917; Peter Bender, *Das Wahlrecht
     des Weltkrieges*, n.p. 1917.

22. V. Klitzing to Westarp, September 19, 1917, in ZStA I,
     NL Westarp, Nr. 20, Bl.159. In December, Admiral
     Tirpitz, one of the Fatherland Party leaders, wrote
     to Westarp informing him that the Executive Committee
     of the Fatherland Party had not solicited the
     Conservatives for their views since "we are convinced
     that the Conservative Party will use all its power
     to work for the kind of peace that the German Fatherland

Party is striving towards." Tirpitz to Westarp,
December 21, 1917, in ZStA I, NL Westarp, Nr. 23,
Bl.66.

23. Heydebrand to Westarp, November 10, 1917, in H-W.

24. Heydebrand to Westarp, December 29, 1917, in H-W.

25. See Chapter VIII, pp.195f,

26. See the notes in II/c2, p.40ff., HFs.

27. See the letter of February 2, 1917, Roesicke to
Wangenheim: "We are now convinced that it is
necessary at present to utter no mistrust of the
Government and let it know that we are satisfied
with its actions." See also Wangenheim to Roesicke,
February 3, 1917, stating a similar view. Both
letters are in ZStA I, NL v. Wangenheim 12, Bl.26ff..

28. See the report of the annual conference of the BdL
(forbidden by governmental decree in 1916) held in
the concert hall of the Berlin Symphony, printed in
the *Norddeutsche Allgemeine Zeitung*, February 22, 1917,
Nr. 52,

29. Roesicke to Wangenheim, March 28, 1917, in ZStA I,
NL v. Wangenheim 12, Bl.55-56 and the report of
General Boy-Ed of August 25, 1916 in *Militaer und
Innenpolitik*, #170, p.420. See also Zechlin, *Die
Deutsche Politik und die Juden*, p.521.

30. Roesicke to Wangenheim, August 6, 1917, in ZStA I,
NL v. Wangenheim 12, Bl.81 : "We are experiencing quite
a bit of bitterness between the large and small
landowners."

31. Roesicke to Wangenheim, January 19, 1917, in ibid.,
Bl.22-23. Among the groups that were to be involved:
BdL, *Christliche Bauernverein*, CDI, BdI, RDMV,
Christliche Gewerkschaften, *Freie Gewerkschaften*, etc.,

32. Kapp had attempted to create a *Kriegsausschuss der
deutschen Landwirtschaft* (War Committee of German
Agriculture). After several meetings, the War
Committee floundered and dissolved. See a report
of the Committee meeting of April 28, 1917, in ZStA II,
Rep. 92, NL Kapp, D I 13. Also see Kapp to Mehnert,
July 5, 1917, in same, Rep. 92, NL Kapp, D III 15,

33. See following pages of this chapter,

34. Roesicke to Wangenheim, August 6, 1917, and Wangenheim to Roesicke, August 10, 1917, both in ZStA I, NL v. Wangenheim 12, Bl.81 and 90.

35. Wangenheim to Roesicke, September 12, 1917, in ibid., Bl.101.

36. See page 61f. According to Georg Schiele, Kapp had been "discovered" by Johannes v. Miquel and launched upon his career. See Schiele to Gebsattel, April 8, 1916, in ZStA I, NL Gebsattel 6, Bl.250.

37. Wangenheim to Roesicke, August 10, 1917, in ZStA I, NL v. Wangenheim 12, Bl.90 : "Don't forget that Kapp has not, up to now, been a BdL member, since he likes to be unattached and he only works where he can be completely independent."

38. See the memorandum dated "Anfang 1917," in ZStA II, Rep. 92, NL Kapp, D IV 22-24.

39. The pamphlet can be found in ibid., Rep. 92, NL Kapp, D X 1, Bl.132-148.

40. See the pamphlet in ibid., Rep. 92, NL Kapp, D IV 22-24.

41. Kapp to Hoensbroech, February 8, 1917, in ibid., Rep.92, NL Kapp, D IV 17.

42. Kapp to Ludendorff, July 11, 1917, in ibid., Rep. 92, NL Kapp, D IV 19.

43. Kapp to Mehnert, July 15, 1917, in ibid., Rep. 92, NL Kapp, D III 15.

44. Wangenheim to Kapp, June 28, 1917, in ibid., Rep. 92, NL Kapp, D III 15.

45. See the memorandum marked "secret": "Notes concerning the German Fatherland Party," in ibid., Rep. 92, NL Kapp, D X 97.

46. Andreas Gildemeister to Kapp, August 22, 1917, in ibid., Rep. 92, NL Kapp, D X 1: "My Bremen friends have declared that they would support a Hanseatic cities plan, but a gentleman from the far east (of Prussia-- meaning Kapp-AJP) who is after all a conservative agrarian, is not acceptable as a co-founder."

47. Kapp to Scharnegel, October 30, 1917, in ibid., Rep. 92, NL Kapp, D X 62.

48. Lenz to Bendixen, August 21, 1917, in ibid., Rep. 92, NL Kapp, D X 1.

49. "Notes concerning the German Fatherland Party," in ibid., Rep. 92, NL Kapp, D X 97,

50. See the Executive Committee list (organizations and individuals) in ibid..

51. A full listing of Fatherland Party speakers may be found in ibid., Rep. 92, NL Kapp, D X 63.

52. See the guidelines for speakers, point #8, in ibid : "The mention of domestic and party-political polemics is to be avoided under all circumstances." Each speaker had to write an elaborate report on his or her speech so that the Executive Committee could ascertain its impact. One speaker wrote that in Waldeck-Pyrmont he had spoken to a group of 279 individuals. Of these, 221 were not members of the Fatherland Party. At the end of the speech, 148 people had signed up as new members.

53. One of Kapp's essential reasons for founding the Party was to gain those results that the Independent Committee for a German Peace had been unable to achieve. See the memorandum in ibid., Rep. 92, NL Kapp, D IV 17.

54. See Stegmann, *Die Erben Bismarcks*, p.499.

55. This is clearly shown in "Notes concerning the German Fatherland Party," in which it is stated that "Kapp, in his letters, ascertains that he wishes to come out strongly against the groups on the Left, that is, he wishes to strengthen the domestic struggle against these parties." In ZStA II, Rep. 92, NL Kapp, D X 97.

56. See ibid., and Stegmann, *Die Erben Bismarcks*, p.499.

57. Stegmann, *Die Erben Bismarcks*, p.499f..

58. Class to Gebsattel, April 7, 1917, in ZStA I, NL Gebsattel 4, Bl.144.

59. See HFs, II/c2, Bl.55. See also Kruck, *Die Geschichte des Alldeutschen Verbandes*, pp.97ff., and Jochmann, "Die Ausbreitung des Antisemitismus." p.428, F.N. 64.

60. Ibid., Bl.66 and Gebsattel to Class, a copy of a
    letter that Gebsattel wrote to Duke Albrecht,
    April 24, 1917, in ZStA I, NL Gebsattel 4, Bl.194.

61. See II/c2, HFs, Bl.87f. and Gebsattel to Ludendorff,
    April 16, 1917, in ZStA I, NL Gebsattel 4, Bl.179.

62. Gebsattel to Class, February 16, 1917, Class to
    Gebsattel, February 19, 1917, both in ZStA I,
    NL Gebsattel 4, Bl.32 and 41.

63. Gebsattel to Class, in ibid., February 16, 1917, Bl.132.

64. Class to Gebsattel, February 19, 1917, in ibid., Bl.41.

65. Gebsattel to Class, February 20, 1917, in ibid., Bl.55.

66. Gebsattel to Wildgrube, February 22, 1917, in ibid.,
    Bl.66.

67. See the article in *Der Reichsbote*, February 1, 1917,
    "Herr Heydebrand und die Alldeutsche Blaetter," in
    which an account is given of *ADB* attacks against
    the Conservative leader.

68. Keim to Gebsattel, March 1, 1917, in ZStA I,
    NL Gebsattel 4, Bl.77.

69. Gebsattel to v. Grumme-Douglas, March 1917, in
    ibid., Bl.? Also see the attacks against both
    Westarp and Heydebrand in *ADB* 21, May 19, 1917.

70. Gebsattel to Schmidt-Gibichenfels, April 1, 1917,
    in ibid., Bl.161-162.

71. Jochmann, "Die Ausbreitung des Antisemitismus," pp.428f..

72. See Schaeffer, *Mein Leben*, p.168.

73. See the report of the Chancellor, dated September 15,
    1916, in ZStA I, ADV 1418, Bl.116: "In 1916, the
    war-aims question was relegated into the background...
    Even the political parties began to see that the plan
    for conquest arising from a patriotic spirit--which
    had arisen from a mistaken understanding of our
    military situation--was a political mistake."

74. See Gebsattel's letter to Bavarian Minister of War,
    v. Hellingrath, March 9, 1917, in ZStA I, NL Gebsattel 4,
    Bl.99: "After the peace, a battle will have to be
    fought simultaneously against both the red and golden

internationals. It will be a battle that will
dwarf any such attempt to date." Also see the
report of the *Mitteilungen aus dem Verein zur Abwehr
des Antisemitismus* (Notes from the Association for
the Defence against anti-Semitism), January 24, 1917,
in ZStA I, ADV 1418/2: "The Pan-German League is
today building the shock troop of racial anti-Semitism."

75. Jochmann, "Die Ausbreitung des Antisemitismus," p.441.

76. For the activities involved in the building of a
voelkisch press in 1916, see ZStA II, Rep. 92, NL Kapp,
C VII 24, D V 5, D VIII 5 and ZStA I, NL v. Wangenheim 11.
Both Wangenheim and Roesicke played a leading role
in the creation of *Deutschlands Erneuerung*, one of
the most viciously anti-Semitic publications to emerge
during the War.

77. Lehmann to Kapp, 1916, in ZStA II, Rep. 92, NL Kapp,
D VIII 5.

78. See Westarp, *Konservative Politik* II, pp.167, 168.

79. V. Graefe was by far the most anti-Semitic of the
influential members in the Party. See his numerous
letters to Westarp in *Konservative Politik* II, *passim*.

80. Gebsattel, "Alldeutsch-vielleicht alljudisch?", in
Deutsche Zeitung (DZ) 22, June 18, 1917. Also
Jochmann, "Die Ausbreitung des Antisemitismus," p.432.

81. "Das internationale Judentum," June 28, 1917, and
"Das Ostjudentum," June 29, 1917, in *DZ* 321 and 323.

82. Minutes of the meeting of July 8, 1917, in HFs, ADV 412.
As late as June 23 and July 2, Gebsattel was still
wondering if the ADV should publicize the "Jewish
Question." Gebsattel to Bodelschwingh, June 23, 1917,
in ZStA I, NL Gebsattel 4, Bl.351 and HFs, ADV 412,
Bl.45-46.

83. Minutes of meeting of July 8, 1917, in HFs, ADV 412.

84. "Judenwahle, Judenfriede," September 21, 1917, in *DZ* 480.

85. Ibid.

86. See Zechlin, *Die Deutsche Politik und die Juden*, p.549.

87. Quoted in Stegmann, "Zwischen Repression und Manipulation,"
p.397.

88. HFs, II/c2, Bl.28.

89. Ibid.

90. Ibid., Bl.211ff..

91. Ibid.

92. Ibid., Bl.216 and see the notes pertaining to the meeting in ZStA II, Rep. 92, NL Kapp, D X 21.

93. HFs, II/c2, Bl.220.

94. Ibid., Bl.225.

95. At a meeting of the ADV, December 8, 1917, in HFs, ADV 412.

96. HFs, II/c2, Bl.226.

97. Class to Gebsattel, October 10, 1917, in ZStA I, NL Gebsattel 4, Bl.498.

98. Gebsattel to Class, December 31, 1917, in ibid., Bl.566.

99. L. Plate to Westarp, December 28, 1917, in ZStA I, NL Westarp, Nr. 21, Bl.194.

100. Stegmann, "Zwischen Repression und Manipulation," p.396.

101. Gebsattel to Class, September 17, 1917, in ZStA I, NL Gebsattel 4, Bl.476.

102. Kapp to Ludendorff, December 31, 1917, in ZStA II, Rep. 92, NL Kapp, D IV 19.

103. George L. Mosse, *The Culture of Western Europe*, Chicago 1961, pp.369f..

104. The all-embracing blame upon the Jews even went so far as having the ADV charge that Jewry wanted to break up the large estates of the *Junkers*--an aim that the ADV had propogated officially since 1912! See Gebsattel to Baumann, July 19, 1917, in ZStA I, NL Gebsattel 4, Bl.395.

105. Stegmann, "Zwischen Repression und Manipulation," p.396.

106. This was the term used by Roesicke in a letter to Westarp. See Roesicke to Westarp, October 31, 1917, in ZStA I, NL Westarp, Nr. 22, Bl.71-73.

107. The growing antipathy to the Kaiser can be noted
     in the ADV files in ZStA I, *passim*.

Chapter X

1. Roesicke to Westarp, January 19, 1918, in ZStA I,
   NL Westarp, Nr. 30, Bl.44.

2. Westarp to Roesicke, January 22, 1918, in ibid., Bl.45.

3. For the negotiations at Brest-Litovsk see Fischer,
   Griff nach der Weltmacht, pp.627ff...For agrarian
   desires concerning the soon-to-be-acquired Russian
   territories, see Dr. Friedrich Freund, "Der Haus
   an der Grenze," in *Die Grenzboten* 22, 1918, pp.217f..

4. Class to Gebsattel, January 18, 1918, in ZStA I,
   NL Gebsattel 5, Bl.31f.. See also the memorandum
   written by Schiele, "Konservative Partei und
   staedtisches Buergertum," (1918), in ZStA II, Rep. 92,
   NL Kapp, D V 13.

5. Pretzel to Class, July 6, 1918, in ZStA I, NL Gebsattel 5,
   Bl.46.

6. Westarp to Theodor Heck, May 31, 1918, in ibid.,
   NL Westarp, Nr. 27, Bl.14.

7. Westarp to Count v. Stolberg, June 20, 1918, in ibid.,
   NL Westarp, Nr. 28, Bl.62.

8. Westarp to Kube, August 28, 1918, in ibid., Bl.104-105.

9. Speech of January 11, 1918, in ibid.

10. Paul Meyer to Westarp, August 21, 1918, in ibid.,
    NL Westarp, Nr. 29, Bl.85.

11. See Feldman, *Army, Industry and Labor*, pp.431f..

12. Limburg-Stirum to Westarp, June 3, 1918, in ZStA I,
    NL Westarp, Nr. 29, Bl.18ff..

13. V. Kleist to Heydebrand, July 5, 1918, in H-W.

14. Fritz Hartung in *Das Neue Deutschland*, (June 1918).
    See also Dr. Jaeger, *Konservative Partei i. Preussen*,
    n.p., 1918, p.835: "Today there is no Conservative
    policy, only the complete destruction of conservative
    thought."

15. The memorandum may be found in ZStA I, NL Westarp, Nr. 25, Bl.49ff..

16. See Reinhard Patemann, *Der Kampf um die Preussische Wahlreform im Ersten Weltkrieg*, Duesseldorf 1964, pp. 182ff.. Also see Westarp to Heydebrand, September 6, 1918, and September 7, 1918, in H-W.

17. Westarp to Heydebrand, September 28, 1918, in H-W.

18. Westarp to Heydebrand, October 10, 1918, in ibid.

19. See Westarp's memo of October 15, 1918, in ZStA I, NL Westarp, Nr. 74, Bl.94-95.

20. V. Klasing to Westarp, October 18, 1918, in ibid., NL Westarp, Nr. 28, Bl.140. Also see Annelise Thimme, *Flucht in den Mythos. Die Deutschnationale Volkspartei und die Niederlage von 1918*, Goettingen 1969, p.162, F.N. 8.

21. For Westarp's fears of *Parlamentarisierung* see his letter to Count Behr, September 29, 1918, in ZStA I, NL Westarp, Nr. 25, Bl.82. See the *Herrenhaus* and *Abgeordnetenhaus* declarations of acceptance in Cuno Graf Westarp, *Die Regierung des Prinzen Max v. Baden und die Konservative Partei,* Berlin, n.d., pp.94f..

22. See the account of Kapp's speech in the *Hamburg General Anzeiger*, Nr.232, October 3, 1918. Also see Westarp, *Die Regierung des Prinzen Max v. Baden,* p.10.

23. Westarp to New Stettin (Pomerania) group, October 22, 1918, in ZStA I, NL Westarp, Nr. 28, Bl.148.

24. Wahl to Westarp, October 17, 1918, and October 23, 1918, in ibid.

25. Wahl had sent Westarp another letter in July. See Wahl to Westarp, July 12, 1918, in ibid., NL Westarp, Nr. 24, Bl.40. Westarp had acknowledged the "absolute necessity of national workers being represented in the *Reichstag*" as early as August. Westarp to Biegert, August 16, 1918, in same, Nr. 29. See also Stegmann, "Zwischen Repression und Manipulation," pp.383ff..

26. Westarp to Wahl, October (?), 1918, in ZStA I, NL Westarp, Nr. 24.

27. Stegmann, "Zwischen Repression und Manipulation,"
     pp.392ff.. See also an early reference to the
     possibility of the Conservatives aiding the
     Arbeiter and *Angestellte* (new *Mittelstand*). Viktor
     Blobel to Kapp, March 18, 1918, in ZStA II, Rep. 92,
     NL Kapp, D IX 19.

28. Thimme, *Flucht in den Mythos*, p.162, F.N. 5, and see
     Koerting to Westarp, October 5, 1918, in ZStA I,
     NL Westarp, Nr. 28, Bl.116.

29. Hoetzsch to Westarp, October 6, 1918, in ZStA I,
     NL Westarp, Nr. 27, Bl.22-23.

30. Westarp, *Die Regierung des Prinzen Max v. Baden*,
     pp.95f..

31. See the report in ZStA I, NL Westarp, Nr. 28, Bl.350ff..

32. "Die Konservative Partei fuer Verdoppelung der
     Loehnung und gleiche Bekoestigung," in *Mitteilungen
     aus der Konservativen Partei* 11, Nr. 44, November 2, 1918.

33. Among these members were Schiele, Graefe, Salm-Horstmarr,
     v. Grumme-Douglas. Hans Delbrueck had also suggested
     this in 1916 in an article entitled "Die preussische
     Thronrede," in *Die Preussische Jahrbuecher* (1916), p.373.

34. Dr. Richard Fuss to Westarp, November 5, 1918, in
     ZStA I, NL Westarp, Nr. 26, Bl.73ff..

35. Baron v. Hammerstein to Westarp, November 5, 1918,
     in ibid., Bl.62ff..

36. Otto Hoetzsch to Westarp, November 5, 1918, in ZStA I,
     NL Westarp, Nr. 27, Bl.45ff.. See also Peter-Christian
     Witt, "Eine Denkschrift Otto Hoetzsches vom 5.
     November, 1918," in *Viertelgahreshefte fuer Zeitgeschichte
     (VfZ)* 21 (1973), pp.337-353. Professor Witt makes
     no mention of Hoetzsch's letter of October 6, 1918, nor
     of the letters sent by Fuss or Hammerstein. See also
     Thimme, *Flucht in den Mythos*, pp.9ff. and Jochmann,
     "Die Ausbreitung des Antisemitismus," pp.444f..

37. Kapp, of course, had suggested it much earlier. The
     Free Conservative Party member, Adolf Grabowsky, had
     written an essay "The Future of the Right" in 1917,
     suggesting that the Conservative Party had to become
     "a real *Volkspartei*--not a party of the masses."
     Quoted in Dietrich Mende, "Kulturkonservatismus und
     Konservative Erneurungsbestrebungen," in *Adolf Grabowsky*.

Leben und Werk, edited by Hans Thierbach, Berlin
(West) 1963, p.110. Finally, see the article by
Dr. Ulrich Kahrstedt, "Was sollen die Konservativen
tun?" in *Konservative Monatschrift* (November 1918)
and Wahl to Westarp, November 8, 1918, in ZStA I,
NL Westarp, Nr. 24, Bl.57.

38. Westarp to ?, November 8, 1918, in H-W.

39. Westarp, *Die Regierung des Prinzen Max v. Baden*, pp.95f..

40. Ibid., p.82.

41. Westarp to Heydebrand, November 11, 1918, in H-W.

42. Thimme, *Flucht in den Mythos*, p.11.

43. Thus Thimme in ibid., p.12.

44. Westarp, before his little "vacation" on November 11,
    had propogated the idea of organizing a resistance
    against the Left. See Westarp to Kreth, November 7,
    1918, and Kreth to Sandrat-Melle, November 9, 1918,
    both in ZStA I, NL Westarp, Nr. 28, Bl.163ff.. For a
    detailed history of the DNVP in its early phase see
    Werner Liebe, *Die Deutschnationale Volkspartei 1918-1924*,
    Duesseldorf 1956, pp.7ff.; Lewis Hertzman, *DNVP. Right-
    Wing Opposition in the Weimar Republic 1918-1924*,
    Lincoln, Nebraska 1963 and Thimme, *Flucht in den Mythos*.

45. Neither Heydebrand nor Westarp signed the Party's
    Aufruf. Conservatives who did were v. Dewitz, Dietrich,
    Anklam, Kahrstedt, Moltke and Schiele. Westarp was
    also not present at the first meeting of the Party
    on December 19, 1918. See BA, NL Traub, Nr. 50.

46. Liegnitz to Tiele-Winkler, November 30, 1918, in ZStA I,
    NL Westarp, Nr. 32, Bl.197ff..

47. See Westarp's letter to Graf Behr, in which he stated
    that "my task, to bring Conservative influence to an
    equal position in the DNVP, will be difficult and
    not attainable in all respects." Westarp to Graf
    Behr, December 21, 1918, in ZStA I, NL Westarp,
    Nr. 25, Bl.165. See also Westarp to Bonin, in which
    Westarp expressed a hope that the monarchist principle
    would be retained by the DNVP and that the Conservatives
    would influence its survival. "The DNVP *Aufruf*," he
    wrote, "did indicate a clear choice in that direction,
    but not as clearly as I would have wished." Westarp
    to Bonin, December 30, 1918, in same, Bl.176.

48. To Behr, Westarp wrote that in the Executive Committee of the DNVP, at least half were German Conservatives. Westarp to Behr, ibid., December 21, 1918.

49. In a statement urging its members to vote for the DNVP, the Executive Committee of the German Conservative Party issued a statement signed by Westarp and Stackmann. Heydebrand's name was nowhere to be found. See *Mitteilungen aus der Konservativen Partei* 11, November 23, 1918.

50. Niegserlingh to Westarp, November 30, 1918, in ZStA I, NL Westarp, Nr. 28, Bl.187.

51. Carmer to Westarp, November 20, 1918, in ibid., NL Westarp, Nr. 26, Bl.16f.. See also the article "Die Konservativen und der neue Volksstaat," in *Mitteilungen aus der Konservativen Partei* 11, November 23, 1918.

52. Schroeter to Berlin Workers' and Soldiers' Council, November 13, 1918, in ZStA I, NL Westarp, Nr. 28, Bl.170.

53. See Junius, "Wirtschaft Horatio!" in *Die Grenzboten* 37 (1918) and the *Hamburger Echo* 127, June 3, 1918. See also Kocka, *Klassengesellschaft im Krieg 1914-1918*, passim..

54. Wangenheim to Roesicke, June 22, 1918, in ZStA I, NL v. Wangenheim 13, Bl.65.

55. On this see Kocka, *Klassengesellschaft im Krieg 1914-1918*. Industry, too, began to sympathize with these agrarian aims; see Roesicke to Wangenheim, July 27, 1918, in ZStA I, NL v. Wangenheim 13, Bl.80.

56. This concern had first been expressed by Oertel in May 1916. See *Mitteilungen aus der Konservativen Partei* 9, May 20, 1916.

57. Wangenheim to Roesicke, July 30, 1918, in ZStA I, NL v. Wangenheim 13, Bl.81 and *Hamburger Echo*, Nr. 196, August 18, 1918.

58. See Jens Flemming, "Grossagrarische Interessen und Landarbeiterbewegung. Ueberlegungen zur Arbeiterpolitik des Bundes der Landwirte und des Reichlandbundes in der Anfangsphase der Weimarer Republik," in H. Mommsen, D. Petzina, B. Weisbrod (eds.), *Industrielles System und politische Entwicklung in der Weimarer Republik*, Duesseldorf 1974, p.747. See also H. Muth, "Die

Entstehung der Bauern- und Landarbeiterraete im
November 1918 und die Politik des BdL," in *VfZ* 21,
(1973) and the *Norddeutsche Allgemeine Zeitung*,
Nr. 424, "Die Neuordnung der Landwirtschaftskammern,"
August 20, 1918.

59. Flemming, ibid., pp.746f..

60. The fear of military defeat and social upheaval was
also expressed by members of the *Volksbund fuer
Freiheit und Vaterland*, which was founded as a "counter"
to the German Fatherland Party. The *Volksbund* consisted
of individuals such as Friedrich Meinicke, F. Naumann,
Friedrich Thimme and Max Weber, "liberal" imperialists
who sought annexations and internal reforms. See for
instance the extremely "conservative" viewpoint of
Max Weber in a letter to F. Naumann, October 18, 1918:
"No reasonable person in Germany can come out for
revolutionary and republican experiments. It is therefore
imperative that the monarchy continue in whatever
form necessary." In ZStA II, NL Weber 30, Nr. 10,
Bl.18. Such a basically conservative orientation
was demonstrated by the *Volksbund* when it met (in an
extraordinary session) with the German Fatherland
Party on October 18, 1918 to search for common
political grounds. See the minutes of the meeting in
ZStA II, Rep. 92, NL Kapp, D V 3.

61. Flemming, "Grossagrarische Interessen," p.751 and
Feldman, *Army, Industry and Labor*, pp.502ff..

62. Stegmann, "Zwischen Repression und Manipulation,"
p.408, and Feldman, ibid., pp.502ff..

63. Thorwalt (Fritsch) to Gebsattel, August 9, 1918, in
ZStA I, NL Gebsattel 5, Bl.171.

64. Gebsattel to A. B. Thorwalt (Fritsch), August 12, 1918,
in ibid., Bl.177ff..

65. Gebsattel to Class, October 6, 1918, in ibid., Bl.289.

66. Gebsattel to J. H. Lehmann, October 21, 1918, in
ibid., Bl.306. The ADV had already formed a committee
to coordinate anti-Semitic activities in September.
See Jochmann, "Die Ausbreitung des Antisemitismus,"
pp.449ff., and Zechlin, *Die Deutsche Politik und die
Juden*, p.552.

67. See the letter from Wangenheim to Kapp, September 20, 1918, in ZStA II, Rep. 92, NL Kapp, D X 15. In July, according to the *Berliner Tageblatt*, Prince Salm had made an anti-Semitic speech in the *Herrenhaus*.

68. Stegmann, "Zwischen Repression und Manipulation," p.407.

69. Ibid., p.397.

70. Ibid., pp.408f..

71. Gebsattel to Lehmann, October 21, 1918, in ZStA I, NL Gebsattel 5, Bl.306.

72. Quoted in Zechlin, *Die Deutsche Politik und die Juden*, p.558 and Jochmann, "Die Ausbreitung des Antisemitismus," p.448.

73. Quoted in Zechlin, ibid..

Epilogue

1. Hans Delbrueck in *Die Preussische Jahrbuecher*, vol. 174 (October-December 1918), p.285.

2. Thimme, *Flucht in den Mythos*, p.10.

3. "Die Konservative Partei und die Deutschnationale Volkspartei," in *DTZ*, Nr. 657, April 13, 1919.

4. *DTZ*, Nr. 661, July 4, 1919.

5. Flemming, "Grossagrarische Interessen und Landarbeiter-bewegung," pp.761f.

6. HFs, II/c2, Bl.455ff.

7. See *Deutschvoelkischer Blaetter*, Nr. 50, December 13, 1918.

8. Printed in *Auf Vorposten* (July-September 1918), pp.72ff. Among some of the other demands: no Jews as trade union officials; no Jews in the army or navy; no Jewish pupils in German schools; newspapers which employed Jews had to carry the Star of David on their front pages; the Jews had to celebrate their Sabbath on Sunday.

9. Quoted in Saul Friedlaender, "Die politische
    Veraenderungen der Kriegszeit," in *Deutsches
    Judentum in Krieg und Revolution*, pp.53f.

10. Ibid., p.49.

11. Jochmann, "Die Ausbreitung des Antisemitismus," p.463.

12. HFs, II/c2, Bl.450.

13. See Uwe Lohalm, *Voelkischer Radikalismus. Die Geschichte
    des Deutschvoelkischen Schutz-und Trutz-Bundes 1919-1923*,
    Hamburg, 1970,

14. HFs, II/c2, Bl.458.

15. Ibid., Bl.459.

16. "Der Zusammenbruch," *Auf Vorposten*, 4/6 (October-December,
    1918), p.95.

17. This was a reference to the fact that *Auf Vorposten*
    had earlier attacked Tirpitz and the German Fatherland
    Party for its alleged laxity on the *Judenfrage*. See
    "Tirpitz und die Juden," *Auf Vorposten*, 11/12 (May-June 1918),
    pp.590ff.

18. "Die Konservative Parteien," *Auf Vorposten* 4/6, 1919,
    pp.90ff.

19. Thimme, *Flucht in den Mythos*, p.41.

20. Quoted in Jochmann, "Die Ausbreitung des Antisemitismus,"
    pp.490f.

21. Zechlin, *Die Deutsche Politik und die Juden*, p.563.

22. Thimme, *Flucht in den Mythos*, P.41.

23. *Berliner Tageblatt*, Nr. 548, November 18, 1924.

24. Thimme, *Flucht in den Mythos*, pp.44f.

25. Ibid.

26. Ibid.

27. Ibid., pp.55f.

28. HFs, II/c2, Bl.496.

29. Thimme, *Flucht in den Mythos*, p.56.

30. See Erasmus Jonas, *Die Volkskonservativen 1928-1933*, Duesseldorf, 1965.

31. Thimme, *Flucht in den Mythos*, p.49.

32. Dr. Rudolf Fischer, "Nationalismus oder Konservatismus?," in *Deutsches Volkstum*, March 1929, p.255.

33. Georg Decker, "Der Tod Einer Partei," in *Die Gesellschaft*, May 1928, pp.385ff. and for the following quotes.

ARCHIVAL SOURCES

I.   Zentrales Staatsarchiv-Potsdam section

1.   Reichskanzlei (Stammakten)

Nr. 442-443   Verbaende deutscher Kaufleute und
                        Industriellen
Nr. 1128   Bund der Landwirte 1901-1918

Nr. 1391/5-1392   Konservative Parteien

Nr. 1394-1395   Fortschrittliche, freisinnige und
                        Nationalliberale
Nr. 1415-1420   Die Alldeutschen

Nr. 1422, 1422/1   Unabhaengiger Ausschuss f. e. Deutschen
                        Frieden
Nr. 1422/2   Deutsche Vaterlandspartei

Nr. 1422/4   Hansabund

Nr. 1561   Pressgewerbe 1909-17

Nr. 1581   Lage des Scherl-Verlages 1906-17

Nr. 1790   Schaffung eines Reichsoberhauses

2.   Akten des Alldeutschen Verbandes

a.) Hauptleitungsakten
    Nr. 239-245/1   1911-1918

b.) Geschaeftsfuehrender Ausschuss
    Nr. 88-122   1913-1918

c.) Schriftwechsel
    Nr. 355, 356, 357   Gebsattel
    Nr. 633, 634, 635, 637   Class
    Nr. 208   Keim
    Nr. 211   Bang
    Nr. 211/1   Kirdorf
    Nr. 219   Fritz, Hopfen, Kirdorf
    Nr. 453   Otto Fuerst zu Salm-Horstmar

d.) miscellaneous
    Nr. 246   Vereine, Verbaende
    Nr. 391   Deutsche Zeitung

Radicals and Reactionaries

3. Stellvertreter des Reichskanzlers

Nr. 99   Alldeutsche und Vaterlandspartei

Nr. 107   Unabhaengiger Ausschuss f. e. Deutschen
                Frieden

4. Reichsamt des Innern

Nr. 13588   Die Vaterlandspartei

Nr. 14440   Schriftwechsel mit der Reichskanzlei

Nr. 14790   Akten betr. Parteien des Reichstags

5. Nachlaesse

Nr. 1-6   Gebsattel

Nr. 18,288   Hutten-Czapski

Nr. 2a, 85-88   Roesicke

Nr. 8-13   v. Wangenheim

Nr. 1-32, 64, 74, 76, 93, 98,   Westarp
    106, 138, 139, 140, 142, 143, 223

II. Zentrales Staatsarchiv-Merseburg section

1. Ministerium des Innern, Rep. 77

Tit. 496a   Beiakten 5, Entschliessungen von
                Verbaenden und
Nr. 186   Parteien zur Wahlrechtsfrage

Nr. 303   Preussische Herrenhaus (1918)

Nr. 309   Preussische Landtag (1855-1917)

Nr. 667   betr. innern und aussern Politik
                (1914-1916)
Nr. 688, vol. 2 betr. innern und aussern Politik
                (1917-1920)

2. Nachlaesse, Rep. 92 - Nachlass Kapp

Nr. CII   Nr. 1,4,6,8,10,11,22,23

Nr. CVII   Nr. 20,23,24

Nr. CVIII   Nr. 1,2,3

Nr. DI   Nr. 1,3,6,13

Nr. DII   Nr. 1,10

Nr. DIII   Nr. 3,6,15

Nr. DIV   Nr. 2,3,5,7,8,10,12,17,20,21,22,23,24,25,
                 26,27,28,30,31,33,35

Nr. DV   Nr. 1,3,4,5,9,13,14,17

Nr. DVIII   Nr. 5

Nr. DIX   Nr. 1,3,7,8,19,22,23

Nr. DX

(Deutsche Vaterlandspartei) Nr. 1,4,10,11,15,21,45,47,48,
                 51,52,62,63,65,67,68,69,80,
                 81,85,87,88,95,97

Nr. DXI   Nr. 1,4,5,40,53,54

Nr. EII   Nr. 26,27

Nr. 2,4,23   v. Valentini

Nr. 29,30 vol.10 Max Weber

Tit. 863 A   Ostmarken Verein (1914-1917)

Nr. 1a

Tit. 885   Kriegs-und Friedensziele 1915

Nr. 4, vol. 1

Tit. 885   Kriegs-und Friedensziele 1916

Nr. 4, vol. 2

Radicals and Reactionaries

Tit. 885   Kriegs-und Friedensziele 1917

Nr. vol. 3

Tit. 885   Innerpolitische Angelegenheiten im

Nr. 5, vol. 1   Weltkriege 1914-18

Tit. 885   Innerpolitische Angelegenheiten im

Nr. 5, vol. 2   Weltkriege 1918

Nr. 970i   Unabhaengiger Ausschuss f. e.
                            Deutschen Frieden (newspaper
                            clipping)

Nr. 970n   Deutsche Vaterlandspartei and Bund der
                            Kaisertreuen (newspaper clipping)

3. Staatsministerium, Rep. 90a

Abt. TH,D1,4c,Nr. 10   Reichsverband gegen die
                            Sozialdemokratie (1911-18)

Abt. B.Tit.III,2^b,Nr.6,   Staatsministerialsitzungsprotokolle
vol. 161-167, 1912-18

4. Koeniglich Geheimes Zivilkabinett, 2.2.1.

Nr. 269   Preussische Landtag (1907-1916)

Nr. 270   Preussische Landtag (1917-1918)

Nr. 302   Preussische Herrenhaus (1914-1917)

III. Bundesarchiv Koblenz

1. Parteiakten

    Unabhaengiger Ausschuss f. e. Deutschen Frieden
    1915-18 (Mitteilungen und Flugblaetter)

2. Nachlaesse

Nr. 1e,2,3,8,10,11,15-17,20,67	Bauer
Nr. 43,44	Hans Delbrueck
Nr. 40,79,96,136,178,234,242,255,263	Fester
Kl. Erwerb. Nr. 293	Axel Freiherr v. Freytag-Loringhoven
H 08-46/113	Groener
Kl. Erwerb. Nr. 536	Heydebrand (Zeitungsberichte)
Kl. Erwerb. Nr. 576	Limburg-Stirum
Kl. Erwerb. Nr. 197	Posadowsky-Wehner
Kl. Erwerb. Nr. 317-1	Siegfried Graf v. Roedern
Kl. Erwerb. Nr. 230/1-4	Roesicke
Kl. Erwerb. Nr. 427-1	Anton Schifferer
Mappe Nr. 5,7,14-15,42-46,48,67	Traub
Kl. Erwerb. Nr. 341-1	v. Valentini

IV. Staatsarchiv Hamburg

1. Senatskriegsakten

B^{II}d Nr. 15,21,23,28,31,38,41,48	Landwirtschaftlichen Massnahmen
CIIr Nr. 1	Siedlungswesen
F 1	Massnahmen zur Durchfuehrung der Volksernaehrung
WZ 67	Einsendungen, Geschenke, Anfragen
WZ 56	Senatskriegsakten betr. Deutsche Vaterlandspartei

Radicals and Reactionaries

2. Polizeibehoerde - Politische Polizei

Vers. 452	Alldeutscher Verband (Ortsgruppe Hamburg)
S6545, vol. 1-2	Alldeutscher Verband
S5915	Bund der Landwirte
S15829	Deutsche Vereinigung
Vers. 1020	Hamburgische Konservative Vereinigung
S17389	Konservative Vereinigung
S19135	Hamburgische Konservative Vereinigung
SA2016	Preussenbund
S11792	Reichsverband gegen die Sozialdemokratie
S20648	Unabhaengiger Ausschuss f. e. Deutsche Frieden (Hamb.)
S20640	Vaterlandspartei
S20650	Volksbund fuer Freiheit u. Vaterland
S18591	Wehrverein

3. Personalia

S17368	Max v. Schinckel
S15825	Paul G. E. Zimmermann

V. Hamburg Forschungsstelle fuer die Geschichte des Nationalsozialismus in Hamburg

Nr. 7113	Deutschkonservative Partei
Nr. 7533-I	DNVP
Nr. 412	ADV (Geschaeftsfuehrende Ausschuss)
Nr. IIc2	miscellaneous

VI. Privatarchiv Freiherr Hiller v. Gaertringen, Gaertringen

(copy) Briefwechsel Westarp-Heydebrand (1914-1918)

RESEARCH LIBRARIES

VII. Institut fuer Zeitungsforschung Dortmund

Frankfurter Zeitung

Vorwaerts

Kreuz-Zeitung (Neue Preussiche Zeitung)

Taegliche Rundschau

VIII. Colindale Newspaper Library (London)

Kreuz-Zeitung

Alldeutsche Blaetter (ADB)

IX. Staatsbibliothek (Preussischer Kulturbesitz)
     Marburg/Lahn

Konservative Monatschrift, 1912-20

Mitteilungen aus der Konservativen Partei, 1913-18

X. Bibliothek des Volksvereins fuer das Katholische
    Deutschland in Stadtbibliothek Moenchengladbach

Korrespondenz des Bundes der Landwirte, 1914-17

Die Grenzboten 1914-18

Deutschlands Erneuerung, 1917-18

Radicals and Reactionaries

XI. Wiener Library London

Auf Vorposten, 1916-19

XII. Other Magazines, Newspapers

Der Panther, 1915-17

Konservative Kalendar, 1911, 1914

Mitteilungen der Deutschen Vaterlandspartei, 1917-18

Politisch-Anthropologische Revue, 1912-1918

Preussische Jahrbuecher, 1912-18

Berliner Neueste Nachrichten

Hamburger Echo

Hamburger Fremdenblatt

Hamburger Nachrichten

Hamburgisher Correspondent

Weser-Zeitung

General-Anzeiger

Berliner Tageblatt

Berliner-Volks-Zeitung

Elbwart

Deutsch-soziale Blaetter (after 1914: Deutsch-Voelkische Blaetter)

Reichsbote

Archiv fuer Sozialwissenschaft und Sozialpolitik

Deutsche Zeitung

Deutsche Tageszeitung

SELECTED BIBLIOGRAPHY

Aereboe, Friedrich. *Agrarpolitik*. Berlin, 1928.

_____. *Der Einfluss des Krieges auf die landwirtschaftliche Produktion in Deutschland*. Berlin and Leipzig, 1927.

Allen, David Yelling. "From Romanticism to Realpolitik. Studies in Nineteenth Century German Conservatism." Ph.D. thesis, Columbia University, 1971.

Arendt, Hannah. *The Origins of Totalitarianism*. 13th ed. New York, 1969.

Arnim, Hans v. and Below, Georg v. *Deutscher Aufstieg*. Berlin and Leipzig, 1925.

Barkin, Kenneth D. "Germany's Path to Industrial Maturity." *Laurentian University Review* 5 (June 1973): 11-33.

_____. *The Controversy over German Industrialization: 1890-1902*. Chicago and London, 1970.

Berdahl, Robert M. "Conservative Politics and Aristocratic Landholders in Bismarckian Germany." *Journal of Modern History* 144 (March 1972): 1-20.

Berger, H. v. *Der Konservatismus und die Parteien*, n.p., n.d.

Berghahn, Volker R. "Das Kaiserreich in der Sackgasse." *Neue* Politische Literatur 4 (1971): 494-506.

_____. *Der Tirpitz-Plan*. Duesseldorf, 1971.

_____. "Der Tirpitz-Plan und die Krisis des preussisch-deutschen Herrschaftssystems." In *Marine und Marinepolitik im kaiserlichen Deutschland 1871-1914*, edited by Wilhelm Deist and Herbert Schottelius. Duesseldorf, 1972.

_____. "Educated and less Educated Guesses: Kritischen Kommentar zu den Ruestungswettlauf und Eskalationsstudien." In *Konflikt-Eskalation-Krise. Studien zum Ausbruch des Ersten Weltkrieges*, edited by Klaus Juergen Gantzel et al. Duesseldorf, 1972.

_____. "Flottenruestung und Machtgefuege." In *Das kaiserliche Deutschland. Politik und Gesellschaft 1870-1918*, edited by Michael Stuermer. Duesseldorf, 1970.

_____. *Ruestung und Machtpolitik. Zur Anatomie des Kalten Krieges vor 1914*. Duesseldorf, 1973.

344

Radicals and Reactionaries

_____. "Zu den Zielen des deutschen Flottenbaus
unter Wilhelm II." *Historische Zeitschrift* 210 (1970):
34-100.

Bergmann, Klaus. *Agrarromantik und Grossstadtfeindlichkeit.*
Meisenheim a. Glan, 1970.

_____. *Berichte ueber die 37. Konferenz der Vorstaende
der preussischen Landwirtschaftskammern.* Berlin, 1925.

Bergstraesser, Ludwig. *Das alte System ueber sich selbst.
Aus den Errinerungen von Ludendorff, Helfferich, Bethmann,
Tirpitz und Anderen.* Berlin, 1920.

Bergstraesser, Arnold. "Zum Begriff des politischen Stils."
In *Faktoren der politischen Entscheidung (Festschrift* for
Ernst Fraenkel), edited by Gerhard A. Ritter and Gilbert
Ziebura. Berlin (West), 1963.

Bermbach, Udo. *Vorformen parlamentarischer Kabinettsbildung
in Deutschland.* Koelnand Opladen, 1967.

Bertram, Juergen. *Die Wahlen zum Deutschen Reichstag vom
Jahre 1912.* Duesseldorf, 1964.

Bethmann-Hollweg, Theodor von. *Betrachtungen zum Weltkrieg.*
2 vols. Berlin, 1921.

Blaich, Fritz. *Kartell-und Monopolpolitik in Kaiserlichen
Deutschland.* Duesseldorf, 1973.

Boeckenfoerde, Ernst-Wolfgang. *Moderne deutsche
Verfassungsgeschichte 1815-1918.* Koeln, 1972.

Boehm, Ekkehard. *"Ueberseehandel und Flottenbau. Hanseatische
Kaufmannschaft und deutsche Seeruestung."* Ph.D. thesis,
University Hamburg, 1971.

Boehme, Helmut. "Big Business, Pressure Groups and Bismarck's
Turn to Protectionism, 1873-1879." *The Historical Journal* 10
(1967).

_____. *Deutschlands Weg zur Grossmacht.* Koeln and
Berlin (West), 1966.

Boldt, Hans. "Deutscher Konstitutionalismus und Bismarckreich."
In *Das kaiserliche Deutschland,* edited by Michael Stuermer.
Duesseldorf, 1970.

Booms, Hans. *Die Deutschkonservative Partei.* Duesseldorf, 1954.

Born, K. E. "Der soziale und wirtschaftliche Strukturwandel Deutschlands am Ende des 19 Jahrhunderts." In *Moderne deutsche Sozialgeschichte*. 3rd ed. Koeln, Berlin (West), 1970.

_____. *Staat und Sozialpolitik seit Bismarck's Sturz*. Wiesbaden, 1957.

Bowen, R. H. *German Theories of the Corporative State with a special reference to the period 1870-1919*. New York, 1947.

Bueck, H. A. *Der Centralverband Deutscher Industrieller 1876-1901*. 3 vols. Berlin, 1902-05.

Buelow, Bernhard v. *Memoirs*. (trans. F. A. Voigt). London and New York, 1931.

Buerger, Curt. *Die Agrardemogogie in Deutschland*. Berlin, 1911.

Carsten, F. L. *The Origins of Prussia*. 2nd ed. Oxford, 1958.

Cecil, Lamar. *Albert Ballin. Business and Politics in Imperial Germany, 1888-1918*. Princeton, 1967.

Class, Heinrich. *Wider den Strom. Vom Werden und Wachsen der nationalen Opposition im alten Reich*. Leipzig, 1932.

Clemennz, M. *Gesellschaftliche Urspruenge des Faschismus*. Frankfurt a.M., 1972.

Cohn, Norman. *Warrant for Genocide. The Myth of the Jewish World Conspiracy and the Protocols of the Elders of Zion*. London, 1967.

Crothers, George Dunlop. *The German Elections of 1907*. 2nd ed. New York, 1968.

Dahrendorf, Ralf. *Soziale Klassen und Klassenkonflikt in der Industriellen Gesellschaft*. Stuttgart, 1957.

David, E. "Der Bund der Landwirte als Machtinstrument des ostelbischen Junkertums 1893-1920." Ph.D. thesis, Martin-Luther University, Halle-Wittenberg, 1967.

Deetjen, Ernst. *Freikonservativ! Die Nationale Mittelpartei*. Ratibor, 1913.

Deist, Wilhelm and Schottelius, Herbert (eds.) *Marine und Marinepolitik im kaiserlichen Deutschland 1871-1914*. Duesseldorf, 1972.

346

Radicals and Reactionaries

Deist, Wilhelm (ed.) *Militaer und Innenpolitik im Weltkrieg 1914-1918.* 2 vols. Duesseldorf, 1970.

Desai, Ashok v. *Real Wages in Germany 1871-1918.* Oxford, 1968.

Dewitz, Herman v. *Von Bismarck bis Bethmann.* Berlin, 1918.

Diwald, Hellmut (ed.) *Von der Revolution zum Norddeutschen Bund. Aus dem Nachlass von Ernst Ludwig von Gerlach.* 2 vols. Goettingen, 1970.

Dorpalen, Andreas. "The German Conservatives and the Parliamentarization of Imperial Germany." *The Journal of Central European Affairs* 10 (1951): 184-199.

Dueding, Dieter. *Der National soziale Verein 1896-1903.* Muenchen, 1972.

Elm, Ludwig. *Zwischen Fortschritt und Reaktion.* Berlin, 1968.

Epstein, Klaus Werner. *Matthias Erzberger and the dilemma of German democracy.* Princeton, N.J., 1959.

_____. *The Genesis of German Conservatism.* Princeton, N.J., 1966.

Erdmann, Karl Dietrich (ed.) *Kurt Riezler Tagebuecher-Aufsaetze-Dokumente.* Goettingen, 1973.

Ermel, Horst. *Der Uebergang vom Kapitalismus der freien Konkurrenz zum Imperialismus in Deutschland.* Koeln, 1974.

Ernst, Johann (ed.) *Innenansicht eines Krieges.* Frankfurt a. Main, 1968.

Erzberger, Matthias. *Erlebnisse im Weltkrieg.* Stuttgart and Berlin, 1920.

Eschenburg, Theodor. *Das Kaiserreich am Scheideweg.* Berlin, 1929.

Fehrenbach, Elizabeth. *Wandlungen des deutschen Kaisergedankens 1871-1918.* Muenchen, 1969.

Feldman, Gerald D. *Army, Industry and Labor in Germany, 1914-1918.* Princeton, N.J., 1966.

Feuchtwanger, E. J. *Prussia: Myth and Reality.* London, 1970.

Fischer, Fritz. *Griff nach der Weltmacht.* Duesseldorf, 1961.

_____. *Krieg der Illusionen*. Duesseldorf, 1969.

_____. *Weltmacht oder Niedergang. Deutschland im Ersten Weltkrieg*. Frankfurt a. Main, 1965.

Frank, Walter. *Hofprediger Adolf Stoecker und die christlichsoziale Bewegung*. 2nd ed. Hamburg, 1935.

Fricke, Dieter (ed.) *Die buergerliche Parteien in Deutschland. Handbuch der Geschichte der buergerlichen Parteien und anderer buergerlicher Innenorganisationen vom Vormaerz bis zum Jahre 1945*. 2 vols. Berlin, 1968-1970.

_____. "Der Reichsverband gegen die Sozialdemokratie von Seiner Gruendung bis zu den Reichstagswahlen von 1907." *Zeitschrift fuer Geschichtswissenschaft (ZFG)* 2 (1959).

_____. "Die Reichstagswahlen von 1907." *ZFG* 9 (1961): 538-576.

Frymann, Daniel (pseud. for Heinrich Class). *Das Kaiserbuch* (pre-1918 title: *Wenn ich der Kaiser waer*) *Politische Wahrheiten und Notwendigkeiten*. 7th ed. Leipzig, 1925.

Fuelberth, Georg. *Die Wandlung der deutschen Sozialdemokratie vom Erfurter Parteitag 1891 bis zum Ersten Weltkrieg*. Koeln, 1974.

Gabler, Hans. *Die Entwicklung der deutschen Parteien auf landwirtschaftlicher Grundlage von 1871-1912*. n.p., 1934.

Gaertringen, Friedrich Freiherr v. *Fuerst Buelows Denkwuerdigkeiten*. Tuebingen, 1956.

Galos, Adam et al. *Die Hakatisten. Der Deutsche Ostmarkenverein (1894-1934)*. Berlin, 1966.

Gantzel, K. J. et al. *Konflikt - Eskalation - Krise. Sozialwissenschaftliche Studien zum Ausbruch des Ersten Weltkrieges*. Duesseldorf, 1972.

_____. *System und Akteur. Beitraege zur vergleichenden Kriegsursachenforschung*. Duesseldorf, 1972.

Geiss, Imanuel. *Der Polnische Grenzstreifen 1914-1918*. Luebeck and Hamburg, 1960.

Geiss, Imanuel and Wendt, Bernd (eds.) *Deutschland in der Weltpolitik des 19 und 20. Jahrhunderts*. Duesseldorf, 1973.

Geiss, Imanuel. *Studien ueber Geschichte und Geschichtswissenschaft*. Frankfurt a. Main, 1972.

Radicals and Reactionaries

Gerlach, Hellmut v. *Von Rechts nach Links.* Zuerich, 1937.

Gerloff, Wilhelm. *Die Finanz-und Zollpolitik des Deutschen Reiches nebst ihren Beziehungen zu Landes und Gemeindefinanzen von der Gruendung des Norddeutschen Bundes bis zur Gegenwart.* Jena, 1913.

Gerschenkron, Alexander. *Bread and Democracy in Germany,* 2nd ed., New York, 1966.

Gerstenberger, Heide. *Der revolutionaere Konservatismus. Ein Beitrag zur Analyse des Liberalismus.* Berlin (west) 1969.

Goehring, Martin. *Bismarck's Erben 1890-1945.* Wiesbaden, 1959.

Goerlitz, Walter. *Die Junker.* Limburg a.d. Lahn, 1964.

Goertz, Hartmann. *Preussens Gloria.* Muenchen, 1962.

Goldschmidt, Hans. *Das Reich und Preussen im Kampf um die Fuehrung von Bismarck bis 1918.* Berlin, 1931.

Grebing, Helga. *Geschichte der Deutschen Parteien.* Wiesbaden, 1962.

_____. *Konservative gegen die Demokratie.* Frankfurt a. Main, 1971.

Greiffenhagen, Martin. *Das Dilemma des Konservatismus in Deutschland.* Muenchen, 1971.

Groh, Dieter. "Negative Integration und Revolutionaerer Attentismus. Die Sozialdemokratie im Kaiserreich." *Internationale Wissenschaftliche Korrespondenz* 5 (April 1972): 1-20.

_____. *Negative Integration und revolutionaerer Attentismus. Die deutsche Sozialdemokratie am Vorabend des Ersten Weltkrieges.* Frankfurt a.M., 1973.

_____. "Waiting For and Avoiding Revolution: Social Democracy and the Reich." *Laurentian University Review* 5 (June, 1973): 83-109.

Grosser, Dieter. *Vom monarchischen Konstitutionalismus zur parlamentarischen Demokratie.* Den Haag, 1970.

Gutsche, Willibald. *Aufstieg und Fall eines Kaiserlichen Reichskanzlers. Theobald von Bethmann Hollweg 1856-1921. Ein politisches Lebensbild.* Berlin, 1973.

_____. "Bethmann Hollweg und die Politik der 'Neuorientierung.' Zur innenpolitischen Strategie und Taktik der deutschen Reichsregierung waehrend des ersten Weltkrieges." *ZFG* 13 (1965): 109-234.

Guttmann, Bernhard. *Schattenriss Einer Generation 1888-1919*. Stuttgart, 1950.

Hallgarten, George W. F. *Imperialismus vor 1914*. 2 vols. Muenchen, 1963.

Hamel, Iris. *"Voelkischer Verband und Nationale Gewerkschaft. Die Politik des Deutschnationalen Handlungsgehilfen - Verbandes, 1893-1933."* Ph.D. thesis, Hamburg University, 1966.

Handbuch der Deutschkonservativen Partei. 4th ed. Berlin, 1911.

Hardach, Karl W. *Die Bedeutung wirtschaftlicher Faktoren bei der Wiedereinfuehrung der Eisen - und Getreidezoelle in Deutschland 1879*. Berlin, 1967.

Heffter, Heinrich. *"Die Kreuzzeitungspartei und die Kartellpolitik Bismarcks."* Ph.D. thesis, Leipzig University, 1946.

Hertzmann, Lewis. *DNVP. Right-Wing Opposition in the Weimar Republic 1918-1924*. Lincoln, Nebraska, 1963.

Herwig, Holger H. *The German Naval Officer Corps. A Social and Political History 1890-1918*. Oxford, 1973.

Herzberger, C. v. *"Die Stellung der preussischen Konservativen zu sozialen Fragen."* Ph.D. thesis, Leipzig University, 1914.

Heydebrand und der Lasa, Ernst v. "Beitrage zu einer Geschichte der Konservativen Partei in den letzten 30 Jahren 1888 bis 1919." *Konservative Monatschrift* 28 (1920).

Horn, Hannelore. *Der Kampf um den Bau des Mittellandkanals*. Koeln, 1964.

Hildebrand, Klaus. *Bethmann Hollweg Der Kanzler ohne Eigenschaften?* Duesseldorf, 1970.

_____. *Deutsche Aussenpolitik 1933-45. Kalkul oder Dogma?* Mainz, 1971.

Hobohm, Martin and Rohrbach, Paul. *Chavinismus und Weltkrieg: vol. 2. Die Alldeutschen*. Berlin, 1919.

Hoffmann, W. G. and Mueller, J. H. *Das Deutsche Volkseinkommen 1851-1957*. Tuebingen, 1959.

Radicals and Reactionaries

Hutten-Czapski, Bogdan Graf. *Sechzig Jahre Politik und Gesellschaft* - 2 vols. Berlin, 1936.

Iggers, George G. *The German Conception of History.* Middletown, Conn., 1968.

Jaeger, Hans. *Unternehmer in der deutschen Politik (1890-1918).* Bonn, 1967.

Jaffe, Edgar. Review of *Innere kolonisation und Selbstverwaltung* by Wolfgang Kapp. *Archiv fuer Sozialwissenschaft und Sozialpolitik* 2 (1909).

Janssen, K-H. *Macht und Verblendung. Kriegsziel politik der deutschen Bundesstaaten, 1914-1918.* Goettingen, 1963.

Jonas, Erasmus. *Die Volkskonservativen 1928-1933.* Duesseldorf, 1965.

Jordan, Erich. *Die Entstehung der Konservativen Partei und die preussischen Agrarverhaeltnisse von 1848.* Muenchen, 1914.

Jochmann, Werner. "Die Ausbreitung des Antisemitismus." In *Deutsches Judentum in Krieg und Revolution, 1916-23,* edited by Werner Mosse. Tuebingen, 1971.

Kaelble, Hartmut. *Industriele Interessenpolitik in der wilhelminischen Gesellschaft.* Berlin (West), 1967.

Kardorff, Siegfried v. *Wilhelm von Kardorff. Ein nationaler parlamentarier im Zeitalter Bismarcks und Wilhelms II - 1828-1907.* Berlin, 1935.

Kehr, Eckart. *Der Primat der Innenpolitik,* edited by Han-Ulrich Wehler. Berlin (West) 1965.

_____. *Schlachtflottenbau und Parteipolitik, 1894-1901.* Berlin, 1930.

Kielmansegg, Peter Graf. *Deutschland und der Erste Weltkrieg.* Frankfurt a. Main, 1968.

Kiesenwetter, Otto v. *Zehn Jahre wirtschaftspolitischen Kampfes.* Berlin, 1903.

_____. *Fuenfundzwanzig Jahre wirtschaftspolitischen Kampfes.* Berlin, 1918.

Kitchen, Martin. *The German Officer Corps. 1890-1914.* Oxford, 1968.

Klein, Fritz. *Deutschland 1897/98-1917.* 3rd ed. Berlin, 1972.

_____. (ed.) *Deutschland im Ersten Weltkrieg.* 3 vols. Berlin, 1970.

_____. (ed.) *Politik im Krieg 1914-1918.* Berlin, 1964.

Klemperer, Klemens v. *Germany's New Conservatism.* Princeton, New Jersey, 1957.

Kocka, Juergen. *Klassengesellschaft im Krieg 1914-1918.* Goettingen, 1973.

Koselleck, Reinhart. *Preussen zurischen Reform und Revolution.* Stuttgart, 1967.

Koch, H. W. (ed.) *The Origins of the First World War.* London, 1972.

Krieger, Leonard. *The German Idea of Freedom.* Boston, 1957.

Kroeger, Karl Heinz. *Die Konservativen und die Politik Caprivis.* Rostock, 1937.

Kruck, Alfred. *Geschichte des Alldeutschen Verbandes, 1890-1939.* Wiesbaden, 1954.

Kuczynski, Juergen. *Die Geschichte der Lage der Arbeiter unter dem Kapitalismus.* (vol. 4). Berlin, 1967.

Kuhn, Axel (ed.) *Deutsche Parlamentsdebatten 1871-1918.* (vol. I). Frankfurt a. Main, 1970.

Kurze, Dietrich (ed.) *Aus Theorie und Praxis der Geschichtswissenschaft. Festschrift fuer Hans Herzfeld zum 80 Geburtstag.* Berlin (West), 1972.

Lambi, Ivo N. "Die Organisation der industriellen Schutzzollinteressen." In *Moderne deutsche Wirtschaftsgeschichte,* edited by Karl Erich Bom. Koeln, 1966.

_____. *Free Trade and Protection in Germany.* Wiesbaden, 1963.

Land, Hanne-Lore. "Die Konservativen und die Preussische Polenpolitik (1886-1912)." Ph.D. thesis, Free University, Berlin, 1963.

Radicals and Reactionaries

Landes, David S. *The Unbound Prometheus, Technological Change and Industrial Development in Western Europe from 1750 to the Present.* London, 1969.

Lebovics, Herman. *Social Conservatism and the Middle Classes in Germany, 1914-1933.* Princeton, New Jersey, 1969.

_____. "Agrarians versus Industrializers." *International Review of Social History* 12 (1967): 31-65.

Leuss, Hans. *Wilhelm Freiherr von Hammerstein.* Berlin, 1905.

Levy, Richard S. *The Downfall of the Anti-Semitic Political Parties in Imperial Germany.* New Haven, 1975.

Liebe, Werner. *Die Deutschnationale Volkspartei 1918-1924.* Duesseldorf, 1956.

Limburg-Stirum, Friedrich Wilhelm Graf von. *Aus der konservativen Politik der Jahre 1890-1905.* Berlin, 1921.

Lindig, Ursula. *"Der Einfluss des Bundes der Landwirte auf die Politik des Wilhelminischen Zeitalters 1893-1914."* Ph.D. thesis, Hamburg University, 1953.

Lohalm, Uwe. *Voelkischer Radikalismus. Die Geschichte des Deutschvoelkischen Schutz - und Trutz Bundes 1919-1923.* Hamburg, 1970.

Luebbe, Hermann. *Politische Philosophie in Deutschland.* Stuttgart, 1963.

Ludendorff, Erich. *Deutsche Abwehr, Antisemitismus gegen Antigojismus.* Muenchen, 1934.

_____. *Kriegfuehrung und Politik.* Berlin, 1922.

_____. *Meine Kriegserrinerungen 1914-1918.* Berlin, 1919.

Lutz, Ralph Haswell (ed.) *The Causes of the German Collapse in 1918.* 2nd ed. n.p. 1969.

Mann, Thomas. *Betrachtungen eines Unpolitischen.* Frankfurt a. Main, 1956.

Martin, Frederick. *The Junker Menace.* New York, 1945.

Massing, Paul W. *Rehersal for Destruction. A Study of Political Anti-Semitism in Imperial Germany.* New York, 1949.

Matthias, Erich and Muller, Suzanne (eds.) *Das Kriegstagbuch des Reichstagsabgeordneten Eduard David 1914-1918.* Duesseldorf, 1966.

Matthias, Erich and Morsey, Rudolf. *Die Interfraktionelle Ausschuss 1917/1918.* 2 vols. Duesseldorf, 1959.

Mayer, J. P. *Max Weber and German Politics.* 2nd ed. London, 1946.

Meinecke, Friedrich. *Erlebtes - 1862-1919.* Stuttgart, 1964.

_____. *Probleme des Welt Krieges.* Berlin, 1917.

Mendelssohn-Bartholdy, Albrecht. *The War and German Society. The Testament of a Liberal.* New York, 1971.

Messerschmidt, Manfred. "Reich und Nation in Bewusstsein der wilhelminischen Gesellschaft." In *Marine und Marinepolitik,* edited by Deist and Schottelius. Duesseldorf, 1972.

Meyer, Henry Cord. *Mitteleuropa in German Thought and Action 1815-1945.* The Hague, 1955.

Minchinton, W. E. (ed.) *Essays in Agrarian History.* vol. 2. Devon, 1968.

Mogk, Walter. *Paul Rohrbach und das "Groessere Deutschland." Ethischer Imperialismus im wilhelminischen Zeitalter.* Muenchen, 1972.

Molt, Peter. *Der Reichstag vor der improvisierten Revolution.* Koeln, 1963.

Mommsen, Wilhelm. *Deutsche Parteiprogramme.* Muenchen, 1960.

Mommsen, Wolfgang J. *Die Geschichtswissenschaft jenseits des Historismus.* Duesseldorf, 1971.

_____. "Die Latente Krise des Deutschen Reiches 1909-1914." In *Handbuch der deutschen Geschichte,* sections II, IV, edited by Leo Just. Frankfurt a.M., 1972.

_____. "Domestic Factors in German Foreign Policy before 1914." *Central European History* 6 (March 1973): 3-43.

Muncy, Lysbeth Walker. *The Junker in the Prussian Administration under William II, 1888-1914.* Providence, 1944.

Mosse, George L. *Germans and Jews.* New York, 1970.

Radicals and Reactionaries

_____. *The Crisis of German Ideology.* New York, 1964.

Mueller, Karl Alexander v. *Mars und Venus.* Stuttgart, 1954.

Nettl, Peter. *Rosa Luxemburg.* Koeln, 1967.

Neumann, Sigmund. *Die Stufen des preussischen Konservatismus.* Berlin, 1930.

Nichols, J. Alden. *Germany After Bismarck: The Caprivi Era, 1890-1894.* Cambridge, Mass., 1958.

Nichtweiss, Johannes. *Die auslaendische Saisonarbeiter in der Landwirtschaft der oestlichen und mittleren Gebiete des Deutschen Reiches.* Berlin (West), 1959.

Nipperdey, Thomas. *Die Organisation der deutschen Parteien vor 1918.* Duesseldorf, 1961.

_____. "Interessenverbaende und Parteien in Deutschland vor dem ersten Weltkrieg." In *Moderne deutsche Sozialgeschichte* edited by Hans-Ulrich Wehler. Koeln, 1970.

_____. "Ueber einige Grundzuege der deutschen Parteigeschichte." In *Moderne deutsche Verfassungsgeschichte 1815-1918.*

Nolte, Ernst. *Die Krise des Liberalen Systems und die faschistischen Bewegungen.* Muenchen, 1968.

Oldenburg-Januschau, Elard v. *Erinnerungen.* Leipzig, 1936.

Pareto, Vilfredo. *The Rise and Fall of the Elites. An Application of Theoretical Sociology.* Totowa, New Jersey, 1968.

Patemann, Reinhard. *Der Kampf um die preussische Wahlreform im Ersten Weltkrieg.* Duesseldorf, 1964.

Pikart, Eberhard. "Die Rolle der Parteien im deutschen konstitutionellen System vor 1914." In *Moderne deutsche Verfassungsgeschichte 1815-1918.*

Poels, Werner. *Sozialistenfrage und Revolutionsfurcht in ihren Zusammenhang mit den angeblichen Staatsstreichplaenen Bismarcks.* Hamburg and Luebeck, 1960.

Pogge von Strandmann, Hartmut. "Domestic Origins of Germany's Colonial Expansion under Bismarck." *Past and Present* 42 (February 1969): 140-159.

_____. "Nationale Verbaende zwischen Weltpolitik und Kontinentalpolitik." In *Marine und Marinepolitik im kaiserlichen Deutschland, 1871-1914.*

_____. "Rathenau, die Gebrueder Mannesmann und die Vorgeschichte der zweiter Marokkokrise." In *Deutschland in der Weltpolitik des 19 und 20. Jahrhunderts.*

Pommer, Otto. *Die Konservativen.* Berlin, 1912.

Pross, Hanz (ed.) *Die Zerstoerung der deutschen Politik: Dokumente 1871-1933.* Frankfurt a. Main, 1959.

Puhle, Hans-Juergen. *Agrarische Interessenpolitik und preussischen Konservatismus im wilhelminischen Reich (1893-1914).* Hannover, 1967.

_____. "Der Bund der Landwirte im wilhelminischen Reich - Struktur, Ideologie und politische Wirksamkeit eines Interessenverbandes in der konstitutionellen Monarchy 1893-1914." In *Zur soziologische Theorie und Analyse des 19 Jahrhunderts,* edited by Rueegg, Walter and Neuloh, Otto. Goettingen, 1971.

_____. "Parlament, Parteien und Interessenverbaende 1890-1914." In *Das kaiserliche Deutschland.*

_____. *Von der Agrarkrise zum Praefaschismus.* Wiesbaden, 1972.

Pulzer, P. G. J. *The Rise of Political Anti-Semitism in Germany and Austria.* New York, 1964.

Rauh, Manfred. *Foederalismus und Parlamentarismus im wilhelminischen Reich.* Duesseldorf, 1973.

Rein, Gustav Adolf. *Die Revolution in der Politik Bismarcks.* Goettingen, 1957.

Reiss, Klaus-Peter. *Von Bassermann zu Stresemann. Die Sitzungen des Nationalliberalen Zentralvorstandes 1912-1917.* Duesseldorf, 1967.

Ringer, Fritz K. *The Decline of the German Mandarins.* Cambridge, Mass., 1969.

Ritter, Gerhard A. *Enstehung und Wandel der modernen Gesellschaft. Festschrift fuer Hans Rosenberg zum 65 Geburtstag.*

_____. (ed.) *Die deutschen Parteien vor 1918.* Koeln, 1973.

Ritter, Gerhard. *Die preussischen Konservativen und Bismarcks deutsche Politik.* Heidelberg, 1915.

_____. *Staatskunst und Kriegshandwerk.* 4 vols. Muenchen, 1964.

Roehl, J. C. G. *From Bismarck to Hitler.* London, 1970.

_____. *Germany without Bismarck.* London, 1967.

_____. "The Disintegration of the *Kartell* and the Politics of Bethmann's Fall from Power 1887-1890." *Historical Journal* 9 (1966): 60-89.

Roesler, Konrad. *Die Finanzpolitik des Deutschen Reiches im Ersten Weltkrieg.* Berlin (West), 1967.

Rohrmann, Elsabea. *Max von Schinckel. Hanseatischer Bankmann im wilhelminischen Deutschland.* Hamburg, n.d.

Rosenberg, Hans. "Die Pseudodemokratisierung der Rittergutsbesitzerklasse." In *Moderne deutsche Sozialgeschichte.*

_____. *Grosse Depression und Bismarckzeit.* Berlin (West) 1967.

_____. *Probleme der deutschen Sozialgeschichte.* Frankfurt a. Main, 1969.

_____. "Wirtschaftskonjunktur, Gesellschaft und Politik in Mitteleuropa, 1873-1896." In *Moderne deutsche Sozialgeschichte.*

Rostow, W. W. *Politics and the Stages of Growth.* London, 1971.

_____. *The Stages of Economic Growth.* London, 1960.

Roth, Guenther. *The Social Democratis in Imperial Germany. A Study in Working-Class Isolation and National Integration.* Totowa, New Jersey, 1963.

Rothfels, Hans (ed.) *Bismarck und der Staat.* 4th ed. Stuttgart, 1964.

Rueegg, Walter and Neuloh, Otto (eds.) *Zur soziologischen Theorie und Analyse des 19 Jahrhunderts.* Goettingen, 1971.

Sarason, Dr. D. (ed.) *Das Jahr 1913.* Leipzig, 1913.

Sauer, Wolfgang. "Das Problem des deutschen Nationalstaates." In *Moderne deutsche Sozialgeschichte.*

Saul, S. B. *The Myth of the Great Depression 1873-1896.* London, 1969.

Schieder, Wolfgang (ed.) *Erster Weltkrieg: Ursachen, Entstehung und Kriegsziele.* Koeln, 1969.

Schiedler, Gert Udo. "Parliament, Parteien und Regierung im wilhelminischen Reich 1890-1914." *Aus Politik und Zeitgeschichte (Beilage to Das Parlament)* 12 (1971): 16-24.

Schilling, Konrad. "Beitraege zu einer Geschichte des radikalen Nationalismus in der wilhelminischen Aera, 1890-1909." Ph.D. thesis, Koeln University, 1968.

Schleier, Hans and Seeber, Gustav. "Zur Entwicklung und Rolle des Antisemitismus in Deutschland von 1871-1914." *ZFG* 9 (1961): 1592-97.

Schmidt, Gustav. "Deutschland am Vorabend des Ersten Weltkrieges." In *Das kaiserliche Deutschland.*

_____. "Innenpolitischen Blockbildungen in Deutschland am Vorabend des Ersten Weltkrieges." *Aus Politik und Zeitgeschichte (Beilage to Das Parlament)* (May 13, 1972): 3-32.

Schroeder, Hans-Christoph. *Sozialismus und Imperialismus.* Hannover, 1968.

Schuecking, Lothar Engelbert. *Die Misregierung der Konservativen unter Kaiser Wilhelm II.* Muenchen, 1909.

Schulthess' Europaeische Geschichtskalendar. Muenchen, 1903-1918.

Schumacher, Martin. "Gruene Front - kontinuitaet oder Wandel?" *NPL* 4 (1971): 520-531.

Schwabe, Klaus. *Wissenschaft und Kriegsmoral.* Goettingen, 1969.

_____. "Zur politischen Haltung der deutschen Professoren im Ersten Weltkrieg." *Historische Zeitschrift* III (1961): 601ff.

Schwarz, Max. *MdR: Biographisches Handbuch der Reichstage.* Hannover, 1965.

Schwerin-Loewitz, Glans Graf von. *Aufsaetze und Reden.* Berlin, 1911.

Radicals and Reactionaries

Senghaas, Dieter. *Ruestung und Militarismus*. Frankfurt a. Main, 1972.

Sheehan, James J. "Political Leadership in the German Reichstag, 1871-1918." *American Historical Review* (1968): 511-528.

Sontheimer, Kurt. *Antidemokratisches Denken in der Weimarer Republik*. Muenchen, 1962.

Stegmann, Dirk. *Die Erben Bismarcks*. Koeln, 1970.

_____. "Wirtschaft und Politik nach Bismarcks' Sturz: Zur Genesis der Miquelischen Sammlungspolitik." In *Deutschland in der Weltpolitik des 19 und 20. Jahrhunderts*.

_____. "Zwischen Repression und Manipulation: Konservativer Machteliten und Arbeiter und Angestelltenbewegung 1910-1918. Ein Beitrag zur Vorgeschichte der DAP/NSDAP." *Archiv fuer Sozialgeschichte* 12 (1972): 351-432.

Stenkewitz, Kurt. *Gegen Bajonett und Dividende*. Berlin (West), 1960.

Stern, Fritz. *Bethmann Hollweg und der Krieg: Die Grenze der Verantwortung*. Tuebingen, 1968.

_____. *The Failure of Illiberalism*. London, 1972.

Stillich, Oscar. *Die Konservativen*. Leipzig, 1908.

Stock, Erich. *Wirtschafts und Sozialpolitische Bestrebungen der deutschkonservativen Partei unter Bismarck 1876-1890*. Berlin, 1928.

Stolberg-Wernigerode, Otto Graf zu. *Die unentschiedene Generation*. Muenchen, 1968.

Stuermer, Michael. "Bismarck in Perspective." *Central European History* 4 (1971).

_____. *Bismarck und die Preussisch-deutsche Politik 1871-1890*. Muenchen, 1970.

_____. "Bismarckstaat und Caesarismus." *Der Staat* 12, (1973): 467-498.

_____. (ed.) *Das kaiserliche Deutschland*. Duesseldorf, 1970.

_____. "Konservatismus und Revolution in Bismarck's Politik." In *Das kaiserliche Deutschland*,

_____. "Machtgefuege und Verbandsentwicklung in wilhelminischen Deutschland." *NPL* 14 (1969): 490-507.

_____. "Staatstreichgedanken in Bismarckreich," *Historische Zeitschrift* 209 (1969).

Thieme, Hartwig. *Nationaler Liberalismus in der Krise*, Boppard am Rhein, 1963.

Thimme, Annelise. *Flucht in den Mythos*. Goettingen, 1969.

_____. *Hans Delbrueck als Kritiker der wilhelminischen Epoche*. Duesseldorf, 1955.

Thimme, Friedrich. *Vom inneren Frieden des deutschen Volkes*, 2 vols. Leipzig, 1916.

Tims, Richard Wonser. *Germanizing Prussian Poland*. New York, 1941.

Tirrell, S. R. *German Agrarian Politics after Bismarck's Fall*. New York, 1951.

Tormin, Walter. *Geschichte der deutschen Parteien seit 1848*, Stuttgart, 1966.

Unold, Dr. Johannes. *Kultur und Fortschritt*, n.p., 1913.

Wagener, Bruno. *Vaterlandslose Gesellen? Die Wahrheit in der Flottenfrage*. Hamburg, 1897.

Wallraf, Lothar. "Deutschkonservative Partei." In *Die Buergerlichen Parteien*,

_____. "Zur Politik der Deutschkonservativen Partei in den letzten Jahrzehnten Ihre Bestchens (1898-1918) unter den Bedingungen der Imperialistischen Epoche." Ph.D. thesis, Friedrich-Schiller-University, Jena, 1970.

Valentini, Rudolf v. *Kaiser und Kabinettschef*. Oldenburg, 1931.

Vogel, Barbara. "Deutsche Russlandpolitik Das Scheitern der deutschen Weltpolitik unter Buelow (1900-1906)." Ph.D. thesis, Hamburg University, 1972.

Wangenheim, H. Freiherr v. (ed.) *Conrad Freiherr von Wangenheim-Klein - Spiegel*. Berlin, 1934.

Radicals and Reactionaries

Wawrzinek, Kurt. *Die Entstehung der deutschen Antisemitismus (1873-1890)*. Berlin, 1927.

Weber, Hellmuth. *Ludendorff und die Monopole*. Berlin, 1966.

_____. "Zur Problem der Wahlrechtsreform in Preussen waehrend den Jahren 1917-1918." *ZFG* 13 (1965): 189-203.

Weber, Max. *Gesammelte Politische Schriften*. Muenchen, 1920.

Wehler, Hans-Ulrich. *Bismarck und der Imperialismus*. Koeln, 1969.

_____. *Das Deutsche Kaiserreich 1871-1918*. Goettingen, 1973.

_____. *Krisenherde des Kaiserreiches 1871-1918*. Goettingen, 1970.

_____. (ed.) *Moderne deutsche Sozialgeschichte*. Koeln, 1970.

_____. "Sozialimperialismus." In *Imperialismus*, edited by H. U. Wehler. Koeln, 1970.

_____. "Sozialoekonomie und Geschichtswissenschaft." *NPL* 14 (1969): 344-374.

Weiss, Dr. Max (ed.) *Der Nationale Wille. Werden und Wirken der Deutschnationalen Volkspartei 1918-1928*. Berlin, 1928.

Wernecke, Klaus. *Der Wille zur Weltgeltung*. Duesseldorf, 1970.

Werner, Lothar. *Der Alldeutsche Verband*. Berlin, 1935.

Wertheimer, Mildred S. *The Pan-German League 1890-1914*. New York, 1924.

Westarp, Kuno Graf v. *Das Ende der Monarchie am 9 November 1918*, edited by Werner Conze. Berlin (West), 1952.

_____. *Die Regierung des Prinzen Max von Baden und die Konservative Partei*. Berlin, n.d.

_____. *Konservative Politik im letzten Jahrzehnt des kaiserreiches*. 2 vols. Berlin, 1935.

Winkler, Heinrich August. "Der rueckversicherte Mittelstand: Die Interessenverbaende von Handwerk und Kleinhandel im deutschen Kaiserreich." In *Zur Sociologischen Theorie*.

_____. *Mittelstand, Demokratie und National-sozialismus.* Koeln, 1972.

_____. *Pluralismus oder Protektionismus?* Wiesbaden, 1972.

Witt, Peter-Christian. "Der preussische Landrat als Steuerbeamter, 1891-1918." In *Deutschland in der Weltpolitik des 19 und 20. Jahrhunderts.*

_____. *Die Finanzpolitik des Deutschen Reiches von 1903 bis 1913.* Luebeck and Hamburg, 1970.

_____. "Eine Denkschrift Otto Hoetzschs vom 5 November 1918." *Vierteljahrescheft fuer Zeitgeschichte* 21 (July 1973): 337-353.

_____. "Reichsfinanzen und Ruestungspolitik 1898-1914." In *Marine und Marinepolitik.*

Wortmann, Karl. *Geschichte der Deutschen Vaterlands Partei 1917-1918.* Halle, 1926.

Wulf, Amandus. "Die Rolle der Flottenbewegung bei der Durchsetzung einen imperialistischen Politik in Deutschland 1897-1900." Ph.D. thesis, Rostock University, 1965.

Wurm, Emanuel. *Die Finanzgeschichte des Deutschen Reiches.* Hamburg, 1910.

Zechlin, Egmont. *Die Deutsche Politik und die Juden im Ersten Weltkrieg.* Goettingen, 1969.

Zmarzlik, Hans Guenter. *Bethmann Hollweg als Reichskanzler 1909-1914.* Duesseldorf, 1957.

GERMAN CONSERVATIVE PARTY PAMPHLETS DURING THE WAR
(Schriften zur Tagespolitik)

Heydebrand und der Lasa, Ernst v. *Fuer Preussen.*

Kahrstedt, Ulrich. *Das rueckstaendige England.*

_____. *Konservative Fuersorge fuer die Kriegsschaedigten und Hinterbliebenen im kriege Gefallenen.*

Kaufhold, Josef. *Die konservative Partei und der Weltkrieg.*

Radicals and Reactionaries

Ohm, Willy. *Kriegsteuerung und Beamtenbesoldung.*

_____. *Sozialdemokratie und Vaterland.*

Wach, Eckart. *Die Kriegsverlaengerer.*

Westarp, Kuno Graf. *Auswaertige Politik.*

Adlon Action, 204, 210, 214
ADV, see Alldeutscher Verband
Africa, 151, 152
Agrarian League, see Bund der
    Landwirte
Agriculture, 119. See also
    Bund der Landwirte; Conser-
    vatives; Sammlungspolitik
Ahlwardt, Hermann, 23, 90
Algeciras Conference, 54
Alldeutsche Blaetter, 129-130
Alldeutscher Verband (ADV or
    Pan Germans), 55, 56, 67,
    78-79, 80-81, 143, 145,158,
    182, 184, 185, 190, 240;
    and anti-Semitism, 92, 95,
    96, 141, 175, 200, 201, 202,
    2160217, 219, 220, 234-235,
    236-237; and Bund der Land-
    wirte, 76, 107-109, 129,
    135-136, 150, 155, 160, 161,
    164, 165, 166-167, 168, 170,
    171-173, 178, 182-183, 190,
    191, 192, 195, 196, 198,
    203, 207-208, 222; and Con-
    servatives, 76, 79-80, 109-
    111, 132-133, 138, 154-155,
    158, 160-163, 164-167, 168,
    169, 170, 172, 178, 179-180,
    181-185, 200, 203-204, 205,
    214-215, 222, 223, 241-242;
    and inner colonization, 59,
    140; and National Opposition
    and war aims, 128-134, 139,
    150-155, 160-163, 164-165,
    166, 167, 168-169, 170, 171,
    173, 177-179, 180, 181, 183,
    187, 189, 192, 194, 196,
    197, 198, 199, 213-216; and
    Sammlungspolitik, 129-130,
    217-218, 219, 220, 223
Alsace-Lorraine, 74, 151
Alter, Junius, 199
Anti-Catholicism, 8, 12, 83
Anti-Semitic League, 89
Anti-Semitism, 2, 3, 23, 25, 28,
    42, 84, 85-97, 131, 133, 141,
    142, 154, 171-172, 174-177,
    200-202, 213, 214, 215, 216-

217, 218, 220, 230, 234-235,
    236-237, 238-239
Anti-Socialist Law, 13, 17, 29.
    See also Ausnahmegesetze;
    Umsturzgesetzes; Zuchthaus-
    vorlage
Antrag Kanitz, See Kanitz pro-
    posal
Army, 64, 80, 98, 100, 101, 102
Army League, see Wehrverein
Arnim, von (Conservative), 142
Association against Presumption
    of Jews, see Verband gegen die
    Ueberhebung des Judentums
Association for Preservation of
    Material Interests of All
    Classes of Prussian People,
    7
Association of Christian German
    Farmers, see Christliche
    deutsche Bauernvereine
Association of German Iron and
    Steel Industrialists, see
    Verein Deutscher Eisen und
    Stahl Industrieller
Association of Tax and Economic
    Reformers, see Vereinigung
    der Steuer und Wirtschafts-
    reformer
Auf Vorposten, 237, 238
Auskunfstelle Vereinigte Verbaende,
    170
Ausnahmegesetze laws (exceptional
    laws), 77, 158, 172, 175
Austria-Hungary, 122, 145, 151,
    152, 191, 201

Baden, Max von, 227
Baecker (Conservative), 192
Ballin, Albert, 78
Baltic, 159, 165-166
Bankers, see Hansabund
Barth, Theodor, 37, 105
Basserman, Ernst, 99, 114, 160,
    169, 171, 172
Bauer, Max, 202, 233
Bavaria, 141
BdI, see Bund der Industriellen

BdL, *see* Bund der Landwirte
Belgium, 151, 152, 158, 161,
  166, 167, 178, 180, 183,
  223
Below, von (Deutsche Vaterlandspartei), 212
Berlepsch, Hans Hermann Freiherr
  von, 32
Berliner Bewegung, 12
Berliner Tageblatt, 138, 239
Bernhardi, General von, 151,
  214
Bethmann Hollweg, Thebold von,
  72-74, 79, 80, 82-83, 97,
  99, 100, 101, 102, 103, 104,
  125, 126, 128-129, 131, 143,
  145, 149, 150, 152, 153, 157,
  158, 164, 167, 168, 169, 170,
  177-180, 181, 184, 185, 187,
  188, 190, 191-193, 194, 195,
  197-198, 199, 201, 203, 204,
  205, 207, 209, 211, 214,
  215, 216
Beutler, Dr. (Pankower Movement),
  70
Bieberstein, von (Conservative),
  148
Bismarck, Otto von, 1, 3-4, 8,
  9, 12-15, 17, 19, 28-29, 35,
  37, 219
Bismarck Kartell, *see* Kartell of
  1887
Bjoerkoe treaty, 54
Black-Blue Block, 82, 98, 105
Bleichroeder, Gershon, 3
Blettnitz, Block von, 226
Bodelschwingh-Schwarzenhasel,
  Baron F. von, 142, 174, 192,
  201, 212
Boeckel, Otto, 23, 90
Boehlendorf, von (Conservative),
  148
Boetticher (government minister),
  32
Bohlen, Krupp von, 62, 151, 160,
  197
Bonin, von, (Conservative Deputy,
  Neustettin), 174-175, 227
Bourgeois, *see* Mittelstand Pol-
  itics

Brandt, Otto, 115
Brederick (Berlin attorney-
  Pankower Movement), 70
Bremen, 211
Bremen Committee for a German
  Workers' Peace, 227-228
Brentano, Lujo, 63
Breusing, Admiral, 107, 108-109
Briey, 190
Bueck, Henri Axel, 77
Buelow, Bernhard von, 32, 34,
  38, 44-45, 53, 55-56, 63,
  180
Buelow Block, 53, 56-57, 62-63,
  66, 67, 68, 69, 71, 74-75.
  See also Sammlungspolitik
Bulgaria, 191
Bund der Industriellen (light
  industry), 117, 118, 120,
  121, 149, 160, 161, 164,
  170, 171, 172, 173. *See also*
  National Liberals
Bund der Landwirte (BdL or
  Agrarian League), 24, 34,
  98, 139, 211, 214, 233, 236;
  and origins, 26; and Alldeutscher Verband, 76, 107-
  109, 129; and National Opposition and war aims, 135-
  136, 150, 155, 160, 161, 164,
  165, 166-167, 168, 170, 171-
  173, 178, 182-183, 185, 190,
  191, 192, 195, 196, 198, 203,
  207-208, 222; and anti-Semitism, 83, 86-87, 90-91, 94,
  95, 96, 141, 234; and Conservatives, 25-28, 39, 42, 46-
  47, 51-52, 54, 70-71, 75, 80,
  135, 136, 137, 138, 188, 189,
  195-196, 222, 232; and economic protectionism, 30, 33,
  40-41, 45-46, 47, 83, 112,
  118, 121-124, 126-128, 156-
  157, 173, 195, 207-208, 232;
  and elections, 40-42, 52, 53,
  56, 58, 82, 84, 93-94, 113;
  and inner colonization, 59-
  62, 140, 155-156; and Mittelstand politics, 27, 31, 35,

41,87-88, 90-91, 95, 107,
112, 113, 138; and Samm-
lungspolitik, 32-33, 37,
39, 41-43, 44, 45, 53, 56,
67, 68, 77-78, 98, 111-112,
113, 115, 116-117, 118,
126, 135, 136, 137, 138,
149, 208-209, 212; and tax
reform, 67-68, 99
Bundesrat, 74, 99, 100, 102,
103
Burgfreiden policy, 146, 148,
149, 150, 157, 158, 173,
174, 175, 177, 181, 182,
191, 192, 200, 216
Caprivi, Leo von, 17, 18-20,
126
Carmer, Count (Conservative
Deputy), 231-232
Cartel of the Creative Estates,
see Kartell der schaffenden
Staende
Catholics, see Anti-Catholicism;
Center Party
CBV, see Christliche deutsche
Bauernvereine
CdI, see Centralverband der
Industriellen
Censorship, 165, 174, 177, 184,
197, 200, 215, 216
Center Party, 11, 12, 25, 41,
49, 53, 56, 57, 63, 68, 72,
82, 83, 98, 99, 101, 103,
105, 113, 132, 135, 143,
160, 168, 169, 170, 212
Central Association of German
Industrialists, see Centralverband der Industriellen
Centralverband der Industriellen
(heavy industry), 35, 36-37,
45, 49, 50, 69-70, 77-78,
84, 106, 111, 112, 113, 115,
116, 117, 118, 119, 120, 121,
124, 125, 137, 149, 160, 161,
162, 164, 165, 166, 168, 169,
170, 172, 174, 183, 188, 189,
192, 195, 197, 207, 209, 212,
233, 234. See also Economic
protectionism; National Liberals; Sammlungspolitik

Chamberlain, Houston Stewart,
91-92, 95, 96, 199
Christian Social Party, 22, 23,
228, 236, 238, 239
Christliche deutsche Bauernvereine, (CBV or Association
of Christian German Farmers),
113, 170
"Circle of Producers," 113-114.
See also Kartell der Schaffenden Staende
Class, Heinrich, 55, 79, 195,
207, 212, 217-218, 219,
240; and anti-Semitism, 92,
94-96, 176, 200, 217, 234,
235, 237; and Conservatives,
76, 107-111, 140, 199-200,
223, 225, 227; and National
Opposition and war aims,
128-129, 130-131, 133, 134,
150-151, 154-155, 160-161,
162-163, 164, 165, 169, 171,
172, 177, 183, 184, 186,
187, 196, 197-198, 205, 213-
214, 215
Colonial Society, see Kolonialverein
Colonialism, 13, 14, 79, 83, 151,
152, 154
Committee of Eleven, see Elfer
Ausschuss
Committee of Fifty, see Fuenfziger Ausschuss
Conservatives, 58, 72, 73, 121,
144, 145-146, 148, 150, 210,
216, 220-221, 224, 228, 232,
233; and party origins, 5-7,
9-10; and Alldeutscher Verband, 75-76, 79-80, 109-111,
241-242; and National opposition and war aims, 132-
133, 138, 154, 155, 158,
160-163, 164-167, 168, 169,
170, 172, 178, 179-180, 181-
185, 186-187, 188, 190, 191,
192, 193, 194, 199, 200, 203-
204, 205, 214-215, 222, 223;
and anti-Semitism, 23, 85-
86, 90, 94, 96-97, 142, 174-
175, 238; and Bund der Landwirte, 25-28, 39, 42, 46-47,

48, 51-52, 54, 70-71, 75, 80, 135, 136, 137, 138, 188, 189, 195-196, 222, 232; and Deutschnational Volkspartei, 230-231, 236, 240, 241; and economic protectionism, 8, 9, 19, 22, 31, 40-41, 43, 44, 45, 46, 83, 124, 195; and elections, 11, 40-41, 56-57, 69, 82-84, 85, 93-94, 113; and Prussian voting law, 74, 140-141, 225-227; and Sammlungspolitik, 9, 12-15, 17-18, 20, 30, 32-33, 39, 41, 57, 63, 68, 69, 71, 74-75, 77-78, 104, 105, 106, 111, 115, 124, 136-138, 174, 206-207, 222-223, 229-230; and tax reform, 65-66, 67-68, 69, 97, 98, 99, 100, 101, 102, 103-104, 195; and voelkisch ideology, 138, 142-143; and inner colonization, 61, 139-140

Courland, 186

Daily Telegraph Affair, 67
Dallwitz , von (Interior Minister), 73
Danzig, 124
Das Deutsche Reich, 166
David, Ernst, 192-193
Dawes Plan, 239
Decker, Georg, 241
Deetjen, Ernst, 138
Delbrueck, Hans, 30, 104-105, 123, 125, 126, 127, 128, 149, 150, 156, 158-159, 178, 189, 209, 236
Delbrueck, Rudolf von, 7
Denmark, 152
Deutsche Arbeiter und Angestellte Partei, 228
Deutsche Arbeitgeberzeitung, 112
Deutsche Bauernbund, 69, 82, 170
Deutsche Handlungsgehilfen Verband (DNHV or Deutschnationaler Handlungsgehilfenverband), 129, 236, 238
Deutsche Partei, 228

Deutsche Reformpartei (DRP or German Reform Party), 86, 87, 236
Deutsche Tageszeitung, 43, 45, 171, 178
Deutsche Vaterlandspartei (German Fatherland, Party), 206-207, 208, 210, 211-213, 217, 218, 219-220, 222-223, 229, 232, 233, 234
Deutsche Vereinigung, 212
Deutsche Zeitung, 190, 217
Deutscher Handelstag, 35
Deutscher Landwirtschafts Rat (German Agricultural Council), 35, 127
Deutschlands Erneuerung, 216
Deutschnationale Volkspartei (DNVP or German National Peoples' Party), 230-231, 236, 238, 239-240, 241
Deutschnationaler Handlungsgehilfen Verband, *see* Deutsche Handlungsgehilfen Verband
Deutschsoziale Partei (DSP or German Social Party), 86, 87, 236
Deutschsoziale Reformpartei (DSRP or German Social Reform Party), 86-87
Deutschvoelkischer Schutz und Trutzbund, 237
DHT, *see* Deutscher Handelstag.
Die Wirklichkeit, 216
Dietrich (Conservative Deputy), 162, 228
DLR, *see* Deutscher Landwirtschafts Rat
DNHV, *see* Deutsche Handlungsgehilfen Verband
DNVP, *see* Deutschnationale Volkspartei
DOV, *see* Hakatisten
DRP, *see* Deutsche Reformpartei
DSP, *see* Deutschsoziale Partei
DSRP, *see* Deutschsoziale Reformpartei
Duehring, Eugen, 89-90
Eastern Marches, *see* Ostmarken
"Economic Election Manifesto," 40-41

Economic protectionism, 7, 8,
9, 19-20, 22, 31, 40-41, 43,
44, 45-46, 47, 49, 55, 64,
77, 83, 112, 118, 120, 121,
122, 124, 152, 156-157, 173,
181, 195, 207-208. *See also*
Tax reform.
Economic Union, *see* Wirtschaft-
liche Vereinigung
Eisendecher (Baden), 69
Eisenhart, Wolfgang, 142
Elections: *1881*,58; *1887*, 13;
1898, 40-42; *1903*, 52, 53;
1907, 56-57; *1909*, 69;
1912, 82-85; *1913*, 113;
1928, 240; *1930*, 240
Electoral law, *see* Prussian
Voting Law
Elfer Ausschuss, 136
Employment laws, 193
Endell, Major, 28, 95
England, 13, 20, 54, 78, 145,
149, 153, 159, 171, 181, 182,
188, 189
Entail law, *see* Fideikommis law
Erzberger, Matthias, 99, 168,
183, 202, 205
Estates of the Realm, 5
Eulenburg, Phillip, 32, 38
Exceptional laws, *see* Ausnahme-
gesetze laws
Expropriation Act, 61
Ex-Servicemen's Association, 112

Falkenhayn, General von, 194
Fatherland Party, *see* Deutsche
Vaterlandspartei
Feiler, Arthur, 120
Fideikommis law, 194
Finance reform, *see* Tax issue
Finland, 152
Flottenverein (Navy or Naval
League), 40, 56, 67, 129
Foreign policy, 13, 34, 54, 78,
145, 146-147. *See also*
Colonialism; Economic protec-
tionism; Kriegszielen; Military
strength
Fortschrittliche Volkspartei
(Progressive People's Party),
75, 82, 84

France, 13, 151, 166, 171, 183,
191
Frankfurter Zeitung, 115
Free Conservatives, *see* Reichs-
partei
Free Fatherland Association, *see*
Freie Vaterlaendische Vereini-
gung
Freemasons, 177
Freie Vaterlaendische Vereingung,
171
Freisinnige Vereinigung, 37
French Congo, 79
French Revolution, 147
Friedrich Wilhelm IV, 5
Friedrich Wilhelm the Great
Elector, 5
Fritsch, Theodor, 87-88, 90,
95, 176, 200, 233-234
Fryman, Daniel, 129, 151, 225
Fuenfziger Ausschuss, 136
Fuhrmann, Paul, 192, 212
Fuss, Richard, 229

Gayl, General von, 170
Gebsattel, Constantin von, 110,
158, 219; and anti-Semitism,
133, 175-176, 200, 202, 217,
234-235, 237; and National
Opposition and war aims, 129,
130-132, 150, 153-154, 155,
160-161, 162-163, 164, 165,
167, 168, 169, 172, 177, 178-
179, 187, 192, 198-199, 214,
215
Gerlach, Helmuth von, 184
German Agricultural Council,
see Deutscher Landwirtschafts
Rat
German Eastern Marches Associa-
tion, *see* Hakatisten
German Fatherland Party, *see*
Deutsche Vaterlandspartei
German National Peoples' Party,
see DeutschnationaleVolkspartei
German Party, *see* Deutsche Partei
German Reform Party,*see* Deutsche
Reformpartei
German Social Party, *see* Deutsch-
soziale Partei

German Social Reform Party, *see*
Deutschsoziale Reformpartei
German Voelkisch Freedom Party,
239
German Workers and Employees Party,
see Deutsche Arbeiter und Anges-
tellte Partei
Gesellschaft zur Forderung der
inneren Kolonization, 167
Gildemeister, Andreas, 212
Gobineau, Arthur de, 89
Gossler, Alfred von, 204
Graef, Walter, 113-114, 192
Graef-Anklam (Conservative Deputy),
226
Graefe, Albrecht von, 132, 178,
184, 185, 192, 199, 216, 226,
228, 230, 238, 239
Grain policy,*see* Economic protec-
tionism
"Great Depression," 2
Grodno, 161
Groebern, Count, 184
Grossgrundbesitzer, *see*
Junkers
Gruenderjahre, 2, 3, 86
Grumme-Douglas, Admiral von, 132,
159, 161, 165, 185, 187, 192,
223
Guelphs, 56
Gwinner, Arthur von, 152

Hahn, Diederich, 28, 42, 43, 61,
84, 87, 112, 115, 137, 141, 212
Hakatisten (DOV), 59, 60, 62, 170,
198. *See also* Inner coloniza-
tion
Halbach (industrialist), 62, 151,
160, 197
Halem, von (Free Conservative Deputy),
204
Halle, Ernst von, 66-67
Hamburg, 211
Hamburg Association for Combatting
Social Democracy, 112
Hamburg Conservative Union, *see*
Hamburg Konservative Vereinigung
Hamburg Konservative Vereinigung,
136, 137, 224, 227
Hamburgerische Correspondent,117-
118

Hammerstein-Schwartow, W. von,
12, 21, 229
Hansabund, 69, 75, 76-77, 78,
82, 84, 95, 105, 112, 117,
118, 121, 149, 170, 171
Hartung, Fritz, 225
Hassel, Ulrich von, 180
Hatzfeld, Count, 172
Heavy industry, *see* Central-
verband der Industriellen
Heinrichs (Under Secretary of
State), 148
Helldorff-Breda, von, (Con-
servative Party chairman),
17, 21-22
Henning (German Voelkisch
Freedom Party), 239
Henningsen, Johann, 95
Hergt, Oskar, 238, 239
Herold (Center Party), 172
Herrenhaus Conservatives, 61,
184, 188, 203, 204
Hertzberg-Lottin, von, 185,
192, 223, 237
Heydebreck, von (Herrenhaus
Conservative), 184
Heyderbrand und der Lasa,
Ernst von, 83, 144, 145,
153, 160, 186, 189, 190,
192, 200, 203, 204, 207,
215, 221, 222, 223, 225-
226, 228, 230, 231, 239;
and Alldeutscher Verband,
76, 79-80, 109-110,132,
134, 139; and National
Opposition and war aims,
143, 148, 154, 161, 163,
164, 166, 167, 169, 172,
180-181, 182, 183-184,
186-187, 188, 189, 190,
198, 205, 223; and Bund
der Landwirte, 75, 188;
and economic protection-
ism, 124, 159; and inner
colonization, 61; and
Sammlungspolitik, 111,
136, 137, 174, 189; and
tax reform, 65, 97, 101,
104, 187
Hindenburg, General von, 188,
194-195, 198, 204, 211

Hirsch (Essen, National Liberal),
    168, 174, 179, 213
Hitler, Adolf, 4, 237
HKT Society, See Hakatisten
Hoensbroech, Count, 200, 204,
    210, 214
Hoetzsch, Otto, 124, 159, 160,
    163, 165, 166, 169, 171, 183,
    187, 190-191, 192, 212, 222,
    223, 228, 229-230, 238, 239
Hohenlohe-Schillingsfurst, Prince,
    29, 31, 39, 52
Hopfen, O. H., 197
Horstmar, Salm, 184
"Hottentott" Election, 5
Hugenberg, Alfred, 60, 151, 153,
    154, 156-157, 162, 163, 165,
    170, 172, 174, 195, 218, 240
Hutten-Czapski, Bogdan von, 75

"Ideas of 1914," 147, 182
Imperial League Against Social
    Democracy, see Reichsverband
    gegen die Sozialdemokratie
Imperial Mittelstand Association,
    87
Imperialism, see Foreign policy
Independent Committee for German
    Peace, see Unabhaengiger
    Ausschuss fuer einen deutschen
    Frieden
Industry, 140, 153, 157, 190,
    199. See also Bund der
    Industriellen; Centralverband
    der Industriellen; Hansabund
Information Center of the United
    Associations, see Auskunft-
    stelle Vereinigte Verbaende
Inner colonization, 58-62, 139-
    140, 155-156, 161, 167-168,
    172, 173, 198, 206, 225, 229
Italy, 152

Jaffe, Edgar, 62
Jesuits, 158
Jews, see Anti-Semitism
Jungdeutschlandbund, 129
Jungkonservativen Reichsverband
    (Young Conservatives or Pan-
    kower Movement), 70-71, 143-
    144

Junkers, 1, 2, 3, 7, 8, 9, 10,
    17, 18-19, 20, 22, 23, 26,
    30, 34, 37, 39, 50, 58-59,
    61-62, 64, 66, 73, 86, 109,
    120, 122, 123, 137, 140, 142,
    155, 156, 167, 182, 185, 194,
    208, 225, 229, 230, 240, 241.
    See also Bund der Landwirte;
    Conservatives

Kamarilla court, 6, 11
Kanitz, Count, 101
Kanitz proposal, 33, 42, 45,
    50, 156, 157, 173
Kapp, Wolfgang, 53, 57, 61-62,
    167-168, 188, 192, 193, 195,
    199, 203, 208-211, 213, 217-
    218, 219, 221, 222, 224, 227,
    228
Kapp Putsch of 1920, 239
Kardorff, von (Reichspartei
    leader), 31
Kardorff compromise, 46, 47, 51
Kartell der schaffenden Staende,
    111-113, 114, 116-117, 118,
    121, 124, 125-126, 129-130,
    135-138, 149, 150, 154-155,
    167, 172-173, 174, 189, 213,
    219. See also Deutsche
    Vaterslandpartei; Sammlungs-
    politik
Kartell of 1887, 8, 9, 12, 13,
    14, 15, 16, 28, 35, 37.
    See also Sammlungspolitik
Karwowski, Professor von, 83
Kaufhold (Bund der Landwirte),
    28, 52
Keim, General, 56, 215
Kessel, von (Prussian House of
    Deputies), 184, 188
Kiderlen-Waechter (Foreign
    Secretary), 73, 78-79
Kiefer, Wilhelm, 216
Kiesenwetter (Bund der Land-
    wirte), 28
Kirdorf (Industrialist), 170,
    234
Kjellen, Rudolf, 147
Klassing, von (Conservative),
    226

Kleist, General von, 142, 223
Klitzing, von (Conservative), 207
Koenigsberg, 114, 111
Koerte (Fatherland Party), 212
Koerting, Berthold, 198-199, 200
Kolberg program, 67-68
Kolonialverein (Colonial Society), 67, 129
Konservative Monatschrift, 136, 137
Konservative Volkspartei, 240
Korrespondenz der BdL, 42
Kreisordnung laws, 6
Kresse (Conservative Deputy), 190, 204
Kreth (Conservative Deputy), 148, 154, 226
Kreuzzeitung, 3. 12, 40, 94, 110, 111, 118, 142, 143, 159, 163, 165, 188, 193, 205, 223
Kreuzzeitung faction, 10, 12, 13, 17, 22
Kriegsausschuss der deutschen Industrie, 149
Krieszielen (land annexation aims), 110, 151-152, 153, 154, 155, 159, 160, 161, 162-163, 164, 166, 168, 170, 171, 177, 178, 180, 181, 182-183, 184, 186, 189, 190, 191, 203, 222, 223
Kroecher (Conservative Party), 52
Krupp (industrialist), 40
Kuehn (Reichtreasury Secretary), 99, 100, 101
Kyffhauserbund, 129

Landesgemeindeordnung of 1891, 18-19
Landowners, large estate, see Junkers; small, see Bund der Landwirte
Left Liberals, 12, 63, 69, 72, 78, 103, 113, 117, 135, 182, 206, 212, 217, 218
Lehmann (voelkisch publisher), 176-177, 192
Leipzig Kartell, see Kartell der schaffenden Staende
Lezius, Professor (Koenigsburg), 184
Liebert, Eduard von, 56, 108, 132-133

Liebig, Hans von, 177, 192, 193, 199, 205, 216, 218
Liegnitz (Conservative), 221
Light industry, see Bund der Industriellen; Hansabund
Limburg-Stirum, Count, 20, 33, 39, 40, 140-141, 225
Lissauer, Ernst, 174
Lithuania, 183, 186
Loebell, Friedrich Wilhelm von, 53, 70, 150, 191
Lohmann (government minister), 32
Ludendorff, General, 194-195, 198, 210-211, 219, 233
Luecke (Bund der Landwirte), 42, 84
Lutherans, 5, 12

Malkewitz, Gustav, 28
Maltzahn, von (government official), 182
Manteuffel-Krossen, Otto von, 22, 33, 39, 40, 42
Marr, Wilhelm, 89
Marschall (government minister), 32
Mecklenburg, Johann Albrecht von, 200, 212, 214, 218
Merchants, see Mittelstand politics
Meyer, Paul, 52, 224
Military strength, 34, 35-36, 39-40, 42-43, 44, 54, 55, 56, 64, 70, 80, 98, 99, 100, 101, 102, 120, 121, 122, 126, 187
Minsk, 161
Miquel, Johannes von, 12, 32, 34, 35, 36, 37, 38, 39-40, 44, 219
Mirbach-Sorquiten, Count, 42, 76, 112, 140, 142, 145, 159
Mittelland Canal Proposal, 43, 45
Mittelstand Association (Union), 87, 168

Mittelstand politics, 27, 31, 35, 41, 87-88, 90-91, 95, 107, 112, 113, 230. *See also* Kartell der schaffenden Staende

Moroccan policy, 79, 83

National Economic Council, *see* Volkswirtschaftrat

National Liberale Zeitung, 137-138

National Liberals, 3-4, 11, 12, 15, 41, 42, 57, 63, 69, 72, 75, 77, 82, 84, 98, 99, 103, 105, 113, 114, 117, 132, 135, 139, 143, 144, 160, 161, 168, 169, 170, 179, 180, 185, 192, 212, 227, 228. *See also* Hansabund; Left Liberals; Sammlungspolitik

National Opposition (vs. Bethmann), 128-134, 135, 138, 149, 177, 178-179, 187-188, 191-193, 194, 196, 197-198, 199, 201, 203, 204, 205, 209, 210, 213-215, 218. *See also* War aims

National Socialist Workers' Party, 228, 237, 239

National-Sozialer Verein, 37

Nationalism, 1, 4, 5, 25, 31, 36, 37, 55, 58, 70, 93, 224. *See also* Foreign policy; Voelkisch ideology

Naumann, Friedrich, 10, 37, 105, 171

Navy, 34, 35-36, 39-40, 42-43, 44, 54, 55, 64, 187

Navy (Naval) League, *see* Flottenverein

Near East, 145

Netherlands, 152

Neumann, Senator (Lubeck), 107, 192

New Orientation policy, 158, 159, 209, 210, 215, 216

Norddeutsche Allgemeine Zeitung, 87

Normann, von (Conservative Party chairman), 52, 67, 74, 97

North German Confederation, 6

Norway, 152

NSDAP, *see* National Socialist Workers' Party

Oertel, Georg, 28, 148, 171

Oerter (Center Party), 172

Oertzen, Dietrich von, 193

Oettingen, Erich von, 107

OHL, *see* Supreme Military Command

Oldenburg-Januschau,von (Bund der Landwirte), 47, 57, 65, 74, 84, 130, 133

Oppenfeld, Frieherr von, 67

Osten-Warnitz, von dem (Conservative Deputy), 184, 205-206, 226

Ostmarken, 53, 58, 183, 206. *See also* Hakatisten

Pan German League, *see* Alldeutscher Verband

Pankower Movement, *see* Jungkonservativen Reichsverband

Panther, 216

Pappenheim, von (Conservative in Prussian Landtag), 77

Peace Resolution of *1917,* 233

Pfister, Otto, 139

Plauener Verbandstag, 109

Podbielski,von (Bund der Landwirte and Prussian Minister of Agriculture), 45

Poland, 151, 152, 159, 182, 183, 191, 201

Poles (German), 56, 58, 59-60, 61, 83, 167, 171-172, 191, 206

Polish seasonal workers, *see* Slav seasonal workers

Political-Anthropological Journal, 202

Pomerania, 200

Pomeranian Economic Society, 15

Posadowsky (government minister), 32, 38, 44

Posen, 58, 61

Praetorius (Conservative
(Party), 52
Pretzel (Junker), 223
Preussenbund, 141, 142
Preussische Jahrbuecher,
176
Progressive Peoples' Party,
see Fortschrittliche Volkspartei
Protective Association for
Landed Property, *see* Schutzverband fuer Deutschen Grundbesitz
*Provinzialausschus der Provinz
Ostpreussen,* 183
Prussia, 4-5, 6-7, 8, 9, 11,
18-19, 20, 30, 32, 36, 39,
48, 58, 61, 62, 63, 66, 74,
80, 93, 100, 102, 104, 110,
113, 125, 135, 140, 142,
182, 191, 194, 200, 205,
206, 215, 228. *See also*
Inner colonization; Junkers,
Prussian voting law
Prussian School Bill, 21
Prussian voting law, 6, 11,
74, 77, 141, 150, 153, 158,
173, 174, 185, 203, 205,
206, 209, 215, 222, 225,
226
Pudor, Heinrich, 192

Racialist theories, 89, 91-92,
93
Rathenau, Emil, 152
Rathenau, Walter, 237
RDMV, *see* Reichsdeutscher
Mittelstandsverband
Recession of *1912-1914,* 119-
120
Reichsdeutscher Mittelstands-
verband (RDMV), 112, 113,
170, 212
Reichshammerbund, 95
Reichslandbund, 236
Reichspartei (Free Conserva-
tives), 11, 13, 41, 46, 57,
84, 99, 135, 138-139, 160,
168, 170, 204, 228, 236

Reichsverband gegen die Sozial-
demokratie, 56, 129, 130,
171
Reismann-Gronc, Theodor, 130,
134, 171
Reventlow, Ernst Graf von, 159,
171, 192
Revolution of *1848,* 4-5
Rheinbaben, von (Prussian Minister of Finance), 65, 66, 180
Rheinisch-Westfaelische Zeitung,
171
Richthofen, von (State Secretary
of Foreign Office), 53
Richthofen-Mertschuetz, von (Conservative), 192
Riesser, Jacob, 77
Riezler, Kurt, 79, 152
Rippler, Heinrich, 108
Rittergutsbesitzer, *see* Junkers
Roesicke, Gustav, 42, 84, 208;
and Alldeutscher Verband war
aims, 155, 156, 162, 167,
173, 182-183, 185, 191, 192,
207, 222; and economic protectionism, 43, 122, 123,
127, 173, 195; and Prussian
voting law, 150; and Sammlungspolitik, 172-173, 174;
and tax reform, 67-68
Roetger, Max, 77, 149
Rohrbach, Paul, 171, 177
Roon, Count, 52, 192
Rumania, 152
Russia, 20, 54, 55, 78, 122, 123-
124, 128, 145, 151, 156, 159,
160, 162, 163, 165-166, 171,
181-183, 184, 188, 189, 203,
211, 222, 225

Salm-Horstmar, Prince, 132, 187,
192, 197, 223
Salomonsohn (business figure),
152
Sammlung Salm, 197
Sammlungspolitik, 34, 35, 36-38,
39-44, 45-46, 49-51, 64, 72,
78, 84, 98, 104-105, 106,
111, 112, 121, 138-139.
Buelow Block; Deutsche

Vaterslandpartei; Kartell der schaffenden Staende; Kartell of *1887*, War aims

Schaefer, Deitrich, 151, 192, 198, 212, 214

Schiele, Georg, 198, 199, 200, 208, 226

Schiemann, Theodor, 159-160, 165, 166, 179

Schifferer, 212

Schmitz-Huebsch (Bund der Landwirte), 192

Schlorlemer-Lieser, Baron von, 73

Schroeter, Bruno, 193, 232

Schuckmann, von (Prussian House of Deputies), 184

Schulenberg, Count, 184

Schutzverband fuer Deutschen Grundbesitz, 140

Schwerin, Friedrich von, 167, 168, 207

Schwerin-Loewitz, Graf von, 40, 44, 62, 82, 142

Seidlitz-Sandreczki, Count, 184, 203

"September Programme," 152

Serbia, 145

Silesia, 58

Slav seasonal workers, 59, 61, 123, 124, 128, 140

Social Democrats (SPD), 1, 29-30, 35, 41, 55, 56, 57, 63, 69, 72, 73, 75, 77, 78, 84, 85, 86, 93, 102, 103, 104, 105, 113, 115, 117, 119, 121, 131, 135, 145, 146, 148, 153, 157-159, 172, 173, 174, 182, 191, 198, 203, 206, 209, 217, 219, 224, 233. *See also* Anti-Socialist law.

Society for Promotion of Inner Colonization, *see* Gesellschaft für Forderung der inneren Kolonization

Somnitz, von (Conservative), 185

Sonnenberg, Max Liebermann von, 87

Sontag, Franz, 111, 134, 193, 199, 205

Spahn (Center), 169, 183

SPD, *see* Social Democrats

Staendestaat concept, 5-6

Stahl, Friedrich Julius, 6, 184, 238

Stahlhelm, 240

Stein, Felix Freiherr von, 3

Stengel, von (Reich Treasury Department), 65

Stillich, Oscar, 24

Stinnes (Industrialist), 151, 156-157, 170, 172, 195, 236

Stock speculation, 1-2, 31

Stoecker, Adolf, 12, 21, 22

Strantz, Kurd von, 177, 201

Streseman, Gustav, 149, 160, 181

Sueddeutsche Monatshefte, 216

Suffrage issue, *see* Prussian voting law

Supreme Military Command (OHL), 202, 204, 210, 222, 224

Suwalki, 161

Sweden, 152

Switzerland, 152

Tarriffs, *see* Economic protectionism

Tax reform, 63-71, 75, 97-104, 113, 141, 195, 206, 229

Theuden, Rudolf, 177

Thielman (Reich Treasury Office), 44

Thimme, Friedrich, 193

Thompson, Admiral Hans von, 175

Thyssen (Industrialist), 170

Tiele-Winkler, Count, 184

Tirpitz, Alfred von, 32, 34, 35-37, 38, 39, 44, 64, 180-181, 194, 198, 212, 214, 217, 218, 219

Tivoli meeting, 23, 24, 25, 228

Trade, *see* Economic protectionism

Trade unions, 99, 153, 192, 194, 206, 227-228, 233

Trimborn (Center), 183

Turkey, 191

Ukraine, 151
Umsturzgesetzes, 30
Unabhaengiger Ausschuss fuer
einen deutschen Frieden
(Independent Committee for
a German Peace), 192, 198,
212, 217
United States, 20, 145
Unold, Johannes, 116

Valentini, von (Government
minister), 188
Verband gegen die Ueberhebung
des Judentums, 95
Verein Deutscher Eisen und
Stahl Industrieller, 7
Vereinigung der Steuer und
Wirtschaftsreformer (Association of Tax and Economic
Reformers), 8, 9, 112, 141-
142
Vietinghoff-Scheel, von (Alldeutscher Verband), 176, 214
Voelkisch ideology, 58-62, 88-
89, 90, 91, 92, 93, 94, 95,
110, 138-140, 141, 142-143,
172, 193, 194, 195, 201,
202, 204, 213-214, 215,
216, 220, 240. See also
Anti-Semitism; Inner colonization.
Volkswirtschaftrat, 115
Voting law, see Prussian voting
law

Wadehn (Bund der Landwirte),
107
Wagener, Leo, 60
Wahl (Breman Committee for a
German Workers' Peace), 227
Waldersee, von (Prussian conservative), 30,32
Wangenheim, Conrad Freiherr von,
25-26, 80, 87, 130, 208, 211,
212, 213, 218; and Alldeutscher Verband, 107, 108, 109;
and anti-Semitism, 95; and
economic protectionism, 46,
47, 51-52, 127-128, 156-157,
195; and inner colonization,

140, 155; and Sammlungspolitik, 53, 112, 114, 116, 117,
126, 149, 150, 172; and tax
reform, 67-68
War aims, 150-155, 160-163, 164-
171, 172, 173, 177-178, 179,
180, 181-185, 186-187, 188,
189, 190-191, 197, 198, 203,
210, 215-216, 219, 222, 223.
See also National opposition
War Committee of German Industry,
see Kriegsausschuss der deutschen Industrie
Warburg, Max, 201
Warsaw, 190
Wehrverein (Army League), 56,
129, 198
Weilnboeck (Bund der Landwirte),
192
Weimar Republic, 237
Weltpolitik, see Foreign policy
Wermuth (Reich Treasury Secretary),
98, 99
Werner, Rev. Julius, 137
Westarp, Count Cuno, 83-84, 99,
144, 175, 192, 224, 225; and
Alldeutscher Verband, 132-
133, 153; and National Opposition, 104, 143, 177, 179-
180, 188, 193, 204; and war
aims, 158, 160, 161, 162,
164-165, 166, 178, 181, 182,
185, 188, 190-191, 194-195,
203, 205, 221, 222, 223, 227;
and Bund der Landwirte, 188;
and Deutschnationale Volkspartei, 230-231, 238, 239-
240, 241-242; and Prussian
voting law, 158, 226; and
Sammlungspolitik, 137, 174;
and Social Democrats, 147-
148; and trade unions, 193-
194, 227-228
Wilamowitz-Moellendorf (Conservative), 142
Wildgrube (Conservative Deputy),
215
Wilhelm II, 14, 17, 30, 31-32,
33, 34, 36, 43, 45, 129, 130,
131, 146, 147-148, 153, 188,
191, 204, 207, 211, 219, 230

Wilna, 161
Winckel, Henning aus dem, 84,
    107, 111
Wirtschaftliche Vereinigung
    (Economic Union), 41, 84,
    87, 88, 103
Wirtschaftlicher Ausschuss,
    35, 40, 126, 127, 128
Workhouse Bill, *see* Zuchthaus-
    vorlage
Working class, *see* Social Demo-
    crats
Worms, Heinrich, 192
Wulle, Reinhold, 239

Yorck, Count (Conservative
    Deputy), 142
Young Conservative Imperial
    Association, *see* Jungkon-
    servativen Reichsverband
Young Liberals, 105

Zabern, 131
Zuchthausvorlage (Workhouse
    Bill), 30, 43

ABOUT THE AUTHOR

Abraham J. Peck is the assistant director of the American Jewish Archives at the Hebrew Union College-Jewish Institute of Religion in Cincinnati, Ohio. He also serves as the assistant editor of that institution's semi-annual historical journal, American Jewish Archives.

He was born in Germany in 1946 and came to the United States in 1949. Peck received his B.A. and M.A. degrees from the School of International Service, American University, Washington, D. C. He did his doctoral work at the University of East Anglia, Norwich , England under Volker R. Berghahn and at the University of Hamburg under Peter-Christian Witt. He has written and lectured on the Holocaust and is presently at work on an article dealing with the significance of a visit to America by the notorious nineteenth -century German anti-Semite, Hermann Ahlwardt.

U.N. CIVILIAN OPERATIONS IN THE CONGO
House, Arthur H., United States Senate
350pp   0-8191-0321-7 $9.45   January, '78
The definitive account of U.N. civilian operations in the Congo.
Focuses on economic, as well as political and diplomatic aspects.

AMERICAN FOREIGN POLICY IN SOUTHERN AFRICA: THE STAKES AND THE
  STANCE
Lemarchard, René, Ed., University of Florida
400pp   0-8191-0324 $9.75   December, '77
Herskovits award winner Lemarchand and his contributors, Larry
Bowman, William Foltz, Allen Isaacman, Edgar Lockwood, Tilden
Lemelle and Hunt Davis, address such issues as corporate influence,
the role of the CIA, the impact of Black Americans and other timely
topics. "...the papers are of uniformly high quality." CHOICE

CZECHOSLOVAKIA'S ROLE IN SOVIET STRATEGY
Josef Kalvoda, Saint Joseph College
391pp   0-8191-0413-2 $9.25   January, '78
"...a thoroughly researched, well-documented, timely and persuasive work of lasting value." - Rudolph C. Krempl, Secretary
General, Comenius World Council. "...one of the better books
about contemporary Czechoslovakia." -M.K. Dziewanowski, Professor of History, Boston University.

PALESTINIANS WITHOUT PALESTINE: A STUDY OF POLITICAL SOCIALI-
ZATION AMONG PALESTINIAN YOUTHS
Alice and Yasumasa Kuroda, Chaminade University and University
of Hawaii
287pp   0-8191-0479-5 $9.75   February, '78
Based on a recent survey of Palestinian youths, this study ex-
amines the roots of Palestine/Israeli anomosities and offers
helpful suggestions for understanding the political matura-
tion process of the Palestinian young people.

THINKING THE THINKABLE: INVESTMENT IN HUMAN SURVIVAL
Ed., Nish Jamgotch, Jr., University of North Carolina at
Charlotte
360pp   0-8191-0402-7 $9.75   February '78
A collection of nine essays dealing with population, food
shortages, energy depletion, ecological abuse and other global
concerns. Contributors include Robert McNamara, Denis Hayes,
Russell Peterson and Edward Azar.

POLITICS AND ADMINISTRATION IN BRAZIL
Ed., Jean-Claude Garcia-Zamor, Howard University
ca. 450pp   0-8191-0509-0 $12.75   August '78
A collection of articles by Brazilian and American scholars
covering the gamut of political, military and administrative
affairs.

CHICANO POLITICS: A THEORETICAL AND BEHAVIORAL ANALYSIS OF
CHICANOS IN AMERICAN POLITICS
Vigil, Maurilio E., New Mexico Highlands University
375pp.   0-8191-0110 $9.45   January, '77
Employing a conceptual approach, this comprehensive study ex-
amines the political development of the Southwest's most
activist minority group "...libraries interested in strengthening their collections in (American politics and Chicano studies)
should have this volume on their shelves." - CHOICE

THE CHIT'LIN CONTROVERSY: RACE AND PUBLIC POLICY IN AMERICA
Charles P. Henry, Dennison University
Lorenzo Morris, Massachusetts Institute of Technology
157pp   0-8191-0471-X $7.25   February, '78
"...a rare book...I don't think there is anything like it in
the field." - Theodore J. Lowi, Cornell University

INTERPRETERS AND CRITICS OF THE COLD WAR
Kenneth W. Thompson, University of Virginia
ca. 110pp   0-8191-0504-X $5.75   ca. September, '78
An attempt to analyze the views of a group of interpreter
critics who fall neither within the school of revision historians nor of orthodox writers on the cold war.

THE FEDERALIST WITHOUT TEARS
Stearns, Jean, Brandywine College
178pp   0-8191-0106-0 $5.50   January, '77
Twenty six of the most important papers have been rewritten in
contemporary language. A unique sourcebook for high school and
undergraduate history and political science courses.

POLICY-MAKING IN THE AMERICAN SYSTEM: THE CASE OF THE MANPOWER,
DEVELOPMENT AND TRAINING PROGRAM
George T. Menake, Montclair State College of New Jersey
387pp   0-8191-0409-4 $10.50   January, '78
A study of American policy-making in the area of social welfare
legislation.

THE PRESIDENCY AND THE MASS MEDIA IN THE AGE OF TELEVISION
William C. Spragens, Bowling Green State University
428pp   0-8191-0476-0 $10.75   February, '78
The author, a former newsman, traces the development of the
relationship between the White House and the Washington correspondent corps since 1945 and offers valuable insights into the
nature of this very important interplay.